Reflections on
The Principles of Psychology

William James After a Century

Photograph used by permission of the Archives of the History of American Psychology.

Reflections on
The Principles of Psychology

William James After a Century

Edited by

Michael G. Johnson
University of Tennessee, Knoxville

Tracy B. Henley
University of Tennessee, Knoxville

LEA LAWRENCE ERLBAUM ASSOCIATES, PUBLISHERS
1990 Hillsdale, New Jersey   Hove and London

Lawrence Erlbaum Associates, Inc., Publishers
365 Broadway
Hillsdale, New Jersey 07642

Library of Congress Cataloging-in-Publication Data

Reflections on *The Principles of Psychology*: William James after a century /
edited by Michael G. Johnson, Tracy B. Henley.
    p. cm.
   Includes bibliographical references and index.
   ISBN 0-8058-0205-3
   1. James, William, 1842–1910. 2. Psychology. 3. James, William,
1842–1910. Principles of psychology. I. James, William,
1842–1910. II. Johnson, Michael G. (Michael Geoffrey), 1943–   .
III. Henley, Tracy B. IV. Reflections on *The Principles of Psychology*.
BF109.J28R44   1990
150'.92—dc20   90-35867
                                            CIP

Printed in the United States of America
10 9 8 7 6 5 4 3 2 1

For Esther, Greg, and Lani

Contents

Chapter 13

James on the Will   295

James Deese

List of Contributors

Ronald Baenninger, Temple University
Roger Brown, Harvard University
Herbert Crovitz, Duke University
James Deese, University of Virginia
Rand Evans, University of Baltimore
Amedeo Giorgi, Saybrook Institute
Mary Henle, The New School for Social Research
Tracy Henley, University of Tennessee
Michael Johnson, University of Tennessee
Stephen Kosslyn, Harvard University
David Leary, University of Richmond
John Malone, University of Tennessee
Sohee Park, Harvard University
Howard Pollio, University of Tennessee
Edward Reed, Drexel University
Irvin Rock, University of California, Berkeley
Eugene Taylor, Harvard Medical School

Foreword

Roger Brown
Harvard University

The writing style and contents of James's *Principles* evokes our lasting admiration and on some topics, especially Attention, Stream of Thought, and Consciousness of Self, he was something of a poet. One thing that poetry does is name "what hath oft been thought but ne'er so well expressed." That namelessness is compatible with existence (I: 251) is a famous James dictum, and it is true, but to it one must add that the giving of a good name, not just a lexical tag but a description that brings a universal experience universally to mind, adds something to existence. It makes the experience available to thought, available as an object of thought, available even as an object of experiment.

> Suppose we try to recall a forgotten name. The state of our consciousness is peculiar. There is a gap therein but no mere gap. It is a gap that is intensely active. A sort of wraith of the name is in it, beckoning us in a given direction, making us at moments tingle with the sense of our closeness and then letting us sink back without the longed-for term. If wrong names are proposed to us, this singularly definite gap acts immediately so as to negate them. They do not fit into its mould. And the gap of one word does not feel like the gap of another, all empty of content as both might seem necessarily to be when described as gaps. (I: 251)

This mental state had not gone entirely nameless before James wrote his description. People would say: "I know the word; it's on the tip of my tongue." What does James's phenomenalist name add? The sense of an active process striving for completing something between the brink of a sneeze and the approach of an orgasm, but, more importantly, an awareness of paradox, of the mystery James always loved, because how can the gap of one word not feel like the gap of another, "all empty of content as both might seem necessarily to be when described as gaps?"

A state of consciousness is one of the "hard facts of psychology" that has been well described; yet it remains to seek out the causal conditions of that state not by way of atomistic introspection but by experimental study of material circumstances, especially brain states. James always acknowledged that it was a metaphysical mystery how brains could give rise to consciousness, but he judged that psychology could only function as a science by assuming that its data, mental states, are brought about by physical states. And the paradox in his description of the tip of the tongue (TOT) state—an empty gap that rejects candidates coming forward to fill its emptiness—motivates a search for a causal mechanism, for something material to supplant his beckoning "wraith of the name." The material could not soon, nor even in a century, be turned into a brain state but only into the kind of thing we call a "model."

The model that David McNeill and I proposed for the TOT phenomenon (Brown & McNeill, 1966) was a Rube Goldberg apparatus, absurdly clumsy even for its date, but it does account for the extremely regular data that are obtained when the mental state is converted into other people's behavior. The number of syllables in the name and the locus of primary stress turn out to be properties of the wraith.

Initial and final phonemes (or letters) are most likely to be recalled and the probability of recall is lowest in the middle of a word. But the middle of the word, when still unrecalled, must be present, whether less distinctly outlined or less elaborately connected, because when incorrect words are presented, which satisfy all recallable properties, they are still confidently negated.

Models of the architecture of the mental lexicon, although not yet of the full TOT phenomenon, are now well past the Rube Goldberg stage. There is, for instance, the Augmented Addressed Morphology Model of Alfonso Caramazza and his associates (Caramazza, Laudanna, & Romani, 1988). TOT studies derived ultimately from James's poetic description have produced results relevant to the serious models of today and the brain models still to come. David Rubin (1975), for instance, has shown that when TOT states are precipitated by words composed of multiple morphemes, such as *usurer* and *altimeter*, constituent morphemes (e.g., the agentive *-er* and instrumental *-meter*) are recalled as units. Such results suggest that lexical items are represented in the mind as morphologically decomposed. I think William James would not have grown bored with experimental psychology as, of course, he did, if it had been able to tackle problems like the structure of the mental lexicon.

Nowadays my memory is so fallible that I can pass a pleasant hour sitting in the sunshine doing TOT experiments on my own mind. And I have discovered a number of things not yet demonstrated in other people's behavior. For instance, when a name comes to mind that is just one phoneme away from a target, and the target then promptly pops up, the phoneme in the name first recalled is usually just one distinctive feature away from the phoneme in the target; as when, today, trying to recall an Italian restaurant named *Ida's* I thought first of *Ina's*. The phoneme /d/ is a voiced, alveolar stop that is not nasalized whereas the phoneme /n/ is a voiced alveolar stop that is nasalized. From data of this kind I hypothesize that phonemes are represented in memory, as some linguists have proposed, as bundles of distinctive features. The explanation may be wrong, and it will take experiments to tell, but data like these seem to me, as they did to James, the hard facts of psychology.

With *Principles* completed, the "interminable black cloud" lifted, at last, after 12 years, James came to feel rather proud of having written one of the biggest books on psychology in any language. He was also a bit surprised at the accomplishment because he had always considered himself to be a "thing of glimpses, of discontinuity, of aperçus" (H. James, 1920, p. 295). In this self-assessment he was not altogether wrong, and we miss something of his genius if we submerge in the systematic thinker the brilliant impressionist.

REFERENCES

Brown, R., & McNeill, D. (1966). The "tip of the tongue" phenomenon. *Journal of Verbal Learning and Verbal Behavior, 5*, 325–337.

Caramazza, A., Laudanna, A., & Romani C. (1988). Lexical access and inflectional morphology. *Cognition, 28*, 297–332.

James, H. (Ed.). (1920). *The letters of William James*. Boston: Atlantic Monthly Press.

James, W. (1890). *The principles of psychology* (Vols. 1–2). New York: Holt.

Rubin, D. C. (1975). Within word structure in the tip-of-the-tongue phenomenon. *Journal of Verbal Learning and Verbal Behavior, 14*, 392–397.

Preface

Over the past several years, in conversations with colleagues and students, and in the more rigorous atmosphere of various graduate seminars, it has become clear to us that William James's *Principles of Psychology* still offers fresh insights (and delights) to the psychologist who takes the trouble to read it. We, along with several of our contributors, are not the first to note that in many instances our discipline has failed to advance very far beyond the intellectual legacy that James has left for us. It is this context which supplied the impetus for our undertaking the editorial project which has resulted in this volume commemorating the 100th year since the original publication of the *Principles*—a century in which it has never been out of print.

The specific idea for this book began in the Fall of 1987, a time when a few voices began to be heard concerning the advent of 1990, and the significance of the centennial of the publication of James's *magnum opus*. It was the first editorial undertaking of this kind for each of us and we learned a lot along the way, including an occasional appreciation of Sartre's observation that "hell is other people"—an opinion probably shared by one or two of our authors. Through it all it has been an interesting experience and, even through the boring bits, a true labor of love.

Our overall plan was to ask our contributors to provide a chapter that would examine some portion of the *Principles* from the perspective of their own current interests and expertise. Other than attempting to select authors with a range of substantive backgrounds—along with a common interest in James, of course—our contributors were given a free hand in their choice of subject matter and the way in which they chose to cover it. The result is a volume that samples a good deal of the diversity of James's thought, without attempting (or pretending) to cover everything. That is a task beyond the range of our undertaking, and commentators on James frequently complain about the problem of deciding what to cover and what to leave out.

Along the way, we lost four of our original contributors, added two, and regained two who had withdrawn. Two of our authors left faculty positions to become administrators during the course of this project. Of the (surprisingly, to us) few who turned down our request to participate in this project, one wrote a most memorable comment to the effect that James was such a compelling writer that he (the person asked to contribute) didn't want to participate in exposing James's potentially dangerous ideas to the unwary!

There are a number of people who contributed directly and indirectly to the success of this book. We would like to thank our colleagues and students at the University of Tennessee for providing the intellectual context and stimulation to sustain this project, and especially Nancy Skeen and Patricia Hinton, without whose help we would not have been able to complete it at all. Most of all, we thank the authors of the chapters in this volume, for their patience and enthusiastic interest in William James—without whom, of course, none of this would have happened at all!

Michael G. Johnson
Tracy B. Henley

EDITOR'S NOTE

As might be expected, this volume contains a great many references to James's *Principles of Psychology*. Since all but one of the contributors has utilized the 1890 Holt edition (or the identically paginated Dover edition), we have adopted this simplifying convention of using only volume and page number (e.g., I: 37) where references are to those editions of the *Principles*. APA style is followed in all other cases.

Introduction

Tracy B. Henley
Michael G. Johnson
University of Tennessee

William James's *Principles of Psychology* (1890) took 12 years to complete. Before it was done, several chapters had appeared in other forms and locations such as *Mind, Scribner's*, and *Popular Science Monthly*. By the time of its completion, some 10 years past due, James referred to it as a *rat*, and remarked to his publisher Henry Holt that it testified both that "there is no such thing as a *science* of psychology, and *2nd*, that W. J. is an incapable" (Evans, 1981). It has now been 100 years since James published the *Principles* in 1890, and yet James and his work still offers insights and inquiries into the contemporary concerns of psychology.

Around 1942, marking 100 years since the birth of William James (1842–1910), Blanshard and Schneider (1942) edited the first commemorative anthology with the purpose of reviewing and assessing the continual impact of James's thought. Nearly 25 years later, during the American Psychological Association's 75th Anniversary Convention, a special part of the program was devoted to a discussion of four major themes (the mind-body problem, instinct, consciousness, and the will) considered by James in the *Principles*. The emphasis was on the progress that psychology had made on these topics, all central to James, and which were of special interest at that time (1966). MacLeod (1969) remembers the occasion:

> It consequently seemed appropriate that on the seventy-fifth anniversary we should step back to 1890, ask again some of the questions James was asking, and review our progress toward their solution. The planning of the series was entrusted to a subcommittee: C. W. Bray, E. G. Boring, R. B. MacLeod, and R. L. Solomon. We found it difficult to agree on which of James's questions we should select, because there were so many of them. Should we, for in-

stance, had included "the self", "the James-Lange theory of emotion", James as the forerunner of modern existentialism, etc.? (p. iii)

In putting together this volume, nearly 25 years later, we have faced a similar problem. This very fact—that after 100 years it is not an issue of finding *something* relevant in James but of deciding *what* relevant material should be included in a single volume—is testimony to the durability of James's contribution to psychological thought. Among the contemporary concerns of 1990 that this volume considers are: the nature of the self and the will, conscious experience, associationism, the basic acts of cognition, and the nature of perception. The developments in each of these areas during the last 100 years have been legion; nevertheless the views of William James as presented in the *Principles* still remain important and provocative.

In order to provide a context for William James, his *Principles*, and this volume commemorating them both after 100 years, we have included chapters devoted primarily to new scholarship about James himself. These works focus on the time the *Principles* were written, relevant intellectual influences, and considerations of James's understanding of this new science of psychology. The balance of this volume is devoted to specific topics that James dealt with. Despite the diversity of topics the contributors to this anthology have chosen to focus on, one theme, like a ribbon, is woven into almost every chapter. This theme concerns the tension between the role of experience (or phenomenological data) within a scientific psychology, and the viability of a materialistic (biologically reductive) account of mental life.

Although psychology as a topic within philosophy had been part of American universities since the middle of the 19th century, nothing written before compared to James's *Principles*. It is certainly a defensible claim that no other work since then has had so great an impact on American psychology. In Chapter 1 of this volume **Rand Evans** advances his own earlier works (e.g., Evans, 1981) to produce a fresh look at William James, which rivals much lengthier biographies (e.g., Allen, 1967; Bjork, 1988; Feinstein, 1984; Knight, 1950; Myers, 1986; Perry, 1935; Roback, 1942) for completeness with respect to James's intellectual heritage and life leading up to the time the *Principles* were written.

Evans focuses on William James's family life, especially the intellectual milieu established by his father. Special attention is given to the writing of the *Principles*, and to James's interactions with the Henry Holt publishing company. Evans completes his chapter with speculations concerning just what it is about the *Principles* that has enabled it to endure for 100 years.

At the close of the preface to the *Principles* James wrote:

Finally, when one owes to so many, it seems absurd to single out particular creditors; yet I cannot resist the temptation at the end of my first literary venture to record my gratitude for the inspiration I have got from the writings of

J. S. Mill, Lotze, Renouvier, Hodgson, and Wundt, and from the intellectual companionship (to name only five names) of Chauncey Wright and Charles Peirce in old times, and more recently of Stanley Hall, James Putnam, and Josiah Royce. (I:vii)

In Chapter 2, **Eugene Taylor** pursues in detail the intellectual influence that several of these thinkers had on James's understanding of experimental psychology. Professor Taylor's essay synthesizes elements of James's biography and James's views about the science of psychology itself. In particular, Taylor considers not only the role of experience within psychology, but the part that various persons and schools of thought played in the development of James's ideas. Taylor concentrates on the influence of Chauncey Wright, Henry Bowditch, and James Putnam, and offers evidence that James was greatly influenced by the "French model of Experimental Physiology." Taylor illustrates how each of these individual factors assisted in shaping James's views as expressed in the *Principles* regarding matters of conscious experience, as well as a variety of other topics.

Chapter 3, by phenomenological psychologist **Amedeo Giorgi**, directly considers the role of experience in a science of psychology—a theme that finds its way into most of the essays that follow. As Giorgi notes, James's *Principles* seems to present a continual paradox between a highly objective scientific realism (indeed an eliminative materialism) and a highly subjective experiential realism (similar to both phenomenology, as Giorgi explains, and to what is currently called Social Constructionism: see Berger & Luckman, 1966; Gergen, 1985; Wittgenstein, 1953). Nevertheless it seems clear that this duality was not one generated by confusion or misunderstanding on James's part, but by an attempt to have a science that used as its fundamental data human experience. In his own introduction James writes:

I have kept close to the point of view of natural science throughout this book. Every natural science assumes certain data uncritically, and declines to challenge the elements between which its own "laws" obtain, and from which its own deductions are carried on. Psychology, the science of finite individual minds, assumes as its data (1) *thoughts and feelings*, and (2) *a physical world* in time and space with which they coexist and which (3) *they know*. Of course these data themselves are discussable; but the discussion of them (as of other elements) is called metaphysics and falls outside the province of this book. This book, assuming that thoughts and feelings exist and are vehicles of knowledge, thereupon contends that psychology when she has ascertained the empirical correlation of the various sorts of thought or feeling with the definite conditions of the brain, can go no farther—can go no farther, that is, as a natural science. (I: v-vi)

Such attempts to have a science with an emphasis on experience characterize later works such as Köhler's *Gestalt Psychology* (1947) and Merleau-

Ponty's *Phenomenology of Perception* (1945/1962). Indeed, direct connections between James and each of these authors have been suggested (see Perry, 1935; and, Schmidt, 1985, respectively). Although links between James and phenomenology abound (e.g., Edie, 1970, 1987; Linschoten, 1968; Stevens, 1974; Wilshire, 1968), Giorgi goes beyond these previous works in an attempt to understand what role experience had for James in his conception of scientific psychology. Giorgi explores just what James meant by "natural science" given such passages as the one just presented. Giorgi examines George Trumball Ladd's original review of James's *Principles*, James's reply to Ladd's review and concludes by relating his findings to contemporary debates about science in psychology in which phenomenologists have continued to argue for the primacy of experience.

In the fourth chapter, **Mary Henle** examines the relationship between William James and Gestalt Psychology. As was the case in the preceding chapter, the connections between James and Gestalt Psychology are many and longstanding (cf. Perry, 1935). Given the family resemblance between phenomenology and Gestalt psychology, it is not surprising that once again the central issues involve the role of direct experience, which Henle sees as an important commonality between James and the Gestaltists, and the proper conception of psychology as a natural science which, Henle argues, separates James from the Gestaltists.

Henle goes on to explore these matters more fully via a well constructed analysis of the similarities and differences between James and the Gestaltists on such topics as mechanism, atomism, associationism, and organization. Henle challenges many of the classically held views about the relationship between James and the Gestaltists and replaces them with a number of new ideas.

Chapter 5, by **David Leary**, concerns James's views on matters of "personality," or Self. Leary's chapter provides a transition from the more general conceptual and biographical essays to specific topics, as his essay concerns the self but is firmly grounded in James's personal history. Leary argues that the place of experience in James's science of psychology is best understood via his conception of self. Leary notes that the chapter concerning the self was among the first started and was the last completed. Leary reasons, as does Evans and Taylor, that James's interest in experience is rooted in his intellectual background. However, Leary focuses more on James the person than external factors in the development of this idea.

Leary concludes the chapter with a most informative review of current views about the self which illustrates the strong degree of continued Jamesian influence. This review is not limited to classical personality theorists but also encompasses a variety of related social and cognitive psychologists (such as Vygotsky), which the reader may find surprising.

Chapter 6, by **John Malone**, argues that part of James's continual influence stems from his rejection of the two popular theoretical alternatives of his day: simple associationism and the mind/soul theory. Malone maintains, somewhat ironically, that a century later both "poor" alternatives, which James dismissed, are as popular among psychologists as they were in James's day, and that both still suffer from the deficiencies James outlined in the *Principles*.

Malone notes that the rapid progress in scientific psychology that James envisioned has not occurred and underscores repeatedly the fact that the "popular" models and the misconceptions they entail remain with us. Malone contends that there is a connection between slow progress in psychology and a reluctance to go beyond the two standard alternative that James rejected. Malone cites the continued popularity of simple associationism, such as modern connectionism, and the work of Bandura as cases in point.

Like Malone, **Herbert Crovitz** in Chapter 7 is most concerned with developments in associationism and related advances in psychology since the time of James. Crovitz notes from the onset the striking similarities between modern connectionism (cf. Rumelhart, McClelland, and the PDP Research Group, 1986) and James's account of associationism as given in the *Principles*.

Crovitz proceeds with an informative and colorful history of associationism beginning with Aristotle, and offers continuing commentary from the perspective of James. This approach affords the reader a scholarly view of the ideas that influenced James, and the directions those ideas have continued along since James. Crovitz's chapter provides an integrative look at the history of associationism with James as centerpiece, and promises to be of interest to those currently involved with associationism, as well as to those concerned with the history of psychology.

Chapter 8, by **Sohee Park** and **Stephen Kosslyn** shares the view developed in the previous chapter that James offers important and underutilized ideas with respect to contemporary movements in cognitive science. The focus for Park and Kosslyn is their own area of empirical work, imagination. Park and Kosslyn offer a brief history of scholarship on imagination and also a consideration of related conceptual and philosophical issues that surround the topic.

Park and Kosslyn proceed to analyze James's views on imagination, and to consider more contemporary advances in the study of imagination, paying special attention to the matters of individual differences and neurological processes, and suggest that many of James's physiological speculations are supported by modern evidence. They conclude with a review of still unresolved issues within the domain, and offer support for the view that a reconsideration of James may well suggest insights into these current problems.

Chapter 9 by **Irvin Rock** begins with a review of James's basic theory of perception which he contends is as theoretically sophisticated as many more contemporary views. Rock considers a number of "facts of perception" which have been learned since James, and attempts to discuss these newer findings in light of James's views. Rock then focuses on the topic of perceptual constancy as a particular example which illustrates that James offers insights that may be of importance to current and future research.

Rock also presents an interesting comparison between James and the phenomenology of perception described by Merleau-Ponty (cf. 1945/1962). Rock concludes his chapter with a critical review of progress in the area of perception, listing 14 unresolved problems, which he feels no contemporary theory of perception can resolve. He suggests that one measure of the viability of James's account is the fact that his views on these issues are just as cogent as most contemporary views, and concludes that James's views of perception were indeed ahead of their time.

Edward Reed provides Chapter 10. Like Rock, Reed's essay is concerned with James's account of perception. Reed's chapter focuses on two classical accounts of space perception. One account, associated with Wundt and Helmholtz, James called the position of the "psychological stimulists." This is contrasted with James's own, opposing view. Reed follows this debated carefully showing how James believed that his opponents had fallen into what James termed the "psychologist's fallacy." James explains:

> It is a case of what I have called the "psychologist's fallacy": mere acquaintance with space is treated as tantamount to every sort of knowledge about it, the conditions of the latter are demanded of the former state of mind, and all sorts of mythological processes are brought in to help. (II: 911)

Reed maintains that by tracing James's arguments carefully valuable insights, as well as an avoidance of pitfalls, can result for contemporary researchers in perception.

Chapter 11 is authored by **Ronald Baenninger** and introduces for this volume one of the most famous of Jamesian topics, consciousness. Baenninger once again emphasizes the place of subjective experience within a scientific psychology; however his perspective on this theme is a novel one.

Being an ethologist, Baenninger considers James's ideas on the "comparative method" as a way of understanding consciousness in relation to other matters, such as habit and instinct. Baenninger traces the place of animals within experimental psychology from the time of James to the present, and considers what the study of animals may offer the study of consciousness. Baenninger offers an intriguing look at the relationship between these two seemingly disparate fields of interest which will interest both cognitive and comparative psychologists.

Chapter 12 by **Howard Pollio** is also concerned with consciousness. Pollio's topic involves perhaps the most famous of all Jamesian metaphors, the "stream of thought." Pollio begins with James's own work: reminding us of James's claim that *"The first fact for us, then, as psychologists, is that thinking of some sort goes on"* (I: 224); and of his metaphor:

Consciousness, then, does not appear to itself chopped up in bits. Such words as 'chain' or 'train' do not describe it fitly as it presents itself in the first instance. It is nothing joined; it flows. A 'river' or a 'stream' are the metaphors by which it is most naturally described. *In talking of it hereafter, let us call it the stream of thought, of consciousness, or of subjective life.* (I: 238)

Pollio then proceeds to explore the evolution of ideas concerning the "stream of consciousness" in both psychology and literature from the time of James up to its treatment by contemporary psychology textbooks. Pollio argues convincingly that consciousness, central to James's *Principles*, has all but been lost in psychology textbooks (see also Henley, Johnson, Herzog, & Jones, 1989).

Pollio provides a detailed exploration of what we know about consciousness not only from literature and introductory psychology, but also, from the perspectives of phenomenology and of modern cognitive scientific metaphoric analysis (cf. Lakoff & Johnson, 1980). Pollio's essay provides an excellent examination of consciousness from the works of James, as well as from many other points of view. It should be noted that his treatment, once again, has as its backdrop the recurrent issue of the relationship between subjective experience and scientific psychology.

In Chapter 13 **James Deese** considers the will, and offers new views of James's ideas about matters of personality interspersed with original insights into how contemporary readers should understand James. Deese suggests new heuristics for Jamesian scholarship, which offer the possibility of resolving some of James's more irritating paradoxes. In particular Deese maintains that the antinomy between free will and determinism (traceable to James's father's interest in Swedenborgian theology) is the underlying source for the tension between the roles of consciousness and materialism (see also Lears, 1987).

Deese believes that James's chapter on the will is the centerpiece for James's own personal intellectual conflicts. Deese argues that within the *Principles* James opted to pay more homage to the "German Science Tradition," but notes that in subsequent volumes concerning the will (cf. *Varieties of Religious Experience*, 1902; *The Will To Believe*, 1905) he largely retracts his materialistic, deterministic stance (see also James, 1904, 1905).

Deese, like Pollio on consciousness, begins his essay with the admonition that "No topic has more completely disappeared from modern psychology than that of the will." However, both chapters raise so many thought provoking ideas that they may signal an end to this state of affairs.

James defined psychology as "the Science of Mental Life, both of its phenomena [conscious experience] and their conditions [physiology and environment]" (I: 1). This interplay between mind and body still serves to define the subject matter of psychology, and is the subject matter of this volume as well. It is true, however, that this definition makes psychology at best an uncomfortable science. As James himself put it:

> According to the assumptions of this book, thoughts accompany the brain's workings, and those thoughts are cognitive realities. The whole relation is one which we can only write down empirically, confessing that no glimmer of explanation of it is yet in sight. That brains should give rise to a knowing consciousness at all, this is the one mystery which returns, no matter of what sort the consciousness and of what sort the knowledge may be. . . . and the mystery of it is unspeakable. (I:687)

As the science of psychology struggles toward the 21st century, it is comforting to know that we are still in good company.

REFERENCES

Allen, G. (1967). *William James*. New York: Viking.

Berger, P., & Luckman, T. (1966). *The social construction of reality*. Garden City, NY: Doubleday.

Bjork, D. (1988). *William James*. New York: Columbia University Press.

Blanshard, B., & Schneider, W. (1942). *In commemoration of William James*. New York: Columbia University Press.

Edie, J. (1970). William James and phenomenology. *Review of Metaphysics, 23*, 481–526.

Edie, J. M. (1987). *William James and phenomenology*. Bloomington: Indiana University Press.

Evans, R. (1981). Introduction. In W. James, *The principles of psychology* (Vol. 1, xli–lxvii). Cambridge, MA: Harvard University Press.

Feinstein, H. (1984). *Becoming William James*. Ithaca, NY: Cornell University Press.

Gergen, K. (1985). The social constructionist movement in modern psychology. *American Psychologist, 40*, 266–275.

Henley, T., Johnson, M., Herzog, H., & Jones, E. (1989). Definitions of psychology. *Psychological Record, 39*, 143–152.

James, W. (1890). *The principles of psychology* (Vols. 1–2). New York: Holt.

James, W. (1902). *Varieties of religious experience*. New York: Longmans, Green.

James, W. (1904). Does 'consciousness' exist? *Journal of Philosophy, Psychology and Scientific Methods, 1*, 477–491.

James, W. (1905). The essence of humanism. *Journal of Philosophy, Psychology and Scientific Methods, 2*, 113–118.

Knight, M. (1950). *William James: A selection from his writings on psychology*. Harmondsworth, England: Penguin.

Köhler, W. (1947). *Gestalt psychology* (rev. ed.). New York: Liveright.

Lakoff, G., & Johnson M. (1980). *Metaphors we live by*. Chicago: University of Chicago Press.

Lears, T. (1987). William James. *The Wilson Quarterly, XI*, 84–95.

Linschoten, J. (1968). *On the way towards a phenomenological psychology*. Pittsburgh, PA: Duquesne University Press.

MacLeod, R. (1969). *William James: Unfinished business*. Washington, DC: American Psychological Association.

Merleau-Ponty, M. (1962). *The phenomenology of perception*. London: Routledge and Kegan Paul. (Original work published 1945)

Myers, G. (1986). *William James: His life and thought*. New Haven, CT: Yale University Press.

Perry, R. (1935). *The thought and character of William James* (Vols. 1–2). Boston: Little, Brown.

Roback, A. (1942). *William James*. Cambridge, MA: SCI-ART Publishers.

Rumelhart, D., McClelland, J., & the PDP research group. (1986). *Parallel distributed processing* (Vols. 1–2). Cambridge, MA: MIT Press.

Schmidt, J. (1985). *Maurice Merleau-Ponty: Between phenomenology and structuralism*. New York: St. Martin's Press.

Stevens, R. (1974). *James and Husserl: The foundations of meaning*. The Hague: Nijhoff.

Wilshire, B. (1968). *William James and phenomenology*. Bloomington: Indiana University Press.

Wittgenstein, L. (1953). *Philosophical investigations*. New York: Macmillan.

Chapter 1

William James
and His *Principles*

Rand B. Evans
University of Baltimore

Just 100 years ago William James published his monumental *Principles of Psychology* (W. James, 1890). The *Principles* has remained in print ever since, a remarkable feat for its hesitant and self-deprecating author. So well known are the author and the book that they hardly need introduction. Still, the centenary of the publication of the *Principles* and the approaching 150th anniversary of James's birth is an appropriate time to stand back and consider the background of his remarkable book.

The *Principles* is certainly James's masterpiece and probably the most significant psychological treatise ever written in America. In its richness of descriptive detail into the varieties of mental life, in its boldness of explanation, and even in its leaps into speculative possibilities, it has no equal in American psychological literature. The *Principles* is also perhaps the best *entree* to any thorough understanding of James's thought (McDermott, 1977, p. xxxiii).

A century ago, however, the *Principles* was just a huge stack of paper on William James's desk being prepared for shipment to Henry Holt for publication. James had reason to anticipate a positive reception for his book. Several of the chapters had already appeared as articles in periodicals and had been well received. When he submitted the manuscript to Henry Holt, however, James was quite self-effacing, calling himself "an incapable" and his manuscript "a loathsome, distended, tumefied, bloated, dropsical mass . . . " (Perry, 1935, Vol. II, p. 48). To his brother Henry, however, James intimated that, "As 'psychologies' go, it is a good one . . . " (H. James, 1920, Vol. I, p. 296).

James's *Principles* was a very personal document. James's philosophy and his life history were tightly intertwined. His emphases of the themes of naturalism, will, and self in his *Principles* was clearly a product of major struggles in his own life. His insights were, at least in part, due to his gaining control of his own self and will from influences that seemed to overcome him in his early life. James tells us that he "drifted" into psychology and philosophy (Perry, 1935, Vol. I, p. 228). The currents on which he drifted, however, can be seen as influenced by his personal struggles. A consideration of some of the major points of James's early life may make that relationship clearer.

LIFE OF WILLIAM JAMES TO 1890

William James was born in New York City on January 11, 1842 (see Allen, 1967; H. James, Jr., 1920; Myers, 1986; Perry, 1935 for more complete biographical details). He was born to wealth and privilege. His grandfather, also named William, had come to America from Ireland in the late 18th century and made his fortune in land speculation. Of this William's 13 children, Henry James Sr. was the father of our William James. Due to his share of the family wealth, Henry James Sr. never had to work in the standard meaning of the word. He spent most of his adult life involved in intellectual pursuits centering primarily around his own religious philosophy, a free-thinking view strongly influenced by the mystical philosophy of Emanuel Swedenborg.

Henry James had five children, the eldest of whom was our William James. The most famous of William's siblings was his brother, Henry, the author of finely crafted "psychological" novels and stories. The other siblings did not reach the attainments of William and Henry. The one sister, Alice, suffered most intensely from the neuroses that seem to have inflicted all of the James children, which chronically disabled her throughout her life. This was particularly unfortunate since Alice showed in her diaries a spark no less than that of William and Henry. The two youngest brothers, Robertson and Garth Wilkinson, in contrast, did little writing and lived, relatively speaking, mediocre lives. Growing up, however, the James children had the benefit of parents who were interested in intellectual attainment. Although the children received a fragmented and somewhat unbalanced education, it was a rich one. The family traveled extensively. William and his siblings attended school in Europe as well as America. He became adept in French and passable in German and Italian, languages that would aid him in his scholarly life. He also spoke a little Portuguese and read Latin and Greek.

Although Henry James Sr. moved in a circle of literary luminaries and there were often visitors in the James home, the family was largely self-contained intellectually, virtually a subculture unto itself. Once, when William James was asked what nationality his brother was, he responded that: "—he's really, I won't say a Yankee, but a native of the James family, and has no other country . . . "(Perry, 1935, Vol. I, p. 412). Because of this unusually self-contained family situation and its famous products, the James family has been the subject of intense scrutiny. Every extant and available line written by any member to or about any other member has been evaluated and interpreted from every standpoint imaginable. The result of all this, as is probably the case with other over-analyzed and over-interpreted individuals and families, is that the James family, which was certainly an unusual one, sometime appears merely eccentric (Bjork, 1983, pp. 15–36; Myers, 1986 pp. 18–34).

It is clear that the members of William James's family shared a neurotic predilection called, in the late 19th century, neurasthenia. The term represented a congeries of illnesses and was vague at best, although perhaps no more vague than the term, neurosis, that replaced it (Carlson, 1980; Gosling, 1987). Although the origin and nature of his ailments is not really known with any precision, his dealing with such symptoms appears to have shaped much of his approach to understanding mental life.

Perhaps the greatest single influence on William's early intellectual life was his father, Henry Sr. Although William claimed he never understood his father's religious philosophy, the environment in which William grew up and in which he lived into his late thirties, was permeated by his father's ideas and their application in the family's domestic sphere.

Henry James wrote of his hopes for William's future:

> I desire my child to become an upright man, a man in whom goodness shall be induced not by mercenary motives as brute goodness is induced, but by love for it or a sympathetic delight in it. And inasmuch as I know that this character or disposition cannot be forcibly imposed upon him, but must be freely assumed, I surround him as far as possible with an atmosphere of freedom. (H. James, Sr., 1855, p. 170)

This freedom and desire for self-actualization Henry Sr. gave to William and his other children, along with a loving, even coddled environment. Henry Sr. believed that his children should remain innocent and unworldly as long as possible and sought a family atmosphere that would foster such unworldliness. In doing so he and his wife, Mary, effectively extended the childhoods of their offspring well into the age when others were expressing the independence of their adulthood. This artificial, hothouse approach to child rearing was not given without cost to William and the other children. When the realities of the world had to be faced, the children, although chronologically adults, were largely unprepared.

William's childhood extended well into his thirties and it might be argued that his transition into adulthood, as it is ordinarily understood, was completed only after his marriage to Alice Howe Gibbons in 1878 and his move from his family's house. This extended adolescence was quite likely the source of some of William's personal tendencies, particularly those involving the avoidance or forestalling of commitments, as well as avoiding firm definitions, hardened concepts, or fixed situations. These tendencies, although they contributed to aspects of James's psychological thought that we prize so much in the *Principles*, were also a source of stress and conflict in his own personal life. I would argue that the ailments and the convalescence that made up so much of James's life before the publication of the *Principles* was a product of William's artificially extended childhood in the James family and the conflicts that resulted from his being presented with an adult world after enrolling at Harvard and being unable to deal with them.

Henry Sr. impressed on his children that they should pursue intellectual delights without consideration to mundane matters such as income. Henry Sr. could and did pursue his own intellectual delights in just this way. Being independently wealthy, he could afford to do so. His children, however, were the generation who would be unable to support themselves only on their shares of the diluted family fortune. It was, in particular, the conflict between individual self-actualization and the practicalities of making a living that would plague William, perhaps most of all, as he attempted to make his way in the world.

A negative influence of Henry Sr. on William was Henry's deterministic belief that an individual's life was controlled by the will of God and that the individual must subjugate his own will to God's. The story of William James's transition from childhood to adulthood is, in many ways, the story of his rejection of his father's notions and his recognition of the necessity for an individual to project his ego into the world through the exercise of his own free will rather than a submissive acceptance of any determinism.

Henry James Sr.'s influence on his children was aided and abetted by his wife, Mary. Although she was the most emotionally stable member of the family and was the glue that held the family together, she also helped create the atmosphere that legitimized and promoted hypochondriasis among the children. She appears to have been a firm believer in overwork as the source of nervous exhaustion and was continually cautioning members of the family against any exertion, lest they overtax themselves and require convalescence. The fact that the James family could afford extended convalescence may have been a contributing factor as well.

In his late teens, William began seeking a direction for his life. He was having some difficulty in finding it, not an uncommon problem for someone born into independent wealth. William found that he had an aptitude for and an interest in painting, and had thoughts of art as a career. On one of the family's sojourns to Newport William came to know the artist, William Morris Hunt. Henry Sr., however, believed that William was better suited for science than for art. Perhaps to avoid the kind of break he had experienced with his father and to maintain at least the appearance of the freedom he declared available to his children, Henry Sr. did not openly forbid his son's dabbling in art. After it became apparent that William was determined to be an artist, Henry Sr. allowed him to study for a while with Hunt in Newport. After a period of study, William, either by his own decision or one influenced by Henry Sr., decided that he did not have sufficient talent to become an artist of quality.

In the fall of 1861, William gave up the notion of becoming an artist and entered the Lawrence Scientific School at Harvard to study chemistry. This shift from art to science on William's part and its supposed role in the onset of William's neurosis has been the subject of several studies, perhaps the most notable of which is found in Howard M. Feinstein's *Becoming William James* (1984). One aspect of the argument has been that the emergence of William's nervous symptoms at this time was incited by his being dragooned from a life of art into a life of science. The argument is interesting but not entirely compelling. There seems to be no clear evidence that Henry Sr. did more than allow William to see whether he had sufficient talent to make art a career. Apparently William decided he did not have the talent. The fact that William apparently had expressed "ardor" for chemistry before he left for Harvard (H. James, Jr., 1920, Vol. I, p. 43) and that there was no sign of acrimony between him and his father, makes the case for a father–son conflict somewhat questionable. The fact that James later seemed to lament his not pursuing art is not sufficient in itself to support the frustrated artist hypothesis since James tended to lament any lost possibility (See, H. James, Jr., 1920, Vol. I, p. 128).

It is a fact, however, that William showed signs of ill health during his first year and a half at college. His instructor in chemistry, Charles W. Eliot, recalled that James's work during those first three semesters was "much interfered with by ill-health, or rather by something which I imagined to be a delicacy of nervous constitution" (H. James, Jr., 1920, Vol. I, p. 32). Eliot's notes taken at the time indicate that James had "irregular attendance at laboratory" (H. James, Jr., 1920, Vol. I, p. 32fn). William showed ability to learn from the texts but seemed not to have a devotion to the study of chemistry or the perseverance for laboratory work (H. James, Jr., 1920, Vol. I, pp. 31–32). James complained for instance, "This chemical analysis is so bewildering at first that I am entirely 'muddled and beat' and have to employ most all my time reading up" (Perry, 1935, Vol. I, p. 210). It is quite likely that these periods of ill health and William's inability to hold to a task or a study for great lengths of time were due to the onset of neurotic episodes. The cause of the episodes is open to question, however. It is entirely possible, for instance, that the largely undemanding, self-paced and even dilettantish educational background William had experienced all his life left him unprepared for the more intense and stringent demands of college life. The onset of symptoms, such as William's, among students suffering the "culture shock" of a transition from a high school environment to that of college is not unusual even today. Eliot noted that James's educational preparation had been irregular, "it did not conform to the Boston and Cambridge traditional method." He also noted that his education had been slanted strongly in the direction of the biological sciences and was "in large proportion observational" (Perry, 1935, Vol. I, p. 207). The nature of James's early education could well have made a transition into the college environment difficult. Whatever the source of William's nervousness and ill-health, which began that fall of 1861, the ailment made laboratory work difficult for him.

William would spend a year and a half in the study of chemistry until he found that his ardor for the field had become "somewhat dulled" (H. James, Jr., 1920, Vol. I, p. 43). He then spent the following semester and summer at home. The fall of 1862, William returned to Harvard, this time transferring from chemistry to comparative anatomy under Jeffries Wyman.

Coming to the end of his sophomore year, he was expected to come up with "finally and irrevocably 'the choice of a profession' " (H. James, Jr., 1920, Vol. I, p. 43). He pointed out that he had four alternatives:

Natural History, Medicine, Printing, Beggary. Much may be said in favor of each. I have named them in the ascending order of their pecuniary invitingness. After all, the great problem of life seems to be how to keep body and soul together, and I *have* to consider lucre. To study natural science, I know I should like, but the prospect of supporting a family on $600 a year is not one of those rosy dreams of the future with which the young are said to be haunted. Medicine would pay, but I should still be dealing with subjects which interest me—but how much drudgery and of what an unpleasant kind is there! Of all departments of Medicine that to which Dr. Prince devotes himself is, I should think, the most interesting. And I should like to see him and his patients at Northampton very much before coming to a decision.

The worst of this matter is that everyone must more or less act with insufficient knowledge—"go it blind," as they say. Few can afford the time to try what suits them. However, a few months will show. (H. James, Jr., 1920, Vol. I, p. 44)

"Beggary," according to Feinstein, is James's word for the life of a student gaining income from his family. William had gone through a bit of a strain with his mother about his demands for money (Feinstein, 1984, p. 162). The Dr. Prince mentioned here was an alienist to whom William's cousin Katharine was married. This letter gives an early indication on James's part of an interest in the study of mental science.

William's conflict between developing his highest interest and making a living can be traced directly to his father's view of the "Artist" and the perfect life. Henry James Sr. had long impressed a distinction between the artist and artisan. Art, in Henry James's meaning, is meant in the broad sense of creation, not in its narrow sense of creation of specific works. Henry James wrote in 1852, for instance:

The sphere of Art properly so called, is the sphere of man's spontaneous productivity. I say his spontaneous productivity, in order to distinguish it on the one hand from his natural productivity, or that which is prompted by his physical necessities, and on the other by his moral productivity, or that which is prompted by his obligations to other men. Thus the sphere of Art embraces all those products of human genius, which do not confess the parentage either of necessity or duty. It covers whatsoever is produced without any external constraint, any constraint imposed by the exigencies either of our physical or social subsistence. We do not call the shoemaker an artist, because we know very well that he is animated in his vocation not by any inward attraction to it, not by any overmastering love of making shoes, but simply by the desire of making a living for himself and his family. What prompts him to work is not any spontaneous and irrepressible delight in it, any such delight as makes the work its own reward, but simply a feeling of obligation to himself and his family. He makes no shoe for the pure pleasure of making it, but because he would so put bread into the mouths of his family. Thus his productivity, being enforced both by necessity and duty, being enforced by the necessity of providing for himself and the duty of providing for those whom society makes dependent on him, is not spontaneous or free, does not in other words obey an internal attraction and consequently fails utterly without the sphere of Art. The shoemaker is not an Artist. He is only an Artisan or Workman. (H. James, Sr., 1852, pp. 101–108)

To Henry James Sr., "The Artist . . . is the Divine Man,—the only adequate image of God in nature. . . . He is that true creature and son of God, whom God pronounces very good, and endows with the lordship of the whole earth" (H. James, Sr., 1852, pp. 101–108).

The artisan or workman was not living up to man's highest possibilities and thus could not share fully in the Divine Will. This notion runs through a great deal of Henry James Sr.'s writings. Henry James, of course, was describing himself as "Artist." He could well afford a life without the demands of making a living. After growing up in a household that set such a high standard for living life, it is not surprising that William and the other James children had great difficulty selecting a life's work. We can only imagine what internal conflicts they had when they realized that they would, by necessity, make their way in life as mere artisans.

The question of selecting a life's work, and having to make a decision that might be irrevocable, clearly weighed on William. He could choose the life of "Artist" in his father's meaning and live life in "penury" with no hope of supporting a wife and family or he could choose a career in the practical world and support a family but live as a mere artisan. He wrote to his mother:

I feel very much the importance of making soon a final choice of my business in life. I stand now at the place where the road forks. One branch leads to material comfort, the flesh-pots; but it seems a kind of selling of one's soul.

The other to mental dignity and independence; combined, however, with physical penury. If I were the only one concerned I should not hesitate an instant in my choice. But it seems hard on Mrs. W. J., "that not impossible she," to ask her to share an empty purse and a cold hearth. On one side is *science*, upon the other *business* (the honorable, honored and productive business of printing seems most attractive), with *medicine*, which partakes of [the] advantages of both, between them, but which has drawbacks of its own. I confess I hesitate. (H. James, Jr., 1920, Vol. I, pp. 45–46; Perry, 1935, pp. 215–216)

William, at this time, seems to have preferred naturalism of some sort as the highest realization of his future life's work but saw in medicine a compromise. In the 19th century, medicine was often the professional pursuit for individuals who were really interested in science but who needed an occupation that would guarantee income.

William's great fear seems to have been setting his sights too low, selling out for money and suffering "some anguish in looking back from the pinnacle of prosperity . . . over the life you might have led in the pure pursuit of truth" (H. James, Jr., 1920, Vol. I, p. 46). He felt that he might be able to stick with science over medicine if he could get a position as a naturalist in Louis Agassiz's museum at Harvard.

Jeffries Wyman, with whom William would study comparative anatomy and physiology, was also a naturalist and was a man who met the highest standards of the kind of man William's father thought represented the "higher attainments." William's description of Wyman in his letters (H. James, Jr., 1920, Vol. I, pp. 48–49), agrees quite closely with his father, Henry's, description of the sort of person he wanted his sons to become.

Although William seems to have "committed" himself to medicine, at least for the sake of Harvard's requirements, and entered into the course of study for a medical degree, it is clear that he was not committed for himself. In spring of 1865, he set aside his medical studies to go with Louis Agassiz on the Thayer expedition up the Amazon.

William soon discovered that the life of the naturalist, at least the field naturalist, was not for him. He felt that his coming on the expedition was a mistake in terms of what he expected the trip to be, and felt that he would learn "next to nothing of natural history as I care about learning it" (H. James, Jr., 1920, Vol. I, p. 61). He had discovered that finding objects and packing them away for later study too mundane. He rationalized for himself a speculative rather than an active life. He wrote to his brother, Henry, that "When I get home, I'm going to study philosophy all my days" (H. James, Jr., 1920, Vol. I, p. 53).

James seems to have been led by the possibilities of one pursuit or the other throughout his life. He tended to view those possibilities in an idealized way without considering the drudgery that often accompanies them.

This tendency may account for his life-long search for the field of his own "highest attainment."

William returned to his medical studies in fall of 1866 after having served in a summer internship at Massachusetts General Hospital. He threw himself into his studies. He initially seemed to be in good health, physically and mentally, even though he had had a bout with smallpox on the Amazon trip.

After his return, James made contacts that would allow him to pursue philosophy as he had declared his intent on the Amazon trip. He entered into regular discussions on philosophical matters with such figures as Charles S. Peirce, Chauncey Wright, Oliver Wendell Holmes, and others. These men were either professional philosophers or individuals deeply interested at the time with philosophical questions. They, among others, would be members of the informal philosophy club called later by C. S. Peirce the Metaphysical Club. The James family had by that time moved nearby and their parlor was also often the site of philosophical discussion, particularly with Chauncey Wright. These individuals and discussions would be of significant influence on James's "drifting" into philosophy and psychology (Perry, 1935, Vol. I, p. 228).

After taking up his studies in the medical school and preparing to attempt joining the hospital, it is clear that William came to regard medicine in a negative light. The "toadying" of the students to the professors who controlled entrance to the hospitals he viewed with disdain. He played the game, however. He wrote his friend Tom Ward in December of 1866, however, that:

> The present time is a very exciting one, for ambitious young men at the Medical School who are anxious to get into the hospital. Their toadying the physicians, asking them intelligent questions after lectures, offering to run errands for them, etc., this week reaches its climax; they call at their residences and humbly solicit them to favor their appointment, and do the same at the residences of the ten trustees. So I have sixteen visits to make. I have little fears, with my talent for flattery and fawning, of a failure. The appointments are published in January. (Perry, 1935, Vol. I, p. 213)

James did not enter the hospital that spring. The reason given by James's biographers is ill-health. He is said to have been plagued since the fall of 1866 by several discomforts: "insomnia, digestive disorders, eye-troubles, weakness of the back, and sometimes deep depression of spirits followed each other or afflicted him simultaneously" (Perry, 1935, Vol. I, p. 233; H. James, Jr., 1920, Vol. I, p. 84). James reported later that during the winter of 1866-67 he had been "on the continual verge of suicide" (H. James, Jr., 1920, Vol. I, p. 129). William's son, Henry, tells us that William was "compelled" to end his medical studies "partly by the pressure of a conviction that his health required him to stop work or continue elsewhere under different conditions, and partly by a desire to learn German and study physiology in the German laboratories" (H. James, Jr., 1920, Vol. I, p. 84). It may be that the high energy expended in studies since his return from Brazil had taken its toll. James had expressed during that fall the belief that "each man's constitution limits him to a certain amount of emotion and action, and that, if he insists on going under a higher pressure than normal for three months, for instance, he will pay for it by passing the next three months below par" (H. James, Jr., 1920, Vol. I, p. 78). Were this not written in 1866, one would think that William had read George M. Beard's article that largely popularized and defined the term neurasthenia. Beard, however, wrote in 1869 (Beard, 1869). James knew Beard, however, and may have been influenced by his ideas at the time. His symptoms were precisely those of neurasthenia or nervous exhaustion. There appears to have been almost a cult of ill-health in the James family. They were not alone, of course. The symptoms were rampant among the well-to-do in the urban eastern United States. Howard Feinstein has made an interesting case for the role of illness in the James family as a means of competition among the James children for family resources, particularly resources for travel and relaxation in Europe (Feinstein, 1984, pp. 182–205). Such travel for pleasure would not have been supported by the family, but recuperation from nervous exhaustion was a legitimate expenditure. Feinstein points out that the James children had to be careful in writing home not to show improvement too quickly. Otherwise they would be called back. It is possible that Feinstein makes his case too strongly. He appears to attribute a fully conscious and scheming intent to the James children. That is a stronger argument than I would make, but I think that illness and its necessary convalescence, whether consciously or unconsciously motivated, appears to have occurred in William James's case whenever he was faced with making a commitment on his life's work.

It appears that William James, again at a decision point, chose the possibilities of a study of physiology in Germany over the realities of the hospital. Whatever the actual nature of William's health, the fact is that he did not intern in the hospital. Instead, he left his medical studies for a recuperative stint in Germany. There, although he availed himself of the spa cures, his symptoms did not go away. His tendency toward self-possession, referred to as introspective, made things even worse. His intention to study physiology, came to very little. He did attend some lectures at the University of Berlin in November, 1867. It was that November that he mentioned psychology as a serious study.

It seems to me that perhaps the time has come for psychology to begin to be a science—some measurements have already been made in the region lying between the physical changes in the nerves and the appearance of consciousness-at (in the shape of sense perceptions), and more may come of it. I am going on to study what is already known, and perhaps may be able to do some work at it. Helmholtz and a man named Wundt at Heidelberg are working at it, and I hope I live through this winter to go to them in the summer. (H. James, Jr., 1920, Vol. I, pp. 118–119)

All this sounds very eager and positive, but in the same letter, James mentions being unable to do work in the laboratory at Berlin because of his "present" condition and adding that he was not ". . . working straight ahead—towards a definite aim. Alas no! I finger book-covers as ineffectually as ever. The fact is, this sickness takes all the spring, physical and mental, out of a man . . . " (H. James, Jr., 1920, Vol. I, p. 119).

James had decided that, even if he received his medical degree from Harvard, he would not practice (H. James, Jr., 1920, Vol. I, p. 123). He believed that he would be an invalid, passing his years writing for medical journals. Still, he emphasized that he had made no firm plans about his future (H. James, Jr., 1920, Vol. I, p. 125). He again expressed regrets for possibilities that might be lost. In a letter to Tom Ward, who was also going through a depressive period, he wrote:

> But I really don't think it so *all*-important what our occupation is, so long as we do respectably and keep a clean bosom. Whatever we are *not* doing is pretty sure to come to us at intervals, in the midst of our toil, and fill us with pungent regrets that it is lost to us. I have felt so about zoölogy whenever I was not studying it, about anthropology when studying physiology, about practical medicine lately, now that I am cut off from it, etc., etc., etc.; and I conclude that that sort of nostalgia is a necessary incident of our having imaginations, and we must expect it more or less whatever we are about. (H. James, Jr., 1920, Vol. I, p. 128)

James left Berlin in January of 1868 for the cure at Teplitz with the hope of getting back his health sufficiently to be able to pursue physiology the following summer with the thought of its becoming his career (H. James, Jr., 1920, Vol. I, pp. 133–136). Although the spa at Teplitz apparently did little to help him, he was able to go to Heidelberg in the spring to attend some lectures by Helmholtz. The summer he was to spend studying physiology, however, was spent in Divonne at another spa. The stay at Divonne was not helpful either. Its only contribution was the fact that it was there that James learned of the French philosopher, Renouvier, who would be such a great influence in his future.

In November, 1868, James returned to his family in Cambridge, Massachusetts, where, after gaining his medical degree from Harvard in June, 1869, he spent the next 3 years again in semi-convalescence. It was a period spent in reading and contemplation, particularly on philosophical and psychological topics (H. James, Jr., 1920, Vol. I, p. 154). In 1870 William James suffered the most severe episode of his illness, brought on, perhaps, by the untimely death of a particularly beloved cousin. The illness was accompanied by a devastating fear of his own inability to control his own destiny. It was during this period that James, after reading Renouvier and Wordsworth, resolved to take possession of his life. The often repeated quote is worth repeating again:

> I think that yesterday was a crisis in my life. I finished the first part of Renouvier's second "Essais" and see no reason why his definition of Free Will—"the sustaining of a thought because I choose to when I might have other thoughts"—need be the definition of an illusion. At any rate, I will assume for the present—until next year—that it was no illusion. My first act of free will shall be to believe in free will. For the remainder of the year, I will abstain from the mere speculation and contemplative *Grüblei* [grubbing among subtleties] in which my nature takes most delight, and voluntarily cultivate the feeling of moral freedom, by reading books favorable to it, as well as by acting. (H. James, Jr., 1920, Vol. I, pp. 147–148)

Whether this decision was the factor that led James to rouse himself from his ailment or merely an indication of that rousing, it was definitely the beginning of a new phase in his life. Free will took over from passivity. The self was no longer subjugated to inexorable external forces. James also willfully turned away from the search for possibilities that would meet his father's criterion of spontaneous delight. He sought, instead, for practical solutions that were needed for coping with real life. We should not be surprised, then, to find the deep significance that free will and expression of self held for James in his exposition of mental life in the *Principles*. William had always viewed his own ailments as apart from himself, being instead physiologically based visitations that, if not ameliorated by physical "cures," were to be borne as patiently as possible. Earlier James had written his friend, Tom Ward, who was suffering symptoms similar to his own, saying: "Take for granted that you've got a temperament from which you must make up your mind to expect twenty times as much anguish as other people need to get along with. Regard it as something as external to you as possible, like the curl of your hair" (H. James, Jr., 1920, Vol. I, p. 128). The medical definition of neurasthenia largely supported this notion of a strictly somatic explanation. William's father's deterministic notion that one should subjugate one's will to the Divine Will may also have influenced William to view ailments as unavoidable visitations. Only when William was able to view his own symptoms as being psychological in nature and perhaps within reach of his own intervention could he pull himself from his depression. Henry James Sr. asked William what had brought about the change. Henry reported that:

> He said several things: the reading of Renouvier (particularly his vindication of the freedom of the will) and of Wordsworth, whom he has been feeding on now for a good while; but more than anything else, his having given up the

notion that all mental disorder requires to have a physical basis. This had become perfectly untrue to him. He saw that the mind does act irrespectively of material coercion, and could be dealt with therefore at first hand, and this was health to his bones. (H. James, Jr., 1920, Vol. I, pp. 169–170)

Henry Sr. rejoiced not only because of the improvement in William's health but also because he appeared to be "shaking off his respect for men of mere science as such, and is even more universal and impartial in his mental judgments than I have known him before" (H. James, Jr., 1920, Vol. I, p. 170). However, William's declaration of free will was also a declaration of independence from the determinism of his father's religious philosophy just as much as from the determinism of somatic psychiatry.

In August, 1872 Charles Eliot, once William James's chemistry instructor, now president of Harvard, intervened in James's life. Eliot, in devising his system of electives at Harvard, decided that undergraduates should have instruction in anatomy and physiology. He proposed that William James and Thomas Dwight, an anatomist, serve as instructors in such a course. James's interests were, by then, more philosophical and psychological than physiological. Still, here was a chance to do something. Thus, at the beginning of the fall term in 1872, William James became an instructor in physiology at Harvard, although his duties did not begin until the spring term of 1873. James's work with Wyman and his reading in Germany had not been in vain after all. Although his duties were primarily directed toward teaching anatomy and physiology, his interests would remain centered on philosophical and psychological questions.

The work seemed to benefit James. His father reported in March, 1873 that William had exclaimed to him, "Bless my soul, what a difference between me as I am now and as I was last spring at this time! . . . Then so hypochondriacal and now with my mind so cleared up and restored to sanity. It's the difference between death and life" (H. James, Jr., 1920, Vol. I, p. 170).

At the end of that term, William was faced with another situation in which he had to make a decision. The appointment he was serving under had only a year's duration, but Eliot wished to give James complete control over the course he then taught in conjunction with Dwight. He was placed in a difficult situation. Either he had to accept the appointment, which would put him in a more permanent position and cause him to declare himself as a physiologist or anatomist or he had to strike out and seek for a position in philosophy, his dominant interest. Philosophy as an interest was one thing, but he expressed as part of his indecision the feeling that "Philosophical activity as a business is not normal for most men, and not for me . . . " (H. James, Jr., 1920, Vol. I, p. 170). James accepted Eliot's offer, at last, but then postponed it for a year and went abroad again. The difference between this trip and the previous one is that the period in Europe was not spent in morbid self-introspection but in undisguised enjoyment and that he returned with a new unction to carry out his university duties. Although James would have recurrences of his nervous malady throughout his life, the worst was over and a productive career lay before him. James returned to Harvard as instructor in anatomy and physiology.

In 1875 James offered his now famous course in physiological psychology, titled "The Relation Between Physiology and Psychology," for graduate students in the Lawrence Scientific School and established his demonstration laboratory in the subject for his students. The following year he offered the course for undergraduates under the title "Physiological Psychology." These courses were offered in the Department of Natural History of the Lawrence Scientific School. In 1876, James became assistant professor of physiology. In 1877, he offered his "Psychology" course in the Department of Philosophy at Harvard as an elective. This was done over the opposition of Francis Bowen, who was then Alford Professor of Philosophy at Harvard and held the chair in philosophy (Hall, 1879). Bowen had offered a course that went under the title of "Psychology" since 1872. Bowen had as his texts in the course, works by Locke, Cousin, and John Stuart Mill. Bowen was of the older generation of philosophical psychologists, a theist and strong supporter of the views of Sir William Hamilton. Bowen may have questioned James's credentials since James's degree was in medicine and he had no formal training in philosophy. Bowen's opposition was overruled by President Eliot, however, and James's course was instituted in the Department of Philosophy (Evans, 1983).

By the fall of 1879 James was teaching "Physiological Psychology" to graduate students, a course on Renouvier to seniors and a class on Spencer's *First Principles* to juniors. He also offered a lecture once a week on physiology (Allen, 1967, p. 229). By 1889, James's title changed again, this time to professor of psychology. By then, James's version of the new psychology was firmly established at Harvard. His teaching and the articles that would come from his pen during the 1880s would establish him as one of the leaders of American psychology. The publication of his *Principles of Psychology* in 1890, just a year after his promotion to professor of psychology, established him not only as the premier American psychologist of his generation but, in the minds of many, the founder of American psychology itself.

There were many factors that had led James to "wander" into psychology, but his own search for will and self seem to me to be paramount motivations. It may be that the intensely personal nature of James's search is what energizes his writing in the *Principles* and keeps it green and compelling for generations of readers.

THE WRITING OF THE *PRINCIPLES*

In the 1870s the topic of psychology had become popular in American colleges. With the spread of the elective system, initiated by Eliot of Harvard, to other institutions, the variety of courses available to students expanded quickly. Courses in psychology, although under varying titles, were added to the curriculum, usually in departments of philosophy.

This was not the beginning of psychological thought in America, however. Textbooks containing psychological exposition had been popular in American classrooms for 60 years before the appearance of James's *Principles*. Thomas Upham had begun the trend in 1827 with his *Elements of Intellectual Philosophy* and remained perhaps the best of the lot. It was revised and renamed *Elements of Mental Philosophy* in 1831 and was as thoroughgoing a psychology as was James's *Principles*, even though it appeared under the philosophical rubric. The first psychology under that name to be published in America by an American, although an emigrant from Europe, was Frederick A. Rauch's *Psychology or, A View of the Human Soul: Including Anthropology . . .* which appeared in 1840.

The textbooks that followed Upham's demonstrated the clear differentiation of psychological thought from other subject matters. Francis Wayland, professor of moral philosophy and president of Brown, wrote both an intellectual philosophy and a moral philosophy. Wayland's "Intellectual Philosophy" covered psychology in its narrow sense of "knowing, feeling and doing," in terms of mental states. His "Moral Science" also touched on psychological matters, but was more concerned with ethics and general concepts of morality—how one should behave rather than how one does behave. Similarly, Joseph Haven wrote very popular books covering mental philosophy and moral philosophy as separate topics with the psychological material primarily lodged in the mental philosophy. Such attempts by one person to cover both the psychological and ethical aspects of the field lasted well into the proliferation of psychology courses after the introduction of the elective system into colleges in the 1870s.

Noah Porter, professor of moral philosophy and metaphysics and president of Yale, brought this intellectual and moral philosophy model to its apex with *The Human Intellect* (1868) and *The Elements of Moral Science: Theoretical and Practical* (1885). (See Evans, 1983).

The courses on intellectual and mental philosophy of the first half of the 19th century gradually became the psychology courses of the second half, although many still used the older titles. New books to serve as texts in these reorganized courses were not long in coming. Spencer's *Principles of Psychology* was imported from England, for instance. Taine's *l'Intelligence* came over from France. In America, John Bascom produced his *Principles of Psychology* in 1869 and his *Comparative Psychology* in 1878. During the 1870s McCosh and Hopkins both added books on psychology to the literature (see, Fay, 1939, pp. 224–226).

In the mid-1870s Henry Holt of New York City sought to add a psychology text to his list and began seeking an author. His intention seems to have been to commission a typical textbook of the time, a volume of approximately 500 pages. Holt approached John Fiske, who was a well-known disciple of Herbert Spencer and was librarian at Harvard. It is unclear how long Fiske worked on the book, but by spring of 1878, he decided to give up the attempt at writing it. Fiske was a member of the Metaphysical Club already mentioned (Madden, 1963, pp. 21–22). In writing to Holt and giving up the book, Fiske suggested James:

> As for psychology, William James knows more about it than I do. He has been studying little else for several years, while I, for the past four years, have done little but peg away at early history, and have hardly looked at a book in philosophy or psychology. I am getting rusty on the details of psychology while James is always keeping right up to the times on such matters. Go for James. . . . (E. Fisk, 1940, p. 271)

In May of 1878, Holt approached James to do the book and he accepted. James predicted that he could have a manuscript ready by the fall of 1880 (James Papers, Harvard University, bMS 1092). James delayed partly because of his impending marriage, which he felt would bring about a certain disruption to the order of his life. Holt thought James's estimate was excessive, but he accepted it with the hope that James could complete the manuscript in less than 2 years. Holt wanted the manuscript no later than June, 1880. Had Holt known that James would take not 2 years but 12 to complete the book, he might have gone elsewhere for his author. What Holt finally received, however, was certainly worth the wait.

The *Principles* did not appear all at once. Several of the chapters appeared as articles in various publications between 1879 and 1890. For this reason, James's contemporaries often used 1879 or 1880 as their date for the separation between the old and new psychologies in America. That was when James's articles that became the nucleus of the *Principles* began to appear.

James's *Principles* appeared at last in two volumes totalling almost 1400 pages. Holt finally got the book he originally expected in 1892 with the publication of James's *Psychology: Briefer Course*. This book was called "Jimmy" by generations of undergraduate students as opposed to the big book called "The James." The *Briefer Course* was just short of Holt's original 500 page preference.

James's *Principles*, when it appeared, had several competitors already on the market. The year 1886 alone had seen the introduction of three major psychologies: James McCosh, President of Princeton and leader of the Scottish philosophical psychology, a giant in his day, had published his *Psychology: The Cognitive Powers*. John Dewey, still showing the strong imprint of Hegel, had published his simply titled *Psychology*. Bordon P. Bowne also released his *Introduction to Psychological Theory* that year.

Holt, patiently waiting year after year for James's manuscript, had reason to be concerned as the field suddenly seemed to fill up with psychological books. These are the books, however, that James quite likely had in mind in 1890 when he declared that " . . . psychology is in such an ante-scientific condition that the whole present generation of them is predestined to become unreadable old medieval lumber, as soon as the first genuine tracks of insight are made. The sooner the better for me! . . . " (H. James, Jr., 1920, Vol. I, p. 296).

This was a prophetic statement, for the insights of James's *Principles* would so eclipse the earlier American psychologies that not only would James be credited with the founding of American *scientific* psychology, but of American psychology itself. James McKeen Cattell, writing in 1898, declared of American psychology that:

> The history of psychology here prior to 1880 could be set forth as briefly as the alleged chapter on snakes, in a natural history of Iceland—"There are no snakes in Iceland."
>
> But the land lay fallow and twenty years ago the seed was sown. James, at Harvard, began the publication of a series of striking articles, culminating in the issue, in 1890, of the *Principles of Psychology*, a work of genius such as is rare in any science or in any country. (Cattell, 1898)

Cattell knew of the early philosophical work, of course, and even cited it. But, to Cattell and most of his generation, psychology was synonymous with scientific, experimental psychology, the psychology of Wundt's laboratory and of William James's *Principles*. To these individuals, the earlier philosophical psychologies did not represent psychology at all and could be ignored as though they were of another subject matter entirely. Tensions increased between the philosophers and experimental psychologists then housed together in departments of philosophy. When psychology departments emerged on their own, their break with philosophy often would be bitter and complete, even to the rewriting of the history of the field. Not only were the philosophical psychologies before James's *Principles* eclipsed, but also less imposing contemporary scientific works such as George Trumbull Ladd's *Elements of Physiological Psychology* (Ladd, 1887). Ladd's book was based on the program of Wilhelm Wundt's *Grundzüge der physiologischen Psychologie* [The principles of physiological psychology]. Ladd's *Elements* was positively received at the time of its publication, even by Cattell and G. Stanley Hall. Ladd, however, in his last chapter, inserted a soul hiding behind the mind. For all its positive contributions, this last metaphysical chapter discredited the work for most antimetaphysical and positivistic psychologists of that generation. Edward Bradford Titchener, for instance, recalled his first encounter with Ladd's book while he was student at Oxford: "I well remember my excitement on finding this book in the library of the Oxford Union, and the shock of disappointment at reading that mind was a real unit-being" (Titchener, 1921, p. 600).

It is interesting that James's *Principles*, even today, is sometimes represented as being an experimental psychology (Myers, 1986, p. 2). It was not. It was a scientific, non-metaphysical psychology but not an experimental one. James was writing a scientific psychology in much the same way as Darwin had written a scientific biology. It was science based on observation but not necessarily on experimentation. If anything, James was hostile to laboratory experimentation, taking refuge in the traditional reflective approach of classic philosophy, the approach G. Stanley Hall would later label as "armchair psychology" (Hall, 1895; W. James, I: 191–193).

In fact, William James was much the same type of transitional figure in America as Wilhelm Wundt was in Europe. They both stood at the margin between the new, experimental psychology and the older, philosophical psychology. James, even more than Wundt, was unable to let go of philosophy and devote himself entirely to the psychology of the laboratory.

If all this is true, why are we celebrating the centennial of James's *Principles*? Why has it survived and remained green when all the other books of its generation have become the old, unreadable, medieval lumber he predicted? First, aside from the significance of its contents, James's *Principles* became a totem for the new, experimental psychology in America. Although its break with the earlier philosophical psychologies was not complete, it was a genuine divergence from the past. It was the first significant non-metaphysical psychology produced in America (Evans, 1981). In many respects it made possible the psychology that was to come—the psychology of the laboratory. This is true, even though experimental psychology was a subject that James had neither interest in nor patience with. A contribution of no less importance, however, is the fact that James communicated to his readers in ways unmatched before or since, the *possibilities* of a scientific psychology, one without the need for appeal to metaphysics. The possibilities James posed ranged far beyond the limits set by Wundt's experimental psychology. James's *Principles* had within it the possibilities of new studies in mental life. The new generation of psychologists, influenced by the growing atmosphere of positivistic science, welcomed this sort of psychology and its possibilities. In it they saw a new beginning. In the long run James's scientific but non-experimental book probably influenced more experimental research than did Wundt's more experimental book.

Long after William James turned away from psychology, he would influence psychologists through his *Principles*. E. L. Thorndike, who was a student at Harvard in the 1890s expressed the view that the "influence of James on psychology means essentially the influence of the *Principles of Psychology*" (Thorndike, 1943). It was Thorndike's encounter with the *Principles* that brought him to Harvard to study with its author. John Dewey was also dramatically influenced by James's *Principles*. He revised his own *Psychology*, rebuilding it around James's stream of thought metaphor. It was Dewey who introduced James's *Principles* to James Rowland Angell, leading Angell to go to Harvard to study with James. Angell recalled later, "That book unquestionably affected my thinking for the next 20 years more profoundly than any other" (Angell, 1930, p. 5). Later, Dewey and Angell would found an experimental extension of James's psychology, Chicago Functionalism.

It may have been, after all, James's long childhood that made his psychology what it was. Unlike the "adult" psychology of Wundt, James eschewed limits and hard definitions. Even James's non-metaphysical position holds only for psychology. For the "important questions" of philosophy, James was quite open to metaphysical notions. The very factors that made it difficult for James to commit himself to positions led him to leave as many intellectual doors open as possible in his psychologizing.

In the end, the new psychology was too narrow to hold William James. The very metaphysical questions that he had eliminated from psychology, the global questions of philosophy, drew him away from the field. By the time the *Briefer Course* appeared in 1892, James was already moving into those bigger questions of philosophy. His title was changed in 1898 to professor of philosophy. The psychology James had helped send on its way was going in a direction that he was unwilling or temperamentally unable to follow.

Many of the issues raised by William James in his *Principles of Psychology* remain at issue today. After a long avoidance of the study of mental life, many psychologists have returned to grapple with some of the same topics that fascinated James. Modern psychologists would do well to read again James's writings for, in many respects, we are still working through the program James laid down in his *Principles* and we still stand in the long intellectual shadow cast by the book and its author.

ACKNOWLEDGMENT

I am indebted to Eugene Taylor for his criticisms of an earlier form of this chapter and suggestions for improvements.

REFERENCES

Allen, G. W. (1967). *William James: A biography*. New York: Viking Press.

Angell, J. R. (1930). James Rowland Angell. In C. Murchison (Ed.), *A history of psychology in autobiography*, (Vol. III). Worcester, MA: Clark University Press.

Bascom, J. (1869). *Principles of psychology*. New York: Putnam.

Bascom, J. (1878). *Comparative psychology; or, the growth and grades of intelligence*. New York: Putnam.

Beard, G. M. (1869). Neurasthenia, or nervous exhaustion. *Boston Medical and Surgical Journal, 80,* 245–59.

Bjork, D. W. (1983). *The compromised scientist: William James in the development of American psychology.* New York: Columbia University Press.

Bowne, B. P. (1886). *Introduction to psychological theory.* New York: American Book Company.

Carlson, E. T. (1980). George M. Beard and neurasthenia. In E. R. Wallace IV & L. C. Pressley (Eds.), *Essays in the history of psychiatry.* Columbia, SC: Wm. S. Hall Psychiatric Institute.

Cattell, J. McK. (1898). *Proceedings of the American association for the advancement of science, 47,* 3–15.

Dewey, J. (1886). *Psychology.* New York: Harper and Brothers.

Evans, R. B. (1981). Introduction: The historical context. In F. H. Burkhardt & F. Bowers (Eds.), *William James's Principles of Psychology* (pp. xli–lxviii). Cambridge, MA: Harvard University Press.

Evans, R. B. (1983). The origins of American academic psychology. In J. Brozek (Ed.), *Explorations in the history of psychology in the United States.* Lewisburg, Pa: Bucknell University Press.

Fay, J. W. (1939). *American psychology before William James.* New Brunswick, NJ: Rutgers University Press.

Feinstein, H. (1984). *Becoming William James.* Ithaca, NY: Cornell University Press.

Fisk, E. (Ed.). (1940). *The letters of John Fiske.* New York: Macmillan.

Gosling, F. G. (1987). *Before Freud: Neurasthenia and the American medical community, 1870–1910.* Champaign, IL: University of Illinois Press.

Hall, G. S. (1879). Philosophy in the United States. *Mind, 6,* 97.

Hall, G. S. (1895). Editorial. *American Journal of Psychology, 7,* 3–4.

James, H., Jr. (Ed.). (1920). *The letters of William James.* Boston: Atlantic Monthly Press.

James, H., Sr. (1850). A scientific statement of the Christian doctrine of the lord, or divine man. In H. James, Sr., *Moralism and Christianity.* Reprinted in H. Gunn (Ed.), *Henry James, Senior: A selection of his writings* (p. 133). Chicago: American Library Association, 1974.

James, H., Sr. (1852). The principle of universality in art. In H. James, *Lectures and miscellanies.* Reprinted in G. Gunn (Ed.), *Henry James, Senior: A selection of his writings.* Chicago: American Library Association, 1974.

James, H., Sr. (1855). *The nature of evil.* Quoted in R. B. Perry (1935). Vol. I, p. 170.

James, W. (1890). *The principles of psychology.* New York: Holt.

Ladd, G. T. (1887). *Elements of physiological psychology.* New York: Scribner and Sons.

Madden, E. H. (1963). *Chauncey Wright and the foundations of pragmatism.* Seattle: University of Washington Press.

McCosh, J. (1886). *Psychology: The cognitive powers.* New York: Scribner.

McDermott, J. J. (1977). Person, process, and the risk of belief. In J. J. McDermott (Ed.), *The writings of William James: A comprehensive edition.* Chicago: University of Chicago Press.

Myers, G. (1986). *William James: His life and thought.* New Haven: Yale University Press.

Perry, R. B. (1935). *The thought and character of William James.* Boston: Little, Brown.

Porter, N. (1868). *The human intellect: With an introduction upon psychology and the soul.* New York; Charles Scribner.

Porter, N. (1885). *Elements of moral science: Theoretical and practical.* New York: Scribner and Sons.

Rauch, F. A. (1840). *Psychology or, a view of the human soul: Including anthropology.* New York: M. W. Dodd.

Spencer, H. (1870). *Principles of psychology.* New York: Appleton and Company.

Taine, H. (1869). *L'Intelligence [On Intelligence]* (T. D. Haye, Trans.). New York: Holt and Williams.

Thorndike, E. L. (1943). James's influence on the psychology of perception and thought. *Psychological Review, 50*, 87.

Titchener, E. B. (1921). George Trumbull Ladd. *American Journal of Psychology, 32*, 600.

Upham, T. (1827). *Elements of intellectual philosophy*. Portland: Shirley and Hyde.

Upham, T. (1831). *Elements of mental philosophy*. Portland: William Hyde.

Chapter 2

New Light on the Origin of William James's Experimental Psychology

Eugene Taylor
Harvard Medical School

Experimental psychology in the hands of William James at Harvard had its genesis in primarily three sources: James's personal interest in the problem of how to regard inner experience, James's dialogues with C. S. Peirce and Chauncey Wright on evolutionary theory and the philosophy of science, and James's attraction to French experimental physiology in the tradition of Claude Bernard.[1] William James produced by this fusion an empirically based program within the broad domain of mental science that wrested the subject matter of psychology from the moral philosophers and defined psychology anew as the scientific study of consciousness.[2]

More than recovery from his near-suicidal crisis impelled James toward this endeavor. From the standpoint of personal experience, there was, first of all, James's struggle with his father's religious epistemology of consciousness. Henry James Sr., independently wealthy, eccentric Swedenborgian philosopher of religion, friend and confidant of Emerson, was a prolific writer on themes of Christian socialism. His two main obsessions in life were spreading the gospel of the science of creation and raising his children. At first blush, he appears to have failed at both, but retrospective analysis delivers up the conclusion that his success must be measured in terms of the subsequent impact of William and Henry on the course of modernism in the 20th century, which was enormous. Even Tolstoi, who chastised Americans for not knowing how great was the genius of the soul they were harboring, had a complete set of Henry James Sr.'s writings.

---

[1]The distortion that James's experimental psychology originated from the tradition of Helmholtz, Fechner, and Wundt continues to be perpetrated. See E. G. Boring (1950).

[2]The overthrow of Francis Bowen's brand of psychology as moral philosophy at Harvard by William James and the Harvard Overseers is told by Stern (1965).

The key to understanding William James's dilemma rests in understanding Henry James Sr.'s definition of science. Of the hundreds who have approached William James, and of the handful who have dared read his father, only one scholar to date seems to have put his finger on the problem (Croce, 1989). The kernel of it is that Henry James Sr. and his transcendentalist friends advocated a spiritual evolution of consciousness that James the Elder hoped would be systematically elucidated in a set of definable laws by the new methods of scientific empiricism. Science, for Henry James Sr., was a weapon in the arsenal of spiritual truth.[3] Because the natural law was in fact derived from the spiritual, and not the other way around, he untiringly delivered his piquant barbs and thrusts to all who would demean or distort this one great spiritual truth. James the Elder attacked the organized churches, which he thought not only had imprisoned the spirit in ritual and professional requirements, but also had sold out by accommodating their teachings to the demands of the reductionistic scientists, and he attacked the scientific positivists, whom he regarded as perverted because they preached that nothing existed but the facts of the natural world. James found the right kind of philosophy in the writings of the transcendentalists, but Emerson's only fault, he thought, was an excess of spirituality without the rigor of scientific laws.[4] His true model was the life and writing of Emanuel Swedenborg, 18th century scientist and interpreter of religious experience (Taylor, 1984). William and Henry fell heir to this Swedenborgian and transcendentalist literary legacy, but both were forced to square the older religious psychology of consciousness with the new literary and scientific dictates of the late 19th century.

The legacy through Emerson and Henry James Sr. requires more of an extensive analysis than has yet been undertaken. One example, however, that undoubtedly led James to an interest in the problem of consciousness was the early contact that both William and Henry had with Henry James Sr.'s close friend, James John Garth Wilkinson. Wilkinson, whom James the Elder had met through Emerson's friend, Thomas Carlyle, was an En-

---

[3]In the a priori mode of the idealists, these thinkers believed, as Emerson did, in the Swedenborgian idea of correspondences, "that every natural fact is a symbol of some spiritual fact." Even Benjamin Peirce, who was no transcendentalist, but rather America's foremost mathematician of the era, believed that it was impossible for God to have writ large his message in nature and a contradiction of it in the Gospels. The material, natural world, in short, was but a manifestation of the larger spiritual reality in which we constantly move and have our being. However much they may have differed in their religious outlook, a wide range of writers in the 19th century thus held the conviction that scientific investigation into the natural world would lead to a harmonious relationship between science and religion. See Hoovenkamp (1978).

[4]"I am led to seek the laws of these appearances that swim around us in God's great museum . . . [while] you continually dishearten me by your apparent indifference to such laws" (H. James Sr., to R. W. Emerson, 1842, quoted in Croce, 1989, pp. 3-4).

glish physician and a translator of Swedenborg's scientific writings. A close family friend since the 1840s, Wilkinson had the Jameses as neighbors in England during the mid-1850s. We are indebted to Professor Saul Rosenzweig for his perceptive analysis of Wilkinson's likely influence on the James boys as a major source for the stream of consciousness technique, which William later developed into a metaphor in the *Principles of Psychology* (1890) to describe the flow of thought and feeling, and which Henry adopted as a style for writing the modern psychological novel (Rosenzweig, 1956).

Wilkinson had been studying the automatic writing productions of mediums at his home the winter of 1855, which could not have escaped the notice of the two inquisitive boys next door, one 12 and the other 13. Thereafter, he developed a technique for spontaneous drawing, speaking, and writing, which he described in *Improvisations from the Spirit* (Wilkinson, 1857a), a volume of a thousand poems automatically written. He followed this with a pamphlet on the homeopathic treatment of insanity, which advocated the use of spontaneous artistic productions as a form of self-therapy in the asylums (Wilkinson, 1857b). We know too, that while Swedenborg was the basis of the relationship between Wilkinson and James the Elder, topics in psychopathology formed the basis for the later professional communications between Wilkinson and William James (Wilkinson, n.d.).

There is also the interesting influence to consider of James's youthful experiments with mind-altering drugs. William's brother Henry has left accounts of these self-induced experiments as William was growing up, and James's biographers have given us many additional clues (Allen, 1967, p. 193; Taylor, 1982a, 170 fn.5). Such behavior appears to have been sanctioned as a social event in the 1860s and 1870s. Ether intoxication, for instance, had been a form of parlor entertainment since the 1840s, and accounts given in letters attest to William's continued participation in such endeavors.[5] As well, in the crude scientific atmosphere of the chemical laboratory James had unlimited access to various substances which he was forever trying on himself, a not uncommon procedure among physicians and medical students.[6] There is also evidence that the mind-altering properties of some substances facilitated the production of insights that, it was thought, could be useful in the development of self-knowledge and charac-

---

[5]One documented account, at a slightly later time, is the following: ". . . that horrid story of Willie James having broken off that needle in his hand. I felt awfully about it. How can he do such things as stick needles into himself? Do ask him about it, for I shan't be easy till I know he has got that needle out" (Fay, 1871).

[6]For his graduating thesis at the Harvard Medical School, James's colleague, Henry Pickering Bowditch, presented a review of observations on the physiological action of potassium bromide, "some of them personal" (Cannon, 1922, p. 184).

ter formation. Later, James himself was to proclaim, that in the midst of the anaesthetic revelation, *the genius of being is revealed![7]*

James was also attracted to the field of mental life through his association with William Henry Prince, a physician and superintendent of the Northampton State Hospital. Dr. Prince had married James's Aunt Kitty, who had been a patient in the Asylum, and, in fact, was in and out of hospitals all her life. James had at one time mentioned to his aunt that in the search for a vocation, psychiatry in the line of Prince's work was a possible consideration.[8]

But the most important line of interest fusing science and consciousness began for James during the 1860s because of his growing involvement with C. S. Peirce and Chauncey Wright. Their dialogues, which centered on questions about evolutionary theory, were carried on in what came to be known as the pragmatist circle.[9] Peirce and Wright became major influences on James's scientific career from the very beginning and both were implicated with James in the early debates over evolutionary theory.

Through his father's transcendentalist and Swedenborgian literary connections, James came to Harvard in 1861 to study under Louis Agassiz at the Lawrence Scientific School, just as the theory of natural selection was being hotly debated between Agassiz, the leading American scientist who stood for creationism, and Asa Gray, the Harvard botanist who was Darwin's American confidant (Dupree, 1959, pp. 216–331). Agassiz's

---

[7]The only problem, he continued, was that most of it was forgotten upon coming to (James, 1898a).

[8]In all likelihood, William was attracted to the idea rather than the reality of the profession. William Henry Prince, 1817–1883), was graduated with the MD from Harvard in 1841, and he became Superintendent at the Northampton State Hospital in 1858 when it opened. An immediate issue became the high number of annual deaths, and accusations were evidently laid at the feet of the Superintendent. The hospital records show, however, that from the very first a large number of terminal patients were received that kept the mortality rate high for a number of years. Thirty patients out of a population of 315 died during 1861 alone, primarily from tuberculosis. Most of the patients suffered from alcoholism, but the largest class were labeled "insanity of unknown origin" (*Sixth Annual Report of the Trustees of the State Lunatic Hospital at Northampton*, 1861, p. 17). Prince retired in 1864, when he was succeeded by Pliny Earl. He died in Newton, Massachusetts in 1883, having committed suicide. That James reconsidered is shown by Feinstein. Aunt Kitty had responded with a list of the ideal qualities of an alienist, and James had replied, "As for 'live lunatics' I am very much afraid that I am little fitted by nature to do them any good and your catalogue of the graces wh. shd. deck any one who undertakes to 'treat' them tends to make my fears a certainty. I verily believe that I shd catch their contagion & go as mad as any of them in a week for on reading Dr. Winslow on Obscure Diseases of the Mind not long since my reason almost fled, it was so redly shaken by the familiar symptoms the Doctor gave of insanity." James's expressed interest thus sounds like a veiled cry for help. (Quoted in Feinstein, 1984, p. 304.)

[9]A case can be made that Henry James Sr. and Emerson promulgated their own forms of a science of consciousness, albeit a spiritual one, and that William fell heir to this literary psychology but was forced to square it with the dictates of the more empirical age in which he lived (Croce, 1989; Taylor, 1988).

staunch allies in this battle were Benjamin Peirce, the Harvard mathematician and astronomer, and others, such as Francis Bowen, a leading Boston Unitarian and Harvard professor of philosophy. Gray, on the other hand, had not only the prestigious American Academy of Arts and Sciences on his side, but also Jeffries Wyman, the comparative anatomist, Charles William Eliot, instructor in chemistry who would later become president of Harvard, and Chauncey Wright, a calculator at the Harvard Observatory, arch positivist, and philosopher *extraordinaire*, whose mission in life was to fuse the ideas of Darwin with the utilitarian theory of John Stuart Mill.

Almost immediately, William James befriended the hot-headed and irascible Charles Sanders Peirce, Benjamin Peirce's son (Perry, 1935; Taylor, 1986). Peirce, in turn, introduced James to the logic of the scientific method and to the German psychophysical literature (Cadwallader & Cadwallader, 1972). Wright soon became Peirce's and James's "intellectual boxing master," and with Peirce introduced James to the British Empiricists, to Wright's brand of strict positivism, and to Wright's interpretation of how language is shaped by self consciousness in the evolutionary process (Perry, I. 1935, pp. 520–528). With Wright, James and Peirce, along with Nicholas St. John Green, John Fisk, and others, founded the so-called Cambridge metaphysical Club, beginning in the early 1870s. The group convened alternately at the Peirce and James houses, and became the setting for Peirce's first enunciation of pragmatism (Weiner, 1949, pp. 22–23) and for the origin of functional psychology, what James later said was the only true psychology worthy of the name.

Allied with his exposure to Peirce and Wright in the mid-1860s, and one of the chief sources for his concept of the experimental method, was James's contact with Charles Edouard Brown-Sequard. Brown-Sequard was Harvard's first professor of neurology and an important influence on Henry Pickering Bowditch and James Jackson Putnam, as well as James. For as young medical students, all three came to know Brown-Sequard in the late 1860s. Brown-Sequard was an English subject from the island of Mauritius, whose blood line was French and Irish-American. He had received his medical training in Paris and distinguished himself for his experimental laboratory research on the nervous system and the endocrine glands before he came to America. When he became professor of neurology at the Harvard Medical School in 1864, he brought with him the latest techniques of experimental medicine, which applied laboratory research to the understanding of clinical problems important to the practicing physician. His appointment was an attempt to expose medical students to the "new physiology," that is, the experimental (meaning surgical) demonstration of the relation of structure to function, in the French scientific tradition of Francois Magendie and Claude Bernard. Although dissection on non-living organisms had long been a standard procedure, Brown-Sequard was in fact the first to introduce vivisection into the medical curriculum as an experimental technique (Tyler & Tyler, 1984).

We have some indication of Brown-Sequard's philosophy of science from a published lecture he delivered opening the medical year at Harvard in November, 1866, which we know William James, Henry Pickering Bowditch, and probably James Jackson Putnam, attended. The talk, entitled "Advice to Students," summarized the importance of the experimental method, and then suggested that the medical students meet in small groups of three or four every day, with one student lecturing. Brown-Sequard enjoined the students to study nature, in addition to books, and he suggested that students devise their own experiments for the practical study of physiology. Careful observation of the facts should also be accompanied by the critical study of conclusions (Brown-Sequard, 1867).

Contrary to recent historical analysis, Brown-Sequard gave more lectures on neuropathology than presently accounted for, because we have William James's medical school notebook, which dates from the late fall of 1866 or early months of 1867, in which there are extensive notes.[10] The notebook is particularly important for the glimpse it gives of the state of medical school training at the time. There are notes on muscle and cell physiology and of the differential effects of chemicals on living tissue. References are made to the works of Huxley, Busk, and particularly Carpenter, and chemical notations appear throughout. The majority of the notebook contains details of Brown-Sequard's lectures. The most interesting feature of the content of these notes is the level of discourse, in that they convey extensive correlation of mental symptoms with physical pathology in describing diseases of the nervous system. In terms of the clinical picture of disease, no attempt was made to reduce consciousness strictly to the language of physiology. Rather, the signs and symptoms of the patient's mental state were presented as equally important to a description of the accompanying organic picture.

One cannot underestimate, in this regard, the effect that French experimental physiology had on William James's subsequent definition of consciousness in the context of scientific psychology. Unlike in Germany, where experimental laboratory research became the ideal pursued in the universities and pure science was seen as the mother of clinical application,

---

[10]The notebook, dated 1866-67, contains several interesting features in addition to James's class notes. One is a note in an unidentified hand, probably Mrs. Bailey Aldrich, referring to Ralph Barton Perry, saying that Perry did not want the notebook to be a part of the William James Collection at Harvard College. Another is a letter, dated July 22, 1942, from the historian of experimental psychology at Harvard, Edwin G. Boring, to Charles Burwell, Dean of the Medical School, where Boring offered to give the notebook to the Medical School archives. Boring had intended to include it as part of a centenary James exhibit at the American Psychological Association meeting that year, but the meeting was cancelled because of the war. With a background limited to psychophysics and engineering, Boring was unable to draw any inferences relevant to James's scientific training. He wrote: "I have gone through the notebook but do not find anything of great interest in it" (James, 1867–88).

in France, the ideal of *la clinique,* bedside teaching and the care of the patient, had held sway. Since the French Revolution, when medical schools were founded around the Paris teaching hospitals, *la clinique* had been the focus, and scientific research, especially experimental physiology, grew up as its handmaiden, and hence had to fight for its own independent recognition (Foucault, 1973). In the early part of the 19th century, American physicians flocked to Paris to study at the patient's bedside and to tour the wards with greats such as Corvisart, Louis, Laennec, and Bouillar. Professors on the faculty at Harvard Medical School, Oliver Wendell Holmes Sr., and Jeffries Wyman, two of James's mentors, in particular, drew their inspiration from French clinical medicine, at a time when other medical institutions looked to Germany, and this French influence at Harvard was to continue until well into the late 19th century (Ackerknecht, 1967, pp. 121–127; Beecher & Altschule, 1977, pp. 61–62; Lesch, 1984, pp. 197–224). Because of this emphasis, the French experimental tradition was also to have a significant later influence on the development of experimental psychopathology and scientific psychotherapy in Boston.

What constituted the principal attraction for James in the 1860s was likely the refinement of French culture as compared to the boorishness and pessimism of the Germans (James, 1875). Although he eventually mastered the language of both cultures, he was most proficient in French, which he learned earlier than German. But, after the near-suicidal crisis in 1870, his attraction was undoubtedly a more personal one, based on his reading of Renouvier, which led to the opening of a life-long correspondence with this thoroughly French philosopher.[11] Renouvier, in turn, was sufficiently impressed with the young American to begin translating his psychological and philosophical essays into French and publishing them in *Critique Philosophique*. Thus from the very start of his career, James was read by the French as a Frenchman, whereas he never enjoyed such notoriety in German speaking countries.

The backdrop of James's introduction into scientific medicine as a student in the 1860s was the experimental physiology of Claude Bernard, at a time when physiology in general was at the forefront of changes occurring in the biological sciences and in medical education. Bernard took his MD in 1843 and after interning in the Paris hospitals entered into a series of pioneering investigations on the nervous system with his teacher Francois Magendie, experimental physiologist at the College de France, who is remembered for his discovery of the function of the dorsal and ventral nerve roots. Eventually, Bernard made numerous important physiological discoveries of his own, among them, he showed the role of the pancreas in digestion; he discovered the existence of the vasomotor nerves; he demonstrated

---

[11]Leary (1988) has analyzed the additional influence of Wordsworth on James at this critical period.

the effect of curare on neuromuscular transmission; and he identified the glycogenic function of the liver. For his accomplishments, Bernard achieved the prize on physiology on four occasions from the French Academy of Sciences, had a chair in physiology created for him at the Sorbonne, and finally succeeded Magandie at the College de France.

Bernard's text, *Introduction a l'etude de la Medecine Experimentale* [Introduction to the Method of Experimental Medicine] (1865) remains today one of the most important original sources for understanding the relation of the Paris clinical school to the development of the experimental sciences. In it, Bernard propounded an active, interventionist, and laboratory based determinism, over against the prevailing passive, contemplative, and descriptive medicine of the hospitals. Instead of merely trying to coordinate the use of experimental and clinical material, he argued for subsuming clinical pathology under experimental physiology as the only was to transform medicine into a science. It is important to note that "experimental," for Bernard, meant operating under laboratory conditions in order to gain surgical control over an animal's physiological reactions. Such control, repeatably produced, demonstrated the relationship between structure and function. It was this demonstration of function that gave physiology its dynamic character, separate from mere anatomical description.

Although Bernard abhorred philosophical speculation, he was inexorably drawn into articulating a number of far-reaching theoretical constructs arising out of his experimental work, which attracted William James's attention. He is perhaps best known for his formulation of the *melieu interior*, the condition of the internal environment that holds the variously changing systems in constant equilibrium, on which Walter Cannon later based his concept of homeostasis, and historians of medicine note that William James gave the earliest American review of this idea in 1868 when he commented on Bernard's *Rapport sur le Progres et la Marche de la Physiologie general en France* [Report on the progress and march of general physiology in France] (1867) in *The North American Review* (James, 1868a, p. 326; Olmstead, 1967, pp. 26–27).

Bernard, as one of the leading scientific men in France, had been commissioned to review the status of physiology as a natural science, and James lauded the report as one of those rare occasions when an experimentalist and man of the laboratory stood back and allowed himself to make a statement about the implications of his research. Despite certain egotistical predilections by Bernard to emphasize his own works, James said, the piece had real philosophy in it that merited attention.

Bernard claimed that physiology had differentiated itself enough from the other branches, such as chemistry, to be deemed an independent science. Its basic unit was the cell, the largest conglomeration of which is the organism. Interestingly, James pointed out, although man sees himself as a land animal, he is preeminently an aquatic one, by virtue of the fact that everything about him that is alive exists in a watery medium. His only dry parts—skin surface, hair, and nails—are dead, and their offices mechanical, not vital. The organism is, in fact, an enormous republic of separate entities, which blindly perform their respective tasks and thereby furnish the means for their fellows to subsist.

James then takes up the idea of the *melieu interior*. In this equilibrium, function is defined in a way that wholly transcends the individual properties of organic elements. A piece of nerve tissue, for instance, can be taken out and placed under the skin in some random place and months later found to be still alive, even though no longer fulfilling is original function. The description of function thus defines the purview of physiology.

Bernard closed his piece with a plea for public endowment of laboratories with apparatus for the study of living animals, if physiology is to become someday the light in which medicine is to work. "Experiments must be separated and controlled with a patience that would drive a chemist, for example, to despair, in order to eliminate the variations caused by the immense number of unknown conditions that accompany each given case" (Bernard, 1865). But James pointed out that the science Bernard envisioned was still in its infancy and already too much had been claimed and too much expected of it. On this point, James invoked the word of his then present teacher, Oliver Wendell Holmes Sr., as evidence that there was growing in medicine a decided impatience with the mass of so-called science, which was intruding upon medical education to an increasing degree. Quoting Holmes, James said: "The amount of baggage which a doctor is now expected to carry in his head is growing too great for the medical brain. The use of the ever-increasing number of scopes and graphs, and meters for diagnosis alone is more than any one man is adequate to: and when we think of the facts we must remember besides, to be considered 'scientific,' we grow fairly dizzy" (James, 1868a, p. 326).

Holmes said, and James echoed, that most knowledge recorded in physiological treatises had yet to find its practical application, and for this reason Holmes stated emphatically that we must not expect too much from science as distinguished from common experience: "There are ten thousand experimenters without apparatus, for every one in a laboratory. Accident is the great chemist and toxicologist. Battle is the great vivisector. Hunger has instituted researches on food, such as no Liebig nor any academic commission has ever recorded. . . . Medicine appropriates from every source. . . . 'Science' is one of her benefactors, but only one out of many" (James, 1868a, p. 326).

But James then took Holmes to task for posing an artificial dichotomy between science and common sense. Experience is complex and often indecipherable in its various forms; science is, on the other hand, more simplistic, in the sense of more elementary, yet it is more exact. A single discovery can have a wide field of various applications. In this regard, the pretensions of the scientist are not false, only premature: "The absurdity they may contain is not that of a frog trying to look like an ox, but rather that of the embryo alligator furiously snapping its harmless jaws, while yet encased by the eggshell" (James, 1868a, p. 326). James's final comment was that both Bernard, the experimentalist, and Holmes, the practitioner, came to the same conclusion; that is, both advocated the separation of experimental and clinical physiology.

Even at this early stage in his career, James became both a critic and supporter of the scientific method, supporting science for its precision, but chiding scientists for using the atomistic requirements of the method as an automatic metaphysical injunction about what can and cannot be legitimately studied. James expressed this attitude in two important statements—one on psychotherapeutics in medicine and the other on the attitude of science toward spiritualism—during the late 1860s while he was still a medical student. Some facts of biography prior to his near-suicidal episode help to understand this interest.

In April, 1867, James, suffering from a variety of non-specific symptoms, fled from the strain of living with his family and, under the pretension of furthering his scientific training, sailed for Europe. His first stop was Paris, after which he spent the summer in Dresden and Bohemia, leisurely preparing to enter one of the German Universities in the fall by taking the water cure and brushing up on his German. By September, he was hardly more improved than when he had arrived, for rather than cure him, the baths at Teplitz had made him feel like his brain had been boiled. Nevertheless, he enrolled in five courses and three lectures on psychology and physiology at the University of Berlin. He attended classes as his health permitted, avoided the laboratories, but read voraciously on the physiology of the nervous system.[12]

To Henry Pickering Bowditch, he wrote:

I live near the University, and attend all the lectures on physiology that are given there, but am unable to do anything in the Laboratory, or attend the clinics or Virchow's lectures and demonstrations, etc., Du Bois-Raymond, an irascible man of about forty-five, gives a very clear, yea, brilliant, series of five lectures a week. . . . The opportunities for study here are superb, it seems to me. Whatever they may be in Paris, they cannot be better. The physiological laboratory, with its endless array of machinery, frogs, dogs, etc., etc., al-

[12]To his friend, Tom Ward, James complained, "If I had been *drilled* further in mathematics, physics, chemistry, logic, and the history of metaphysics, and had established, even if only in my memory, a firm and thoroughly familiar *basis* of knowledge in all these sciences (like the basis in human anatomy one gets in studying medicine), to which I should involuntarily refer all subsequently acquired facts and thoughts,—instead of having now to keep going back and picking up loose ends of these elements, and wasting whole hours in looking to see how the new facts are related to them, or whether they are related to them at all,—I might be steadily advancing" (Quoted in H. James, Jr., 1920, I: 119–120).

most 'bursts my gizzard,' when I go by it, with vexation. . . . The general level of thoroughness and exactness in scientific work here is beyond praise; and the abundance of books in every division of every subject is something we English have no idea of. . . . [But] the general impression the Germans make on me is not at all that of a remarkably intellectually gifted people; and if they are not so, their eminence must come solely from their habits of conscience and plodding work. (H. James, Jr., 1920, Vol. I, pp. 120–124)

He added a number of additional points on national gossip, before proposing to Bowditch that when he returned from Europe the two of them go into medical practice together; James doing all the reading, since he was fit for nothing else, with Bowditch doing all the clinical work. It was a plea of despair for his present, and consequently future, state (H. James, Jr., 1920).

The episode lasted 12 weeks. James left without finishing his courses and returned to the baths at Teplitz and Divonne, promising his father, who was paying for it all, that he would return in the spring to study science at Heidelberg with Helmholtz and Wundt. When he did return, he was in Heidelberg only 6 days before he again retreated to the baths. Finally, he returned to Cambridge after 18 months. One of his last stops was Paris, where he spent a delightful 2 weeks with Bowditch, who by then had come abroad to study physiology.

While James's health had remained poor, his reading had been voluminous. During 1868 alone, while he was staggering through the German medical literature trying to master physiology, he also read Homer, Shakespeare, Renan, Cousin, Taine, Kant, Paul Janet, Lessing, Goethe, and Schiller, and he managed to publish five reviews, which he distributed between *The Nation, The Atlantic Monthly*, and *The North American Review*. The content of these pieces is significant for the pattern of James's thinking, and for a hint of the subject matter in which he felt most fluent. He produced two separate reviews of Darwin's *Variation of Animals and Plants Under Domestication*, and three reviews of works from the French. One was his piece on Claude Bernard. Another was a notice of Feydeau's *La Comtesse de Chalis*, published as "The Manners of the Day" in Paris. But most important was a short essay entitled "Moral Medication," his review of A. A. Liébeault's *Sleep and Analogous States* (James, 1868b).

Auguste Ambroise Liébeault, a small, talkative, and vivacious man, with a wrinkled face, a dark complexion, and the appearance of a peasant, was a hard working country doctor in Pont-Saint-Vincent, a village outside Nancy in France. As a young medical student he had discovered an old treatise on magnetism and later incorporated the induction of trance states into his practice. But because hypnosis, as it came to be called, had been repudiated by the French medical and scientific community, it was not considered official medicine. Liébeault's tack was to offer his patients the choice of undergoing hypnotic treatments for their ailments, for which there was no charge, or of receiving conventional medical treatment at the customary fee. He was an excellent hypnotizer and soon had an immense practice, from which he derived almost no income. He thus decided to take a 2 year leave of absence from his practice, during which he wrote about his hypnotic method and its effect. The result was *Du Sommeil et des Etats analogues* [On Sleep and analogous states] (Liébeault, 1866), a work that 20 years later became the primary text of the Nancy School of psychotherapeutics under Hippolyte Bernheim. Its publication, however, was barely noticed. Only one copy was thought to have been sold in 10 years, but Ellenberger has shown that Liébeault had readers in France and Russia (Ellenberger, 1970, pp. 86–87). At the same time, William James published the only review of it to appear in the English language (Ellenberger, personal communication; Hale, 1971).

James cautiously praised Liébeault's work as a somewhat diffuse, but sturdy, honest, and sensible book, the main point of which was to show the identity between ordinary sleep and certain pathological conditions, such as fascination and hallucination, and to advocate the application of hypnosis to the treatment of various forms of disease. The focus of the theoretical explanation of the phenomenon was one of attention. Attention, the great working agent which presides over all the changes, bodily or mental, conscious or unconscious, which we undergo is diffused equally over all the senses when we are in the normal waking state. When we are absorbed or abstracted, it flows more particularly toward one form of sensibility. When we are asleep, it withdraws itself entirely from the reach of the senses and retires into unconscious caverns, where it can be recognized only afterwards by its effects. When attention then emerges from this latent condition and shows only a one-sided connection to the world, we are dreaming, somnambulistic, cataleptic, and so on.

It was a justifiable extension of the normal definition of attention, James said: "The phenomena of somnambulism, mania, etc., are connected with those of what is commonly called attention by such a number of gradual steps, all characterized by a diminution of mental activity in some directions, running parallel to its exaltation in others, a narrowing of its channel proportional to its deepening, that it seems quite justifiable to grasp all the terms of this series of facts of mental concentration under the name by which the most familiar term is known to us" (James, 1868b, p. 50).

But at the same time, James had numerous criticisms of Liébeault's conceptions. He objected, for instance, to the author's gratuitous assumption that the sum of the mind's operations, conscious and unconscious, should at all times be a constant quantity. Thus, the reason why we sleep, according to Liébeault, is because the mind adopts the idea of repose. The reason why we awaken the next morning is because a portion of the mind remains fixed on this resolve. Far from the attention to the senses being merely distracted elsewhere in the mind during sleep, James said, studies in cerebral circulation definitely show that during sleep most cerebral functions as a whole are depressed.

James then took up several of the topics associated with the magnetic sleep: the phenomenon of rapport between the patient and the hypnotist, the dissociation that comes from a narrowing of focus, the hypersuggestibility of the somnambule, and the increased sensitivity that allows for the perception of sensory changes more minute and subtle than would normally be possible. James then reviewed Liébeault's comments on the phenomenon of post-hypnotic suggestion: hemorrhages of mucous membranes can be timed in advance, pulse can be voluntarily slowed, and all kinds of actions can be commanded, all without the knowledge of the doer at the moment the instructions are carried out, or where there was actually consciousness of the act, the perpetrator of the action assured all that it was performed under his own willful control, although he had no knowledge of his prior instructions. Thus, pains, such as that of a toothache, can be both suggested and suggested away at will by implanted hallucinations.

Liébeault's pronouncement was that the powers of the mind should be enlisted in the service of therapeutics. Not all subjects are susceptible to it, and it was not a universal panacea. But in people disposed toward its influence, the power of thought, he said, was superior to drugs. James then presented some statistics based on Liébeault's treatment of patients with anemia, showing different rates of cure depending on the depth of the trance.

James recommended the book to physicians for its many sagacious practical hints, besides many observations promising to be of scientific importance. He said finally in praise of Liébeault's efforts.

> It seems high time that a realm of phenomena which have played a prominent part in human history from time immemorial should be rescued from the hands of uncritical enthusiasm and charlatanry, and conquered for science; and this will never be done unless educated medical men, who are daily forced up to the very threshold, shake off the discreditable shyness which has hitherto characterized them, and walk boldly in to take possession. (James, 1868b, p. 50)

In March, 1869, James also published his first critique of the spiritualists, a review of Epes Sargent's *Planchette: Or the Despair of Science*, which was printed in the *Boston Daily Advertiser* (James, 1869b). It was no coincidence. Sargent, a journalist and cousin to the famous Boston painter, John Singer Sargent, was friends with W. T. Fields and Nathaniel Hawthorne, and a member of the same literary circle in which Henry James Sr. circulated. In addition, he was also the editor of *The Boston Advertiser*. Sargent was interested in spiritualism and endeavored to produce a work that would reflect the facts of the phenomenon, as collected by himself and as reported by others. His contention was that the planchette, or small wooden plank sold in all the bookshops that had lately become a popular form of entertainment in New England, revealed aspects of human experience that, since the Hydesville rappings in 1848, had become firmly established and could not well be ignored by science. Sargent's text was a mix of anecdote, rumor, and personal observation about the rise and diffusion of spiritual manifestation in America, England, and especially in France that confused potentially interesting observations about psychological processes with spiritualist manifesto. According to Sargent, the trance state entered by mediums, the unconscious forces at work among participants of planchette writing, and the mesmeric condition induced by the physician, all gave clues to a complete rational assurance of our immortal destiny.

James thought the book a good popular account, but superficial in its treatment of so much anecdotal data. "A reader with scientific habits of thought would have been more interested by a very few cases described by the author over his own signature, and with every possible detail given, in which pedantically minute precautions had been taken against illusion of the senses and of deceit" (James, 1869b). He chided the spiritualists for their self-complacency. After all why would one with a season ticket over the Stygian ferry, and daily enjoying the privileges it confers in conversing with the "summer land," have any sympathy with the critical vigilance and suspicion of earthbound naturalists? Then he poked fun at the scientists, who always "seem to demand that spiritualists should come and demonstrate to them the truth of their doctrine, by something little short of a surgical operation upon their intellects" (James, 1869b). On the one hand, James was wont to agree with the critics of spiritualism, who, unable to find much that was attractive, useful, or original in spiritualists' productions, exclaimed, "If this is the spirit-world,—it is much better to be a respectable pig and accept annihilation, than to be cursed with such an immortality" (James, 1869b). On the other, if the capacity for mediumship, clairvoyance, and the like was actually within the realm of human experience, then James could not understand why scientists rejected the phenomena on a priori grounds and made such a big issue out of it. For if true, it would seem to have no more claim upon each individual than any special problems one would find taken up in organic chemistry or pathological anatomy.

BOWDITCH, PUTNAM, AND JAMES

Perhaps the greatest impetus to the development of psychology as a science at Harvard in the post-Darwinian period was the establishment of the first laboratory for instruction in experimental physiology in America under Henry Pickering Bowditch in 1871. Experimental psychology at Harvard began in this laboratory as a result of the collaboration between James,

Bowditch, and Putnam on problems having to do with the structure and function of the nervous system.

Henry Pickering Bowditch was born April 4, 1840 into a wealthy Boston family known for its medical and scientific interest. On his maternal side he was related to the astronomers, Edward and William Pickering, and the mathematician, Benjamin Peirce. His paternal grandfather was Nathaniel Bowditch, also a mathematician, renowned author of *The American Practical Navigator*, and translator of La Place's *Mechanique Celeste* [Celestial Mechanics]; and his father, Jonathan Ingersoll Bowditch, was a Harvard Overseer and Boston businessman with a scientific turn of mind. His uncle, Nathaniel Ingersoll Bowditch, was Jackson Professor of Clinical Medicine at Harvard Medical School and distinguished local physician, known for his knowledge of auscultation and percussion.

Young Henry prepared for college at the school of Epes S. Dixwell, who later became the father-in-law of one of Henry's classmates, Oliver Wendell Holmes Jr.. Bowditch was graduated from Harvard in 1861 and immediately enrolled in the Lawrence Scientific School with the intention of studying chemistry and natural history. The Civil War had just broken out, however, and Bowditch enrolled in the First Massachusetts Cavalry as a second Lieutenant. He saw extensive active service, was furloughed with wounds, but reenlisted, and did not resign his command until June, 1865. Major Henry Lee Higginson described him during this time as upright, reserved, even unbending in manner, but unflagging in faithfulness and unflinching in courage, "a handsome, refined, and homebred looking youth, with a fondness and faculty for keeping face and clothing neat when these attributes were a rarity" (Cannon, 1922, p. 184).

On leaving the army, Bowditch reentered the Lawrence Scientific School to study comparative anatomy with Jeffries Wyman. He combined his study with courses in the Medical curriculum and was graduated with the MD in 1868. Embarking on the traditional medical grand tour, he left for Paris in the late summer of 1868, intent, at least in the beginning, on combining scientific interests with medical practice. His desire to pursue scientific study in physiology with Brown-Sequard was thwarted, and so Bowditch attended clinics held by Broca, Charcot, and Louis, before turning to work in physiology with Claude Bernard and in microscopy with Ranvier. It was during this period that he was joined briefly by William James and other American students, who with Ranvier would embark on frog-hunting parties to collect specimens for their experiments.

Bowditch's experience in France confirmed in him the desire to devote himself purely to scientific work, despite the apparent impracticality of the plan, but he was determined to get as thorough a training in experimental physiology as the European universities could offer. Jeffries Wyman wrote to him from Harvard with a note of assurance to continue along this line, as something was sure to turn up in his favor. Bowditch's sojourn came to an end in Paris when he was advised by the German physiologist, Kuhne, to go on to Germany and study with such greats as Schultze, Ludwig, Virchow, and Helmholtz. Bowditch spent the summer of 1869 at Bonn studying microscopic anatomy with Schultze, before moving on to Leipzig, where he became one of the star American pupils in the laboratory of Carl Ludwig. There Bowditch made friends with numerous figures who became famous in physiology, and earned Ludwig's respect by inventing an automatic recording device for the kymograph, which was used to record physiological activity on a moving surface.

Meanwhile, events were taking place at Harvard that would have an important influence on Bowditch's future career.[13] Charles William Eliot had been elected the new president, and James wrote to Bowditch, informing him about their old chemistry Professor. "His great personal defects, tactlessness, meddlesomeness, and disposition to cherish petty grudges seem pretty universally acknowledged, but his ideas seem good and his economic powers first-rate. So in the absence of any other candidate, he went in" (James, 1869a).

In his inaugural address, Eliot proposed a major reorganization of the Harvard curriculum, which included expanding instruction in the sciences and developing adequate laboratory facilities. Eliot had been following Bowditch's progress with real interest and wanted him to return from Europe to teach a course at Harvard in 1870. Bowditch, however, on the advice of both his father and his former professor, resisted, determined instead to continue his training in the German laboratories. Eliot's offer was tempting, but Bowditch was already conscious of bigger plans, which entailed nothing less than raising the standards of scientific education at Harvard. As subsequent events would show, refusing Eliot benefited Bowditch tremendously, for he was soon able to become Harvard's first full-time research professor in the Medical School, with his own department and laboratory. And once installed, he became a willing instrument for Eliot's continued reforms.

Eliot's plans, in the meantime, provoked much controversy among the older faculty. Eliot wished to introduce the European style of experimental physiology, which employed advanced teaching and research. Oliver Wendell Holmes, on the other hand, preached that everything needed to be learned can be learned at the bedside. He was joined by the surgeons, Henry Jacob Bigelow and Richard M. Hodges. Not the least of their concerns was the increased cost of supporting full-time salaried research professors, expensive laboratory apparatus, and the new buildings that would be required to house facilities for scientific instruction.

Eliot's plan for reform, by no means hastily thought out, addressed these issues and more. In the first place, physiology had to be freed from its

---

[13]I have relied heavily in the following paragraphs on the analysis by Fye (1987).

traditional conjunction with anatomy. At the time, Oliver Wendell Holmes occupied the dual chair of anatomy and physiology under the Parkman professorship. Left to his own system, the Poet-at-the-Breakfast-Table spent the majority of his class lectures on anatomy, reserved a few tasks on physiology, and provided no laboratory opportunities for the students whatever. Eliot's advance was signalled in May, 1871, when the Harvard Corporation voted to separate physiology from the Parkman chair.

In the second place, resistance to vivisection as an experimental method had to be overcome. The Old Guard proclaimed that few facts of immediate considerable value to the race had been exhorted "from the dreadful suffering of dumb animals" (Fye, 1987, p. 108). As Bigelow pronounced before the Massachusetts Medical Society in 1871:

> It is dreadful to think how many poor animals will be submitted to excruciating agony, as one medical college after another becomes penetrated with the idea that vivisection is part of modern teaching, and that, to hold sway with other institutions, they, too, must have their vivisector, their mutilated dogs, their guinea pigs, their rabbits, their chamber of torture and of horrors to advertise as a laboratory. (Fye, 1987, p. 108)

The younger men, such as Putnam and bowditch, were Eliot's staunch supporters. Writing to his father, Putnam exclaimed:

> How Dr H[olmes] would open his eyes if he could spend a day or two in Leipzig and see how Physiology is taught there. If they make Henry Professor as soon as he comes home, as they will if they know anything, he will teach the students more than they have been taught for many a year. He expects to meet with a good deal of opposition from the practical men in trying to introduce so much pure science, but I hope that they will soon see that the discovery of as many physiological facts as possible whether apparently important or not, must in the end lead to the discovery of some simple law which put into the hands of practitioners all over the world will benefit two men for every one animal that was slaughtered in the cause. (Quoted in Fye, 1987, p. 110)

Eliot, in this case, was finally able to win Holmes over, weaning him from Bigelow's influence and thus severely weakening the strongest opposition.

Third, Eliot had to confront the issue of finding funds necessary to support increased salaries and the construction of new laboratory space. Private donations had to be found to support the idea of improved scientific education in the United States, whereas such endeavors had been automatically supported by the state controlled universities in Germany. In the particular case of physiology, Bowditch's father was only too glad to make available to his son considerable sums to purchase any and all equipment that was thought necessary. At the same time, Calvin Ellis and James White were laying plans for the construction of new chemical and physiological labs. The physiology laboratory was composed of two rooms, situated in the attic of the Medical School building on Grove Street, situated just opposite from the Massachusetts General Hospital. Half of the $7,000 needed to build this laboratory came from the estate of one of Bowditch's friends.

Shortly after marrying Selma Nauth, daughter of a Leipzig Banker, Bowditch returned to Harvard in the summer of 1871. He was more thoroughly trained in the German approach to physiology than any other American. He had his own independent department, a new laboratory, and as a full-time research professor he was freed from the need to maintain a private practice. The only immediate drawbacks were a lack of paid assistants and the immediate demand placed on him to begin teaching. He thus had to build his own apparatus when necessary, prepare his own demonstrations, and develop the physiology curriculum. Nevertheless, he was well launched, and would soon be able to resume his own scientific investigations.

This, of course, is something of an overstatement. For novel as Bowditch's lab was, and generous as his father had been, the circumstances under which the early physiologists pursued their studies for the first 12 years, while serviceable, must also have been barely tolerable. Frederick W. Ellis, an early student of Bowditch's later described the medical school as housed in a dingy building at the end of North Grove Street amid decidedly humble surroundings that had probably seen better days, with the morgue and the local jail both readily at hand (Ellis, 1938). The main room of the laboratory was not large, and contained only a table for experiments, a sink, a workbench and foot lathe, and a tub for frogs. A smaller room, which physiology shared with histology, contained apparatus and books. Nevertheless, important work emanated from these environs, which had its effect not only on the development of physiology throughout the United States, but also on other laboratory-based sciences at Harvard.

James Jackson Putnam, born in 1846, was descended from a distinguished New England lineage of physicians and jurists, related to both the Cabots and the Lowells. His father, an unassuming and unobtrusive man, was an early specialist in obstetrics and women's diseases, while his mother's father was James Jackson, a found of the Massachusetts General Hospital and for decades one of the leading physicians in the city. Putnam grew up in an intellectual atmosphere saturated with liberal and scientific idealism. The heros of his youth were men such as Johannes Kepler, the astronomer, and William Ellery Channing, the Unitarian divine. Ideas, for him, were what mattered. Moral principles, the vision of a good community, and the discovery of truth were to be uncompromisingly sought. Unpopular causes were to be pursued in the name of truth, even if their adherents were few. His motto, reflecting an almost religious devotion to the process of character development, may as well have been, "Only those who could withstand temptation and the severest moral tests were truly virtuous" (Quoted in Hale, 1971, p. 5).

Putnam attended Harvard during the dark years of the Civil War and was graduated in 1866 at the age of 20, having been too young for military service. He entered Harvard Medical School that same year and, after completing the 3-year course in 1869, published his medical dissertation, "A Report of Some Experiments on Reflex Contraction of Blood Vessels," in the *Boston Medical and Surgical Journal* (Putnam, 1874), which was based on observations originally made by Brown-Sequard, and which was highly praised by Oliver Wendell Holmes Sr.

In May, 1870, full of youthful enthusiasm, Putnam embarked on a 2 year medical grand tour of Europe. Accompanied by his sister, Annie, their aim was to combine pleasure with enlightenment. They sailed first to England, where they toured for 2 weeks, and then proceeded on to Belgium and down the Rhine. By June, they reached Leipzig, where they met Henry Pickering Bowditch, already hard at work in Ludwig's laboratory, and where Putnam got his first look at European medical science. To his father, Putnam reported that during the first summer months, he had attended lectures on pathological anatomy and daily autopsy sessions, and heard Carl Wunderlich, one of the founders of modern thermometry, lecture on clinical medicine and typhoid diseases.

In August, Putnam and his sister moved on to Dresden, Prague, and Salzburg, where they met their brother Charles, who had been studying pediatrics in Germany. The three toured Switzerland and Italy in the autumn, until December, when Charles returned to Boston to begin his medical practice, while Jim and Annie settled in Vienna, where Putnam resumed his post-graduate medical studies. There he fell under the influence of Benedict and Meynert. Moritz Benedict, professor at the University of Vienna, pioneer in medical electricity, and director of the Vienna Polyclinic, with Heidenhain and others, would later become an early defender of hypnotism, but he is best known as a contributor to modern neurology for his studies in 1872 of brain lesions in the pons. Theodore Meynert, probably the more important of the two for Putnam, was professor of neurology and psychiatry at Vienna, and involved in investigations of the anatomy and physiology of the brain. Writing to his mother, Putnam described the pair: "I . . . heard Benedict show himself off to uncommon poor advantage, mentally and morally (i.e., scientifically and personally)," because he had made public statements based on shoddy evidence criticizing "a previous lecture of Meynert in much the same manner as he might that of a well-known quack." "Professor Meynert," Putnam said, "certainly deserves respect. His observations on the pathology of the brain has for a basis more than 800 specimens which have all been examined and weighed, etc. by himself with a care." He then gave his impression of German medicine: "Still with all their hard work and knowledge most of the Germans in Vienna are far behind the American Drs. in care of their patients and in general refinement and respect for principle. Knowledge is all in all with them in most cases. When we at home change some of our hospitals and school (from primaries to colleges) regulations and learn to get up earlier in the morning, and to live with less money and a few other things, we shall soon get ahead of them" (Quoted in Cohen, 1966, pp. 3–4).

Putnam became enamored with medical electricity during this time and sought to inform himself on the most recent advances in this burgeoning field. At one point, he planned to translate a text on electricity by a German professor from Berlin, but this never materialized, probably due to his ambivalence to becoming known as a mere "battery doctor" when he returned to Boston. He confided some of his misgivings to his sister, Elizabeth, noting that it was "easy at home to make a reputation and a 'pile' on the strength of a new fashioned remedy." However, he felt that there is no reputation that is less worth having than one so made. Although electricity was valid, he could not bear being relegated to the role of "apothecary," and he vowed to become known as a doctor who studied disease rather than a mechanic who dealt only in one phase of treatment.

To this end he was also attracted to the work of Johannes von Oppolzer, one of his instructors who was a premier diagnostician. Each morning, Putnam would spend 3 hours with Oppolzer making clinical visits. "Oppolzer's clinic is very crowded and I consider myself fortunate to get jammed in behind him near enough to see and watch the two holes in his old and rusty stock, for he wears no collar at all. With all his roughness he is a capital leader and whether from habit alone or greater knowledge tells more about his cases than anybody else that I have been with yet" (Quoted in Cohen, 1966, p. 5).

The summer of 1871, Putnam left Vienna for an extended vacation by himself, while his sister returned to Boston. By autumn, he was situated in Berlin, where he resumed his studies. He attended the lectures, demonstrations, and autopsies of Rudolf Virchow, the famous cell pathologist and politician. He also took courses with Herman Eulenberg, a pioneer in industrial diseases, and Carl Westphal, who first described agoraphobia.

During the winter of 1871-72, Putnam completed a translation and analysis of Meynert's "Anatomy of the Mammal Brain," which he published a year later (Meynert, 1873). He left Berlin in the spring of 1872 and went to Paris, where, among other medical experiences, he went to observe Jean Martin Charcot at the Salpetriere. Writing to his mother of these visits, he said: "I have been twice to Salpetriere where I am going hereafter pretty regularly. Charcot, who speaks English as I discovered today, looks like Booth fattened up. He doesn't talk much but seems to be friendlily disposed and today put me in the way of attending an ophthalmoscopic clinic" (Quoted in Cohen, 1966, p. 8).

Putnam further reported that, accompanied by a nephew of Brown-Sequard, he also attended a . . .

seance of the Societe de Biologie, where all the swells make reports. . . . Claude Bernard, a fine looking, old man in a velvet cap and fur-trimmed coat presided and Charcot and Vulpain and Ranvier all had their say, of which I understood more or less. Its odd enough that both laboratory and society-room are in an old Gothic church which they share with Dupuytren's anatomical museum. Their government does nothing it seems for science and for the last 40 years this famous society has held its meetings in this dirty barnlike, room which would be looked twice at by a country school committee. For all their French blood the members behaved a good deal like school boys and for all the ringing of his bell M. Bernard couldn't keep the room quiet. (Cohen, 1966, p. 8)

A week later he wrote:

I am a trifle disappointed at what the Salpetriere has to offer in the way of advantages, the cases are good enough or bad enough but the Dr. altho' polite is rather taciturn and they don't examine with the same carefulness and system as at Berlin. There is a charming variety of hysterical patients who will have fits for you at the shortest notice which amuses M. Charcot very much, but as to treatment you don't hear a word of it. (Cohen, 1966, p. 8)

After but a few months stay in Paris, Putnam set sail for Boston, having been most thoroughly indoctrinated into the ways of German medical science and somewhat put off by the French. His experience had confirmed in him the importance of neuropathological investigation and he had been exposed to the most advanced research and clinical methods that Europe had to offer. On his triumphant return home, he was immediately appointed Lecturer on the Application of Electricity in Nervous Diseases at Harvard Medical School and Chief of Electrization at the Massachusetts General Hospital, appointments that would eventually be expanded as Putnam became known as one of the early pioneers in modern neurology. The laboratory situation at Harvard and the MGH was practically nonexistent. For this reason Putnam was drawn into continuing his experimental studies of the nervous system in the only facilities in existence at the time, the newly opened laboratory of his old friend Henry Pickering Bowditch.

JAMES BEGINS TEACHING AT HARVARD

Sometime during 1870, while both Bowditch and Putnam were abroad, William James had about reached rock-bottom. The onset had been partly foretold by numerous signs, one in a letter to Bowditch, where James, who had stopped writing for some months, resumed his correspondence by admitting that he had been in low spirits and plagued with thoughts "of the bowl and the knife." He had first mentioned the possibility of a medical partnership with Bowditch in 1867 in which James would keep up with the reading and Bowditch would maintain the practice. James humorously tried to change the arrangement in a letter written in early 1870, when he proposed that, in the interest of science, the sick, and the proposed firm of B. & J., Bowditch might become the superintendent of an insane asylum where James could be the grateful patient.

His plummet was deep and his recovery only gradual. The hospital in which he sequestered himself for the nearly year-and-a-half that followed, was, paradoxically, the Cambridge home of his father, Henry James Sr. Outwardly, he accomplished little, yet inwardly, he kept up his reading and expanded his European contacts. Not insignificantly, he began what was to become an extensive exchange with Charles Renouvier. In the larger view, however, prospects for a permanent vocation were nil and his inability to decide on anything definite was a force that slowed his improvement.

But then, Bowditch's return from Europe, and a little meddling by James's parents, proved his God-send. With the separation of anatomy from physiology, Eliot had put the entire responsibility for physiology in Bowditch's hands. Bowditch first of all needed an assistant, and his natural choice was William James. Then, in July 1872, Bowditch offered to let James teach the course in anatomy and physiology in Harvard College, if Eliot assented. When James's mother heard about the plan, she went right down to the pier where Eliot tied his yacht and was there with Bowditch's letter in here hand when the president sailed into the dock. He said nothing except that he promised to write to Bowditch. She, however, had little doubt of his agreeing. In August, Eliot offered William the job.

The effect on William's health was instant and dramatic. In the fall he could write: "I go in to the Medical School nearly every morning to hear Bowditch lecture, or paddle around in his laboratory. It is a noble thing for one's spirits to have some responsible work to do. I enjoy my revived physiological reading greatly, and have in a corporal sense been better for the past four or five weeks" (Quoted in Feinstein, 1984, p. 320). Although there is some discrepancy in accounts as to his teaching load, in the fall of 1872, James began teaching Natural History 3, "Comparative Anatomy and Physiology," with Dr. Dwight in the Museum of Comparative Anatomy, then located in Harvard's Boylston Hall. He also taught a course on physiology and hygiene, an elective in Eliot's new system that drew 50 students, which began in January, 1873. By the end of the semester, despite the low caliber of the students, he found the work salutary and the response to his teaching positive. Eliot, for his part, was so pleased he offered James the opportunity to take full responsibility for anatomy and physiology the following year. James declined and went abroad for the academic year 1873-74, but in the summer of 1873, just before he left, he evidently participated in a number of experiments with Putnam in Bowditch's lab.

One of these studies, undertaken by Putnam, with the assistance of James and Bowditch, was published in January, 1874, under the title "Contributions to the Physiology of the Cortex Cerebrii" (Putnam, 1874). The problem under investigation involved a much discussed topic in the scientific literature at the time on localization of brain function. Specific centers of the brain in live animals had been surgically exposed and then electrically stimulated, and entire maps had been drawn showing the relation of specific brain sites to bodily functions. The primary criticism of such endeavors was methodological, in that one could not definitely tell whether the superficial stimulation of surface tissue in the cortex was activating more deeply embedded brain centers.[14]

Putnam, James, and Bowditch devised a unique approach to answer this question. Etherized dogs had a portion of their skulls surgically removed and a partial incision was then made around the area of the cortex to be tested, creating a flap of tissue which prevented electrical stimulation from penetrating more deeply into the brain at that site. Stimulation of the surface confirmed the recognized specificity of function, thus answering the questions of the critics.

Mills, in reporting on early scientific advances in American neurology in the 1870s, highlighted Putnam, Bowditch, and James's experiments and faradic currents on the cerebral cortex and subcortex. Ellis, Bowditch's student in the 1880s, recalled with some reverence the importance attached to the early collaboration of these experimenters. And Cannon in the 1930s echoed this same theme as a major first step in the development of physiology at Harvard.[15] Their significance in the present context is that Bowditch's facilities became the prototype for Putnam to develop a laboratory in neuropathology at Harvard Medical School and for James to develop the laboratory of experimental psychology in Harvard College. Their collaboration also marked the kind of mutual interaction the three would continue throughout their respective careers in physiology, neurology, and psychology. Bowditch became the great facilitator; Putnam was preeminently the clinician; which James became the theoretical philosopher. Between them, the activities of three intertwined laboratory disciplines defined the new mental science at Harvard and significantly expanded the vistas of the biological and social sciences in America.

IMPLICATIONS FOR PSYCHOLOGY

It is clear from this analysis that Bowditch and Putnam's conception of science was rooted in German laboratory empiricism, while James represented the French experimental tradition, which blended the clinic with the scien-

---

[14]For a thorough overview of the specificity of function debate, with important implications for psychology, see Harrington (1987).

[15]Benison, Barger, and Wolfe (1987) have given important details of the early laboratory and apparatus manufacture, as well as the growth pains of the physiology laboratory under Bowditch. For recognition of the work by Putnam, James and Bowditch during this early period, see, for instance, Mills (1904). For further elaboration of the experimental studies that James, himself, believed were his contribution to the scientific literature, see Taylor (1989b).

tific experiment. For James's conception of psychology was at all time person-centered. He sought to blend the techniques of the English, French, and German laboratory traditions into a uniquely American functional psychology that had practical consequences.

Such a person-centered approach is inferred by the content of James's early laboratories in psychology at Harvard described by Harper (1949, 1950).[16] Psychophysical apparatus and reaction-time equipment were in use, questionnaire data was collected, but the Dane Hall laboratory was dominated by an experimental arrangement to study hypnosis and automatic writing. And on the shelves beside all the brass instruments were anatomical models, as well as the famous jars of human and animal brains.

The person-centered approach is also reflected in the content of James's courses, taught between 1872 and 1907 (Burkhardt, Bowers, & Skrupskelis, 1988). The array of topics included anatomy and physiology, physiological psychology, social darwinism, the British empiricists, German philosophy, and a range of topics in scientific psychology, such as the senses and the intellect, the self and nature, and mental pathology. We are struck by a profound emphasis, not on merely the details and methodology of empiricism, but on an examination of the philosophical assumptions of modern scientific psychology.

This emphasis, then, inexorably led to a conception of psychology rooted at once in physiology and philosophy. James had even once said that physiologists should study philosophy to keep from becoming too narrow, and that philosophers should study physiology so the field would not be left to the reductionists (James, 1876). Science, he maintained, was a tool to understand our experience, not a weapon to dictate it.

But the person-centered view that James espoused went into eclipse, beginning in the 1880s, when the first waves of Wundt's American students returned from Leipzig to establish experimental laboratories in the major American universities. Professional boundaries between psychology, philosophy, medicine, and other disciplines became more rigid, graduate schools soon proliferated that were exclusively modeled after the German PhD system, and psychology increasingly became a discipline determined at all costs to associate itself with the physical sciences. Methodology took precedent over subject matter, and the person became insignificant next to the more important task of generating scientific data.

James attempted to redress this imbalance through his philosophy of radical empiricism (see, for instance James, 1904, 1907, 1910), but an international dialogue over the meaning and implications of pragmatism diverted his attention in the last years of his life, psychoanalysis gained prominence even before he died, and then behaviorism ushered in what can

---

[16]The concept of a person-centered science is my choice of words, of course, not James's, but the intent for psychology is the same as his radical empiricism. See Taylor (1987).

only be described as the dark ages of consciousness in American psychology. Thus, James's agenda for a person-centered approach in psychology went unheeded.

Yet, the Jamesian view of psychology as a science of the whole person had its effect, both while he was alive and after his death. This view initially attracted, but then repelled, James's first PhD student in psychology at Harvard, G. Stanley Hall. Hall had come to Harvard because it was the only place in America to study the new scientific psychology. But later, after studying with Wundt in Germany, Hall proceeded to expunge James's name from the history of scientific psychology by editorial fiat (see, for instance, James, 1895).

This Jamesian view also brought Münsterberg to Harvard. For James did not merely want to give up the laboratory. Rather, he detested the idea of spending his time teaching German experimental laboratory methods to graduate students, because he wished to focus on experimental psychopathology and psychical research instead. He brought Münsterberg in because of his attraction to Münsterberg's act psychology, because Münsterberg had been a student of Wundt's, but then surpassed Wundt in reputation, and, besides holding the PhD, Münsterberg also had the MD, which meant to James a balanced view between the mental and the physical sciences. James eventually did draw Münsterberg into the Boston School of Psychotherapy (Münsterberg, 1909), but they eventually broke over the issue of psychical research. Münsterberg then reverted to his own agenda of defining German experimental psychology in a host of applied American settings.

It was also this larger view of the whole person that turned experimental psychologists and scientifically oriented medical men against James in the 1890s. First, James was attacked for his support of the mental healers, when the medical men sought through the legislature to have all unorthodox practitioners licensed (James, 1894, 1898c).[17] Later, James was again vilified for the way he spoke out on vivisection. Although he defended it under proper safeguards, he also criticized most scientists as second-rate for the cavalier way in which they treated animals as experimental subjects (James, 1909). It was actually easier to censure James for these transgressions and thus dismiss him as a throw-back to moral philosophy than it was to confront the real epistomological issues he raised.

But at the same time, this larger Jamesian view had a selective impact on subsequent developments in pastoral counseling and the psychology of religion (Taylor, 1978), on personality, abnormal, social, and clinical psychology (Allport, 1967; Leary, chap. 5 in this volume; Murphy, 1987; Murray, personal communication; Taylor, 1982b), on counter-culture developments

---

[17]For a related incident, see James's controversy with Titchener over the experimental analysis of telepathic whispering (James, 1898b).

in existential, humanistic, and transpersonal psychology (Taylor, in press), and which now has the potential of influencing the emerging field of psychoneuroimmunology (Taylor, 1989).

It is a curious fact of history that modern academic psychologists usually read only James's *Principles of Psychology*, while ignoring his other works, and in reading *The Principles*, are familiar with only those chapters appropriate to their parochial interests. Yet, even with such a limited reading, it is still easy to see why James's thought continues to have such vitality. A pioneer in the uniquely American tradition of functionalism, he remains eclectic without succumbing to chaos; pragmatic without becoming merely utilitarian; and empirical without losing a vision of the whole person. There is no possibility of a perfectly closed philosophical system, he once said, for in every absolute statement, the juices of metaphysical assumptions leak in at every joint. He was a pluralist, he said, instead of a monist, because for the pluralist, monism could always be one of the options. The monist, however, really had no choices before him. And when he bought his summer home in Chocorua, he exclaimed, "It has fourteen doors, and they all open outward." One hundred years after the publication of James's *Principles*, psychology, it seems to me, which has strayed away from its roots and become hopelessly mired in a methodological, positivistic, and behavioral nihilism, could still do with a good strong dose of this Jamesian philosophy.

REFERENCES

Ackerknecht, E. H. (1967). *Medicine at the Paris hospital, 1794–1848*. Baltimore: Johns Hopkins University Press.

Allen, G. W. (1967). *William James: A Biography*. New York: Viking.

Allport, G. W. (1966). William James and the behavioral sciences. *Journal of the History of the Behavioral Sciences, 2*, 145–147.

Beecher, H. K., & Altschule, M. (1977). *Medicine at Harvard: The first three hundred years*. Hanover, NH: University Press of New England.

Benison, S., Barger, A. C., & Wolfe, E. (1987). *Walter Bradford Cannon: The life and times of a young scientist*. Cambridge, MA: Harvard University Press.

Bernard, C. (1865). *Introduction à l'étude de la médecine expérimentale* [Introduction to the study of experimental medicine]. Paris: Baillière.

Boring, E. G. (1950). *History of experimental psychology* (2nd Ed.). New York: Appleton, Century, Crofts.

Brown-Sequard, C. E. (1867). *Advice to students: An address delivered at the opening of the medical school lectures of Harvard University*. Cambridge, MA: Wilson and Son.

Burkhardt, F., Bowers, F., & Skrupskelis, I. (Eds.). (1988). *Manuscript lectures: The works of William James* (Vol. 17). Cambridge, MA: Harvard University Press.

Cadwallader, T. C., & Cadwallader, J. V. (1972). America's first modern psychologist: William James or C. S. Pierce? *Proceedings of the 80th Annual Convention of the American Psychological Association, Contributed papers and Symposia, VII* (pp. 773–774). Washington, DC: American Psychological Association.

Cannon, W. B. (1922). Biographical memoir of Henry Pickering Bowditch, 1840–1911. *Memoirs of the National Academy of Sciences, 17,* 184.

Cohen, S. (1966). *A medical grand tour: James Jackson Putnam in Europe.* Typescript on deposit at Rare Books, Countway Library of Medicine, Harvard Medical School, Cambridge, MA., pp. 3–4.

Croce, P. (1989). A scientific spiritualism: The elder Henry James's adaptation of Swedenborg. In J. Williams-Hogan (Ed.), *Swedenborg and his influence* (pp. 251–262). Bryn Athyn, PA: Swedenborg Scientific Association.

Dupree, A. H. (1959). *Asa Gray, 1810–1888,* Cambridge, MA: Belknap/Harvard University Press.

Ellenberger, H. (1970). *Discovery of the unconscious.* New York: Basic Books.

Ellis, F. W. (1938). Henry Pickering Bowditch and the development of the Harvard Laboratory of Physiology. *New England Journal of Medicine, 219,* 819–828.

Fay, A. (Oct. 18, 1871). Letter to Melusina Fay Pierce, Berlin. Courtesy of the late Silvia Mitarachi, from the unpublished biography of Melusina Harriet Fay.

Feinstein, H. (1984). *Becoming William James.* Ithaca, NY: Cornell University Press.

Foucault, M. (1973). *The birth of the clinic: An archaeology of medical perception.* London: Tavistock.

Fye, W. B. (1987). *The development of American physiology.* Baltimore: Johns Hopkins University Press.

Hale, N. G. (1971). *James Jackson Putnam and psychoanalysis.* Cambridge, MA: Harvard University Press.

Harper, R. S. (1949). The laboratory of William James. *Harvard Alumni Bulletin, 51,* 169–173.

Harper, R. S. (1950). The first psychological laboratory. *Isis, 41,* 158–161.

Harrington, A. (1987). *Mind, medicine and the double brain.* Princeton, NJ: Princeton University Press.

Hoovenkamp, H. (1978). *Science and religion in America, 1800–1860.* Philadelphia: University of Pennsylvania Press.

James, H., Jr. (Ed.). (1920). *The letters of William James* (Vols. 1–2). Boston: Atlantic Monthly Press.

James, W. (1868a). Review of Bernard's *Rapport sur le Progres et la Marche de la Physiologie general en France* (1867). *North American Review, 107,* 322–328.

James, W. (1868b). Moral Medication, a review of A. A. Liebault's *Du Sommeil et des états analogues, considérés surtout au point de vue de l'action du moral sur le physique* (1866). *The Nation, 7,* 50.

James, W. (1867–68). Medical School Notebook, (Archives CB 1869.42). Rare Books, Countway Library of Medicine, Harvard Medical School, Cambridge, MA.

James, W. (May 22, 1869a). Letter to H. P. Bowditch. Bowditch Papers. Countway Library of Medicine, Harvard Medical School, Cambridge, MA.

James, W. (March 10, 1869b). Review of E. Sargent's *Planchette: Or the Despair of Science. Boston Daily Advertiser.*

James, W. (1875). Review (unsigned) on German Pessimism. *Nation, 21,* 233–234.

James, W. (1876). Review (unsigned) on the *Revue Philosophique. Nation, 22,* 147.

James, W. (1890). *The principles of psychology* (Vols. 1–2). New York: Holt.

James, W. (March 24, 1894). Letter on the Medical Registration Act. *Boston Transcript.*

James, W. (1895). Experimental psychology in America. *Science,* n.s., *2,* 626.

James, W. (1898a). Consciousness under nitrous oxide. *Psychological Review, 5,* 194–196.

James, W. (1898b). Lehman and Hansen "on the Telepathic Problem." *Science,* n.s. *8,* 956.

James, W. (March 2, 1898c). Speech before the Committee on Public Health on Medical Registration Bill. *Boston Evening Transcript.* (Also in *Banner of Light,* March 12, 1898).

James, W. (1904). Does "consciousness" exist? *Journal of Philosophy, Psychology and Scientific Methods, 1,* 477–491.

James, W. (1907). The energies of men. *Philosophical Review, 16,* 1–20.

James, W. (May 22, 1909). Letters on vivisection. *New York Evening Transcript.*

James, W. (1910). A suggestion about mysticism. *Journal of Philosophy, Psychology, and Scientific Methods, 7,* 85–95.

Leary, D. (1988). *Poetry and science: William Wordsworth's influence on Charles Darwin and William James.* Invited address presented at the annual meeting of the American Psychological Association, Atlanta, GA.

Lesch, J. E. (1984). *Science and Medicine in France: The Emergence of experimental physiology, 1790–1855.* Cambridge, MA: Harvard University Press.

Liébeault, A. A. (1866). *Du Sommeil et des états analogues, considérés surtout au point de vue de l'action de moral sur le physique* [Concerning sleep and similar states considered especially from the perspective of the action of mind on the body]. Paris: Masson.

Meynert, T. (1873). "The Anatomy of the mammal Brain: Analyzed by J. J. Putnam, M. D., of Boston," Reprinted from Dr. Brown-Sequard's *Archives of Scientific and Practical Medicine,* in Collected Papers of James Jackson Putnam, 1 (1873–1899). Putnam Papers, Rare Books, Countway Library of Medicine, Harvard Medical School, Cambridge, MA.

Mills, C. K. (1904). Neurology in Philadelphia from 1874 to 1904. *Journal of Nervous and Mental Disease, 31,* 353–367.

Münsterberg, H. (1909). *Psychotherapy.* New York: Moffat, Yard and Co.

Murphy, L. B. (July, 1987). *Gardner Murphy and William James.* Unpublished manuscript.

Olmstead, E. H. (1967). Historical phases in the influence of Bernard's scientific generalizations in England and America. In F. Grande & M. B. Visscher (Eds.), *Claude Bernard and Experimental Medicine* (pp. 26–27). Cambridge, MA: Schenkman.

Perry, R. B. (1935). *The thought and character of William James* (Vol. 1–2). Boston: Little, Brown.

Putnam, J. J. (July 16, 1874). Contributions to the physiology of the cortex cerebrii, *Boston Medical and Surgical Journal.* Author's reprint. Putnam Papers, Rare Books, Countway Library of Medicine, Harvard Medical School, Cambridge, MA.

Rosenzweig, S. (1956). The Jameses' Stream of Consciousness. *Contemporary Psychology, 1,* 250–257.

Sixth Annual Report of the Trustees of the State Lunatic Hospital at Northampton. (1861). Boston: William White.

Stern, S. M. (1965). William James and the new psychology. In P. Buck (Ed.), *Social sciences at Harvard, 1860–1920; From inculcation to open mind* (pp. 175–222). Cambridge, MA: Harvard University Press.

Taylor, E. I. (1978). Psychology of Religion and Asian Studies: The William James legacy. *Journal of Transpersonal Psychology, 10,* 66–79.

Taylor, E. I. (1982a). *William James on exceptional mental states: Reconstruction of the 1896 Lowell lectures.* New York: Scribner's.

Taylor, E. I. (1982b). Louville Eugene Emerson: Psychotherapy, Harvard, and the early Boston scene, *Harvard Medical Alumni Bulletin, 56,* 42–46.

Taylor, E. I. (1984). Some Historic Implications of Swedenborg's Spiritual Psychology. *Studia Swedenborgiana, 4,* 5–38.

Taylor, E. I. (1986). Peirce and Swedenborg. *Studia Swedenborgiana, 6,* 25–51.

Taylor, E. I. (1987). Prospectus for a person-centered science: The unrealized potential of psychology and psychical research. *Journal of the American Society for Psychical Research, 81,* 313–337.

Taylor, E. I. (1988). Ralph Waldo Emerson: The Swedenborgian and transcendentalist connection. In R. Larsen (Ed.), *Emanuel Swedenborg: The vision continues* (pp. 127–146). New York: Swedenborg Foundation.

Taylor, E. I. (1989a, April). *The current status of William James's psychology of the emotions*. Public lecture sponsored by the William James Society of Harvard College and the Swedenborg Society of Cambridge, Swedenborg Chapel, Cambridge, MA.

Taylor, E. I. (1989b). *Experimental psychology and psychical research at Harvard, 1872–1910*. Paper presented at the annual meeting of the History of Science Society, Gainesville, FL.

Taylor, E. I. (in press). Williams James and the humanistic tradition. *Journal of Humanistic Psychology*.

Tyler, H. R., & Tyler, K. L. (1984). Charles Edouard Brown-Sequard: Professor of physiology and pathology of the nervous system at Harvard Medical School, *Neurology, 34*, 1231–1236.

Weiner, P. P. (1949). *Evolution and the founders of pragmatism*. Cambridge, MA: Harvard University Press.

Wilkinson, J. J. G. (n.d.). The Welsh Fasting Girl, James Papers, Houghton Library, Harvard University (Bms Am 1092.9 #4595).

Wilkinson, J. J. G. (1857a). *Improvisations from the spirit*. London: W. White.

Wilkinson, J. J. G. (1857b). *The homeopathic principle applied to insanity: A proposal to treat lunacy by spiritualism*. Boston: Otis Clapp.

Chapter 3

The Implications of James's Plea for Psychology as a Natural Science

Amedeo Giorgi

Saybrook Institute

and

University of Quebec at Montreal

It is well known that James was an unsystematic, and even paradoxical, writer (Allport, 1943) and that throughout his works he spiced his observations with personal biases and whimsies. He would open an article or section of a book with a guiding idea and immediately proceed to outstrip its logical boundaries. Perhaps the novelist in him kept him close to a descriptive attitude, which in turn kept his attention riveted on a concretely unfolding phenomenon so that its logical borders mattered less than the interesting twists and turns that the phenomenon was taking. In any event, this discursive side of James is what keeps him interesting and why it is vital still to return to his works even a century later. It is also why even his explicit statements have to be taken with a grain of salt and have to be understood contextually.

The thesis of this chapter is that James's style also surrounded his plea for psychology as a natural science. At face value, it seemed as though James's voice was simply one more plea in the chorus of the time making the case for a natural scientific approach to psychology. Yet, his attitude toward scientific psychology was that it was, at best, only "the hope of a science," and his antipathy toward the Fechnerian and Wundtian style of research was equally well known (James, 1890, I: 192–193, 549; Perry, 1936, p. 30). But he did insist that psychology should be a natural science even as he researched and commented on multiple personalities, witchcraft, and religious experiences (Taylor, 1982). The purpose of this chapter is to tease out, to the extent possible, what James meant by making psychology a natural science and then to draw out some implications of that meaning for contemporary psychology.

THE MEANING OF PSYCHOLOGY AS A NATURAL
SCIENCE IN THE *PRINCIPLES*

When James's *Principles of Psychology* came out in 1890, there was a section in the work entitled "Psychology Is A Natural Science." In this section, James attempted to articulate, briefly, the principles on which psychology as a natural science would be based that would differentiate it from the "faculty psychology" or the metaphysical psychology of the earlier period. James (I: 183) writes,

> . . . the mind which the psychologist studies is the mind of distinct individuals inhabiting definite portions of a real space and of a real time. . . . To the psychologist, then, the minds he studies are *objects*, in a world of other objects. (Italics in original)

By such phrasing, James was trying to establish that the proper object of the science of psychology was to be conceived analogously to the way that the natural sciences delineated their objects of study. On the one hand, he was trying to get away from metaphysical postulates such as absolute minds, souls, and so forth, by insisting that all the minds psychologists have to deal with were individuated, and on the other, he was trying to indicate that even when a psychologist reflects on his own mental processes (i.e., uses the method of introspection), the procedure does not involve the utilization of personal intimacy with our own processes. That is, the objectivity required by science could be met because introspection correctly understood was an objective procedure. Mind, for psychology, according to James (I: 199) "is an object in a world of objects" and thus one had to understand its relation to other objects, and merely assume, as in other sciences, that the psychologist could have access to its subject matter. It was the task of the metaphysics to wonder more deeply how this was possible.

James also discussed the methods of psychology in broad perspective, citing three: introspection, experimentation, and comparison. He noted that introspection was not infallible, but psychologists nevertheless had to rely on it. He referred to experimentation as the new method arising in Germany at that time and merely listed the areas to which it had been applied. The comparison method, he noted, assumed "a normal psychology of introspection to be established" (I: 194) since the results of work with primitives, children, abnormal, and other types of consciousness presupposed it.

Finally, James mentioned the sources of error and "snares of psychology," but these snares have to be understood in the light of his conception of psychology's definition and scope. As is well known, James (I: 184) divided the scope of psychology into four parts: the psychologist, the thought or mental state studied, the thought or mental state's object, and finally, the psychologist's reality. Now, one of James's points about psychology being a natural science is that the psychologist need not trouble himself over how he knows the psychologist's reality any more than "the geometer, the chemist, or the botanist do" (I: 184). Yet, James was aware that, somehow, such an attitudinal assumption for psychology was perhaps more problematic than with the other sciences he mentioned because he went on to show that the execution of such a directive was fraught with difficulties. Basically, the adoption and execution of the proper psychological attitude was hampered by speech and the psychologist's fallacy.

Psychology, James claimed, was limited by ordinary speech because the latter was primarily outer directed and psychology was concerned essentially with subjective phenomena. As a consequence, James believed that subjective facts did not receive the degree of articulation they deserved. In addition, language tended to deceive one by the use of words as labels so that if a group of phenomena were named, one was motivated to posit a substantive entity existing behind and supporting them. On the other hand, the lack of a word inclined one not to see an entity where there was one in fact, and so either way, language was as deceitful as it was helpful. Finally, James pointed out all of the difficulties associated with psychology's dependence on common speech in the sense that there tended to be a confusion between the thought and the object. James (I: 196) writes:

> The continuous flow of the mental stream is sacrificed, and in its place an atomism, a brickbat plan of construction, is preached, for the existence of which no good introspective grounds can be brought forward, and out of which presently grow all sorts of paradoxes and contradictions, the heritage of woe of students of the mind.

The confusion between the experience of the object and the object experienced leads James directly into a discussion of the psychologist's fallacy, the second snare of psychology. In the section of the *Principles* that is being covered here, James (I: 196–197) gives two versions of the psychologist's fallacy:

> The *great* snare of the psychologist is the *confusion of his own standpoint with that of the mental fact* about which he is making his report. . . . *Another variety of the psychologist's fallacy is the assumption that the mental state studied must be conscious of itself as the psychologist is conscious of it.*
> (italics in original)

In effect, both varieties of the psychologist's fallacy involve a confusion of standpoint: the second variety being an intersubjective confusion since the psychologist assumes that the consciousness of the experiencer is identical to his own; and the first is a "knowledge versus experience" confusion, since the psychologist here believes that the experiencer experiences the conscious state along the lines that the psychologist *knows* it (see Giorgi, 1981). What the snares of psychology show are the difficulties one would have in attempting to capture the proper object of psychology.

In the Preface to his text, James is even clearer about the natural science viewpoint on psychology that he adopted. He writes:

> Every natural science assumes certain data uncritically, and declines to challenge the elements between which its own 'laws' obtain, and from which its own deductions are carried on. Psychology, the science of finite individual minds, assumes as its data (1) *thoughts and feelings*, and (2) *a physical world* in time and space with which they coexist and which (3) *they know*. Of course these data themselves are discussable; but the discussion of them (as of other elements) is called metaphysics and falls outside the province of this book. (I: vi)

Thus, James admits that the units of psychological analysis could be criticized, but to do so would be to be metaphysical. He presumed that laws for psychology could be found because he (I: vi–vii) said "I have therefore treated our passing thoughts as integers, and regarded the mere laws of their coexistence with brainstates as the ultimate laws for our science." It was the attitude that the last sentence expressed that triggered off a mild controversy with G. T. Ladd.

LADD'S REVIEW OF THE *PRINCIPLES*

Ladd (1892), in the very first issue of the *Philosophical Review* used the appearance of the *Principles* as an excuse to start a debate with James about the meaning of psychology as a natural science. Ladd (1892, p. 24) began his article by stating that the issues concerning the "nature, problem and legitimate methods of Psychology, and the relations which it sustains to other forms of science and to metaphysics" were far from being settled and so that James raised the issues was not surprising. Moreover, he affirmed that James's book was learned and lively and written in an engaging and personal style. Although this made good reading, according to Ladd, it also made certain interpretations less than clear. Ladd felt that he often experienced that he had to guess at what James meant. He also thought that James's selectivity with respect to topics was never justified, and that even though, theoretically speaking, he picked a consistent perspective to speak from, there was a lack of unity to the volumes.

Ladd more or less went on in this vein, alternatively praising and criticizing James in small ways until he came to a key question, which he posed as follows:

> What, then, does Professor James understand psychology to be; and how does he propose to give to his own psychological opinions the character of a

science? The answer to this twofold inquiry will introduce another closely connected: What does he conceive to be the relation between metaphysics and psychology as a "natural science"? (Ladd, 1892, p. 27)

Ladd then went on to quote and paraphrase James as he answered this question. The phenomena of psychology are the states of consciousness of the individual and the science of psychology is to be both descriptive and explanatory, the latter task achieved by relating the conscious phenomena to their conditions. But it is precisely here that Ladd lodged his complaint. He (Ladd, 1892, p. 28) wrote:

> . . . the author's conception of psychology as a natural science results in a most astonishing abbreviation of the rights of the psychologist. The treatment is to be explanatory, . . . (but) [h]ow greatly disappointed we are, therefore, when an advocate of the new "natural science" of psychology restricts all legitimate explanation, by his very conception of such science, to one class of conditions only. . . .

Ladd's complaint was that James wanted to explain the realm of descriptive psychology only in terms of "brain-states." He refused to do it in any other way, according to Ladd, for fear of introducing metaphysics into psychology. Yet, complains Ladd (1892, p. 29), ". . . a vast amount of conjectural metaphysics of physics is woven into the very texture of both volumes." Thus, Ladd wondered why metaphysics of a physical sort was permitted whereas all metaphysics relating to experience and consciousness was cast away. This inspired Ladd (1892, p. 30) to call psychology as a natural science a "wholly cerebral psychology," because James was seeking "A blank unmediated correspondence, term for term, of the succession of states of consciousness with the succession of total brain-processes."

Ladd perceived the above ambition to be a most restricted conception of explanatory psychology because it excluded all of introspective psychology as well as what was then called "physiological psychology" (psychophysics). Ladd found that vision to be too restrictive, and offered the opinion that James himself did, too, because in the *Principles*, he did not remain faithful to his own conception of natural scientific psychology and he covered all sorts of issues that should have been banned. Thus, Ladd (1892, p. 31) concluded that "The attempt to establish psychology as a natural science upon such an extremely tenuous and cloudy foundation as our present or prospective knowledge of cerebral explosions and overlappings is doomed to failure from the very beginning." Ladd made this point the central theme of his review, showing over and over again how James himself could not keep to his own narrow definition and how most of the *Principles* indulged in metaphysics anyway. Ladd (1892, p. 38) finally summarized his critique:

Of the conception of psychology, its nature, problems, and method, which is proposed in these volumes, and of the defense in detail of this conception, the following statements seem to me true: The conception is such, and so narrow, that a consistent adherence to it compels us to admit the utter impossibility of establishing psychology as a natural science. It excludes almost all the really scientific data and conclusions; it includes only those data and conjectures which are most remote from genuine science. But the author does not adhere to this conception. Neither does he adhere to his determination to exclude metaphysics. The metaphysics of mind is often admitted, with confession of apparent inconsistency; the metaphysics of physics is freely admitted, generally without confession or apparent consciousness of inconsistency. As descriptive science, the work is admirable; for its author is a born, and thoroughly trained, psychologist. As explanatory science also,—wherever it departs most widely from its own conception—it is generally admirable. As explanatory science, without metaphysics, in the form of the aforesaid "blank unmediated correspondences," it is, at best, *not science at all*.

RESPONSES TO LADD'S REVIEW

Ladd's review triggered off two quick responses, one from Gordy (1892) and one from James (1892) himself. Gordy (1892, p. 299) claimed that James's *Principles* had two important distinguishing features: "(1) its point of view, its conception of psychology as a natural science; (2) its contention that all our so-called ideas at any moment form one undivided mental state." His objection to Ladd's review is that Ladd confined himself almost exclusively to the first point, and even then, according to Gordy, he did not really clinch his argument. Gordy contended that James did not say that psychology *was already* a natural science, but that it hoped to be. Yet, Ladd said that it could *never be* one, and Gordy wanted to know how Ladd could be so sure since psychology had barely started. Finally, with respect to this first point, Gordy showed that when James claimed that psychology as a natural science would consist in "blank unmediated correspondence, term for term, of the succession of states of consciousness with the succession of total brain processes," he meant that this would be an ultimate state of affairs, not a current one. Gordy then argued that that possibility could not be eliminated. With regard to James's position that all our ideas at any moment formed one undivided mental state, Gordy showed that James's position was superior to those of his contemporaries, namely, the associationistic position or the transcendentalist metaphysical claim. Thus, Gordy defended James's natural scientific conception of psychology, even if he admitted that its fulfillment lay far in the future.

James (1892) began his article, in response to Ladd's critique, by denying that he meant that psychology was a natural science at the time he was writing. "Psychology," he (James, 1892, p. 146) wrote, indeed, is today hardly more than what physics was before Galileo, what chemistry was before Lavoisier. It is a mass of phenomenal description, gossip and myth, including, however, real material enough to justify one in the hope that with judgment and good will on the part of those interested, its study may be so organized even now as to become worthy of the name of natural science at no very distant day.

James (1892, p. 146), then, went on to say, "I wished, by treating Psychology *like* a natural science, to help her become one" (Italics in original). James then admitted that some of Ladd's sallies struck home, and that his book was "uncouth enough," but then he suggested that one leave the book behind and that one concentrate on the key issue—what psychology as a natural science could possibly mean.

James then asked the general question, what is a natural science? James's (1892, p. 147) answer was "It is a mere fragment of truth broken out from the whole mass of it for the sake of practical effectiveness exclusively. *Divide et impera*" (italics in original). Thus, James's theory of science was that it must be practically effective. This accounted for all of the other assumptions he held. Thus, he went on to articulate that, as a result, special sciences had to make certain assumptions about their subject matter and not be held responsible for other questions that the mind might make about their phenomena. He used physics as an example, showing how it assumed a material world without trying to get metaphysical and showed how it was "possible," and how it merely assumed that bodies interact, and that laws of sequence could be established, and so on. Then James (1892, p. 147) wrote:

If, therefore, psychology is ever to conform to the type of the other natural sciences, it must also renounce certain ultimate solutions, and place itself on the usual commonsense basis by uncritically begging such data as the existence of a physical world, of states of mind, and of the fact that these latter take cognizance of other things. What the 'physical world' may be in itself, how 'states of mind' can exist at all, and exactly what 'taking cognizance' may imply, are inevitable further questions; but they are questions of the kind for which general philosophy, not natural science, is held responsible.

Thus, for James, psychology as a natural science meant the ability to draw certain boundaries. James admitted that in everyday life one could raise issues related to the Infinite, the Absolute, and so forth, but on the other hand, he (James, 1892, p. 147) claimed that there was an aspect of our mental being "which falls wholly within the sphere of natural history." Thus, it is clear at this point, at least, that James, in arguing for a natural scientific psychology was also arguing for naturalism. He (1892, pp. 147–148) continued his argument by stating:

As constituting the inner life of individual persons who are born and die, our conscious states are temporal *events* arising in the ordinary course of nature—events, moreover, the conditions of whose happening or nonhappening from one moment to another, lie certainly in large part in the physical world.

James, showing his pragmatic bias, then launched into a discussion of how valuable in a practical sense it would have been if psychology could control the conditions of mentation. He claimed that the achievements of the other natural sciences would seem pale compared to this. Thus, although legitimating philosophy, James nevertheless wanted to restrict psychology to the collection of facts and wanted the philosophers to stick to the metaphysics of the soul. He wanted the term "psychology" to be reserved for scientific psychology and he wanted to overcome the distinction of his time, "rational psychology" and "empirical psychology."

From the above position, James argued that both the philosopher and the biologist could accept mental states as the data of psychology because "they form a practically admitted sort of object whose habits of coexistence and succession and relations with organic conditions form an entirely definite subject of research" (James, 1892, pp. 150–151). But with this definition, James still hoped that the correlation of mental states with brain states could be possible. And James ended the defense of his position with the idea that one would be compelled to choose a practical psychology over a metaphysical one.

IMPLICATIONS OF JAMES'S PLEA
FOR PSYCHOLOGY
AS A NATURAL SCIENCE
FOR CONTEMPORARY PSYCHOLOGY

In brief, then, for James, natural scientific psychology was a nonmetaphysical psychology that tried to stay close to facts and tried to understand conscious phenomena, as much as possible, as natural events. However, as Ladd pointed out in his review, James himself, did not stay within his own definition. The question is, could anyone?; that is, what would it mean to keep at the level of psychic facts with respect to conscious phenomena without being metaphysical? For example, when James said that he was looking for "A blank unmediated correspondence of the succession of states of consciousness with the succession of total brain processes" (James, 1892, p. 6), was that strictly a scientific statement? Isn't a strong dosage of metaphysics implied in the very assumption that conscious states would be wholly determined by brain processes? Or, indeed, even if James had claimed the opposite, would metaphysics not be as deeply implicated?

Moreover, did James himself avoid all of the snares of psychology? In one passage, James (1892, p. 147) appealed to common sense ways of thinking as a possible way to stick with facts. But didn't James himself tell us that we had to be wary of language, and especially with common sense expressions? Indeed, psychologists from very different perspectives have been denouncing the perfidious role of common sense. Titchener (1912, p. 104) called it "the enemy!" Skinner (1963) has criticized the prevalence and popularity of the mentalistic expressions of everyday life because they are interpreted as terminal data whereas in his view they merely reflect insufficient analyses. Skinner would want to translate all the mentalistic expressions of everyday life into the language of radical behaviorism. That is, common sense is an obstacle to the advance of behaviorism. Lacan (1977) has lamented that Freud has been tamed by culture and everyday life and that in order to be properly understood, he has to be read in a radical way. In other words, contact with common sense mollified the impact of Freud's views and in order to understand them properly Lacan has argued that they must be detached from common sense interpretations.

Now, if such different perspectives as these are all calling attention to the seductions of common sense, how could James naively appeal to it as a way of avoiding metaphysics? But, of course, it is simply another one of his paradoxes! He tells us not to be deceived by common sense, but in order to avoid another pitfall, metaphysics, he appeals to common sense! In such a way were James's productive paradoxes constituted! But behind them there was always a legitimate problem, the solution of which would certainly advance the state of the art of psychological praxis.

It is important, therefore, to clarify the primary meaning of James's attempt to establish psychology as a natural science. He did not mean that the natural sciences had to be slavishly imitated. He meant, first and foremost, that metaphysics had to be overcome as a factor constraining the descriptions of psychologists. That is, connotations of words like soul, transcendental, and so forth, should not influence psychological descriptions. Thus, James wanted to be concrete and specific in his descriptions in order to uncover the facts of psychological experience, but without committing himself to a specific metaphysics. But how was this to be done? What perspective needed to be assumed, what language was to be used, and within what context should the psychologist place him or herself to accomplish this task?

I shall try to show the dilemmas within which James was caught as he tried to answer those questions, and I will then suggest that phenomenological thought has advanced the problem of how to begin psychological analyses in an important way without claiming that the issue is completely solved. Before proceeding, I simply want to mention that James did, of course, make many descriptive contributions to psychology, some of which have stood for a century, but as Ladd showed, he was not as nonmetaphysical as he had hoped. Indeed, according to Linschoten (1968, p. 38), James later admitted that he could not describe psychological reality without some philosophical presuppositions concerning the nature of experience. Consequently, the challenge of understanding the contributions of descriptive science is still with us. But now, let us turn to James's dilemma.

Although James desired to be nonmetaphysical with respect to psychological reality, and wished to avoid the snares of language, he was not always successful in avoiding either. We saw earlier that James wanted to understand mind naturalistically, which is a metaphysical position, and the difficulties that James sometimes had in describing bodily sensations (James, 1940/1912 shows that he sometimes presupposed the distinctions of common sense language (e.g., inner-outer). In other words, James's descriptions are ambiguous. Sometimes he implicitly broke from the perspective of common sense (e.g., does consciousness exist?) or what phenomenologists call the natural attitude, while at other times he was clearly ensconced in it. Thus, either James was naturalistic (an explicit metaphysical position) or else he was writing from the perspective of the natural attitude, which is scientifically and philosophically naive, containing an implicit, sedimented metaphysics. Either way, James theoretically did not reach a genuine nonmetaphysical position nor a position that would escape the snares of linguistic expression.

I would now like to introduce three phenomenological concepts that I believe can help advance the problem of nonmetaphysical description. The first is the idea of essence. Husserl (1913/1931) believed that if one could grasp the essence of a phenomenon, then one's concrete work could be better guided because some sense of the legitimate variations of the phenomenon could be ascertained. For Husserl, essential intuition, by the way, is grasped and described within the perspective of ontological neutrality. Phenomenologically, if psychology were to be defined as the study of mental life, as James postulated, then one's concrete work should have been guided by the essential understanding. However, James did not even raise the issue of what guided his descriptions. He only knew that minds were "objects in a world of other objects" and set about describing them with the language of everyday life. (Of course, in other sections of the *Principles* James did, implicitly at least, exceed the naturalistic understanding of mental life, but he did not relate these transgressions to the concept of psychology as a natural science.) In any event, concern for the essence of a phenomenon, even if limited, would help guide a researcher in his or her concrete descriptions.

The second concept is the well-known notion, intentionality, which Husserl, following, but modifying, Brentano, described as the essence of consciousness. Intentionality refers to the fact that all objects of consciousness transcend the acts in which they appear. In other words, consciousness is essentially directedness toward objects, understood in the broadest possible sense. Again, the concept as used here is essentially purely descriptive and not ontological, and so James could have spoken more freely of the psychological realm as an epistemologically neutral realm. As we saw earlier, James placed a cognitive relationship between the mind and its object. An intentional relationship, a relationship that describes the directedness of consciousness as such, could support more varieties of relationship, including a cognitive one, than a specifically cognitive relation.

Finally, Husserl introduced the phenomenological reduction as a methodological device to help investigators obtain a more purified description. The phenomenological reduction refers to the assumption of an attitude on the part of a researcher in which all knowledge *about* an object of consciousness is put aside so that the experience of the object in the present can be freshly attended to. In addition, the phenomenological reduction entails the withholding of the existential claim with respect to the presented object. In other words, in such an attitude, the object precisely as experienced is described, but knowledge claims are only made with respect to its presence. No claim is made that it *is* the way it presents itself.

Now, we stated earlier that James assumed either a naturalistic position or one described as partaking of the natural attitude. Naturalism, as indicated, is a metaphysical position that assumes that the laws, concepts, properties, and so forth, that are found in researching nature are equally appropriate for conscious phenomena as well. To the extent, then, that James assumed naturalism, he did not escape metaphysics.

On the other hand, in taking up the position of the natural attitude as implicitly justifiable, James was forced to deal with the very snares he cautioned us about. James neither argued theoretically for, nor practiced, describing at a critical distance. But the role of the phenomenological reduction is precisely to introduce an attitude that has some chance of escaping the pitfalls of the natural attitude by withholding the existential claims that the objects of consciousness offer. That is, all objects of consciousness are considered precisely insofar as they are given to consciousness, not as they are in themselves. Because no realist claim is made, surprising aspects of the phenomena can have as good a chance of being described as expected ones. All objects or states of affairs that appear are given the status of "phenomenon," that is, appearances for consciousness, rather than the status of existing beings. Moreover, in tapping into what is called "pretheoretical experience" the researcher within the reduction has a greater chance of being present at the very constitution of psychological reality because the pretheoretical level is below the attitude required by the discipline of psychology.

In order to appreciate the theoretical advance that phenomenology brings to the point of departure of psychology as a science, a return to James's own schema for psychology will be helpful. It will be recalled that James conceived of the science of psychology in terms of four categories: (1) the psychologist, (2) the thought or feeling studied by him or her, (3) the thought's object, and (4) the psychologists's reality, which must be distinguished from physical reality. Now, James himself, at the time of the *Principles*, in order to avoid metaphysics, simply assumed that the thoughts that coexisted with the physical world in time and space could know the physical world on which they were also dependent. He did not try to explain the cognitive relation involved. Indeed, everything that was interesting—and still problematic about psychology's point of departure—was left unanalyzed in the name of metaphysics: How the psychologist constituted psychological reality, how the thought or feeling being studied grasped its object, and just how psychological reality specifically differed from the physical reality on which it depended.

The phenomenological reinterpretation of James's schema would look as follows. The psychologist, from within the reduction, observes and describes the thought or feeling studied by him as it is intentionally related to its object. The intentional relation, of course, is much broader than the cognitive relation because it refers to any directedness of consciousness to its object and not just that specific direction we call "cognition." Thus, affective and conative relationships would also be varieties of intentionality. Because of the reduction, the attitude assumed by the psychologist not only escapes the metaphysics of naturalism, but it also transcends the natural attitude since what is presented to consciousness is precisely understood in relation to consciousness. Moreover, since it is admitted that psychological reality is constituted (rather than ready-made) out of the pretheoretical experience of everyday life, the snares of the psychologist's fallacy are also avoided. In other words, one could say that what James was looking for when he was searching for a nonmetaphysical way of approaching psychological description was precisely something like essential intuition, intentionality, and the phenomenological reduction, because, as indicated above, all three terms would help psychological researchers become liberated from metaphysical stances. Although the actual achievement of what is theoretically clearly delineated here is still problematic, at least it is clear that the theoretical concepts introduced by phenomenology to help free disciplined inquiry from metaphysics converges with James's hesitation to enter into the realm of metaphysics.

Still, one should not forget that the psychological schema that phenomenology is reinterpreting was introduced by James, and it is still a viable one. Indeed, until psychology finds a way of working through the relationships among the psychologist and the psychologist's reality and the mental state and the mental state's object, in an adequate way, its praxis and disciplinary status will have to be considered to be merely tentative. Insofar as this problem is still unsolved 100 years after its introduction, one could say that James was well ahead of his times.

REFERENCES

Allport, G. (1943). The productive paradoxes of William James. *Psychological Review, 50,* 95–120.

Giorgi, A. (1981). On the relationship among the psychologist's fallacy, psychologism and the phenomenological reduction. *Journal of Phenomenological Psychology, 12*, 75–86.

Gordy, J. P. (1892). Professor Ladd's criticism of James's psychology. *Philosophical Review, 1*, 299–305.

Husserl, E. (1931). *Ideas* (W. R. B. Gibson, Trans.) New York: Collier. (Original work published 1913)

James, W. (1890). *The principles of psychology* (Vols. 1–2). New York: Holt.

James, W. (1892). A plea for psychology as a natural science. *Philosophical Review, 1*, 146–153.

James, W. (1940). A world of pure experience. In W. James, *Essays in radical empiricism* (pp. 39–91). New York: Longmans, Green. (Original work published 1912)

Lacan, J. (1977). *Ecrits*. (A Sheridan, Trans.) New York: Norton.

Ladd, G. T. (1892). Psychology as so-called natural science. *Philosophical Review, 1*, 24–53.

Linschoten, J. (1968). *On the way toward a phenomenological psychology: The psychology of William James*. Pittsburgh, PA: Duquesne University Press.

Perry, R. B. (1936). *The thought and character of William James* (Vol. 2). Boston: Little, Brown.

Skinner, B. F. (1963). Behaviorism at fifty. *Science, 140*, 951–958.

Taylor, E. (1982). *William James on exceptional mental states*. New York: Scribner's Sons.

Titchener, E. B. (1912). Description vs. a statement of meaning. *American Journal of Psychology, 23*, 165–182.

Chapter 4

William James and Gestalt Psychology[1]

Mary Henle
New School for Social Research

William James has been widely claimed as a forerunner of various later developments in psychology (cf. Perry, 1935, Vol. 2, p. 91). Since this chapter concerns William James and Gestalt psychology, it may be remarked at the outset that James was perhaps closer in spirit to Gestalt psychology than were any of his contemporaries, particularly in his respect for direct experience and his faithfulness to it, his sensitivity to its nuances, his welcoming of new problems to psychology, and his lively relation to them. Still, it would be a mistake to call James, as Perry did, "a father of 'Gestalt' psychology, especially in its rejection of 'associationism'" (James, 1892/1948, p. viii; introduction by R. B. Perry).[2] Prior to other considerations to be detailed here, it must be stated that although James was widely familiar with contemporary continental developments in philosophy and psychology, like other psychologists of his time, he was unaffected by the revolution in natural science that took place after his student days (indeed mainly after his floruit), a revolution that so much influenced the Gestalt psychologists. Both treated psychology as a natural science, but their conceptions of natural science were radically different. The Gestalt psychologists relied on field theory, whereas James's thinking rested on an older physics. This difference

---

[1]This chapter will confine itself for the most part to James's *Principles of Psychology*. Others of his works will be drawn upon only sparingly. The 1890 edition of the *Principles* has been used.

James was a prolific user of italics. Many of these will be omitted without comment where, for example, they are used only for a definition or a summary. Only where italics are used for emphasis will they be retained.

[2]In 1935 Perry pointed out that James "did not, of course, deny association."

In that place he stated more correctly, "James's antiatomism is closely related to the contemporary *Gestalt* movement" (1935, Vol. 2, p. 79, n. 22).

cannot fail to influence any further comparisons between James's psychology and Gestalt psychology. The emphasis of this chapter will be on a few basic, interrelated assumptions. Although it is possible, and instructive, to find interesting similarities and differences with respect to specific problems, these will be used mainly for purposes of illustration.

The issues to be considered will be mechanism, atomism, associationism, and organization. On all these issues there will be seen to be a conspicuous contrast between the views of James and of the Gestalt psychologists; yet there are sometimes hints in James of attempts to break away from traditional positions (in the case of atomism, more than hints). The chapter will conclude with an attempt to find convergences between William James and Gestalt psychology.

MECHANISM

I use the term mechanism for any conception of the order of events in the brain (and therefore corresponding psychological events) in terms of constraints, innate or acquired. Köhler (1947, chap. 4) has used the expression *machine theory*, because the machine offers a perfect analogy to such thinking. Machines are constructed to control the direction of the forces of nature by the judicious arrangement of man-made constraints. A very simple example, borrowed from Köhler, provides an analogy to the traditional concept of association and recall:

> Just as a railroad train remains on its tracks because these constitute a way of least resistance, and just as the enormous power of the engine has no influence upon the direction of the train, so order in association and recall is a matter of pathways, and the nature of the processes which travel along these pathways has no influence upon their course. (1947, p. 112)[3]

Correspondingly, far from allowing free play to dynamic forces, machines constrain the action of these forces and thus achieve the desired ends, here the direction of the locomotion; the arrangement of structures limits the direction the natural forces can take.

Scientific psychologists have, for the most part, conceived the nervous system in machine terms. The orderly results achieved in perception, memory, thinking, and other psychological functions have been viewed as corresponding to machinelike arrangements in the nervous system,

---

[3]Railroad tracks are not, of course, a machine, but they supply a simple example of the way in which machinelike arrangements constrain the direction of natural forces.

The railroad engine, to be sure, is itself a machine, the direction of whose power is likewise controlled by man-made constraints.

It may be emphasized that Köhler is here referring to the traditional views of association and recall, not to his own.

arrangements of nerve cells, fibers, and other structures. Otherwise, it seems to be taken for granted, anything could happen: Natural forces left to themselves are assumed to lead only to chaos.

The Gestalt psychologists do not, of course, deny the importance of anatomical conditions in the nervous system. And by no means do they deny the influence of learning, which may be viewed as resulting in acquired constraints in the cortex. But within the limits set by these constraints, dynamic processes occur that permit the interactions needed to make understandable many corresponding psychological phenomena. "Both observation and theoretical calculation," wrote Köhler (1947, p. 130) "make [the physicist] conclude that, in general, dynamic interaction within a system tends to establish orderly distributions."

Thus there is an alternative to machine theory. Did James see it?

James (1890) explicitly described the nervous system as a machine: "The whole neural organism, it will be remembered, is, physiologically considered, but a machine for converting stimuli into reactions" (II: 372). Again, speaking of the modification of reflex action through experience, he said:

> It is like the great commutating switch-board at a central telephone station. No new elementary process is involved; no impression nor any motion peculiar to the hemispheres; but any number of combinations impossible to the lower machinery taken alone, and an endless consequent increase in the possibilities of behavior on the creature's part. (I: 26)

Whether James was speaking of reflex action, of the "machinery of association" (II: 575), of "the mental machine" (1899, p. 11), of the "complication of the associative machinery" (II: 391), of habit, he had in mind paths in the nervous system through which currents flow. In a popular lecture, teachers are told that "your pupils, whatever else they are, are at any rate little pieces of associating machinery" (1899, p. 82) and again that "our mind is essentially an associating machine" (1899, p. 116).

Why did James adopt so mechanistic a position? For two reasons that I can see. Most importantly, the brain is a universally admitted bodily condition of mental operations (I: 4), and he saw that organ as demanding such a conception. "The brain-physiology of late years has with great effort sought to work out the paths by which these couplings of sensations with movements take place" (I:27). He cannot escape from the physiology that was the standard view of psychologists of his time.

In addition, James saw that "before . . . indeterminism, science simply *stops*" (II: 576). He saw the alternative to determinism, which for him entails mechanism, as what he calls spiritualism (vitalism). Although he does not rule out a selective role of the soul, "the *existence* of the current, and its *tendency* towards either path, I feel bound to account for by mechanical laws" (II: 584). As others both before and after him, James adopted mechanism to avoid vitalism.

Nevertheless, it must be added that, despite his intention to make psychology a natural (i.e., for him, mechanistic) science, James was sometimes tempted by nonmechanistic orientations. In contrast to the psychophysical parallelism that he maintained through most of the *Principles*,[4] James found a need for mind-body interaction. For example, in his criticism of the automaton theory, he found it necessary to argue for the causal efficacy of consciousness. Pointing out that in higher organisms, consciousness is generally admitted to be more complex and intense than in lower ones, he contended:

> From this point of view it seems an organ, superadded to the other organs which maintain the animal in the struggle for existence; and the presumption of course is that it helps him in some way in the struggle, just as they do. But it cannot help him without being in some way efficacious and influencing the course of his bodily history. (I: 138)

Feelings, interest, and volition can influence physiological events: "The feelings can produce nothing absolutely new, they can only reinforce and inhibit reflex currents" (I: 138). Again, James assigned to "interested attention and volition" the possibility of selecting among the ideas which "the associative machinery has already introduced." But this "mental spontaneity" is enough for "the most eager advocate of free will" (I: 594).

This question of the role of free will in a scientific psychology need not be discussed here. What is relevant is that, as mentioned earlier, for James "before . . . indeterminism science simply *stops*" (II: 576). But free will seems to be equated with indeterminism: To the free-willist, the appearance of indetermination is a reality; and James asserted: "I myself hold with the free-willists" (1899, p. 191).

The intervention of such psychological functions in the course of physiological events suggests that at times James was tempted by vitalism ("mental spontaneity"). A less mechanistic physiological basis for his psychology would have enabled him to avoid such departures from his major aim:

> I have kept close to the point of view of natural science throughout the book. . . . This book . . . rejects both the associationist and the spiritualist

---

[4]A typical statement of James's dominant position:

However numerous and delicately differentiated the train of ideas may be, the train of brain-events that runs alongside of it must in both respects be exactly its match, and we must postulate a neural machinery that offers a living counterpart for every shading, however fine, of the history of its owner's mind. Whatever degree of complication the latter may reach, the complication of the machinery must be quite as extreme, otherwise we should have to admit that there may be mental events to which no brain-events correspond. (I: 128)

theories; and in this strictly positivistic point of view consists the only feature of it for which I feel tempted to claim originality. (I: v–vi)

A couple of additional examples may be given to show that James was not immune to the temptations of vitalism:

It is true that a presiding arbiter seems to sit aloft in the mind, and emphasize the better suggestions into permanence, while it ends by dropping out and leaving unrecorded the confusion. (I: 552)

The objects come before us through the brain's own laws, and the Ego of the thinker can only remain on hand, as it were, to recognize their relative values and brood over some of them, whilst others are let drop. (I: 587)

Possibly neural laws will not suffice, and we shall need to invoke a dynamic reaction of the form of consciousness upon its content. (I: 581)

On the other hand, James knew that "most believers in the ego [i.e., an Ego added to the bundle of ideas to give it unity] make the same mistake as the associationists and sensationists whom they oppose. Both agree that the elements of the subjective stream are discrete and separate. . . . Both make an identical initial hypothesis; but the egoist, finding it won't express the facts, adds another hypothesis to correct it" (I: 277–278).

Both in the nervous system and elsewhere, mechanical or dynamic thinking relates items in an orderly manner. I borrow from Köhler the expression "string connection" for a mechanistic relation. That there are string connections cannot be denied. Almost any items may be connected by a string: an associationist and a spiritualist, a monkey and a fundamentalist, an elephant and a memorandum book. The nature of the items in question does not matter in the case of such mechanical connections. Where the connection is a dynamic one, on the other hand, the nature of the items in their relation to each other is essential: One chemical combination can lead to an explosion, another can produce a valuable new alloy. In another area, one conclusion will follow inevitably from given premises, another will not. The distinction between string and dynamic connections will be of direct concern to us in later contexts. It is introduced here to notice a strange (and commendable) inconsistency in James, a departure from his mechanistic thinking. Thus:

Now, why do the various animals do what seem to us such strange things, in the presence of such outlandish stimuli? Why does the hen, for example, submit herself to the tedium of incubating such a fearfully uninteresting set of objects as a nestful of eggs . . .? Why do [men] prefer saddle of mutton and champagne to hard-tack and ditch-water? Why does the maiden interest the youth so that everything about her seems more important and significant than anything else in the world? Nothing more can be said than that these are human ways, and that every creature *likes* its own ways, and takes to the following them as a matter of course. . . . It is not for the sake of their utility that they are followed, but because at the moment of following them we feel that is the only appropriate and natural thing to do. Not one man in a billion, when taking his dinner, ever thinks of utility. He eats because the food tastes good. . . . The connection between the savory sensation and the act it awakens is for him absolute and *selbstverständlich* [self-evident, understandable]. (II: 386)

We may conclude that, to the animal which obeys it, every impulse and every step of every instinct shines with its own sufficient light, and seems at the moment the only eternally right and proper thing to do. It is done for its own sake exclusively. (II: 387)

Another example again shows how seriously James took such understandable relations:

The aesthetic principles are at bottom such axioms as that a note sounds good with its third and fifth, or that potatoes need salt. We are once for all so made that when certain impressions come before our mind, one of them will seem to call for or repel the others as its companions. (II: 672)

Although he countenances an explanation in terms of habit to a certain extent, he added, "But to explain *all* aesthetic judgments in this way would be absurd; for it is notorious how seldom natural experiences come up to our aesthetic demands" (ibid.).

For James, it does matter, in short, what goes with what, that is, *how* the self is related to phenomenal objects. Not just any object will do; it must be a natural and appropriate one. A casual reference to the "inner fitness of things" is another example (1899, p. 192). In a very different connection, a discussion of classification, logic, and mathematics, the same issue arises. These sciences James derived from the apprehension of series as such and of certain of their properties, which cannot be accounted for as a matter of habitual associations. "The axiom of skipped intermediaries applies, however, only to certain particular series. . . . [It] flows from the nature of the matters thought about" (II: 659–660). Again: "Nothing but the clear sight of the ideas themselves shows whether the axiom of skipped intermediaries applies to them or not. Their connections, immediate and remote, flow from their inward natures" (II: 661).

Shall we call these sciences intuitive, innate, or a priori bodies of truth? asked James. This would be his own preference, but in order not to offend many worthy readers, he referred the whole matter to "the immortal Locke" (II: 661–662).

The term *intuitive* is noncommittal, but to call such "eternal verities" innate or a priori would fail to do justice to the *selbstverständlichkeit* of the relations, to the fact that they flow "from the nature of the matters thought about" (II: 660). These considerations make one wonder whether James had entirely accepted the understandable character of the relations he discussed; nor would the immortal Locke have helped him out in this respect.

Nevertheless, these discussions, both of instinct and of aesthetics, logic, and mathematics, imply a departure from the indifference of the items connected either by innate or by habitual paths in the nervous system. They constitute an inconsistency with James's most basic assumptions but, it seems to me, an improvement on them.

In summary, James's psychology is basically mechanistic. But he was too lively a thinker and too subtly aware of the nature of psychological phenomena to have been satisfied with such a framework. He was aware of understandable relations, though not able to do theoretical justice to them. He was even tempted by vitalism, but such a solution would have violated his most basic aim. Science as he saw it demanded mechanism; where this view did not fit the facts, James was forced into some really productive contradictions. The next step would be a conception of science that supersedes the mechanism–vitalism dilemma, one that the time scarcely permitted.

ATOMISM

An important respect in which James may be compared with Gestalt psychology is on the issue of atomism. The natural science that James knew, as did American psychologists of his time, took atomism for granted. Yet we find in the ever-paradoxical William James a strong attack on this position.

Perhaps best known is James's attack on what he calls the "mind-stuff theory." This is "the assumption that our mental states are composite in structure, made up of smaller states conjoined" (I: 145). For example, Herbert Spencer is cited as arguing that, although a tone appears simple and continuous, it is really compound, since its stimulus is a series of discrete vibrations and, correspondingly, discrete nervous excitations underlie it. The question is: Where does the transformation into a unitary experience take place? "in the nerve-world or in the mind-world?" (I: 154). Spencer assumed that a simple sensation corresponds to each nervous discharge, so that the fusion is one of conscious processes, the discrete sensations compounding with themselves into a continuous state of consciousness. James, on the contrary, maintained that the integration must occur in the nervous system itself, so that a unitary nervous process corresponds to a unitary mental experience.

James argued that the theory of the "mind-stuffists" is logically unintelligible. Every combination we know anything about requires a medium or vehicle (I: 158)—which the mind-stuff theory does not provide. The mind-stuffists do not provide any way for the, say, 20,000 discrete sensations to combine into the experience of a single tone of a given pitch.

The mind-stuff theory will be recognized as an extreme form of what later came to be called the constancy hypothesis. This is the thesis that there is a point-for-point correspondence between local stimulation and local experience. Also known as the mosaic theory, it has repeatedly been attacked by Gestalt psychologists.

It is interesting to note that the arguments of the Gestalt psychologists resemble James's criticisms of the mind-stuff theory. Not only did James criticize the absence of a medium for the needed combinations; he also knew that although this theory (and the constancy hypothesis) fail to do justice to most perceptual phenomena, it is immune from attack on these grounds. Except under the most artificial conditions, local stimulation does not correspond to such perceptual phenomena as size, color, brightness, speed, and so on. But the constancy hypothesis has been protected by a number of auxiliary assumptions that account for the apparently anomalous cases. Thus these assumptions have been the point of attack both of William James and of the Gestalt psychologists. In connection with the phenomena mentioned, James confined his criticism to the doctrine of unconscious inferences.[5] By a process of unconscious inference, "a small human image on the retina is referred, not to a pygmy, but to a distant man of normal size" (I: 168). This interpretation is rejected, although in favor of one of "processes of simple cerebral association" (I: 169), an approach that will be considered later. The Gestalt psychologists extend the criticism, beyond unconscious inferences, to empiristic and other auxiliary assumptions used to bolster up the constancy hypothesis (cf. Köhler, 1913/1971).

In a prophetic passage, James remarked:

> [The psychologist] feels an imperious craving to be allowed to *construct* synthetically the successive mental states which he describes. The mind-stuff theory so easily admits of the construction being made, that it seems certain that 'man's unconquerable mind' will devote much future pertinacity and ingenuity to setting it on its legs again and getting it into some sort of plausible working-order. (I: 176)

That James's prediction of the persistence of the mind-stuff theory, or more generally, of the constancy or mosaic hypothesis, was astute is indicated by the fact that much of the early controversial literature of Gestalt psychology is devoted to combating its supporting hypotheses. This is not the place to trace the history of attempts to rescue the constancy hypothesis and the criticisms of these attempts, but the reader is referred to Koffka (1915/1938; Köhler, 1913/1971, 1925/1938, 1928/1938). The criticisms of

---

[5]It may be remarked that although James rejected *unconscious* inferences to explain anomalous perceptual phenomena, he was not averse to the use of inferences for this purpose: "Note that in every illusion what is false is what is inferred, not what is immediately given" (II: 86).

the doctrine of unconscious inference still have relevance to the present-day psychology of perception.

Since James was writing in a period in which atomism was virtually un-questioned in psychology, his criticisms of it may be counted among his strongest contributions. A couple of additional examples will, therefore, not be out of place:

> Where the elemental units are supposed to be feelings[6], the case is in no wise altered. Taken a hundred of them, shuffle them and pack them as close together as you can (whatever that may mean); still each remains the same feeling it always was, shut in its own skin, windowless, ignorant of what the other feelings are and mean. (I: 160)

> Take a sentence of a dozen words, and take twelve men and tell to each one word. Then stand the men in a row or jam them in a bunch, and let each think of his word as intently as he will; nowhere will there be a consciousness of the whole sentence. (ibid).

In both cases, James was pointing out the need for a medium or vehicle if any combination is to occur.

Having criticized the mind-stuff theory in general terms, James faced the problem of dealing with sensation and perception without falling into atomism. He was willing to allow a role to sensation, but not as "a fractional *part* of the thought (see footnote 6), in the old-fashioned atomistic sense which we have so often criticized" (II: 5).

> We certainly ought not to say what usually is said by psychologists, and treat the perception as a sum of distinct psychic entities, the present sensation namely, *plus* a lot of images from the past, all 'integrated' together in a way impossible to describe. The perception is one state of mind or nothing. (II: 80)

James admitted that he had no rival theory of the elementary processes to propose (II: 103), but repeatedly criticized what later came to be known as the context theory of perception.

In the "time-world" as in the "space-world," "the first known things are not elements, but combinations, not separate units, but wholes already formed" (I: 622). Examples of James's attacks on atomism could be multiplied.

---

[6]James's use of such terms as sensation and feeling is neither so strict nor so exclusive as that of many psychologists of his time (and of the present time). For example, he used the term "thinking" "for every form of consciousness indiscriminately" (I: 224). In another place, discussing the difficulties of terminology, James said:

> My own partiality is for either *feeling* or *thought*. I shall probably often use both words in a wider sense than usual . . . ; but if the connection makes it clear that mental states at large, irrespective of their kind, are meant, this will do not harm. . . . (I: 186–187)

Having rejected mental atoms, James saw that it is necessary to state the relation between thought and brain in an elementary form; "and there are great difficulties about so stating it" (I: 177).

> The consciousness, which is itself an integral thing not made of parts, 'corresponds' to the entire activity of the brain, whatever that may be, at the moment. . . . Our own formula escapes the unintelligibility of psychic atoms by *taking the entire thought . . . as the minimum with which it deals on the mental side.* But in taking the entire brain-process as its minimal fact on the material side it confronts other difficulties almost as bad. (I: 177)

By the use of nervous explanation, James had found a *place* for the interactions that would support his nonatomistic conception; but by his mechanistic view of the *nature* of nervous function, he had precluded such interactions. His mechanism forced him into atomism.

Before examining this unwanted atomism in James, one may speculate that he himself at times glimpsed the relation between atomism and a nervous system that works exclusively by excitations traveling along insulated, though connected, pathways. For this reason, it may be, we find hints of a different conception of nervous activity. I quote a passage that suggests that James may have had doubts about his own dominant view:

> A process set up anywhere in the centres reverberates everywhere, and in some way or other affects the organism throughout, making its activities either greater or less. We are brought again to the assimilation which was expressed on a previous page of the nerve-central mass to a good conductor charged with electricity, of which the tension cannot be changed anywhere without changing it everywhere. (II: 381)

Is the nervous system a conductor or is it a network of insulated fibers, "a machine for converting stimuli into reactions" (II: 372)? This question is of the greatest importance for the issue of atomism in James. It is probably both, thus accounting alike for James's attacks on atomism and his lapses into it.

To these lapses we now come.

John Dewey, in 1896, criticized the atomism of the reflex arc concept in psychology. The first example he chose for analysis (Dewey, 1896, pp. 358ff.) is taken from James's *Principles* (I: 25). To select for criticism the reflex arc concept is to select one of James's central concepts. For example, he derived instinct from reflex: "The actions we call instinctive all conform to the general reflex type; they are called forth by determinate sensory stimuli" (II: 384). The reflex schema is complicated, but not basically altered, by associative paths by means of which the outcome of the originally reflex action is changed, as when "the burnt child dreads the fire."

The problem, as Dewey pointed out (1896, p. 358), is that the reflex arc is not conceived as an organic unity: It consists, rather, of "a patchwork of disjointed parts, a mechanical conjunction of unallied processes." The stimulus is conceived as one thing, the central activity as another, and the response still a third. Because the pieces are unrelated, they can *only* be joined mechanically. It is interesting that Dewey saw, as James probably did not see clearly, that mechanism entails atomism. Because we are here concerned with atomism in James, I will limit myself to this part of Dewey's criticism and not continue with his reinterpretation of James's example.

In perception, James's treatment of the mind-stuff theory has already been discussed. Another example of his rejection of atomism is to be found in connection with color contrast. He adopted Hering's "physiological" theory, rejecting Helmholtz's "psychological" one. This means a rejection of the constancy hypothesis, as corrected by unconscious inferences. "Contrast is occasioned, not by a false idea resulting from unconscious conclusions, but by the fact that the excitation of any portion of the retina—and the consequent sensation—depends not only on its own illumination, but on that of the rest of the retina as well" (II: 19).

On the other hand, Nicholas Pastore (1971, pp. 237–238) has shown that this same constancy hypothesis is implicit in James's treatment of shape constancy and other phenomena. An object seen from various viewing positions occasions any number of retinal images; James believed that experience teaches us to choose one corresponding to the pre-eminent or "normal" position. Such sensations are selected "to be the exclusive bearers of reality" (II: 237). Again, "we attend exclusively to the 'reality' and ignore as much as our consciousness will let us the 'sign' by which we came to apprehend it" (II: 240).

Thus the table top looks square even when seen from an oblique position; the obtuse and acute angles projected on the retina are ignored. But if the correspondence of local sensation to local stimulation (constancy hypothesis) were not assumed, it would be unnecessary to treat such obtuse and acute retinal angles as parts of the "jungle of our optical experiences" (II: 240), only to ignore them. Better not to invite unwelcome guests than to invite them and then ignore them.

Thus we find in James a rejection of atomism along with lapses into it. In the same way, we found a mechanistic conception of the nervous system, along with certain passages suggesting that cortical action is viewed in a more dynamic way. These inconsistencies in James, it seems to me, are not to be deplored. He was rooted in the physiology of his time, but on occasion he seems to see beyond it. The inconsistencies are not, indeed, to be seen as solutions, rather as the glimpsing of problems.

ASSOCIATIONISM

Both William James and the Gestalt psychologists are critics of associationism; indeed, as mentioned earlier, Perry saw this as the most notable respect in which James anticipates Gestalt psychology. Yet James exemplifies just the associationism that Gestalt psychology criticizes. To resolve this apparent puzzle, it is necessary to examine the specific associationisms that each criticizes.

James criticized what he called the historic doctrine of psychological association (I: 553), that of Hobbes, Hume, Hartley, James Mill, Herbart, and others. He rejected the atomism of associationism:

> The whole historic doctrine of psychological association is tainted with one huge error—that of the construction of our thoughts out of the compounding of themselves together of immutable and incessantly recurring 'simple ideas.' It is the cohesion of these which the 'principles of association' are considered to account for. (I: 553–554)

When applied, for example, to personal consciousness, James saw this doctrine as a matter of representing successive feelings and thoughts "as in some inscrutable way 'integrating' or gumming themselves together on their own account, and thus fusing into a stream" (I: 338). He pointed to the incomprehensibilities of the idea of things fusing without a medium, as discussed earlier.

James's criticism of associationism is further directed against its conception of what is associated:

> Association, so far as the word stands for an *effect*, is between things thought of[7]—it is *things, not ideas*, which are associated in the mind. We ought to talk of the association of *objects*, not of the association of *ideas* And so far as association stands for a *cause*, it is between *processes in the brain*—it is these which, by being associated in certain ways, determine what successive objects shall be thought. (I: 554)

The neglect of attention by the English empiricist school is also criticized: Experience, which accounts for the higher mental faculties, is supposed by these authors to be "something simply *given*."

> These writers have, then, utterly ignored the glaring fact that subjective interest may, by laying its weighty index finger on particular items of experience, so accent them as to give to the least frequent associations far more power to shape our thought than the most frequent ones possess. (I: 403)

With these and other criticisms, James rejected the doctrine of the classical associationists. But he is fully aware that he has not thereby diminished the role of association in his own psychology:

> It would be a true *ignoratio elenchi* to flatter one's self that one has dealt a heavy blow at the psychology of association, when one has exploded the the-

---

[7]i.e., phenomenal things or objects.

ory of atomistic ideas, or shown that contiguity and similarity between ideas can only be there after association is done. The whole body of the associationist psychology remains standing after you have translated 'ideas' into 'objects,' on the one hand, and 'brain-processes' on the other. (I: 604)

It is this "whole body of the associationist psychology" that, as we shall see, Gestalt psychology criticizes. This criticism can best be understood when we compare the manner in which associations are conceived and the use that is made of them by William James and by the Gestalt psychologists.

For James, the nature of associations is to be understood in terms of his conception of the nervous system:

> The entire nervous system is nothing but a system of paths between a sensory *terminus a quo* and a muscular, glandular, or other *terminus ad quem*. A path once traversed by a nerve-current might be expected to follow the law of most of the paths we know, and to be scooped out and made more permeable than before; and this ought to be repeated with each new passage of the current. (I: 108)

Thus habits are the result of scooping out of paths in the nervous system; and associations, too, are the result of the "laws of habit in the nervous system" (I: 562). An association is thus the consequence of a path connecting items indifferently, a string-like connection, to return to Köhler's analogy, which can combine any two items regardless of their nature, so long as the path between them is permeable.

The Gestalt psychologists, quite in contrast, hold that an association is an aftereffect of perceptual organization. They reject the traditional view, the one James adopted, that the associated items are "indifferent pieces in a mosaic" (Köhler, 1947, p. 259). For them, associations are not items connected by a bond in which their own characteristics do not matter. Such connections, as the Gestalt psychologists point out, do not occur in nature: "When in physics two objects or events, A and B, become functionally interrelated, this interrelation and its consequences are invariably found to depend upon the characteristics of A and B" (Köhler, 1947, p. 258). If they do not occur in nature, such indifferent connections cannot, of course, be expected to occur in the nervous system.

Rather than seeing associations as indifferent bonds between unrelated items, Gestalt psychology sees organization as "the really decisive condition of what is commonly called association. . . . Where organization is naturally strong, association occurs spontaneously" (Köhler, 1947, p. 268). In the absence of such spontaneous organization, the learner must intentionally organize the items to be associated, as in the learning of nonsense syllables. In either case, the organization achieved leaves a trace of itself in the nervous system: the trace is not of an independent A and B but, corresponding to the organization in experience, of an organized unit of which both items are members.

> The unitary experience indicates that a functional unit is formed in the nervous system, in which the processes A and B have only *relative* independence. . . . Thus only one trace will be established, which represents the functional unit by which it was formed. (Köhler, 1947, p. 270)

Another passage from Köhler further clarifies the Gestalt view of association: "According to our thesis, association loses its character as a special and independent theoretical concept. It becomes a name for the fact that organized processes leave traces in which the organization of these processes is more or less adequately preserved" (Köhler, 1947, pp. 270–271).

In a nervous system whose functional units are cells and pathways, the question arises: How are the connections formed that are responsible for associations? These are, of course, *new* connections, not originally functional. Interestingly, the question was raised both by Köhler and by James. Apart from the other considerations discussed, the hypothesis of increased conductivity of neural pathways connecting the associated processes is not entirely satisfactory, said Köhler (1947, p. 269). "It does not tell us why anything particular should happen to these pathways on the *first* occasion." James, too, remarked in connection with the formation of associations: "The difficulty here as with habit *überhaupt* is in seeing how new paths come *first* to be formed" (I: 562n). He referred to a discussion of habit that will not be repeated here because, as James himself remarked: "All this is vague to the last degree, and amounts to little more than saying that a new path may be formed by the sort of *chances* that in nervous material are likely to occur" (I: 109). More elaborate speculations in terms of drainage from cell to cell (II: 581–592) are perhaps interesting in showing James attempting to face up to, and deal with, a problem that the physiology he employed did not permit him to solve. For our purposes, these discussions are valuable chiefly in showing the contrast between the conceptions of William James and those of the Gestalt psychologists.

It is clear that a concept of organization would obviate the necessity for these speculations on how associations come to be formed in the first place. Either spontaneously, according to known determinants of organization, or by deliberate efforts to organize the data in question, these come to be included in the same experienced organization. An organized trace will be preserved in memory, so that the one fact calls up the other.

For Gestalt psychology, association plays no special role. It is a kind of learning, by no means the most interesting kind. And it is subsumed under the central concept of organization. In the psychology of William James, on the contrary, the concept of association is employed throughout. A few examples will serve to illustrate.

Although James emphasized the ability to deal with novel data as "the technical differentia of reasoning" (II: 330), and although he recognized that "a thing inferred by reasoning need neither have been an habitual associate of the datum from which we infer it, nor need it be similar to it" (II: 329), he still gave great weight to association by similarity in reasoning: "After the few most powerful practical and aesthetic interests, our chief help towards noticing those special characters of phenomena, which, when once possessed and named, are used as reasons, class names, essences, or middle terms, *is this association by similarity*" (II: 347).

It is interesting that a large part of the discussion of problem solving is to be found in James's chapter on association. For example, the scientist who seeks the reason for some phenomenon or who tries to test a hypothesis "keeps turning the matter incessantly in his mind until, by the arousal of associate upon associate, some habitual, some similar, one arises which he recognizes to suit his need. This, however, may take years" (I: 589). "From the guessing of newspaper enigmas to the plotting of the policy of an empire" (ibid.), the process is one of the appearance of the right association to fill an experienced gap.

Likewise in perception, "men have no eyes but for those aspects of things which they have already been taught to discern" (I: 443). Spatial location is given by association of local signs with certain positions (II: 158). "Our rapid judgments of size, shape, distance, and the like, are best explained as processes of simple cerebral association" (I: 169). Many illusions are attributed to our seeing of the "habitual, inveterate, or most probable" object (II: 86). Indeed, the general law of perception is that "whilst part of what we perceive comes through our senses from the object before us, another part (and it may be the larger part) always comes . . . out of our own head" (II: 103).

In connection with the perception of difference, say, between black and white, James rejected an empiristic explanation as "absolutely unintelligible. We now find black and white different, the explanation says, because we have always so found them. But why should we always have so found them?" (II: 643). In this case, James was aware that an empiristic explanation merely pushed the problem back to some previous occasion, without solving it.[8] Why did he not take the same position with regard to other associationistic or empiristic explanations? For further analysis of James's empiristic theories, the reader is referred to Pastore's excellent discussion (1971, chap. 12). It may be emphasized that, without the constancy hypothesis, James would not have need for such explanations.

Enough examples have been given to show that James, the critic of associationism, was associationist to the core. The laws of association, he says, "*run* the mind" (1899, p. 84). And it may be repeated that, although both he and the

---

[8]See also the discussion earlier of how associations are formed in the first place.

Gestalt psychologists criticize associationism, they criticize *different associationisms*.

ORGANIZATION

The discussion thus far leads to another essential respect in which James differs from Gestalt psychology. Organization, which is a central concept for the Gestalt psychologists, was absent in James (as it was for the psychologists of his time). I take Köhler's definition of sensory organization (1947, p. 120):

> The term refers to the fact that sensory fields have in a way their own social psychology. Such fields appear neither as uniformly coherent continua nor as patterns of mutually indifferent elements. What we actually perceive are, first of all, specific entities such as things, figures, etc., and also groups of which these entities are members. This demonstrates the operation of processes in which the content of certain areas is unified, and at the same time relatively segregated from its environment.

Organization corresponds to interactions among processes in the nervous system, the outcome of the interactions depending on the nature of the processes in question in their relation to each other.

James took for granted the *facts* of organization, as must anyone who looks without bias at the world as it presents itself. For example:

> Experience, from the very first, presents us with concreted objects,[9] vaguely continuous with the rest of the world which envelops them in space and time, and potentially divisible into inward elements and parts. These objects we break asunder and reunite. We must treat them in both ways for our knowledge of them to grow. (I: 487)

Again:

> A monotonous succession of sonorous strokes is broken up into rhythms, now of one sort, now of another, by the different accent which we place on different strokes. . . . Dots dispersed on a surface are perceived in rows and groups. Lines separate into diverse figures. (I: 284)

And one more example: "We conceive of a world spread out in a perfectly fixed and orderly fashion" (II: 183).

How did James deal with such facts? It will be recalled that his conception of the nervous system is one of indifferent bonds (cf. e.g., I: 570, Fig. 40), not the continuous medium that, for the Gestalt psychologists, provides the condition of interaction. A network of insulated fibers, no matter how dense, is

---

[9]Here is a contradiction with the "blooming buzzing confusion" of which the newborn's world is said to consist, and which will be considered later.

not a medium in which interactions can occur. As Köhler remarked (1947, p. 120): "The machine theory with its mosaic of separate elements is, of course, incapable of dealing with organization" in the sense defined earlier.

James felt compelled to offer a neurological alternative to the mind-stuff theory, but it did not overcome the difficulties of his mechanistic nervous system. He suggested, for example, that many single fibers connect with higher ones, and these in turn with still higher cells, until some cortical center is reached, characterized as a "massive and slow process of tension and discharge" to which "*as a whole*" the psychological phenomenon corresponds. If the lower fibers correspond to the many vibrations constituting a tone, the highest process "*simply and totally*" corresponds to the feeling of a musical tone (see I: 156, Fig. 26). James offered an analogy:

> It is as if a long file of men were to start one after the other to reach a distant point. The road at first is good and they keep their original distance apart. Presently it is intersected by bogs each worse than the last, so that the front men get so retarded that the hinder ones catch up with them before the journey is done, and all arrive together at the goal. (I: 156)

But the men in the procession, however bunched they may be in the end, remain each separate and distinct and, like the dozen men each of whom knows one word of a sentence, cannot by mere proximity produce an integrated process.

In another connection, James rejected Helmholtz's "psychological" theory of brightness and color contrast in favor of Hering's "physiological" theory. He took it as conclusively proved "that the process on one part of the retina does modify that on neighboring portions, under conditions where deception of judgment is impossible" (II: 20). "There are many other facts," James continued, "beside the phenomena of contrast which prove that when two objects act together on us the sensation which either would give alone becomes a different sensation" (II: 28). Indeed, James believed that in "*all* cases of mental reaction to a plurality of stimuli . . . , the physiological formulation is everywhere the simplest and the best" (II: 30)—that is, as opposed to the "psychological" explanation, such as Helmholtz's view of contrast. Such a physiological explanation would require mutual influences in the nervous system. But James's conception of cortical action, it has been seen, as isolated function in cells and paths (or networks of paths) precludes the necessary interactions. Thus the physiology of his time makes it impossible for him to offer a real alternative to the Helmholtzian theory he so clearly sees to be wrong. That the explanation of contrast and many other phenomena is physiological and not "psychological" (II: 17) says very little if the physiology on which James had to build precluded just such an explanation.

Given this dilemma, how did James handle it? He said, "It must be that the cerebral process of the first sensation is reinforced or otherwise altered by the other current which comes in" (II: 30). In addition to such facilitation, inhibition "is an essential and unremitting element of our cerebral life" (II: 583). How do these processes occur? James prudently suggested that we "relegate the subject of the *intimate* workings of the brain to the physiology of the future" (I: 81–82). To admit of such mutual influences, that future physiology will doubtless have to consider processes other than those that occur in insulated fibers and cells. (It has been suggested earlier that James himself may, at times, have glimpsed a different kind of nervous system.)

Without a concept of organization, how did James deal with perception? Whence the segregated, unified, articulated, "concreted" objects of our experience? James started with an original chaos: "To the infant, sounds, sights, touches, and pains, form probably one unanalyzed bloom of confusion" (I: 496). This idea of the baby's "great blooming, buzzing confusion" (I: 488) is not abandoned. In the posthumously published *Some Problems of Philosophy* (James, 1911, p. 50), the reader is invited to abstract from all conceptual interpretation; he will then find "his immediate sensible life . . . to be what someone has called a big blooming buzzing confusion." The cuts we make in the perceptual flux are purely ideal (i.e., conceptual). Attention, James continued, carves out objects (1911, pp. 49–50).

Criticism of this thesis is unnecessary, since James himself provided it. "Attention *creates* no idea; an idea must already be there before we can attend to it" (I: 450). The same must be true in perception: Attention cannot create phenomenal objects out of a blooming, buzzing confusion. They must be there to be attended to.

Also invoked to produce objects from chaos are "powerful practical and aesthetic interests," traces of previous experience, the partiality or selectiveness of the stream of consciousness. Some examples:

"What are things?" (see footnote 7) asked James. "Nothing . . . but special groups of sensible qualities, which happen practically or aesthetically to interest us, to which we therefore give substantive names, and which we exalt to this exclusive status of independence and dignity" (I: 285).

> Millions of items of the outward order are present to my senses which never properly enter into my experience. Why? Because they have no *interest* for me. *My experience is what I agree to attend to.* Only those items which I *notice* shape my mind—without selective interest, experience is an utter chaos. (I: 402)

"A strong message from the sense-organs" breaks the slumber of the baby. "In a new-born brain this gives rise to an absolutely pure sensation" (II: 8). But this experience leaves its trace ("its 'unimaginable touch'") in the brain and will influence and complicate the next impression. Again, "perception . . . differs from sensation by the consciousness of farther facts associated with the object of the sensation" (II: 77). And "our nerve-centres are an organ for reacting on sense-impressions, and . . . our hemispheres, in particular, are given us in order that records of our private past experience may co-operate in the reaction" (II: 103).

As to the partiality of the stream of consciousness:

> The world *we* feel and live in will be that which our ancestors and we, by slowly cumulative strokes of choice, have extricated out of [matter], like sculptors, by simply rejecting certain portions of the given stuff. Other sculptors, other statues from the same stone! Other minds, other worlds from the same monotonous and inexpressive chaos! My world is but one in a million alike embedded, alike real to those who may abstract them. How different must be the worlds in the consciousness of ant, cuttle-fish, or crab! (I: 289)

Or more simply: "But we do far more than emphasize things, and unite some, and keep others apart. We actually *ignore* most of the things before us." (I: 284).

To all these processes, James's own criticism must be applied. Just as an idea must be there before we can attend to it, so a phenomenal scene must be there before we can be interested in it or select from it. Once it exists, we can select to our heart's content, but our selective interest cannot create it.

The same is true of past experience. The infant's blooming buzzing confusion can only leave a blooming buzzing vestige or trace in the brain; and such a trace can hardly influence and complicate the next impression except possibly by making it familiar. Once an organized form exists, it can lay down any number of memory traces. But we must perceive the form in order for it to influence subsequent experience.

Still speaking of the vagueness of the infant's perception, James remarked:

> In this vague way, probably, does the room appear to the babe who first begins to be conscious of it as something other than his moving nurse. It has no subdivisions in his mind, unless, perhaps, the window is able to attract his separate notice. (II: 344)

But how is the perceived nurse to be accounted for? And the window, we have just seen, must be there before we can take notice of it.[10]

---

[10]I have been concerned with sensation in the sense of "pure sensation," which is almost exclusively the possession of the infant. James also used the term "sensation" to refer to that function which cognizes simple qualities; it is prior to perception. Although sensation and perception are not sharply distinguished, and although, in adults, one never occurs without the other, perception differs from sensation in its "voluminous associative or reproductive processes in the cortex" (II: 3). To the extent to which the two are to be distinguished, the question again arises as to how past experience makes the transition from simple qualities to phenomenal objects. The problem is similar to the one raised in the text.

In short, attention, selective interest, past experience are invoked to account for perception. These are just the kinds of explanation James criticized so well in others. He was aware of the problems for which a concept of organization was needed, but he lacked the conceptual tools with which to solve them.

CONVERGENCES

One could point out various similarities on specific issues between James and the Gestalt psychologists, but these are not my concern.[11] James's criticisms of atomism have already been found to resemble the critique of Gestalt psychology.

Aside from the attitude toward atomism, the most important similarity I can find between James and the Gestalt psychologists is in their use of psychological phenomenology. James remarked: "Psychology is a mere natural science, accepting certain terms uncritically as her data, and stopping short of metaphysical reconstruction. Like physics, she must be naive" (I: 137). Such a statement may meaningfully be compared with those with which Köhler opened his *Gestalt Psychology*:

> There seems to be a single starting point for psychology, exactly as for all the other sciences: the world as we find it, naively and uncritically. The naiveté may be lost as we proceed. Problems may be found which were at first completely hidden from our eyes. For their solution it may be necessary to devise concepts which

---

[11]In a notable footnote, (I: 147n), James remarked:

> The disparity between [the physical facts of the brain and the corresponding facts of consciousness] . . . is somewhat less absolute than at first sight it seems. There are categories common to the two worlds. Not only temporal succession . . . but such attributes as intensity, volume, simplicity or complication, smooth or impeded change, rest or agitation, are habitually predicated of both physical facts and mental facts. Where such analogies obtain, the things do have something in common.

The Gestalt hypothesis of psychophysical isomorphism depends on certain kinds of similarity between physical (neurological) and mental facts.

As another example, in connection with size constancy, James spoke of "the principle of simplifying as much as possible our world" (II: 178). He referred to "the great intellectual law of economy" (II: 183), and he made numerous references to aesthetic demands. Can it be that he was glimpsing a principle of Prägnanz, according to which perceptual forms, groups, and changes tend to assume the greatest possible simplicity and regularity?

Another important footnote discusses the whole-part problem (I: 279n). Speaking of the parts of the thought of a complex object, on which many of his readers will insist, he observed:

> These parts are not the separate 'ideas' of traditional psychology. No one of them can live out of that particular thought, any more than my head can live off of my particular shoulders. . . . Dismiss the thought and out go its parts. . . . Each thought is a fresh organic unity, *sui generis*.

seem to have little contact with direct primary experience. Nevertheless, the whole development must begin with a naive picture of the world. (1947, p. 3)

For James, the primary method of psychology is that of introspection. But what is introspection? "It means, of course, the looking into our minds and reporting what we there discover" (I: 185). James's greatest talent seems to be generally recognized as looking into his own mind and reporting what he there discovered. His descriptions of tendency (I: 249ff.), for example, of the attempt to recall a forgotten name—with different consciousnesses of emptiness, its "aching gap,"[12] his descriptions of feelings of relation, "psychic overtones, halos, suffusions, or fringes" (I: 269) are a few noteworthy examples. "It is . . . the re-instatement of the vague to its proper place in our mental life which I am so anxious to press on the attention," said James (I: 254). Has anybody else so successfully captured this aspect of mental life? In general, his sensitive and differentiated description of the stream of thought, perhaps unparalleled in the psychological literature, remains a remarkable contribution to the science. As Perry put it (1948, p. 46), William James "had a capacity, perhaps never equaled, of seizing and exposing the evanescent moments and fugitive sequences of conscious life. He could see most cunningly out of the corner of his eye."

James's phenomenology is not limited to the stream of consciousness. He prefaced his discussion of sensation and perception with the declaration (II: 1): "After inner perception, outer perception!" Taking a psychological point of view, James admits "knowledge whether of simple toothaches or of philosophical systems as an ultimate fact" (II: 5).

Gestalt psychology has directed its attention more to what James called "outer perception" and, after phenomenology, has relied much more on the experimental method than did James. (It must be added that James himself did a little experimental work, but was often less than enthusiastic about the triviality of the results so laboriously obtained in the psychological laboratories of his time.) But the important point in the present connection is that both James and the Gestalt psychologists start their work with naive description of the phenomena to be investigated.

Like the Gestalt psychologists, James looked for physiological explanations of psychological facts (even though, as has been seen, with a very different conception of the nervous system). But, like the Gestalt psychologists, James realized that "it is probable that for years to come we

---

[12]Again:

The truth is that large tracts of human speech are nothing but *signs of direction* in thought, of which direction we nevertheless have an acutely discriminative sense, though no definite sensorial image plays any part in it whatsoever. . . .

One may admit that a good third of our psychic life consists in these rapid premonitory perspective views of schemes of thought not yet articulate. (I: 252–253)

shall have to infer what happens in the brain either from our feelings or from motor effects which we observe" (I: 137–138).

Köhler goes farther (1959/1971, pp. 252–253):

> Not only is psychology now old enough to stand on her own feet; she is even, in my opinion, sufficiently grown up so that she can occasionally be of assistance to her older sisters, the natural sciences. . . . I will be concerned with tasks which psychological facts set for physiology.

This assistance was given by starting with psychological observation, from which Köhler derived hypotheses of corresponding physiological events. These, in turn, had implications for further physiological relations, which then had to be tested in new psychological investigation, and so on, moving back and forth between the two realms. In this way, the (psychological) facts of figural aftereffects led to hypotheses about corresponding brain facts, and these to further psychological investigation. Eventually, Köhler was led to direct physiological experimentation. (See, e.g., Köhler, 1940, 1959/1971.)

Although James could not, of course, foresee these developments, he did share with Gestalt psychology the view that psychology had to set tasks for brain physiology.

A FINAL WORD

This chapter began with the widespread view of James as a forerunner of specific later developments in psychology. I would prefer to regard him as a transitional figure. But transition to what? Perhaps we may say that William James was trying to bring psychology into the 20th century. That he was not entirely successful, as we have seen in a number of contexts, is a consequence of the fact that he was enmeshed in the physiology of the 19th century. He saw problems that his scientific background did not enable him to solve.

I conclude with an excerpt from a review of the *Principles* by Léon Marillier in the *Revue Philosophique*, as translated and quoted by James's publisher: "In spite of the objections which would necessarily be raised to the theories it contains, it is nevertheless a glorious work."

REFERENCES

Dewey, J. (1896). The reflex arc concept in psychology. *Psychological Review, 3*, 357–370.

James, W. (1890). *The principles of psychology* (Vols. 1–2). New York: Holt.

James, W. (1892). *Psychology, briefer course*. New York: Holt. (Reprinted with introduction by R. B. Perry, 1948. Cleveland & New York: World Publishing Co.)

James, W. (1899). *Talks to teachers on psychology: and to students on some of life's ideals*. New York: Holt.

James, W. (1911). *Some problems of philosophy*. London: Longmans, Green.

Koffka, K. (1915/1938). Reply to V. Benussi. In W. D. Ellis (Ed.). *A source book of Gestalt psychology* (pp. 371–378). London: Kegan Paul, Trench, Trubner.

Köhler, W. (1913/1971). On unnoticed sensations and errors of judgment. In M. Henle (Ed.), *The selected papers of Wolfgang Köhler* (pp. 13–39). New York: Liveright.

Köhler, W. (1925/1938). Reply to G. E. Müller. In W. D. Ellis (Ed.), *A source book of Gestalt psychology* (pp. 379–388). London: Kegan Paul, Trench, Trubner.

Köhler, W. (1928/1938). Reply to Eugenio Rignano. In W. D. Ellis (Ed.), *A source book of Gestalt psychology* (pp. 389–396). London: Kegan Paul, Trench, Trubner.

Köhler, W. (1940). *Dynamics in psychology*. New York: Liveright.

Köhler, W. (1947). *Gestalt psychology* (rev. ed.). New York: Liveright.

Köhler, W. (1959/1971). Psychology and natural science. In M. Henle (Ed.), *The selected papers of Wolfgang Köhler* (pp. 252–273). New York: Liveright.

Pastore, N. (1971). *Selective history of theories of visual perception: 1650–1950*. New York & London: Oxford University Press.

Perry, R. B. (1935). *The thought and character of William James* (Vols. 1–2). Boston: Little, Brown.

Perry, R. B. (1948). *The thought and character of William James. Briefer version*. Cambridge, MA: Harvard University Press.

Chapter 5

William James on the Self and Personality: Clearing the Ground for Subsequent Theorists, Researchers, and Practitioners

David E. Leary
University of Richmond

The fundamental basis of William James's psychology—the rock-bottom foundation on which it is constructed—is "the stream of thought" or "the stream of consciousness."[1]* The first and preeminent characteristic of our flowingly continuous experience of "thought" or "consciousness," James (1890/1983d) said, is that it is personal (pp. 220–224). Every thought, every psychological experience, is *mine*, or *hers*, or *his*, or *yours*. For this reason, he suggested, "the personal self rather than the thought [or consciousness] might be treated as the immediate datum in psychology" (p. 221).[2] Indeed, James was strongly convinced that "no psychology . . . can question the *existence* of personal selves. The worst a psychology can do is so to interpret the nature of these selves as to rob them of their worth" (p. 221).

This issue of the worth of human selves was no trivial concern for James: It was critically important to him from early in his life right up to his death, and it was intertwined not only with his interests in mainstream psychology, but also with his interests in psychical research, the psychology of religion, pragmatism, pluralism, and radical empiricism. Fittingly, James's chapter on the self (Chapter 10) in his masterpiece, *The Principles of Psychology*, was one of the first chapters he began to conceptualize and the final chapter he completed. Or rather, it was the last chapter on which he worked, after postponing its final revision "to the very last, when my wisdom shall be at its unsurpassable climax!" (letter to G. Croom Robertson, 4 November 1888, in Perry, 1935, Vol. 2, p. 44). Yet, however great his wisdom, it was inadequate to the task: In James's own estimation, at least, this crucial chapter was never truly "finished," and he kept returning to the topic of the self and personality throughout the last two decades of his life.

---

*Due to their length, the footnotes in this chapter appear as endnotes.

Why was the self so important to James? What was the context within which he formulated his ideas about the self, personality, and related topics? What exactly *was* James's psychology of the self and of personality, as he expressed it in his *Principles*, and what path did his thoughts on these topics subsequently take? Finally, what influences and echoes has this aspect of his psychology had over the years since it was first enunciated? These are the sort of questions that I want to address in the following chapter. In doing so, I hope to convey the centrality, importance, influence, and current relevance of James's views.

THE CONTEXT OF JAMES'S PSYCHOLOGY

Virtually from the time of his birth on January 11, 1842, William James was surrounded by issues, claims, concerns, and debates about the human self. In this regard it is emblematic that before he was 3 months old the young "Willy" was visited and blessed by Ralph Waldo Emerson, the author of a recent, startling essay on "Self-Reliance" (1841/1983). In subsequent years, William would imbibe much of Emerson's wisdom, which is to say, much of Emerson's trust in the experience of "isolated" individuals.[3] On the other hand, by the time William was 3 years old, his father had suffered a major spiritual crisis and had become convinced of "the nothingness of Selfhood." From that point on, his father, Henry James Sr., dedicated his life to the development and propagation of a theology espousing the "redemption" of individual selves through their absorption and ablation in social life.[4] Both of these ironic emphases—on the primacy of the individual by the famed transcendentalist and on the illusoriness and need for "social reformation" of individual selves by the amateur theologian, were to echo throughout William's later writings, and throughout the works of his younger brother, the novelist Henry James Jr.[5]

In addition to this dual heritage, which drew attention to the human self even as it raised questions about the self's substantive reality and about its extended network of social relations, James had the privilege and responsibility of growing up and living during one of the most exciting and transformative periods in the history of psychology. During this period—from 1842 to 1910, to use the endpoints of James's own life as markers—psychology moved from being a predominantly philosophical enterprise to being an increasingly scientific and clinical discipline.[6] As one of the major figures involved in this transition, James incorporated philosophical, scientific, and clinical orientations into his system of thought.

Of course, James lived not only among New England transcendentalists, home-grown theologians, and American philosophers and psychologists. Due to his father's unusual childrearing practices, James traveled frequently during his formative years and received much of his education in foreign countries, especially in Europe. Subsequently, he continued to enjoy transatlantic sojourns, so that he benefited throughout his life from firsthand acquaintance with virtually all of the major intellectual and cultural trends of his times, including increasing interest in Eastern thought (see, e.g., Taylor, 1986). Since these trends were necessarily related to the social and historical events of the day—advances in technology, changes in the material conditions of life, increases and shifts in population, social upheavals, the organization of labor, the rise of nationalist movements, the development of educational systems, the emergence of modern medical and psychiatric practice, the professionalization of social roles, and so on—James had occasion to notice and to comment on most of the challenges and opportunities offered by modern life. Many of these challenges and opportunities reinforced the concerns he had inherited regarding the appropriate relations between the individual and society.

However informative his social and historical context, however, James himself would have supposed that his own inner life—his own unique interests and personal concerns—also contributed importantly to the development of his psychological ideas, including especially his ideas about the self and personality (see, e.g., James, 1879/1978a, 1907/1975b, pp. 9–26). And so it did. The question of selfhood, posed so vigorously by Emerson and by his father, was raised even more compellingly by the stresses and strains that James experienced as he grew into manhood. Always sensitive and curious, he did not wear his experience lightly, even early on, and as a young man he more than earned the right to give his own daughter the following advice, many years later:

> Now, my dear little girl, you have come to an age [13 years old] when the inward life develops and when some people (and on the whole those who have most of a destiny) find that all is not a bed of roses. Among other things there will be waves of terrible sadness, which last sometimes for days; and dissatisfaction with one's self, and irritation at others, and anger at circumstances and stony insensibility, etc., etc., which taken together form a melancholy. Now, painful as it is, this is sent to us for an enlightenment. . . . and we ought to learn a great many good things if we react on it rightly.

However, James continued,

> many persons take a kind of sickly delight in hugging [this melancholy]. . . . That is the worst possible reaction on it. . . . we mustn't submit to it an hour longer than we can help, but jump at every chance to attend to anything cheerful or comic or take part in anything active that will divert us from our mean, pining inward state of feeling. When it passes off, as I said, we know more than we did before. (letter to Margaret James, 26 May 1900, in H. James III, 1920, Vol. 2, p. 131)

These were hard-won insights that James was passing along, as anyone who has read his biography can attest (see Allen, 1967; Anderson, 1982; Feinstein, 1984; Fullinwider, 1975; Perry, 1935). The bottom line, he noted, was that

> the disease makes you think of *yourself* all the time; and the way out of it is to keep as busy as we can thinking of *things* and of *other people*—no matter what's the matter with our self. (H. James, III, 1920, p. 132)

This was the crux of James's own earlier torment—his need, in the late 1860s and early 1870s, to escape from the "tedious egotism" associated with his own protracted period of melancholy—and his comments recapitulate his realization, first reached at that earlier age, that he could escape from this debilitating self-obsession only by becoming busily preoccupied with "a constructive passion of some kind" (see Hardwick, 1960/1980, pp. 29, 32, 64). As we know, James found his "constructive passion" and escaped from his melancholy when he turned his attention from his flagging "commitment" to medicine to his more engaging interest in the newly developing discipline of psychology. The context of this switch of vocations suggests an unusually rich confluence of personal and professional factors, and James's subsequent focus on the nature and workings of the ego, self, and personality does nothing to dispel this suggestion. It seems appropriate, therefore, to say a few more words about James's early-life bout with depression, about its causes, and about the conclusions that he drew from it. This brief discussion should clarify some of the ways in which James's personal life seems to have contributed to his later psychological interests, insights, and theories.

As background, it is important to note that even by the age of 16, before he began to suffer from depression, James's personal sense of worth was derived largely from the very high expectations he held regarding the difference that he *as an individual person* would make in this world. "Which of us," he wrote to a youthful friend,

> would wish to go through life without leaving a trace behind to mark his passage. Who would prefer to live unknown to all but his immediate friends and to be forgotten by all thirty years after his death. For what was life given to us? Suppose we do nothing and die; we have swindled society. Nature, in giving us birth, had saddled us with a debt which we must pay off some time or other.

Later in the same letter he indicated the sort of trace he hoped to leave behind:

> If I followed my taste and did what was most agreeable to me, I'll tell you what I would do. I would get a microscope and go out into the country, into

the dear old woods and fields and ponds. There I would try to make as many discoveries as possible. (letter to Edgar B. Van Winkle, 1 March 1858, in Perry, 1948, pp. 52–53)

Though by a somewhat circuitous path, William did find his way, eventually, into science. But when he entered the Lawrence Scientific School at Harvard in the early 1860s, the scientific world into which he was initiated was not as idyllic as he had imagined it would be. The very face of "dear old" nature was just then being radically transformed by the scientists of his day, especially those assuming the new Darwinian perspective, first promulgated the year after his youthful letter (Darwin, 1859/1964). Instead of going out into the countryside to study some aspect of living, purposeful nature, James confronted a world increasingly portrayed as mechanistic, materialistic, and driven by blind chance. Before long, in the later 1860s, he had learned his lessons so well that he had come to fear "that we are Nature through and through, that we are wholly conditioned, that not a wiggle of our will happens save as the result of physical laws" (letter to Thomas W. Ward, March 1869, in H. James, III, 1920, Vol. 1, pp. 152–153). This conclusion—to him a very dreadful one—conflicted with his fundamental desire to "make my *nick*, however small a one, in the raw stuff the race has got to shape, and so assert my reality" (letter to Ward, January 1868, in H. James, III, 1920, Vol. 1, p. 132). Desperately, virtually against all hope, he clung to "the thought of my having a will" and, relatedly, to the thought "of my belonging to a brotherhood of men," for . . .

> if we have to give up all hope of seeing into the purposes of God, or to give up theoretically the idea of final causes, and of God anyhow as vain and leading to nothing for us, we can, by our will, make the enjoyment of our brothers stand us in the stead of a final cause; and through a knowledge of the fact that that enjoyment on the whole depends on what individuals accomplish, lead a life so active, and so sustained by a clean conscience as not to need to fret much. Individuals can add to the welfare of the race in a variety of ways. You may . . . contribute your mite in *any* way to the mass of the work which each generation subtracts from the task of the next; and you will come into *real* relations with your brothers—with some of them at least. (H. James, III, 1920, 130–131)

This hope of entering into "real relations" with others mattered deeply to James, who had come to believe that "*everything* we know and are is through men. We have no revelation but through man" (p. 131).

The echoes of this father's doctrines are apparent in these reflections. So too are James's distinctive concerns about his own personal "salvation." Clearly, having a will and belonging to "a brotherhood of men" were critical components of a practical philosophy of life that James needed for moral support—to give him a purpose for living—in his time of crisis. It was crucially important to him that he be, or at least that he *could* be, in "real relations" with others—in relationships in which he made a concrete, personal difference. In essence he reasoned that if anyone else, placed in his position in time and space, would act exactly as *he* would, then his own *personal* self and life, on the terms specified years before, would be meaningless. If that were the case, he concluded, he would rather forfeit his life—and his dark contemplation of suicide, over several seasons, bears painful testimony to the seriousness with which he pondered this entire matter.

Fortunately, James came to believe that he did have a will, he began to act on this belief, his mental state began to improve, and, in time, he made his nick on the course of human history. As we turn our attention to one aspect of his legacy, I hope it will not seem coincidental that he made his contribution, in good part, through the composition of a major psychological work that addresses the nature of the human self, that insists on the self's development and sustenance within a network of social relations, and that culminates in a chapter on the vital reality and importance of the human will.[7] It should also seem less than surprising, after this brief review of the context of his thought, that James went on to focus on abnormal psychology (Taylor, 1982a), on the psychology of religion (James, 1902/1985), and on a new type of philosophy that espouses the centrality and worth of each individual's distinctive interests and point of view (James, 1907/1975b, 1909/1977, 1909/1975c, 1912/1976b).

JAMES'S CLASSIC CHAPTER ON THE CONSCIOUSNESS OF SELF

When James began to think and read seriously about psychology, starting in the midst of his personal crisis in the late 1860s, he was attracted to recent works by the likes of Herbert Spencer (1855), Hermann Lotze (1856–1864/1988), Alexander Bain (1859), Wilhelm Wundt (1863–1864/1894), and Hippolyte Taine (1870/1875), to cite only a few individuals whose publications were relevant to his concerns about the self. His study also led him back to the classics of empiricism—to Locke's *Essay* (1690/1959) and to Hume's *Treatise* (1739–1740/1978)—as well as to such classics from the rationalist tradition as Kant's *Critique* (1781/1965) and Hegel's *Phenomenology* (1807/1910). He familiarized himself, too, with the texts of mental and moral philosophy that were the main diet in the "psychology" courses offered in American colleges and universities—the texts, for instance, of James McCosh (1860/1882), Noah Porter (1868), and Mark Hopkins (1870)—and before long he became quite knowledgeable about his friend Charles Peirce's (1868/1966) critique of "intuitive self-consciousness" and about his friend Chauncey Wright's (1873/1877) perspective on "self-consciousness." In addition, his reading and thinking drew from the beginning upon the literature on spiritualism (e.g., Sargent, 1869) and upon clinical studies of hypnotism (e.g., Liébeault, 1866), and a decade later he was scrutinizing psychical research (e.g., Gurney, Myers, & Podmore, 1886) and clinical studies of split personality (e.g., Janet, 1889). James also attended, by and large critically, to the views of James Ward (1883a, 1883b, 1886), Josiah Royce (1885), John Dewey (1887/1967), and George Trumball Ladd (1887).[8] Thus, by the time he pulled together his own thoughts on "the consciousness of self," James had touched a great many bases and considered a wide variety of perspectives. Not surprisingly, his chapter reflects, amalgamates, and, in many respects, transcends these multiple points of view.

The two fundamental vantage points, or ways of approaching the self, that James (1890/1983d) adopted in his classic chapter are the view of the self as knower (as a pure or transcendental *I*) and the view of the self as known (as an objective or empirical *Me*).[9] In making this famous distinction between the *I* and the *Me*, James meant "nothing mysterious and unexampled": The terms "are at bottom only names of *emphasis*" (p. 324). But the emphases are significant, and on them James constructed a two-part chapter, the first part devoted to "the empirical self or *Me*" and the second part devoted to "the pure Ego" (or "soul"). This second part is divided, in turn, into a discussion of the sense and theories of personal identity and a review of the phenomena and implications of multiple personality. Within this compass and outline, James treated a vast array of issues and touched off many lines of later conceptual development.

From the very beginning of the chapter, James established that he was going to take a fresh approach to his subject. *"In its widest possible sense,"* he wrote,

> *a man's Self is the sum total of all that he* CAN *call his*, not only his body and his psychic powers, but his clothes and his house, his wife and children, his ancestors and friends, his reputation and works, his lands and horses, and yacht and bank-account. (p. 279)

The explication James offered for this claim is telling: All these various things and persons are part of an individual's self insofar as they give that individual *the same emotions* (pp. 279–280). In pointing thus toward the emotional foundations of the self, James indicated right at the start that he was going to follow Bain (1859, chap. 7) and others in reaching beyond the old rationalist approach to "the soul" in order to ground his treatment of the human self on the experience and makeup of the *whole* person, emotional as well as intellectual.

As is well known, James based his wholistic treatment on an analysis of three different, but interrelated aspects of the empirical self: the *Me* viewed as material, the *Me* viewed as social, and the *Me* viewed as spiritual in nature. In articulating these different points of view, James did not mean to suggest that the "material," "social," and "spiritual" perspectives reveal radically disjunctive or ontologically distinctive dimensions of the self. In describing the "material" aspect of the self, for instance, James was clearly *not* portraying anything like the *materialistic* or *physiological* foundations of the self, as one might expect. Instead, he argued that the body does not even provide the boundaries, much less the determinants, of this aspect of the self. In James's view, the body is simply "the innermost part" of the material self, and even within the body, "certain parts of the body seem more intimately ours than the rest" (p. 280). The key notion here, once again, is emotional feeling: Individuals *feel* the material dimensions of their selves, including those dimensions that extend *beyond* the borders of their bodies. These emotional feelings about particular material aspects of experience are quite distinctively personal, being aimed at things, persons, and experiences that are somehow uniquely "owned" and specially "ours." James recognized, from his own experience, that even one's own body may not be "owned" or experienced as part of one's self at each and every moment, and that rarely if ever are all parts of the body experienced equally intimately, or as being equally "mine." Furthermore, one's clothes, family, home, and property may be just as central to one's sense of self—and sometimes even more central—than one's own body. As James put it with reference to members of one's own immediate family:

> When they die, a part of our very selves is gone. If they do anything wrong, it is our shame. If they are insulted, our anger flashes forth as readily as if we stood in their place. (p. 280)

And regarding material possessions and productions, there are few individuals

> who would not feel personally annihilated if a life-long construction of their hands or brains—say an entomological collection or an extensive work in manuscript—were suddenly swept away. The miser feels similarly towards his gold. . . . [In such instances there is invariably] a sense of the shrinkage of our personality, a partial conversion of ourselves to nothingness. (p. 281)

Having thus extended the sphere of self-consciousness to include any and all personally owned aspects of material existence, James went on to discuss the distinctively social aspect of the self. Here too, James's treatment defies easy presumptions. The social dimension of the self is *not* set against the material and spiritual dimensions, except as a matter of emphasis. After all, social relations begin and are sustained through *material* interactions with others, but soon come to involve such *non*-material factors as love, reputation, fame, and honor. In fact, the essence of the social aspect of self, James said, is "the recognition which [a person] gets from his [or her] mates" (p. 281). Such is our "innate propensity to get ourselves noticed, and noticed favorably, by our kind" that

> No more fiendish punishment could be devised, were such a thing physically possible, than that one should be turned loose in society and remain absolutely unnoticed by all the members thereof. (p. 281)

The result of such ostracism, James said, would be "a kind of rage and impotent despair" in the face of which even cruel treatment by others—*any* form of human interaction—would be a relief (p. 281).

As this example suggests, James recognized that the individual self has a vital need for "felt relations" with others. Following in his father's footsteps and probably drawing on his own personal need for "real relations" with others (as expressed so poignantly in his letter to Thomas Ward in the late 1860s), he argued that it is within the context of such relations that the individual self is constituted. So important is this social dimension of selfhood, in fact, that James suggested (in a now famous passage) that

> Properly speaking, *a man has as many social selves as there are individuals who recognize him* and carry an image of him in their mind. To wound any one of these his images is to wound him. But as the individuals who carry the images fall naturally into classes, we may practically say that he has as many different selves as there are distinct *groups* of persons about whose opinion he cares. He generally shows a different side of himself to each of these different groups. . . . From this there results what practically is a division of the man into several selves; and this may be a discordant splitting, as where one is afraid to let one set of his acquaintances know him as he is elsewhere; or it may be a perfectly harmonious division of labor, as where one tender to his children is stern to the soldiers or prisoners under his command. (pp. 281–282)

It is difficult to realize the remarkableness of this passage and of James's sensitivity to the social dimension of self-consciousness. To do so, one must recall that earlier "psychological" texts of "mental and moral philosophy" treated the mind (or soul) as either an indivisible, autonomous unit or as an accretion of discrete, associated ideas. James was quite innovative in mapping the *larger* dimensions of the self, social as well as material. The self to him was neither autonomous nor simply a unity of internal elements. Although it enjoys a form of independence and wholeness, it is constructed over time and depends on functional relations with the objects and persons of the "external" world. It is in these latter relationships, James recognized, that the "club-opinions"—the norms and values—that constitute "one of the very strongest forces in life" are created and conveyed. The personal empowerment that comes from socialization to these opinions is not, in

James's analysis, the result of *remaking* a preexisting self into a social being, but of *creating* a self that is from the beginning social in nature.

If James redefined common-sense notions about the material and social aspects of the self, he similarly confounded expectations regarding his discussion of the "spiritual" (or subjective) dimension of inner experience. For one thing, he suggested that the experiential core of our spiritual being (our sense of being the subject of our own experience) is *physically* felt—in his own case, in such physiological experiences as "the opening and closing of the glottis" (p. 288)![10] For another, he recast the traditional "abstract" manner of speaking about the faculties of the self into a more "concrete view" of the "spiritual self" as either "the entire stream of our personal consciousness, or the present 'segment' or 'section' of that stream, according as we take a broader or narrower view" (p. 284). In this manner, he connected his discussion of the self with his discussion of the stream of thought, or consciousness, in the preceding chapter of the *Principles*, and he prepared the way for placing the self at very center of his psychology and philosophy.

As regards his definition of "the Spiritual Self, so far as it belongs to the Empirical Me," James stated that he meant this term to refer only to a person's "inner or subjective being . . . taken concretely." It was not to be confused with "the bare principle of personal Unity, or 'pure' Ego," that is to say, with the ultimate ontological nature of the self, which he would discuss later in the chapter (p. 283). Rather, to label one of the dimensions of the empirical self "spiritual" was simply to acknowledge that we are able "to think of subjectivity as such, *to think ourselves as thinkers*," an ability that James admitted to be both "momentous" and "rather mysterious" (p. 284).

"Now, *what is this self of all the other selves?*" James began to answer this question as most of his contemporaries would, but he quickly turned this typical beginning to his own ends:

> [Others] would call it the *active* element in all consciousness. . . . It is what welcomes or rejects. It presides over the perception of sensations, and by giving or withholding its assent it influences the movements they tend to arouse. It is the home of interest,—not the pleasant or the painful, not even pleasure or pain, as such, but that within us to which pleasure and pain, the pleasant and the painful, speak. It is the source of effort and attention, and the place from which appear to emanate the fiats of the will. (p. 285)

Anyone who knows James's psychology will recognize in these few sentences an epitome of his most vital doctrines. Selectivity, interest, effort, attention, and will—these are the critically fundamental concepts in James's psychology, and they are rooted in the self, in that most highly personal and idiosyncratic aspect or segment of the stream of consciousness, in what James sometimes called, succinctly, "the Thinker."

About the ultimate nature of "the Thinker"—that is to say, about the ontological nature of the hypothetical "pure Ego"—James did not venture to conjecture, at least not in the *Principles*, even though he spent a considerable number of pages (27 pages, to be exact) reviewing the pertinent philosophical theories: the "soul theory" of the spiritualists; the associationist theory of Locke, Hume, and their followers; and the transcendental theory of Kant and the idealists. The purpose of James's critical review of these theories was not to resolve a metaphysical issue, but to arrive at an "empirical consensus" that members of each of these schools of thought would be able to accept. That consensus, he believed, was that "personality implies the incessant presence of two elements, an objective person, known by a passing subjective Thought" (p. 350). In other words, James's analysis of the literature on the self, and in particular the literature on the existence and nature of the transcendental ego, confirmed James's own conceptual distinction between the *I* (the "passing subjective Thought") and the *Me* (the "objective person"). However, in yet another innovative digression from traditional treatments of the self, James pointed out that the relation between these two aspects of the self, although real enough, "is only a loosely construed thing, an identity 'on the whole' " (p. 352). By reviewing the recently discovered phenomena of multiple personality, as studied by Edmund Gurney, F. W. H. Myers, Pierre Janet, and others, James demonstrated that there can be rather "grave" alterations, mutations, and multiplications of both the *I* and the *Me*—and of their relationship. Thus, by the time he arrived at the conclusion of his chapter on the self, he had made it clear that the unity of the self or personality—and hence of the stream of thought, or consciousness—*can* become quite deeply problematic.

This was an unexpected thesis with which to *end* a chapter on the self—the recognition that the unity of the self, and by implication the self's very existence is far from guaranteed. Beyond that, in summarizing the central thrust of the chapter, James suggested that if "the passing thought" is all that is ever directly and verifiably experienced, then the passing thought is the safest empirical foundation or starting point for our psychology of the self and indeed, for psychology as a whole. As he had said earlier in the chapter:

> As *psychologists*, we need not be metaphysical at all. The phenomena are enough, the passing Thought itself is the only *verifiable* thinker, and its empirical connection with the brain-process is the ultimate known law. (p. 328)

This being the case, James concluded, "psychology need not look beyond." In the absence of any experience of a *thinker* apart from *thoughts*, we can do no better than to surmise, or at least to accept as a reasonable theoretical postulate, that *"thought is itself the thinker"* (p. 379).

Here, in James's hypothetical reduction of the thinker to the thought, was the seed of John Dewey's (1940/1988) well known argument about "the vanishing subject in the psychology of William James." Here was the kernel of James's later (1904/1976a) questioning of the very nature and existence of "consciousness."[11] Here, too, was the stimulus of many later analyses and debates about the nature of consciousness and the self in James's thought (e.g., Browning, 1975, 1980; Capek, 1953; Edie, 1973, 1987; Ehman, 1969; High & Woodward, 1980; Linschoten, 1968; McDermott, 1980/1986b; Myers, 1986; Shea, 1973; Wilshire, 1968).[12] However, too often lost in these later developments and scholarly commentaries is something that James wrote earlier in the chapter, just before he suggested for the first time that thought is itself the thinker, or self:

> I find the notion of some sort of an *anima mundi* [or world-soul] thinking in all of us to be a more promising hypothesis, in spite of all its difficulties, than that of a lot of absolutely individual souls. (p. 328)

This quiet suggestion, reminiscent of his father's earlier doctrines, had to await future elaboration. When that elaboration began to take place in the later 1890s, it did not suggest that either "the subject" or "consciousness" had vanished from James's thought. Far from it: The self in its all-pervading stream of consciousness became a fundamental category of James's epistemology and metaphysics.[13]

JAMES'S FURTHER THOUGHTS ON THE SELF AND PERSONALITY

James had much more to say about the self, both in his classic chapter on the self and in other parts of the *Principles*. Within the chapter on the self, for instance, he discussed self-feeling, self-seeking, the relations among the various aspects of the empirical self, and the nature of self-love. Mixed into these discussions is a great deal of wisdom about the facts and foibles of human nature. James's discussion of the importance and process of self-esteem and his analysis of the hierarchical relations among the various dimensions of self are but two well known examples.

In other chapters of the *Principles*, too, the self is clearly visible. In fact, no one has really understood James's *Principles* until she or he sees how the self underlies its entire breadth. In the chapters on habit, attention, conception, and will, for instance, and even in the chapter on the psychological grounds of the sense of "reality," the self is frequently and centrally implicated. "Reality," for instance, "means simply relation to our emotional and active life," so that "*whatever excites and stimulates our interest is real*" to us (p. 924). As a consequence,

> *The fons et origo* [source and origin] *of all reality, whether from the absolute or the practical point of view, is thus subjective, is ourselves. . . . As thinkers*

with emotional reaction, we give what seems to us a still higher degree of reality to whatever things we select and emphasize and turn to WITH A WILL. These are our *living* realities; and not only these, but all the other things which are intimately connected with these. Reality, starting from our Ego, thus sheds itself from point to point—first, upon all objects which have an immediate sting of interest for our Ego in them, and next, upon the objects most continuously related with these. It only fails when the connecting thread is lost. A whole system may be real if it only hangs to our Ego by one immediately *stinging* term. (pp. 925–926)

Thus we see, in James's words, that the world of living realities is "anchored in the Ego, considered as an active and emotional term" (p. 926). Such anchoring, so vital to each and every person, is only one of the self's important functions according to James. *Willing* actions by *attending* to ideas that are *interesting* to us also depends on the *selective* and *effortful* functioning of our *personal consciousness* or *self*, and *this willful behaving is what true, "strenuous" living—being an experiencing self and a responsible person—is all about for James*, who provided the following blueprint for the construction of a worthwhile life:

Sow an action, & you reap a habit; sow a habit & you reap a character; sow a character and you reap a destiny.

This pithy summary, written as a marginal notation in his copy of the *Briefer Course* (1892/1984, p. 448), provides a fitting digest of James's psychology and of his philosophy of life, especially as regards the self and personality. It also recapitulates the course of James's own personal development from his earlier melancholy and "tedious egotism" to his subsequent "asserting of his own reality" and hence his "leaving a trace" in the course of human history.[14]

However deeply the *Principles* and the abbreviated *Briefer Course* helped to etch James's "trace" as regards his psychological analyses of the self and personality, it is important to note that James did not cease to ruminate on these topics after the publication of these works. Following up on themes and issues raised in his chapter on the self and in an article on "The Hidden Self" (1890/1983c), James continued to focus on abnormal psychology and altered states of consciousness in his courses in the 1890s.[15] One of the results was his delivery of an important series of lectures on "Exceptional Mental States" at the Lowell Institute in Boston in 1896 (recently reconstructed and published by Taylor, 1982a). In these lectures James discussed dreams, hypnotism, automatism, hysteria, multiple personality, demoniacal possession, witchcraft, degeneration, and genius. One of his central conclusions was that "health [including particularly mental health] is a term of subjective appreciation, not of objective description." In other words, "it is a teleological term" which admits "no purely objective standard" (Taylor, 1982a, p. 163). As a result, we should hold such labels lightly, and more importantly, "we should *not be afraid of life*" on account of "some single element of weakness" or unusualness (Taylor, 1982a, p. 164). If we or others are "exceptional," so be it:

> A certain tolerance, a certain sympathy, a certain respect, and above all a certain lack of fear, seem to be the best attitude we can carry in our dealing with these regions of human nature. (Taylor 1982a, p. 165)

With characteristic openness toward—and even enthusiasm about—individual variation, James thus tried to nurture in his audience a "more positive attitude" toward their own and other selves.[16]

Not unrelated to his interest in "exceptional" phenomena and individuals, James continued to encourage psychical research throughout the 1890s and up to the time of his death in 1910 (see James, 1909/1986b; Leary, 1980b), and he began a serious study of the psychology of religion, leading up to his Gifford Lectures at the University of Edinburgh in 1901–1902. These lectures, published as *The Varieties of Religious Experience* (1902/1985), constitute James's *other* psychological masterpiece and provide a truly remarkable set of analyses that touch at many points on issues pertinent to the psychology of the self and personality. Extracting brilliant insights from his own experience as well as from the psychological literature and from autobiographical reports of religious persons, James shared in the *Varieties* his mature thoughts about the role of meaning in life, about "once-born" and "twice-born" characters, about "healthy-minded" and "sick-souled" personalities, about the "divided self" and the process by which personalities can be integrated or unified, about the significance and process of personal "conversion," about the nature and value of "saintliness," about "mysticism" and the loss or transcendence of "personality," and about the possible "fruits" of the religious orientation. Along the way, he addressed many other issues as well, so that it is clearly not without reason that James subtitled this work "A Study in Human Nature," and it is not surprising that many people, from every walk of life and from many different disciplines, have turned to this book over the past 90 years for insight and self-understanding.

In addition to these developments and publications, James (1985/1983e) wrote the entry on "Person and Personality" for the 1895 edition of *Johnson's Universal Cyclopaedia*. This entry is notable for its historical survey of past uses of these two terms and for its pointed use of "personality" in an unambiguously empirical, psychological sense. Prior to this time, "personality" was not so clearly a psychological term. Even the uses of "personality" in the *Principles* were usually glancing and by the way, generally restricted in reference to "multiple personality." Indeed, the significance of James's use of the term with a specifically psychological meaning in 1895 can be measured against the fact that it was not until the 1930s that the study of personality was formally established as a technical subject matter of scientific and academic psychology.[17]

Characteristically, James made little of his personal role in adding weight to the *empirical* meaning and implications of the term. Noting that "in psychology 'personality' designates individuality, or what is called 'personal identity' " (p. 315), James (1895/1983e) surveyed various theories before suggesting that *"recent psychology* has, in the main, elaborated itself on Lockian lines," thus shifting the focus of attention to "the *empirical self"* (p. 318). Then, after reviewing the results of recent psychological and psychical research, especially research on hypnotized subjects, mediums, and multiple personalities, James concluded:

> All these facts have brought the question of what is the unifying principle in personality to the front again. It is certain that one human body may be the home of many *consciousnesses*, and thus, in Locke's sense, of many *persons*. . . . It is clear already that the margins and outskirts of what we take to be our personality extend into unknown regions. Cures and organic effects, such as blisters, produced by hypnotic suggestion show this as regards our bodily processes; while the utterances of mediums and automatic writers reveal a widespread tendency, in men and women otherwise sane, to personifications of a determinate kind; and these again, though usually flimsy and incoherent in the extreme, do, as the present writer believes, occasionally show a knowledge of facts not possessed by the primary person. The significance and limits of these phenomena have yet to be understood, and psychology is but just beginning to recognize this investigation as an urgent task. (pp. 320–321)[18]

I have already hinted about the direction taken by James as he strove to understand the implications of trance states, automatic writing, multiple personality, and so on—implications having to do with "the margins and outskirts of what we take to be our personality," which James saw as extending into "unknown regions." As he commented in the *Principles* (1890/1983d), the existence of "some sort of an *anima mundi* [or world-soul] thinking in all of us" seemed to him to be "a more promising hypothesis . . . than that of a lot of absolutely individual souls" (p. 328), and a little further on in the same work, he revealed that his thinking about this "promising hypothesis" was further along than his earlier statement might have implied:

> One great use of the Soul has always been to account for, and at the same time to guarantee, the closed individuality of each personal consciousness. . . . [But] it would be rash, in view of the phenomena of thought-transference, mesmeric influence and spirit-control, which are being alleged nowadays on better authority than ever before, to be too sure about that point. . . . The definitely closed nature of our personal consciousness is

probably an average statistical resultant of many conditions, but not an elementary force or fact. (p. 331)

Then, much later in the *Principles*, James wrote:

> *The perfect object of belief would be a God or 'Soul of the World,' represented both optimistically and moralistically . . . and withal so definitely conceived as to show us why our phenomenal experiences should be sent to us by Him in just the very way in which they come.* (pp. 944–945)

Although he had argued earlier in the *Principles* that metaphysics has no place in the realm of empirical psychology, James mentioned the "Soul of the World" [or *anima mundi*] in this context simply to indicate what *would* be an ideal belief about ultimate reality *if* the psychology of belief (as he understood it) were the only determining factor. Still, the passage reveals more about James's incipient belief-system than he may have intended. In the years ahead, as his beliefs grew, he came to realize that he had been wrong to try, and that he had inevitably failed, to banish metaphysics from the *Principles*. In his first presidential address to the American Psychological Association, James (1895/1978b) made a public confession in this regard, admitting that "no conventional restrictions *can* keep metaphysical and so-called epistemological inquiries out of the psychology-books" (p. 88). Since this is the case, he felt it incumbent upon him *as a psychologist* as well as a philosopher to clarify his metaphysical beliefs. That is precisely what he did in the final decade and a half of his life—he clarified his view of ultimate reality, relying on psychological research and on the pragmatic method of inquiry (see James, 1907/1975b; Suckiel, 1982).

As a consequence, a full understanding of James's mature psychology of the self and personality *on his own terms* necessarily involves an understanding of his metaphysical speculation about the ultimate nature of reality. Although this is not the place for a full-scale review of his metaphysics, I hope it is clear why I will conclude this treatment of his thought with a relatively succinct summary of his metaphysics.

From the mid-1890s at least, James began to speculate more and more freely in his psychological seminars, playing with such notions as "point of view" and "field" as alternatives to "self" and "ego" (see James, 1895–1896/1988b, 1897–1898/1988c). The self, by whatever term it was called, remained for James the "centre of knowledge & interest," but he increasingly emphasized the self's connection with what lay "beyond the margin" of consciousness. This speculation was reflected in various publications in the 1890s (e.g., James, 1895/1979b, 1898/1982b), and it culminated in *The Varieties of Religious Experience* (1902/1985), in which he asserted that

> I cannot but think that the most important step forward that has occurred in psychology since I have been a student of that science is the discovery, first

made in 1886, that, in certain subjects at least, there is not only the consciousness of the ordinary field [of "vision" or "awareness"], with its usual centre and margin, but an addition thereto in the shape of a set of memories, thoughts, and feelings which are extra-marginal and outside of the primary consciousness altogether, but yet must be classed as conscious facts of some sort, able to reveal their presence by unmistakable signs. I call this the most important step forward because . . . this discovery has revealed to us an entirely unsuspected peculiarity in the constitution of human nature. . . . In particular this discovery of a consciousness existing beyond the field, or subliminally as Mr. Myers terms it, casts light on many phenomena of religious biography. (p. 190)

The "Mr. Myers" to whom James referred was the same Frederic (or F. W. H.) Myers whom he credited, in large part, with the 1886 discovery of this new arena of psychological and metaphysical reality (Myers, 1886; see also Gurney, Myers, & Podmore, 1886). As James (1901/1986a) had said in his obituary notice on Myers:

Myers's conception of the extensiveness of the Subliminal Self [as Myers called the transmarginal extension of consciousness] quite overturns the classic notion of what the human mind consists in. The supraliminal region, as Myers calls it, the classic-academic consciousness, which was once alone considered either by associationists or animists, figures in his theory as only a small segment of the psychic spectrum. It is a special phase of mentality, teleologically evolved for adaptation to our natural environment, and forms only what he calls a 'privileged case' of personality. The outlying Subliminal, according to him, represents more fully our central and abiding being. . . . This problem of Myers [regarding the subliminal region] still awaits us as the problem of far the deepest moment for our actual psychology, whether his own tentative solutions of certain parts of it be correct or not. (pp. 195–197)

Whether correct or not, James thought Myers's conceptual framework was very useful. Myers's concept of "automatisms," for instance, helped make sense of many unusual phenomena—sensory and motor, emotional and intellectual—that could be seen as "due to 'uprushes' into the ordinary consciousness of energies originating in the subliminal parts of the mind" (James, 1902/1985, p. 191). Such "uprushes" included mystical and religious experiences as well as the manifestations of multiple personality, thought-transference, and so forth. To James, Myers's hypothesis made everything fit, and it accounted for his earlier "obscurer feeling" that there was "something more" underlying conscious experience (see footnote 10). It even made sense of his own personal "observations" of "nitrous oxide intoxication," which had "forced" on his mind the conclusion that . . .

our normal waking consciousness, rational consciousness as we call it, is but one special type of consciousness, whilst all about it, parted from it by the

filmiest of screens, there lie potential forms of consciousness entirely different; but apply the requisite stimulus, and at a touch they are there in all their
completeness. (James, 1902/1985, pp. 307–308)

As a result, James was convinced that . . .

no account of the universe in its totality can be final which leaves these other
forms of consciousness quite disregarded. How to regard them is the question. . . . [But] at any rate, they forbid a premature closing of our accounts
with reality. (James, 1902/1985, p. 308)

Whatever explanation one might give, it was clear to James that when humans identify their "real being" with "the germinal higher part" of themselves, they become *"conscious that this higher part is conterminous and
continuous with a* more *of the same quality, which is operative in the universe"* outside of themselves (p. 400). Looking to the broader significance
of such an awareness, it seemed apparent that "the conscious person is continuous with a wider self through which saving experiences come" and
"higher energies filter in" (pp. 405, 408, italics deleted).

James attempted throughout the last decade of his life, and especially in
A Pluralistic Universe (1909/1977), to give clearer and clearer expression to
his conviction that individual selves are part of a much larger "field," a
truly "cosmic consciousness." He felt that such an hypothesis, developed
by others (e.g., Bucke, 1901/1969) as well as by himself, does a better job
than any other of "saving the phenomena," including the "exceptional"
phenomena of psychological experience. With an array of simple, naturalistic metaphors—comparing each of us to a "wavelet" in the "mother-sea"
of consciousness or to a "tree" whose roots commingle underground with
those of the rest of the forest—James (1909/1977) gave graphic expression
to his confidence that our "present field of consciousness is a centre surrounded by a fringe that shades insensibly into a subconscious more," that
"our *full* self is the whole field, with all those indefinitely radiating subconscious possibilities of increase that we can only feel without conceiving, and
can hardly begin to analyze," that "every bit of us at every moment is part
and parcel of a wider self" (pp. 130–131). Waxing even more speculative, he
even wondered:

May not we ourselves form the margin of some more really central self in
things which is co-conscious with the whole of us? May not you and I be con-
fluent in a higher consciousness, and confluently active there, tho we now
know it not? (p. 131)

In essence, James was wondering whether the universe itself might not be a
Self writ large, a sort of cosmic multiple personality, in which each individual self is a particular, irreplaceable "point of view." The mere possibility

of "a world wider than either physics or philistine ethics can imagine," James said, can "take our breath away" with its promise of "another kind of happiness and power, based on giving up our own will and letting something higher work for us" (James, 1909/1977, p. 138).

Here at the end, once again, we can detect the echo of his father's earlier doctrines, and just as plainly we can sense the open-minded curiosity, the intellectual vigor, and even the youthful zestfulness of the 67-year-old scientist and philosopher, one of whose final questions should give us pause:

> When was not the science of the future stirred to its conquering activities by the little rebellious exceptions to the science of the present? (James, 1909/1986b, p. 375)[19]

ECHOES AND INFLUENCE

The impact of William James on modern thought is well known, yet it still might surprise some to learn that Alfred North Whitehead, the noted logician, mathematician, philosopher, and historian of science, considered James to be one of the four major thinkers in the entire Western tradition, along with Plato, Aristotle, and Leibniz (see Whitehead, 1938, pp. 3–4). Similar and perhaps better known is the estimate of Edwin G. Boring, the eminent historian of psychology, who considered James to be one of the "four great men" in the history of psychology, the others being Darwin, Helmholtz, and Freud (see Boring, 1950, p. 743). Despite these accolades and the widespread awareness of James's historical importance, however, it might not be superfluous to specify a few of the lines of James's influence and to point out some of the echoes of his thought in subsequent developments in the psychology of the self and personality.

I should say at the start that it is *not* the case that James created the 20th-century study of the self and personality all by himself. I have already noted that the study of personality was not even formally established until the 1930s, although there were many earlier works that presaged the founding texts of Gordon Allport (1937), Ross Stagner (1937), and Henry Murray (1938). When the psychology of personality did take off, however, it did so with frequent nods to James's analyses of the self, habit, emotion, and instinct—and to James's contention that psychology should study the *whole* person. (Kurt Lewin's 1935 collection of articles on *A Dynamic Theory of Personality* deserves mention in this latter regard as well.) As for the psychology of the self, others besides James contributed in important ways to its establishment as an area of empirical study, which took place much earlier than that of personality, due in large part to the central place the self had enjoyed in earlier philosophical psychology. Josiah Royce and John

Dewey, whose work was mentioned earlier (see footnote 8), did more than simply lend a hand to James in the advancement of this area of inquiry, as did James Mark Baldwin (1897), G. Stanley Hall (1898), and Mary Whiton Calkins (1900). But however independent their contributions, each acknowledged a debt to James.

Perhaps the most instructive example of how James served as a pushing-off point of future theory and practice is provided by the work of John B. Watson. Although he acknowledged that James was "the most brilliant psychologist the world has ever known" (p. 141), Watson (1924/1963) argued, as is well known, for a purely "objective" account of behavior and personality that rejected the use of any notion of consciousness or inner self (see especially chap. 12). Yet this behavioristic account was conceptualized and worked out in very telling fashion: In place of the Jamesian "stream of consciousness" as the fundamental notion of psychology, Watson simply substituted his own notion of the "activity stream" (Watson, 1924/1963, pp. 137–139). Thus, even though his treatment seemed quite distinct because of its different focal *content*, the logical *form* of Watson's account of individual development and dynamics was very similar to James's. Indeed, by emphasizing behavioral habits rather than the cognitive self, he was simply working out a different aspect of James's legacy.[20]

Such individual instances of James's influence are interesting, but perhaps not as useful given our present concerns as a more systematic review of the lines of development extending from specific aspects of James's thought on the self and personality down to the present time. I would like, therefore, to point out some of the major stepping stones along these lines of development, particularly with regard to James's treatment of the material, social, and spiritual dimensions of the self.

James's ideas about "the material self" were picked up and developed in particular by Gordon Allport, who was perhaps the most "Jamesian" psychologist of his generation.[21] In his discussion of "consciousness of self," Allport (1937) noted how "clothing, ornamentation, and special grooming contribute their share to self-consciousness" (p. 164), and in his treatment of "extensions of the self," he discussed how "possessions, friends, one's own children, other children, cultural interests, abstract ideas, politics, hobbies, recreation, and most conspicuously of all, one's *work*, all lead to the incorporation of interests once remote from the self into selfhood proper" (p. 217). In a later work, Allport (1961) further developed his discussion of the "bodily self," and at the close of his overall analysis of "the evolving sense of self," he noted that William James had been "well aware of additional aspects we have described" and that he had "anticipated our present more detailed analysis in terms of bodily sense, self-identity, self-esteem, self-image, self-extension, and propriate striving" (p. 127). Others have subsequently taken up matters pertinent to James's "material self," but not nearly so many as the topic seems to warrant. Interestingly, in one of the most fascinating and directly relevant of recent instances, Csikszentmihalyi and Rochberg-Halton's *The Meaning of Things* (1981), the authors do not register any awareness of James's contribution, even though they quote James, admiringly, on the selectivity of psychic activity (p. 5).

Regarding "the social self," there is much to say, although it cannot all be said here. The major force in promoting and developing James's ideas along this line was George Herbert Mead. Acknowledging James's priority, Mead actually was a "third generation" Jamesian, who was influenced by the "revisionist" approach of Charles Cooley (1902/1964), who was himself inspired by James. As Mead (1929–1930/1964) saw it:

> James recognized early the influence of the social environment upon the individual in the formation of the personality, [but] his psychological contribution to the social character of the self was rather in showing the spread of the self over its social environment than in the structure of the self through social interactions. The superiority of Cooley's position lies in his freedom to find in consciousness a social process going on, within which the self and the others arise. (p. 300)

Although Mead's reading of James is somewhat questionable, this passage highlights the way in which Cooley and Mead developed James's original insight. Building up a theory of the self on the initiating notion of the communicative gesture, Mead (1934) helped to establish a strong and lasting tradition of the social psychology of the self. Although psychologists have not always taken sufficient advantage of this tradition, it has nonetheless had its impact on the psychological study of the self. One such impact was mediated by Jessie Taft (1933/1962), a former student of Mead, who helped in the 1930s to fan Carl Rogers's (1961) then smoldering interest in the self. (In essence, Rogers's mature psychological theory pivoted around the contrast between James's "social self" and James's "spiritual self," although he did not seem to be aware of this fact.) And as is well known, Harry Stack Sullivan (1953) integrated Mead's insights about the social nature of the self into his "interpersonal theory of psychiatry," which has had its own impact on psychological theory and practice. Most recently, the kinds of theory and research contained in the collections edited by Suls (1982), Gergen and Davis (1985), and Berkowitz (1988), summarized in the review by Snyder and Ickes (1985), and integrated into the textbook by Aronoff and Wilson (1985) represent a strong resurgence of interest in the social dimensions of selfhood and personality.

As if to preserve a healthy "Jamesian" tension regarding current notions of the social contextualization of the self and the distinctive individuality of the self, the elation of some psychologists regarding "the rediscovery of self in social psychology" (Hales, 1985) has been countered by a reciprocal concern for the "whereabouts" of the *person* in personality research

(Carlson, 1971). Such latter concerns point toward James's interest in the "spiritual self," which is to say, in the sense of personal *agency* and *experience* that lies at the core of human selfhood. This aspect of James's psychology of the self was selected as a primary focus of investigation by James's student, Mary Whiton Calkins. Although Calkins's research is now too little known, it was probably more important than James's initial discussion in establishing "self-psychology" and in giving an empirical basis to "personalism" at the turn of the century. Even James acknowledged that Calkins soon outdid her teacher in advocating and advancing this field of study. On a blank flyleaf inside the front cover of his own personal copy of the *Briefer Course*, James wrote "Calkins's Articles Dec. 1907 + ," as a reminder that he wanted to draw upon a several-part treatise by Calkins (1908) if he should ever revise the *Briefer Course*. (Despite E. L. Thorndike's persistent efforts, and even his volunteering of his services, the *Briefer Course* was never revised, although it was often reissued.) Throughout her life, Calkins wrote periodic reviews of the literature on the self, the final review appearing in 1927. One of her last publications was a critical review of the self-psychology of contemporary psychoanalysts (Calkins & Gamble, 1930). All along, she remained a vociferous proponent of the self and its empirical manifestations, which she believed to be amenable to scientific study as well as philosophical reflection.

Although Calkins's work was well enough respected to earn her the presidency of the American Psychological Association in 1905, a very distinct honor for a woman in the early 20th century, it very soon had to battle the rather insistent tides of behaviorism. (Her final publication in 1930, urging "the case against behaviorism," was well aimed, but less effective than she would have wished.) However, others took up James's call for attention to the experiential dimension of the self. Chief among these were the phenomenologists, some of whose descendants subsequently helped lead the way in the revival of James scholarship that began several decades ago. Not surprisingly, the works of these descendants (e.g., Edie, 1987; Linschoten, 1968; Wilshire, 1968) provide better accounts than I can pretend to offer here regarding the developments of the phenomenological aspects of James's psychology. Suffice it to add that many American psychologists (e.g., Rogers, 1961) have given phenomenological analyses of the experiences of the self, and to this extent have been in the Jamesian tradition, without necessarily harkening back to James. Still, much of the research along this line, partially summarized in Singer and Kolligian's (1987) review article and further advanced by Singer's (1987) own research and by that of Czikszentmihalyi (1982) and many others, represents a continuation of a tradition initiated by James a full century ago.

As regards the interrelations of the various aspects of the self, there have been both echoes and influences stemming from James. The echoes resound in such work as Abraham Maslow's (1954/1987) proposition of "the hierarchy of needs," which extend (he said) from the material through the social to the spiritual domain. Although Maslow acknowledged that his theory is "in the functionalist tradition of James and Dewey" (p. 15), he seemed not to be aware of how closely his scheme recapitulated James's (1892/1984) earlier discussion of the various aspects of the self and of their place on "an *hierarchical scale, with the bodily me at the bottom, the spiritual me at top, and the extra-corporeal material selves and the various social selves between*" (p. 170).

The direct influence of James as regards the need to understand the various dimensions of the self as being in some sort of dynamic, integrated union is illustrated by the work of Lev S. Vygotsky. I choose this particular historical example because a great deal of attention is being devoted at the present time (for good reason) to Vygotsky's distinctive program of research, with its attempt to understand the development of the human self within a complex matrix of both the material *and* social dimensions of existence. Little noticed in recent treatments of Vygotsky, however, has been his first publication, which foreshadows all of his later work on the social foundations of consciousness, ego, and self. In this article, Vygotsky (1925/ 1979) relied on James as a critical point of reference. Noting at the end that "it is crucial to point out the agreement between the conclusions I have drawn here and those of the brilliant analysis of consciousness made by William James," Vygotsky wrote that "I should like to regard this as a partial confirmation of my ideas" (p. 32). Conversely, Vygotsky's working out of a multidimensional approach to the self went a long way toward establishing one of the lines of potential development from James's thought.

Much remains to be said about the influence and echoes of James's hypothesis that the thought is the thinker, of his suggestion that "self" is a general term for a range of phenomena experienced by different persons and "on the whole," in similar ways, of his articulation of the significance of the fact that the self can become divided and multiple, of his speculations concerning the relationship between individual selves and the larger context of reality, of his criticism of conceptual and diagnostic labels, of his tolerance of exceptionalness, of his defense of keeping philosophical perspectives alive and well within psychology, of his interest in altered states of consciousness, and so on and so forth. But given the limits of this chapter, I shall simply leave it to the industrious reader to fill in what I cannot possibly say here. I would only suggest that a review of the work of such disparate individuals as Albert Bandura (1978), Carl Jung (1921/1971), R. D. Laing (1961), Robert Jay Lifton (1970), Hazel Markus and Paula Nurius (1986), Thomas Natsoulas (1983), Oliver Sacks (1984), Edward Sampson (1985), Theodore Sarbin and George McKechnie (1986), and M. Brewster Smith (1978) would only begin to indicate the range of reverberations set off by James, along many of the lines suggested by the preceding list of issues and topics.

All in all, it seems more than fair to conclude that the influence of James's psychology of the self and personality has been steady and substantial, and that the echoes of his ideas have been loud and recurrent. Yet for all the echoes and influence, the potential of James's fertile thought does not seem to have been exhausted. As long as psychologists continue to carve up the human person in their attempt to grasp the pieces rather than understand the ensemble of human functioning, as long as theorists of different persuasions squabble about the relative merits of cognitive as opposed to behavioral as opposed to physiological accounts, as long as methods are used to limit and even to dictate the range of thoughtful speculation, as long as white adult males—and middle-class college sophomores—remain the prototypes of human nature, so long will it remain true, as George Mandler (1979) suggested a decade ago, that "too many of us have still not absorbed James's insights" (p. 744). But don't take my word for it: If there is any hope with which I end this chapter, it is that many readers will turn from it to James's *Principles* and begin to make up for lost time.

CONCLUSION

George Santayana (1933) once described John Locke as "a sort of William James of the seventeenth century" (p. 25).[22] Turning Santayana's insightful comparison on its head, the preceding historical and conceptual analysis suggests that we might profitably think of James as a sort of John Locke of the 19th and 20th century—an "under-labourer in clearing the ground a little, and removing some of the rubbish that lies in the way to knowledge," as Locke (1690/1959) too modestly described himself and his own historical role (Vol. 1, p. 14). And, of course, with the development of new knowledge comes the opportunity and inspiration of new practice. In fact, for James as for Locke, the ultimate purpose of science and philosophy "is not to know all things, but those [practical things] which concern our conduct" (Vol. 1, p. 31).[23] Hopefully, in this chapter, I have provided sufficient insight into James's psychology so that readers will have begun to recognize and appreciate the ways in which James *did* clear the road to our current understanding and treatment of the human self and personality. I hope, too, that this chapter will have suggested some of the ways in which James's thought might *still* clear the road to additional future developments, developments that would secure for the self a place at the center of psychology, where James wished it to be.

REFERENCES

Albrecht, F. M. (1960). *The new psychology in America, 1880–1895*. Unpublished doctoral dissertation, Johns Hopkins University, Baltimore, MD.

Allen, G. W. (1967). *William James: A biography.* New York: Viking Press.

Allport, G. W. (1937). *Personality: A psychological interpretation.* New York: Holt.

Allport, G. W. (1961). *Pattern and growth in personality.* New York: Holt, Rinehart and Winston.

Anderson, J. W. (1982). "The worst kind of melancholy": William James in 1869. *Harvard Library Bulletin, 30,* 369–386.

Aronoff, J., & Wilson, J. P. (1985). *Personality in the social process.* Hillsdale, NJ: Lawrence Erlbaum Associates.

Bain, A. (1859). *The emotions and the will.* London: Parker and Son.

Baldwin, J. M. (1897). *Social and ethical interpretations in mental development: A study in social psychology.* New York: Macmillan.

Bandura, A. (1978). The self system in reciprocal determinism. *American Psychologist, 33,* 344–358.

Berkowitz, L. (Ed.). (1988). Social psychological studies of the self: Perspectives and programs. *Advances in experimental social psychology* (Vol. 21). New York: Academic Press.

Boring, E. G. (1950). *A history of experimental psychology* (2nd ed.). New York: Appleton-Century-Crofts.

Browning, D. S. (1975). William James's philosophy of the person: The concept of the strenuous life. *Zygon, 10,* 162–174.

Browning, D. S. (1980). *Pluralism and personality: William James and some contemporary cultures of psychology.* Lewisburg, PA: Bucknell University Press.

Bucke, R. M. (1969). *Cosmic consciousness: A study in the evolution of the human mind.* New York: E. P. Dutton. (Original work published 1901)

Burkhardt, F. (Ed.). (1981). *William James's "The principles of psychology": Vol. 3, Notes, appendices, apparatus, general index.* Cambridge, MA: Harvard University Press.

Burnham, J. C. (1967). *Psychoanalysis and American medicine. 1894–1918: Medicine, science, and culture.* New York: International Universities Press.

Burnham, J. C. (1968). Historical background for the study of personality. In E. F. Borgatta & W. J. Lambert (Eds.), *Handbook of personality theory and research* (pp. 3–81). Chicago: Rand McNally.

Calkins, M. W. (1900). Psychology as science of selves. *Philosophical Review, 9,* 490–501.

Calkins, M. W. (1908). Psychology as science of self. I. Is the self body or has it body? II. The nature of self. III. The description of consciousness. *Journal of Philosophy, Psychology and Scientific Method, 5,* 12–20, 64–68, 113–121.

Calkins, M. W. (1927). The self in recent psychology. *Psychological Bulletin, 24,* 205–215.

Calkins, M. W. (1930). [Autobiography.] In C. Murchison (Ed.), *A history of psychology in autobiography* (Vol. 1, pp. 31–62). Worcester, MA: Clark University Press.

Calkins, M. W., & Gamble, E. A. McC. (1930). The self-psychology of the psychoanalysts. *Psychological Review, 37,* 277–304.

Capek, M. (1953). The reappearance of the self in the last philosophy of William James. *Philosophicl Review, 62,* 526–544.

Carlson, R. (1971). Where is the person in personality research? *Psychological Bulletin, 75,* 203–219.

Cooley, C. H. (1964). *Human nature and the social order.* New York: Schocken Books. (Original work published 1902)

Cotton, J. H. (1954). *Royce on the human self.* Cambridge, MA: Harvard University Press.

Csikszentmihalyi, M. (1982). Toward a psychology of optimal experience. In L. Wheeler (Ed.), *Review of personality and social psychology* (Vol. 3, pp. 13–36). Beverly Hills, CA: Sage.

Csikszentmihalyi, M., & Rochberg-Halton, E. (1981). *The meaning of things: Domestic symbols and the self.* Cambridge: Cambridge University Press.

Darwin, C. (1964). *The origin of species* (facsimile of 1st ed.; E. Mayr, Ed.). Cambridge, MA: Harvard University Press. (Original work published 1859)

Dewey, J. (1967). Psychology. In J. A. Boydston (Ed.), *The early works of John Dewey, 1882–1898* (Vol. 2). Carbondale: Southern Illinois University Press. (Original work published 1887)

Dewey, J. (1969). Psychology as philosophic method. In J. A. Boydston (Ed.), *The early works of John Dewey, 1882–1898* (Vol. 1, pp. 144–167). Carbondale: Southern Illinois University Press. (Original work published 1886)

Dewey, J. (1983). Human nature and conduct: An introduction to social psychology. In J. A. Boydston (Ed.), *The middle works of John Dewey, 1899–1924* (Vol. 14). Carbondale: Southern Illinois University Press. (Original work published 1922)

Dewey, J. (1988). The vanishing subject in the psychology of William James. In J. A. Boydston (Ed.), *The later works of John Dewey, 1925–1953* (Vol. 14, pp. 155–167). Carbondale: Southern Illinois University Press. (Original work published 1940)

Edie, J. M. (1973). The genesis of a phenomenological theory of the experience of personal identity: William James on consciousness and the self. *Man and World, 6*, 322–340.

Edie, J. M. (1987). *William James and phenomenology.* Bloomington: Indiana University Press.

Ehman, R. R. (1969). William James and the structure of the self. In J. M. Edie (Ed.), *New essays on phenomenology* (pp. 256–270). Chicago: Quadrangle Books.

Ellenberger, H. F. (1970). *The discovery of the unconscious: The history and evolution of dynamic psychiatry.* New York: Basic Books.

Emerson, R. W. (1983). Self-reliance. In *Essays & lectures* (J. Porte, Ed.; pp. 257–282). New York: Library of America. (Original work published 1841)

Evans, R. B. (1984). The origins of American academic psychology. In J. Brozek (Ed.), *Explorations in the history of psychology in the United States* (pp. 17–60). Lewisburg, PA: Bucknell University Press.

Feinstein, H. M. (1984). *Becoming William James.* Ithaca, NY: Cornell University Press.

Fontinell, E. (1986). *Self, god, and immortality: A Jamesian investigation.* Philadelphia: Temple University Press.

Fullinwider, S. P. (1975). William James's "spiritual crisis." *The Historian, 38*, 39–57.

Gergen, K. J., & Davis, K. E. (Eds.). (1985). *The social construction of the person.* New York: Springer-Verlag.

Gifford, G. E., Jr. (Ed.). (1978). *Psychoanalysis, psychotherapy, and the New England medical scene, 1894–1944.* New York: Science History Publications.

Gurney, E., Myers, F. W. H., & Podmore, F. (1886). *Phantasms of the living* (2 vols.). London: Trubner.

Hale, N. G., Jr. (1971a). *Freud and the Americans: The beginnings of psychoanalysis in the United States, 1876–1917.* New York: Oxford University Press.

Hale, N. G., Jr. (Ed.). (1971b). *James Jackson Putnam and psychoanalysis.* Cambridge, MA: Harvard University Press.

Hales, S. (Ed.). (1985). The rediscovery of self in social psychology: Theoretical and methodological implications. *Journal for the Theory of Social Behaviour, 15*, No. 3 (entire issue).

Hall, G. S. (1888). [Reviews of psychological textbooks by John Dewey, George Trumball Ladd, and others]. *American Journal of Psychology, 1*, 146–164.

Hall, G. S. (1898). Some aspects of the early sense of self. *American Journal of Psychology, 9*, 351–395.

Hardwick, E. (Ed.). (1980). *The selected letters of William James.* Boston: Godine. (Original work published 1960)

Hegel, G. W. F. (1910). *The phenomenology of mind* (J. B. Baillie, Trans.). London: Macmillan. (Original work published 1807)

High, R. P., & Woodward, W. R. (1980). William James and Gordon Allport: Parallels in their maturing conceptions of self and personality. In R. W. Rieber & K. Salzinger (Eds.), *Psychology: Theoretical-historical perspectives* (pp. 57–79). New York: Academic Press.

Hopkins, M. (1870). *Lectures on moral science*. Boston: Gould and Lincoln.

Hume, D. (1978). *A treatise of human nature* (P. H. Nidditch, Ed.). Oxford: Clarendon Press. (Original work published 1739–1740)

James, H., Jr. (1963). *The portrait of a lady*. Harmondsworth, England: Penguin Books. (Original work published 1881)

James, H., Sr. (1876). The reconciliation of man individual with man universal. *The Index, 7* (3 February), 52.

James, H., III. (Ed.). (1920). *The letters of William James* (Vols. 1–2). Boston: Atlantic Monthly Press.

James W. (1975a). Philosophical conceptions and practical results. In *Pragmatism: A new name for some old ways of thinking* (F. Burkhardt, Ed.; pp. 255–270). Cambridge, MA: Harvard University Press. (Original work published 1898)

James, W. (1975b). *Pragmatism: A new name for some old ways of thinking* (F. Burkhardt, Ed.). Cambridge, MA: Harvard University Press. (Original work published 1907)

James, W. (1975c). *The meaning of truth* (F. Burkhardt, Ed.). Cambridge, MA: Harvard University Press. (Original work published 1909)

James, W. (1976a). Does 'consciousness' exist? In *Essays in radical empiricism* (F. Burkhardt, Ed.; pp. 3–19). Cambridge, MA: Harvard University Press. (Original work published 1904)

James, W. (1976b). *Essays in radical empiricism* (F. Burkhardt, Ed.). Cambridge, MA: Harvard University Press. (Original work published posthumously 1912)

James, W. (1977). *A pluralistic universe* (F. Burkhardt, Ed.). Cambridge, MA: Harvard University Press. (Original work published 1909)

James, W. (1978a). The sentiment of rationality. In *Essays in philosophy* (F. Burkhardt, Ed.; pp. 32–64). Cambridge, MA: Harvard University Press. (Original work published 1879)

James, W. (1978b). The knowing of things together. In *Essays in philosophy* (F. Burkhardt, Ed.; pp. 71–89). Cambridge, MA: Harvard University Press. (Original work published 1895)

James, W. (1979a). Great men and their environment. In *The will to believe and other essays in popular philosophy* (F. Burkhardt, Ed.; pp. 163–189). Cambridge, MA: Harvard University Press. (Original work published 1880)

James, W. (1979b). Is life worth living? In *The will to believe and other essays in popular philosophy* (F. Burkhardt, Ed.; pp. 34–56). Cambridge, MA: Harvard University Press. (Original work published 1895)

James, W. (1982a). Introduction to *The literary remains of the late Henry James*. In *Essays in religion and morality* (F. Burkhardt, Ed.; pp. 3–63). Cambridge, MA: Harvard University Press. (Original work published 1884)

James, W. (1982b). Human immortality: Two supposed objections to the doctrine. In *Essays in religion and morality* (F. Burkhardt, Ed.; pp. 75–101). Cambridge, MA: Harvard University Press. (Original work published 1898)

James, W. (1982c). Emerson. In *Essays in religion and morality* (F. Burkhardt, Ed.; pp. 109–115). Cambridge, MA: Harvard University Press. (Original work published 1903)

James, W. (1983a). The spatial quale. In *Essays in psychology* (F. Burkhardt, Ed.; pp. 62–82). Cambridge, MA: Harvard University Press. (Original work published 1879)

James, W. (1983b). On some omissions of introspective psychology. In *Essays in psychology* (F. Burkhardt, Ed.; pp. 142–167). Cambridge, MA: Harvard University Press. (Original work published 1884)

James, W. (1983c). The hidden self. In *Essays in psychology* (F. Burkhardt, Ed.; pp. 247–268). Cambridge, MA: Harvard University Press. (Original work published 1890)

James, W. (1983d). *The principles of psychology* (F. Burkhardt, Ed.). Cambridge, MA: Harvard University Press. (Original work published 1890)

James, W. (1983e). Person and personality. In *Essays in psychology* (F. Burkhardt, Ed.; pp. 315–321). Cambridge, MA: Harvard University Press. (Original work published 1895)

James, W. (1983f). Introduction to *The psychology of suggestion* by Boris Sidis. In *Essays in psychology* (F. Burkhardt, Ed.; pp. 325–327). Cambridge, MA: Harvard University Press. (Original work published 1898)

James, W. (1983g). On a certain blindness in human beings. In *Talks to teachers on psychology and to students on some of life's ideals* (F. Burkhardt, Ed.; pp. 132–149). Cambridge, MA: Harvard University Press. (Original work published 1899)

James, W. (1983h). What makes a life significant. In *Talks to teachers on psychology and to students on some of life's ideals* (F. Burkhardt, Ed.; pp. 150–167). Cambridge, MA: Harvard University Press. (Original work published 1899)

James, W. (1984). *Psychology: Briefer course* (F. Burkhardt, Ed.). Cambridge, MA: Harvard University Press. (Original work published 1892)

James, W. (1985). *The varieties of religious experience* (F. Burkhardt, Ed.). Cambridge, MA: Harvard University Press. (Original work published 1902)

James, W. (1986a). Frederic Myers's service to psychology. In *Essays in psychical research* (F. Burkhardt, Ed.; pp. 192–202). Cambridge, MA: Harvard University Press. (Original work published 1901)

James, W. (1986b). The confidences of a "psychical researcher." In *Essays in psychical research* (F. Burkhardt, Ed.; pp. 361–375). Cambridge, MA: Harvard University Press. (Original work published 1909)

James, W. (1987a). Review of "Ueber den psychischen mechanismus hysterischer phänomene" [On the psychical mechanism of hysterical phenomena], by Josef Breuer and Sigmund Freud. In *Essays, comments, and reviews* (F. Burkhardt, Ed.; pp. 474–475). Cambridge, MA: Harvard University Press. (Original work published 1894)

James, W. (1987b). Review of *Genie und entartung* [Genius and degeneration], by William Hirsch. In *Essays, comments, and reviews* (F. Burkhardt, Ed.; pp. 509–513). Cambridge, MA: Harvard University Press. (Original work published 1895)

James, W. (1988a). Lowell lectures on "The brain and the mind." In *Manuscript lectures* (F. Burkhardt, Ed.; pp. 16–43). Cambridge, MA: Harvard University Press. (Original lectures delivered 1878)

James, W. (1988b). Notes for Philosophy 20b: Psychological seminary—The feelings (1895–1896). In *Manuscript lectures* (F. Burkhardt, Ed.; pp. 212–230). Cambridge, MA: Harvard University Press. (Original lectures delivered 1895–1896)

James, W. (1988c). Notes for Philosophy 20b: Psychological seminary—The philosophical problems of psychology (1897–1898). In *Manuscript lectures* (F. Burkhardt, Ed.; pp. 234–259). Cambridge, MA: Harvard University Press. (Original lectures delivered 1897–1898)

Janet, P. (1889). *L'automatisme psychologique* [Psychological automatism]. Paris: Alcan.

Jastrow, J. (1915). The antecedents of the study of character and temperament. *Popular Science Monthly*, *86*, 590–613.

Jung, C. G. (1971). *Psychological types* (H. G. Baynes & R. F. C. Hull, Trans.). Princeton, NJ: Princeton University Press. (Original work published 1921)

Kant, I. (1965). *Critique of pure reason* (N. K. Smith, Trans.). New York: St. Martin's Press. (Original work published 1781)

Ladd, G. T. (1887). *Elements of physiological psychology*. New York: Scribner's.

Ladd, G. T. (1918). *The secret of personality: The problem of man's personal life as viewed in the light of an hypothesis of man's religious faith*. New York: Longmans, Green.

Laing, R. D. (1961). *The self and others: Further studies in sanity and madness*. London: Tavistock.

Leary, D. E. (1980a). The intentions and heritage of Descartes and Locke: Toward a recognition of the moral basis of modern psychology. *Journal of General Psychology*, *102*, 283–310.

Leary, D. E. (1980b, September). *William James, psychical research, and the origins of American psychology*. Presentation at the 88th Annual Meeting of the American Psychological Association, Montreal.

Leary, D. E. (1987). Telling likely stories: The rhetoric of the new psychology, 1880–1910. *Journal of the History of the Behavioral Sciences, 23*, 315–331.

Leary, D. E. (Ed.). (1990). *Metaphors in the history of psychology.* New York: Cambridge University Press.

Lewin, K. (1935). *A dynamic theory of personality: Selected papers* (D. K. Adams & K. E. Zener, Trans.). New York: McGraw-Hill.

Liébeault, A. A. (1866). *Du sommeil et des états analogues, considérés surtout au point de vue de l'action du moral sur le physique* [Sleep and analogous states, considered throughout from the viewpoint of the action of moral upon physical factors]. Paris: Masson.

Lifton, R. J. (1970). Self. In R. J. Lifton (Ed.), *Boundaries: Psychological man in revolution* (pp. 35–63). New York: Random House.

Linschoten, H. (1968). *On the way toward a phenomenological psychology: The psychology of William James* (A. Giorgi, Ed.). Pittsburgh: Duquesne University Press.

Locke, J. (1959). *An essay concerning human understanding* (A. C. Fraser, Ed.). New York: Dover. (Original work published 1690)

Lotze, R. H. (1899). *Microcosmus: An essay concerning man and his relations to the world* (E. Hamilton & E. E. C. Jones, Trans.; 4th ed., 2 vols.). Edinburgh: Clark. (Original work published 1856–1864)

Mandler, G. (1979). A man for all seasons? *Contemporary Psychology, 24*, 742–744.

Markus, H., & Nurius, P. (1986). Possible selves. *American Psychologist, 41*, 954–969.

Marx, O. (1968). American psychiatry without William James. *Bulletin of the History of Medicine, 42*, 52–61.

Maslow, A. H. (1987). *Motivation and personality* (3rd ed.). New York: Harper & Row. (Original work published 1954)

Matthiessen, F. O. (1947). *The James family: A group biography.* New York: Alfred A. Knopf.

McCosh, J. (1882). *The intuitions of the mind inductively investigated* (2nd ed.). New York: Carter. (Original work published 1860)

McDermott, J. J. (1986a). Spires of influence: The importance of Emerson for classical American philosophy. In *Streams of experience: Reflections on the history and philosophy of American culture* (pp. 29–43). Amherst: University of Massachusetts Press. (Original work published 1980)

McDermott, J. J. (1986b). The promethean self and community in the philosophy of William James. In *Streams of experience: Reflections on the history and philosophy of American culture* (pp. 44–58). Amherst: University of Massachusetts Press. (Original work published 1980)

Mead, G. H. (1934). *Mind, self, and society* (C. W. Morris, Ed.). Chicago: University of Chicago Press.

Mead, G. H. (1964). Cooley's contribution to American social thought. In A. Strauss (Ed.), *George Herbert Mead on social psychology: Selected papers* (pp. 293–307). Chicago: University of Chicago Press. (Original work published 1929–1930)

Morawski, J. G. (Ed.). (1988). *The rise of experimentation in American psychology.* New Haven, CT: Yale University Press.

Moseley, J. G. (1975). *The idea of self-transcendence in the theology of Henry James, Sr., and the novels of Henry James.* Missoula, MT: Scholars Press.

Murphy, G. (1947). *Personality: A biosocial approach to origins and structure.* New York: Harper & Brothers.

Murray, H. (Ed.). (1938). *Explorations in personality: A clinical and experimental study of fifty men of college age.* Oxford: Oxford University Press.

Myers. F. W. H. (1886). Human personality in the light of hypnotic suggestion. *Proceedings of the Society for Psychical Research* (English), *4*, 1–24.

Myers, G. E. (1986). Self. In *William James: His life and thought* (pp. 344–386). New Haven, CT: Yale University Press.

Natsoulas, T. (1983). The experience of a conscious self. *Journal of Mind and Behavior, 4,* 451–478.

O'Donnell, J. M. (1985). *The origins of behaviorism: American psychology, 1870–1920.* New York: New York University Press.

Osowski, J. V. (1986). *Metaphor and creativity: A case study of William James.* Unpublished doctoral dissertation, Rutgers University, Newark, NJ.

Peirce, C. (1966). Questions concerning certain faculties claimed for man. In *Selected writings* (P. P. Wiener, Ed.; pp. 15–38). New York: Dover. (Original work published 1868)

Perry, R. B. (1935). *The thought and character of William James* (Vols. 1–2). Boston: Little, Brown.

Perry, R. B. (1948). *The thought and character of William James: Briefer version.* Cambridge, MA: Harvard University Press.

Porter, N. (1868). *The human intellect: With an introduction upon psychology and the soul.* New York: Charles Scribner.

Richards, R. J. (1987). The personal equation in science: William James's psychological and moral uses of Darwinian theory. In *Darwin and the emergence of evolutionary theories of mind and behavior* (pp. 409–450). Chicago: University of Chicago Press.

Rogers, C. R. (1961). *On becoming a person.* Boston: Houghton Mifflin.

Ross, B. (1978). William James: A prime mover of the psychoanalytic movement in America. In G. E. Gifford, Jr. (Ed.), *Psychoanalysis, psychotherapy, and the New England medical scene* (pp. 10–23). New York: Science History Publications.

Royce, J. (1885). *The religious aspect of philosophy.* Boston: Houghton Mifflin.

Royce, J. (1916). The hope of the great community. In *The hope of the great community* (pp. 25–70). New York: Macmillan.

Sacks, O. (1984). *A leg to stand on.* New York: Harper & Row.

Sampson, E. E. (1985). The decentralization of identity: Toward a revised concept of personal and social order. *American Psychologist, 40,* 1203–1211.

Santayana, G. (1933). Locke and the frontiers of common sense. In *Some turns of thought in modern philosophy: Five essays* (pp. 1–47). New York: Charles Scribner's.

Sarbin, T. R., & McKechnie, G. E. (1986). Prospects for a contextualist theory of personality. In R. L. Rosnow & M. Georgoudi (Eds.), *Contextualism and understanding in behavioral science: Implications for research and theory* (pp. 187–207). New York: Praeger.

Sargent, E. (1869). *Planchette: Or the despair of science.* Boston: Roberts Brothers.

Scott, F. J. D. (Ed.). (1986). *William James: Selected unpublished correspondence, 1885–1910.* Columbus: Ohio State University Press.

Shea, J. J. (1973). The self in William James. *Philosophy Today, 17,* 319–327.

Singer, J. L. (1987). Private experience and public action: The study of ongoing conscious thought. In J. Aronoff, A. I. Rabin, & R. A. Zucker (Eds.), *The emergence of personality* (pp. 105–146). New York: Springer.

Singer, J. L., & Kolligian, J., Jr. (1987). Personality: Developments in the study of private experience. *Annual Review of Psychology, 38,* 533–574.

Smith, M. B. (1978). Perspectives on selfhood. *American Psychologist, 33,* 1053–1063.

Snyder, M., & Ickes, W. (1985). Personality and social behavior. In G. Lindzey & E. Aronson (Eds.), *The handbook of social psychology* (3d ed., Vol. 2, pp. 883–947). New York: Random House.

Spencer, H. (1855). *The principles of psychology.* London: Longman, Brown, Green, and Longmans.

Stagner, R. (1937). *Psychology of personality.* New York: McGraw-Hill.

Suckiel, E. K. (1982). *The pragmatic philosophy of William James.* Notre Dame, IN: University of Notre Dame Press.

Sullivan, H. S. (1953). *The interpersonal theory of psychiatry* (H. S. Perry & M. L. Gawel, Eds.). New York: W. W. Norton.

Suls, J. (Ed.). (1982). *Psychological perspectives on the self* (Vol. 1). Hillsdale, NJ: Lawrence Erlbaum Associates.

Taft, J. (1962). *The dynamics of therapy in a controlled relationship*. New York: Dover. (Original work published 1933)

Taine, H. (1875). *On intelligence* (T. D. Haye, Trans.). New York: Holt. (Original work published 1870)

Taylor, E. (1982a). *William James on exceptional mental states: The 1896 Lowell Lectures.* New York: Charles Scribner's Sons.

Taylor, E. (1982b). William James on psychopathology: The 1895 Lowell Lectures on "exceptional mental states." *Harvard Library Bulletin, 30,* 455–479.

Taylor, E. (1986). Swami Vivekananda and William James: Asian psychology at Harvard in the 1890s. *Prabuddha Bharata, 91,* 374–385.

Vygotsky, L. S. (1979). Consciousness as a problem in the psychology of behavior (M. Cole, Ed.). *Soviet Psychology, 17* (No.4), 3–35. (Original work published 1925)

Ward, J. (1883a). Psychological principles: I. The standpoint of psychology. *Mind, 8,* 153–169.

Ward, J. (1883b). Psychological principles: II. Fundamental facts and conceptions. *Mind, 8,* 465–486.

Ward, J. (1886). Psychology. *Encyclopedia Britannica* (9th ed.), *20,* 37–85.

Watson, J. B. (1916). Behavior and the concept of mental disease. *Journal of Philosophy, Psychology and Scientific Methods, 13,* 589–596.

Watson, J. B. (1963). *Behaviorism* (rev. ed.). Chicago: University of Chicago Press. (Original work published 1924)

Whitehead, A. N. (1938). *Modes of thought*. New York: Macmillan.

Wilshire, B. (1968). *William James and phenomenology: A study of "The Principles of Psychology".* Bloomington: Indiana University Press.

Wright, C. (1877). Evolution of self-consciousness. In *Philosophical discussions* (C. E. Norton, Ed.; pp. 199–266). New York: Holt. (Original work published 1873)

Wundt, W. M. (1894). *Lectures on human and animal psychology* (2nd ed.; J. E. Creighton & E. B. Titchener, Trans.). London: Swan Sonnenschein. (Original work published 1863–1864)

NOTES

[1]Actually, since James believed that all other psychological phenomena must be analyzed *out of* the primordial stream of experience, it would be more precise to say that James's psychology was *de*constructed *from*, rather than *con*structed *upon*, this stream. However, the use of "deconstruction" would probably confuse some contemporary readers, given recent uses of the term.

As regards the labeling of on-going mental life as either "the stream of thought" or "the stream of consciousness," suffice it to say that James used the first locution in his *Principles of Psychology* (1890/1983d) and the second in the later, abbreviated version of this work (1892/1984). He came to feel that the latter phrase was a more appropriate designation for the all-inclusive whole of mental life. However, he used the terms interchangeably, and they will be so used in this chapter.

[2]Indeed, the stream of thought or consciousness was so intimately and necessarily personal, from James's point of view, that he admitted in 1908 that "I still fail to see any great difference [between "our saying 'Self' or saying 'dynamic entirety of experience,' etc."], and 'Self' and 'Stream' seem to me but two names for the same facts." That being the case, he

said, "I fully admit that the term 'Self' should have the right of way" (letter to Mary Whiton Calkins, 1 February 1908, in Scott, 1986, p. 469). On the equation of "self" and "stream," see also James (1909/1977, p. 111).

[3]James did not fully appreciate the extent of Emerson's influence until he re-read Emerson's works in preparation for an address on the centenary of Emerson's birth (James, 1903/1982c). Regarding Emerson's influence on James, see McDermott (1980/1986a).

[4]Although he continued to distance himself publicly from his father's philosophical and theological positions, the impact of these positions on William's thought is apparent in William's introduction to his father's "literary remains" (see James, 1884/1982a). Regarding the personal crisis and theology of Henry James Sr., and his relation to his famous sons, see Matthiessen (1947, Bk. 1), Moseley (1975), and Perry (1935, Vol. 1, chap. 2). His basic theology is perhaps most succinctly conveyed in Henry James Sr. (1876).

[5]The resolution—or rather, the lifelong sustenance—of this paradoxical set of coordinates with respect to selfhood may have set the pattern for all of James's thought. At least, he tended in all aspects of his thought to seek novel positions that integrated or superseded, rather than selected from among, traditional dichotomies. In this case he learned since early childhood that the self was both central and ephemeral, both deeply personal and intimately related to others. As we shall see, these became vital tensions in his psychology of the self. As for his brother Henry, the following passage suggests a family-wide connoisseurship of the self-in-context:

> When you've lived as long as I you'll see that every human being has his shell and that you must take the shell into account. By the shell I mean the whole envelope of circumstances. There's no such thing as an isolated man or woman; we're each of us made up of some cluster of appurtenances. What shall we call our "self"? Where does it begin? Where does it end? It overflows into everything that belongs to us—and then it flows back again. I know a large part of myself is in the clothes I choose to wear. I've a great respect for *things*! One's self—for other people—is one's expression of one's self; and one's house, one's furniture, one's garments, the books one reads, the company one keeps—these things are all expressive [of the self]. (H. James, Jr., 1881/1963, p. 201)

It is relevant to note that Henry was not alone in bringing the novel to bear, more and more explicitly and exquisitely, upon the human self, especially the self in its social milieu. Among the contemporaries with whom he and William were quite familiar, were Balzac, Dickens, G. Eliot, Howells, Flaubert, Tolstoy, and Zola, to name only a few.

[6]Regarding the transition of psychology from a philosophical to a scientific discipline, see Albrecht (1960), Evans (1984), Leary (1987), Morawski (1988), and O'Donnell (1985). The literature on the transition to a more clinically oriented discipline, especially in reference to the development of William James's thought, is much less satisfactory. Eugene Taylor (1982a, 1982b, chap. 2 in this volume) is among those currently addressing this shortcoming. In the meantime, some of the relevant background can be derived from Burnham (1967), Gifford (1978), Hale (1971a, 1971b), Marx (1968), and Ross (1978), and from Ellenberger's (1970) treatment of Janet (chap. 6). The history of psychical research, which I have discussed elsewhere (Leary, 1980b), is also relevant to this historical topic.

[7]It is not by chance that two of the three longest chapters in *The Principles of Psychology* (1890/1983d) are the chapters on "The Consciousness of Self" (101 pages) and "Will" (96 pages). The longest chapter is James's technical and detailed discussion of "The Perception of Space" (137 pages), the topic on which he had cut his scientific teeth many years before (James, 1879/1983a). All other chapters average 37 pages in length, with the fourth longest being the concluding chapter, "Necessary Truths and the Effects of Experience" (66 pages). In the abbreviated version of the *Principles* (James, 1892/1984), "Will" (37 pages) and "Self" (33 pages) are the longest chapters, and "The Perception of Space" is exactly average in length (13 pages), as compared to all the other chapters.

[8]To James, these works by Ward, Royce, Dewey, and Ladd all reflected, so far as their anal-

yses of the self was concerned, a misplaced commitment to idealist and quasi-idealist modes of thought. Even Dewey (1887/1967), after seeming to move toward a rejection of absolute self-consciousness (Dewey, 1886/1969), "sorely disappointed" James by "trying to mediate between the bare miraculous self and the concrete particulars of individual mental lives." "It's no use," James said; such an approach merely takes "all the edge and definiteness away from the particulars" (letter to G. Croom Robertson, ca. 1887, in Perry, 1935, Vol. 2, p. 516). James wrote this as he worked on his own chapter on the self. Dewey (1887/1967), by the way, defined psychology as "the science of the facts or phenomena of self" (p. 7). No matter how "introspective" or how "objective" its methods, he said, "the ultimate appeal [of psychology] is to self-consciousness" (p. 16). Regarding James's reflections on Royce, Dewey, and Ward, see Perry (1935, Vol. 1, chap. 50, Vol. 2, chaps. 81 & 88, respectively). Royce's views on the self are more fully treated in Cotton (1954). As a close friend, Harvard colleague, and philosophical opponent, Royce served, through his critique of "the detached individual" and his repeated call for "loyalty, the devotion of the self to the interests of the community" (see, e.g., Royce, 1916), to keep James mindful of the social relations of the self. For critical reviews of Dewey's (1887/1967) and Ladd's (1887) doctrines of the self, by a former student of James who was similarly bothered by their idealist nature, see Hall (1888). Ladd's later (1918) work on personality revealed little movement away from his earlier idealism, whereas Dewey (1922/1983) progressively transformed his absolute idealism into what might be called a social naturalism: Individual conduct, like the individual self, is necessarily social in nature, according to the later Dewey. Altogether, the general legacy of the idealist approach to the self is obvious: It reinforced the theme of the social relations of the self, the same theme emphasized earlier by Henry James Sr. (1876) and elaborated later by George Herbert Mead (1934). One of James's contributions, foreshadowing Mead, was to emphasize the *empirical* nature and *temporal* development of the self's social relations.

[9]The following discussion is based on Chapter 10, "The Consciousness of Self," in James (1890/1983d). For clarity's sake, however, I will occasionally use terms from Chapter 12, "The Self," in James's (1892/1984) abbreviated textbook. For example, "the self as knower" and "the self as known" are phrases from the latter work. In no instance, however, do the terms I have borrowed from the *Briefer Course* change James's original meaning.

[10]Although James (1890/1983d) admitted that "what I say [in this regard] will be likely to meet with opposition if generalized (as indeed it may be in part inapplicable to other individuals)" (p. 286), he reported that his own introspection revealed that the "constant play of furtherances and hindrances in my thinking" is always accompanied by *"some bodily process, for the most part taking place within the head,"* whereas *"it is difficult for me to detect in the activity any purely spiritual element at all"* (pp. 286–287). Thus,

> in one person at least, *the 'Self of selves,' when carefully examined, is found to consist mainly of the collection of these peculiar motions in the head or between the head and throat.* I do not for a moment say that this is *all* it consists of. . . . But I feel quite sure that these cephalic motions are the portions of my innermost activity of which I am *most distinctly aware*. If the dim portions which I cannot yet define should prove to be like unto these distinct portions in me, and I like other men, *it would follow that our entire feeling of spiritual activity, or what commonly passes by that name, is really a feeling of bodily activities whose exact nature is by most men overlooked.* (p. 288)

This sensitivity to the physical dimensions of subjectivity was highly refined in James, so much so that his own personal sense of self was intimately related to physical manifestations. For instance, in a letter to his wife soon after their marriage in 1878, James wrote:

> I have often thought that the best way to define a man's character would be to seek out the particular mental or moral attitude in which, when it came upon him, he felt himself most deeply and intensely active and alive. At such moments there is a voice inside which speaks and says: *"This* is the real me!" . . . This characteristic attitude in me al-

ways involves an element of active tension, of holding my own, as it were . . . which translates itself physically by a kind of stinging pain inside my breast-bone (don't smile at this—it is to me an essential element of the whole thing!), and which, although it is a mere mood or emotion to which I can give no form in words, authenticates itself to me as the deepest principle of all active and theoretic determination which I possess. (in H. James, III, 1920, Vol. 1, pp. 199–200)

It is interesting to note that the word "sting" and the epithet "stingless" were often used by James. It is also important to underline the fact that James did not wish to *reduce* subjectivity to its physical correlates, although he sometimes seemed close to doing so. "Over and above these [cephalic movements]," James (1890/1983d) noted, "there is an obscurer feeling of something more" (p. 292). Although he did not discuss this "obscurer feeling" in the *Principles*, he addressed the "something more," with particular reference to nature of the self, in his later work, as we shall see.

[11]Actually, James questioned the nature and existence of "consciousness" as a distinctive ontological *state*, as opposed to a "merely" cognitive *function*, many years before the publication of the *Principles*, and he shared his questions with his students in the 1880s and 1890s, well before giving formal expression to his thoughts in James (1904/1976a).

[12]As regards James's equation of *thought* and *thinker*, about which a lot of ink has been spilled, it should be noted that this formula is simply a different way of expressing James's original, fundamental premise that consciousness (thought) is first and foremost personal (self-ish) in nature. As he told Mary Whiton Calkins in 1908, "self" is merely a different—and better—term for the stream of thought or consciousness (see footnote 2). Self, on this account, is *implicit* within psychological phenomena. If this somewhat indirect voucher for the self makes self more a *quality experienced* than a *substance known*, that seems to be what James intended, at least as regards the empirical self. Just as "the question 'what is *the* truth?' is no real question" because "the whole notion of *the* truth is an abstraction from the fact of truths in the plural, a mere useful summarizing phrase like *the* Latin Language or *the* Law" (-James, 1907/1975b, pp. 115–116), so too *the* self is simply a general name (James implied) for a variety of personal experiences. This approach to the self is certainly in keeping with James's pluralism and pragmatism. The key question about the self, as about anything else, for the pragmatist is not "what?" but "so what?" To the "so what?" question, James's answer was expressed most succinctly by the list of self-referent and self-originating thoughts, emotions, and behaviors discussed in the *Principles*: self-feeling, self-seeking, and self-love, which are bound up with selectivity, interest, effort, attention, and will. An elaboration of these various terms and processes must be left to other chapters and occasions, but it is relevant to note that they constitute the teleological purpose, final cause, or *raison d'être* of the self.

As regards the need for the self or ego to *create* thoughts by unifying supposedly elemental, discrete, and disparate ideas, James was skeptical from at least the early 1880s. In an important article in 1884, in which he argued for the a priori continuity and connectedness of the stream of consciousness, James (1884/1983b) pointed out that "there is no need of an agent [i.e., an ego] to relate together what never was separate" (p. 167). However, he did feel, even then, that the self or ego was a central feature of the on-going stream of consciousness: How are *your* feelings "cognized" by me different from *my* feelings "cognized" by me? My own feelings are characterized, said James, by "a difference of intimacy, of warmth, of continuity, similar to the difference between a sense-perception and something merely imagined—which seems to point to a special *content* in each several stream of consciousness, for which Ego is perhaps the best specific name" (p. 167).

[13]As is well known, the stream of consciousness would become the "pure experience" of James's later philosophy (see, e.g., James, 1912/1976b, pp. 21–44). From this "neutral stuff," James maintained, both the subjective and objective dimensions of experience are extracted by the analytic mind. The fact that James took the self to be a fundamental category of reality is reflected in his statement that "the great continua of time, space, and the self envelope every-

thing, betwixt them, and flow together without interfering" (p. 46). As regards James's philosophy, Suckiel's (1982) critical review reveals that "the teleological subject—with his needs, desires, and interests—plays an indisputably central role in determining the character of the pragmatic world-view" (p. 14).

[14]The foregoing account of James's views on the self, drawing primarily on his chapter on "The Consciousness of Self," inadequately conveys his convictions regarding the relevance of *willing* and *choosing*—of making decisions—in the development of the self. As James (1890/ 1983d) noted in the preceding chapter of the *Principles*, when someone decides to commit a crime, choose a profession, accept an office, or marry a particular person—in a word, when someone has to "choose which *interest* out of several, equally coercive, shall become supreme," the decision is actually between "several equally possible future Characters" or "selves" (p. 276; see also James, 1878/1988a, p. 27). A decision, once made, begins to establish habits that eventually come to rule the day:

> Whether a young man enters business or the ministry may depend on a decision which has to be made before a certain day. He takes the place offered in the counting-house, and is *committed*. Little by little, the habits, the knowledges, of the other career, which once lay so near, cease to be reckoned even among his possibilities. At first, he may sometimes doubt whether the self he murdered in that decisive hour might not have been the better of the two; but with the years such questions themselves expire, and the old alternative *ego*, once so vivid, fades into something less substantial than a dream. (James, 1880/1979a, p. 171)

Substitute a decision between art and science for the one between business and the ministry in this passage, and the autobiographical foundations of James's comments are unmistakable. Regarding James's ideal of "the strenuous life," the life that continually reaches for the "higher interest" and the "morally good," see Browning (1975, 1980).

[15]James's students in the 1890s included many who were influenced by his views on consciousness and the self—for instance, Mary Whiton Calkins, later to be an active proponent and leader in "self-psychology," Gertrude Stein, who was to use stream-of-consciousness and other Jamesian techniques and insights in her literary writing, and W. E. B. Du Bois, whose famous investigations of "black consciousness" followed from James's belief that differences in individual consciousness (and by extension, group consciousness) are worthy of attention and admiration. Among the activities associated with James's seminars were trips to asylums to observe mental patients, and there is little doubt that many of his students were exposed to exhibitions of the trance states and other phenomena associated with mediums. It is also relevant to note that James (1894/1987a) took very early note of Josef Breuer and Sigmund Freud's pioneering work on hysteria, and that some of James's students—for instance, Edmund B. Delabarre—followed his example in experimenting with chemically induced altered states of consciousness. James's psychological seminars of 1895–1896 and 1897–1898 are particularly worthy of mention because of their focus on the self (see James, 1895–1896/1988b, 1897–1898/1988c). So too is his 1890 seminar in which, according to her own (1930) recollection, Mary Whiton Calkins received her introduction to psychology while sitting "at either side of a library fire" with the author of the just-published *Principles of Psychology* (p. 31).

[16]James's use of "*exceptional* mental states" rather than "*abnormal* mental states" reflects his Darwinian belief that individual variation is a simple fact of nature. (On James's "darwinizing" of psychology, see Richards, 1987.) Judgments about whether or not such variations are "good" should depend, James thought, not on comparisons to some "norm," statistical or otherwise, but on the practical results or fruits of these variations. The same welcoming attitude toward individual differences underlies James's analysis of religious personalities (James, 1902/1985), his criticism of our typical "blindness" to the dignity and worth of strangers (James, 1899/1983g), and his thoughts on what makes life significant (James, 1899/1983h). As regards the misuse of diagnostic labels, James (1895/1987b) noted that writers on pathology tend to "use the descriptive names of symptoms merely as an artifice for giving objective au-

thority to their personal dislikes. The medical terms become mere 'appreciative' clubs to knock men down with" (p. 513).

[17]Regarding the history of the study of personality, reaching all the way back to the ancient Greeks, see Burnham (1968). It is interesting to note that Burnham's discussion of James (pp. 63–64), written from the perspective of the study of personality in the 1960s, emphasizes James's treatment of instinct and habit rather than his focus on the self. The self was just beginning to come back into vogue as a subject of psychological research in the 1960s. It is also worth noting that the historical figures reviewed in Burnham's chapter rarely used the word "personality" in their study of factors that are relevant to the 20th-century study of personality. As James himself (1895/1983e) pointed out, both "person" and "personality" were primarily theological and juridical terms prior to the 20th century. It was, by and large, clinical researchers in France and psychical researchers in Britain and the United States who pioneered the use of "personality" in its contemporary psychological meaning, first using the term with reference to multiple personality and later, by reduction, to singular personality. The old theological meaning of "personality" was still very evident in such works as Dewey (1887/1967) and Ladd (1918). The one, true Personality, of course, was taken to be God. Individual selves were understood as mere reflections of, and subservient to, this infinite ideal (see, e.g., the conclusion of Dewey's work and the subtitle of Ladd's). The more traditional conceptual categories for dealing with personal styles of thought, feeling, and behavior were "character" and "temperament." James's (1890/1983d) call for individuals to establish good habits (chap. 4) was definitely related to his concern about the former, and his awareness of the role of what he called instincts (chap. 24) was not unrelated to traditional treatments of the latter. Clearly, the conceptual context of James's thought on the self and personality was more complex than I have been able to convey in this chapter. For some of the historical background on "character" and "temperament," written from the perspective of James's time, see Jastrow (1915).

[18]James more clearly acknowledged the novelty and contours of recent psychological investigations of "personality" in his (1898/1983f) introduction to Boris Sidis's *Psychology of Suggestion*:

> The meaning of personality with its limits and its laws, forms a problem which until quite recently had to be discussed almost exclusively by logical and metaphysical methods. Within the past dozen years, however, an immense amount of new empirical material has been injected into the question by the observations which the "recognition" by science of the hypnotic state set in motion. Many of these observations are pathological: fixed ideas, hysteric attacks, insane delusions, mediumistic phenomena, etc. And altogether, although they are far from having solved the problem of personality, they must be admitted to have transformed its outward shape. What are the limits of the consciousness of a human being? Is "self" consciousness only a part of the whole consciousness? Are there many "selves" dissociated from one another? What is the medium of synthesis in a group of associated ideas? How can certain systems of ideas be cut off and forgotten? Is personality a product, and not a principle? Such are the questions now being forced to the front—questions now asked for the first time with some sense of their concrete import, and questions which it will require a great amount of further work, both of observation and of analysis, to answer adequately. (pp. 325–326)

[19]In such a brief treatment, I have not very adequately explained James's (1909/1986b) belief that "there is a continuum of cosmic consciousness, against which our individuality builds but accidental fences, and into which our several minds plunge as into a mother-sea or reservoir" (p. 374), and I have not even begun to discuss James's related ideas regarding an alternative mode of conceptualizing brain function—as being "permissive" or "transmissive" rather than "productive" with respect to consciousness or thought (see James, 1898/1982b). Regarding these and other matters pertaining to the "wider self" and its implications, see Fontinell (1986). Finally, it is interesting to note that James's teen-age interest in "going out into the country, into the dear old woods and fields and ponds" (Perry, 1948, p. 53) is reflected in his

late-life metaphoric imagery for consciousness and the self. The metaphors James used, like those used by others, were not merely random (see Leary, 1990; Osowski, 1986).

[20]Watson's "rejection" of Freud followed the same basic plot—what was barred entry at the front door was admitted without much ado through the back door (see, e.g., Watson, 1916).

[21]It is interesting to note that in 1947 one of Allport's main competitors for this distinction, Gardner Murphy, also published a pioneering textbook on personality in which the self received focal attention. Clearly, Jamesians are prone to be interested in the self and personality.

[22]Interestingly, the first edition of Locke's major work, *An Essay Concerning Human Understanding* (1690/1959), appeared exactly 200 years before James's masterpiece, *The Principles of Psychology* (1890/1983d).

[23]James acknowledged Locke's priority and influence in this regard. In fact, James referred to Locke's analysis of "personal identity" as the first and exemplary instance of the application of the pragmatic method (see James, 1898/1975a), and in the margins of his own copy of Locke's *Essay*, James reiterated his debt by writing "practicalism" next to a passage in which Locke claims that it does not really matter of what kind of substance the self is composed (see Burkhardt, 1981, p. 1347). Regarding Locke's concerns about conduct or morality, which he (1690/1959) considered *"the proper science and business of mankind"* (Vol. 2, p. 351), see Leary (1980a). It is interesting to note that both Locke and James were motivated by a desire to resolve problems having to do with religion and morality (see Locke, 1690/1959, Vol. 1, pp. xvi–xvii).

Chapter 6

William James and Habit: A Century Later

John C. Malone Jr.

University of Tennessee

> But what is the use of being a genius, unless *with the same scientific evidence as other men*, one can reach more truth than they? (James, 1962a, p. 168)

Many writers have praised James for the great influence he had on the psychology of his time and on subsequent developments. The *Principles* was a masterpiece and it remains so today. But virtually nothing in it was original; all of the ideas that we normally attribute to James, from the stream of consciousness to ideo-motor action to his analysis of the self were taken from the writings of others, both predecessors and contemporaries. In most cases he acknowledged those from whom he borrowed, although David Hume's (1739) contribution to James's description of the spiritual self is an exception.

The book admirably presented much of what was known of psychology at that time but it *was* highly selective. There is virtually no coverage of the "New Psychology" of Wundt and Titchener and the reader who searches for research results or for data of any kind will not find much. Where coverage of experimental work had to be included, as in Chapter 17 (Sensation), we find James relying on a ghostwriter, so that 14 pages come " . . . from the pen of my friend and pupil Mr. E. B. Delabarre" (II: 13).

Research and data were of little interest to James throughout his career; and this book, like his other works, was confined to his perceptive analyses of what were commonly considered the interesting phenomena of psychology. This was very different from other texts of the late 19th century. For example, Bain's *The Senses and the Intellect* appeared in four editions from 1855 to 1879 and was so filled with data and "hard facts" that one wonders that anyone could be so diligent as to compile it all. Bain's final (1879) edition retained all of the "facts" and added a very long appendix, "The Psychology of Aristotle."

Letters collected by Perry (1935) well expressed James's dislike for experimental research and showed that he doubted that he could conduct it. He could not "torture his brain to devise new varieties of insipidity for publication . . . I was bowed down with weight of woe that I couldn't invent original investigations" (Perry, 1935, p. 116). He found texts that did stress experimental findings to be tedious: "Tedious not as really hard things, like physics and chemistry, are tedious, but tedious as the throwing of feathers hour after hour is tedious" (p. 119).

WHY WAS *THE PRINCIPLES* SO INFLUENTIAL?

According to the Social Sciences Citation Index, James was cited 255 times in 1987; 99 of these cited *The Principles*. If James presented little data and if his interpretations of phenomena were not original, why did his work, rather than Bain's, exert such influence? It is almost surely James's unique point of view that makes the book as timeless as it is and that offers valuable lessons to those of us living and working a century after the publication of his masterpiece.

In August of 1890 James included the following in his preface:

> This book consequently rejects both the associationist and the spiritualist theories; and in this strictly positivistic point of view consists the only feature of it for which I feel tempted to claim originality.

In the preface to the later Italian translation he wrote:

> We live at a time of transition and confusion in psychology as in many other things. The classic spiritualistic psychology using the soul and a definite number of distinct ready-made faculties as its principles of explanation, was long ago superceded by the school of association. But it still lingers . . . the older associationism itself retained a half scholastic character . . . it took the mind too statically . . . (Perry, 1935, p. 52)

Both of these theories appear frequently in the book and, despite occasional praise for one or the other, neither is judged acceptable.

The associationist theory to which he referred had been handed down from Aristotle (as a theory of memory) through the British empiricists to John Stuart Mill and Helmholtz as a theory of mind. It assumed that experience is comprised of "simple ideas," elements that were often thought of as sensations and that were assumed in advance. Its most common expression was the crude "mental mechanics" of James Mill and this was the version most frequently attacked by the Gestaltists and others who later criticized what they believed to be the view of Wundt and Titchener. James could not reject associationism outright, no more than anyone can. His version is presented in his Chapter 14; it does not rely on combinations of simple elements and is therefore not "associationism," as the term is ordinarily understood. It is similar to Wundt's interpretation (e.g., Wundt, 1907). The historical alternative to associationism was the "spiritualist" theory. This was also called the "soul" or "mind" theory, exemplified by philosophers from Descartes through Kant and later writers who posited an ego or "knower" that possesses faculties and powers that make experience possible. Wundt discussed and dismissed the same two historical choices.

These two alternatives both provided explanations, although often poor ones. For *practical* purposes associationism is difficult to beat. The textbooks of the 19th century were full of good advice on the application of simple associationist methods for changing habits, training morality, and more. Simple associationism can also account for memory, perception, foresight, knowledge, hallucinations, deja vu, belief, and anything else we might want to explain, as long as we are not too demanding. The main problem with associationism is that the elements into which experience is divided do not seem natural and it is difficult to see how they can be sufficient to account for all of our experience.

The spiritualist/faculty theory usually included associationism and added powers that ordinary people found congenial; do we not differ in our "powers" of memory, reasoning, perception, and attention? James cited A. Lange, who charged that the spiritualist theory, in the form of phrenology, did not divide experience into elements, as did the associationists, but divides it into individual personal beings "of a peculiar character." The problem with the spiritualist theory was illustrated by Lange in a way reminiscent of Skinner's (1964) argument against "inner man":

'Herr Pastor, sure there be a horse inside,' called out the peasants to X after their spiritual shepherd had spent hours in explaining to them the construction of the locomotive. With a horse inside truly everything becomes clear, even though it be a queer enough sort of horse—the horse itself calls for no explanation! (I: 29)

It would be a comfort to believe that these truly poor alternatives, popular only because of their comprehensibility by the masses, had been replaced during the past century. Sadly, were he alive today and made aware of our progress since his time, James would be depressed, as he often was during his lifetime. He would see that the history of psychology during this century has been largely a succession of incarnations of the spiritualist and associationist theories, usually simultaneously present as alternatives, just as they were in his day. From time to time alternatives have been proposed to the poor choices James described and rejected. Although some have and do enjoy some recognition, some version of the spiritualist/faculty or the associationist theories invariably arises and becomes popular for a time; then another edition of one of the two theories replaces it. This endless sequence is evident in many areas of psychology, including cognitive psychology, learning and biological psychology, as well as social and abnormal psychology. James's "positivistic" point of view, devoid of research and data as it is, may at least remind us that it is profitable to look at phenomena in terms other than those provided by his (and our) two poor choices in their various guises. The associationist theory has proven especially durable, often appearing as "habit theory."

Habit is usually viewed as a defining characteristic of behavioral learning theories, but we will see that it actually also characterizes popular cognitive models. This applies to the information-processing models that were recently popular as well as to current connectionist models. Although James would have disapproved of these models, as he disapproved of simple associationism, he would have preferred even them to a monster that owes its existence to the appeal of popular psychology. This includes, of course, the social cognitive theory of Bandura (e.g., 1986). Bandura combines the caricatures of the two alternatives that James rejected, creating a product that is extremely appealing to those whose knowledge of psychology is superficial (Malone, 1987). While this (and other) popular treatments prosper, the "positivistic" view that James preferred to the poor alternatives remains as neglected as it was in his time.

Before considering the history of associationism/habit, it is instructive to examine James's treatment. It will be clear that little was original in his original Chapter 4 *and* in the rest of the *Principles*. Its influence must owe, therefore, to James's constant attention to phenomena and to his rejection of the two traditional interpretations.

ON ORIGINALITY

James honestly began the *Principles* by confessing that he could not claim any originality, aside from the aforementioned "positivistic point of view." This, and his engaging writing style, may indeed be all that was original. Aside from the countless lines of acknowledged direct quotations that fill the book, we find that all of the points that have become synonymous with his name were indeed borrowed from other writers.

For example, his emphasis on the experiencing of "feelings of relation" (Chapter 9) was borrowed from Herbert Spencer, whom James strenuously criticized, yet quoted more often than any other source. The "specious present" (Chapter 15) came from the writings of E. R. Clay, whereas "ideomotor action" (Chapter 26) was a term in common use during the latter half of the 19th century (e.g., by Renouvier and by Lotze). Alexander Bain (1879) treated the volitional power of ideas as did James, although he did not use the term "ideo-motor action."

The characterization of the mental state as a unity and the concept of the fringe of consciousness came from a "Mr. Wills" and seems very similar to John Stuart Mill's (1865) view of reality as the permanent possibility of sensation. Finally, James's long and seemingly sincere analysis of the spiritual self, or "self of selves," almost perfectly parallels (mirrors, follows, shadows) Hume's (1739) similar effort in his "Treatise of Human Nature."[1] And of course, James relied on his "friend and pupil," Mr. E. B. Delabarre, for 14 pages of text discussing the Law of Contrast and the Hering-Helmholtz debate.[2]

JAMES'S CHAPTER 4: HABIT

This was a chapter where it would have been most difficult for James to have been original, even if that were his aim. He called it: "A mere pot-boiler, which I had long had, written, in my drawer. No new thing in it, so I hardly advise you to read it" (Perry, 1935, p. 90). Habit amounts to the law of association by contiguity and, if there were another principle in psychology that could claim similar ancient origin, it would have to be the principle of self actualization (as presented by Aristotle) or the soul theory of Democritus and Plato. But habit is the *great law*, true and beyond doubt, with the only dispute concerning the limits of its application. By the 19th century it was clear that history repeats itself, so to speak, that our acts recur as do our thoughts and that this fact allows us to understand our actions and our experience better than can any other single principle. We will return to the importance of this later.

James's actual chapter was an entertaining and persuasive version of points made by Alexander Bain in his classic *The Senses and the Intellect* (1879) and by W. B. Carpenter in another classic, *Principles of Mental Physiology* (1876). The main points of James's chapter echo from these sources and from an amusing piece in the *Andover Review* (1887) by Miss Vida Scudder. The main points in the chapter follow.

---

[1]James proposed that the "self of selves" may be no more than sensations, particularly those accompanying motor activity, while Hume referred to sensations in general. Hume's analysis was discussed 50 pages later, as if unrelated to James's proposal.

[2]Interestingly, E. B. Delabarre was also mentioned by E. L. Thorndike when describing his 1894–1896 period at Harvard and his thwarted intentions to study mindreading in children (Joncich, 1968). More interesting still, E. B. Delabarre was also mentioned by Skinner (1938). He assisted Skinner in attempts to demonstrate operant conditioning of vasoconstriction in the forearms of human subjects. This must have been at least 40 years after Delabarre's service for James.

1. Living creatures are literally "bundles of habits," a term used by Carpenter, who, like James, interpreted both instinct and reason as instances of habit.

2. The laws of physical nature may also be viewed as habits, an interpretation that was strongly criticized by many of James's readers (Perry, 1935). However, it was a view with which Carpenter concurred.

3. The above assumption leads naturally to the view that the brain is an organ of habit, in which currents passing in and out leave their mark, rearranging and deepening channels, forming the physical basis for retention of habits. Bain had particularly emphasized this theory.

4. Experience thus "molds the brain," which grows according to the mode in which "it is exercised": "La fonction fait l'organe." This occurs more rapidly in the young, since it depends on nutrition, change, and growth. This argument was made especially strongly by Carpenter.

5. Given a stock of habits, we think, feel, and do what we thought, felt, and did the last time the situation was encountered. The practical effect is to diminish the conscious attention necessary to perform all of the routine activities of life, a point also emphasized by Carpenter and Bain.

6. It follows that we should acquire a stock of as many good habits as is possible and James repeated Bain's advice for doing that: start at once, allow no exceptions, and so on.

7. But James emphasized more than did others the importance of *action* in the establishment of habits. As the path to hell is paved with good intentions, dispositions and sentiments are in themselves valueless. As James (1890) wrote:

> There is no more contemptible type of human character than that of the nerveless sentimentalist and dreamer, who spends his life in a weltering sea of sensibility and emotion, but who never does a manly concrete deed. Rousseau, inflaming all the mothers of France, by his eloquence, to follow nature and nurse their babies themselves, while he sends his own children to the foundling hospital, is the classical example of what I mean. . . . The habit of excessive novel-reading and theatre-going will produce true monsters in this line. (I: 125)

By this James meant that novels and the theatre present pure and abstract models of good, evil, pitiful, beautiful, enraging, and other things that should arouse concrete action. But they do not, and the "monsters" thus created are spectators who are accustomed to consider such things only in the abstract and to do nothing about them. It follows that everyday examples of such things will likely not be recognized as such and, if recognized, will lead to no action because that has been the habitual response.

Music plays a similar role, as discussed by Miss Scudder, who was clearly upset with the popularity of symphonies and other concerts. While listening to music, one experiences various emotions without acting on them, an effect that must affect everyday moral behavior. While Miss Scudder could see no solution to the problem, James suggested that emotion felt while listening to music be purposely acted on in *some* way, even if it be expressed in kind words or the giving up of one's seat in a public vehicle.

8. Finally, as did Bain and, especially, Carpenter, James believed that attention is affected by habit. This is of extreme importance, of course, because attention is the key element in the operation of the ideo-motor theory of volition, or will. All three men believed that attention determines what ideas are apt to gain the upper hand and that those ideas that do prevail determine what we do or do not do. As Carpenter suggested, strength of will (attention) depends on exercise and he pointed to the drills that made the British solider the very model of self discipline.

Unlike James, Carpenter believed that improvement of the will and of the intellect in general through the cultivation of proper habits could be passed on to our children and our efforts thus benefit the future of the race! Also unlike James, both Bain and Carpenter were strong believers in hedonism and reference to pleasure and pain occur frequently in their writings. It is to James's credit that he repudiated hedonism, but he did it largely in Chapter 26 (Will).

Related Chapters

Since habit is just another name for the law of association by contiguity, it appears in some form in every chapter of the *Principles*. However, several chapters consider issues closely related to habit and are typically dismissed as unimportant and uninteresting.

For example, Chapter 3, "On Some General Conditions of Brain-Activity," might have been an amplifying of the simple connectionist model that often appears in other chapters. James *did* often refer to the forming of pathways and the firing of chains of connected neurons. But the "general conditions" to which he referred in this chapter concern the opposite, the *failure* of neurons to fire!

This includes discussion of the summation of subliminal stimuli, in which repeated applications of stimuli that apparently have no effect, sum to produce an effect, and of reaction-time experiments. The latter concerned procedures that ostensibly measured mental processes by comparing reaction times in simpler and progressively more complicated tasks. This method was much later named "mental chronometry" and was first used by the Viennese physiologist Exner. Interestingly, Exner noted the same flaw in the method that James pointed out and that led to its abandoning at the beginning of the 20th century. That is, it was clear that the "mental work" that was supposed to be occurring during the period from the presentation of the problem to the subject's response largely occurred before the actual problem was presented. It was the corroboration of this by Kulpe and his colleagues at Würzburg that led to the demise of the "subtractive procedure" until its resurrection in the 1960s.

James's Chapter 23, "The Production of Movement" is also closely related to the nature of habit and is also typically ignored. The point of the chapter is that stimuli acting on us, whether they originate externally or internally, produce "movement of the whole organism." Bain called this the "law of diffusion" and it means that habit is not characterized as the activity of individual S-R or other units. The body acts as an "organic sounding board," a belief clearly evident in James's interpretation of the experience of emotion as a bodily and not purely mental event.

It is also clear that later psychologists who emphasized the importance of habit were influenced by this view. John B. Watson (e.g., 1919) interpreted all psychological phenomena as habit and also repeatedly emphasized that it is always the whole organism that reacts. Pavlov and other Russian physiologists and psychologists have long accepted this fact and it is (belatedly) now recognized by researchers in behavioral medicine (e.g., Ader & Cohen, 1982).

Finally, James's Chapter 5, "The Automaton Theory," presents the powerful argument for the sufficiency of habit embodied in physical mechanism and the superfluity of mind and consciousness. Given the adaptive/ intelligent activity of unconscious spinal reflexes and of the brain stem mechanisms controlling the viscera, isn't it possible that similar reflex (habit) mechanisms account for all of our activity, including that which we call acts of reason? Continuity can work both ways and it is possible to treat the spinal cord as intelligent, since it does intelligent things. Or, since it operates habitually (or mechanically), does reason operate habitually?

This led James to his famous defense of ideas as causes of activity and what amounts to a recasting of the problem of mind/reason versus mechanism/habit. In a "positivistic solution," James suggests that the contiguity of ideas and actions in time suggests causal efficacy for ideas, a position that could be construed as applying Descartes's interactionist solution to the mind-body problem. *Or*, as I prefer, it could be viewed as an appeal for a phenomenal approach: Ideas and physical movements often go together, so we may say that the first "causes" the second.

This implies that mental and physical activity fall into the same category, a view held by many behaviorists, from Thorndike to Watson, to Guthrie, to Skinner. The objection that "mental things cannot cause physical change" is irrelevant to these behaviorists, who did not believe in the usefulness of the mental/physical distinction and it was handled admirably by James. Referring to Messier, who had ridiculed the possibility that "thoughts could affect molecules," James pointed out that since Hume and Kant we have realized that we will never understand *material* causation. How can one object to mental causation, yet treat physical causation as completely understandable, as if Hume and Kant had never been born?

HABIT'S HISTORY: FROM MEMORY TO MIND

The history of habit is actually the history of associationism, especially association by contiguity in time and space. Aristotle is often referred to as the first "real associationist." This is hardly appropriate, since his references to association refer only to its effect in recall. But he was no more an associationist (habitist) than was Pavlov; in neither case was the simple fact of association/habit one of the most important aspects of their point of view. No one denies the bare fact of habit, in memory and in behavior, and everyone who refers to association is not an associationist. In Aristotle's case, so little is known of his message in *de Anima* that his reference to the "white patch" that is interpreted as "the son of Diares" is part of the little that most readers understand. "Ah, he was an associationist," the reader concludes, and misses completely the dialectic that was Aristotle's real point (cf. Holt, 1915).

Descartes's machine is often pointed to as a clear example of "habit theory," it was built of innate habit systems and could acquire new habits (as memories). But it was a dead machine, animated only by the magic of the soul. True, the machine could operate independently of the soul to some extent, but it typically did not. No one can read Descartes (1650) without seeing that he incorporated both of James's terrible alternatives—a mechanism of inherited and acquired habits and a soul with faculties to drive it.

The same could be said of Hobbes and Locke, both of whom emphasized mental habit much more than did Descartes and both of whom (of course) de-emphasized the inherited habits of Descartes. But both were more similar to him than to the later associationists, who built everything out of habit. Both Locke and Hobbes viewed us as copiers of an objective world sequence that chugged by and left its imprint on us. Locke's version was far more sophisticated and influential, but even it assumed that experience consists of the taking in of particles given off by objects of the world (Locke, 1700). The "simple ideas" thus arising were then transformed by every faculty one could imagine, as the "reflection" that led to derived ideas. In fact, this process only *seems* less repugnant than Descartes's "soul"; its workings were equally magical, even though its raw materials all came through the senses.

Real associationism, the placing of complete reliance on habit, came only with Berkeley and Hume. Their views may be treated as identical, despite the difference in their interpretation of the role of God. Although the question of God's existence and influence is certainly important, it is of no great consequence in this brief history of habit. Hume merely went a short step further than Berkeley in explaining the *self* as an instance of habitual groups of sensations, a conclusion that any reader of Berkeley could hardly have failed to consider.

Both of these men had the genius to see that psychology was perfectly capable of existing without philosophy, or at least, philosophy as meta-physics. Following Hobbes and Locke, habitual sensory experiences are per-fectly capable of explaining all of our experience, as well as that of the physical world; the latter is no more than habitual clumps and series of sen-sory experiences . . . habits of mind, so to speak.

This extremely sophisticated conclusion will never be *really* appreciated or understood by most people, even educated ones, although many can speak in such a way that it appears that they understand. John Stuart Mill ad Helmholtz carried empiricism/associationism/habit to the highest level of sophistication and their arguments and interpretations are still consid-ered stock aspects of current theory in sensation and perception (see Hoch-berg, 1979).

The chief accomplishment of this highest level of "Berkeleian associa-tionism" appears in J. S. Mill's (1865) explanation of belief in matter, in which he accounts for the "intuitions" posited by those influenced by Kant. They are the result of habit! We typically attend to a small part of what we "see" and that small part occurs in many different circumstances, along with many different concomitant sensations. We are apt to treat these con-comitants as a "fringe" or cloud of contexts that lends meaning to the core. With experience, the cloud/fringe of possible contexts that have habitually accompanied a given particular object (a tree, sunset, etc.) seem more real than the *particular* object itself. This becomes the basis for the "intuition" that the object is real; it is more than a set of sensations or the memory of them in varying contexts.

HABIT'S DECLINE IN RESPECTABILITY

Popular writers and lecturers of the 19th century were not apt to emphasize John Stuart Mill's associationism or the version of it promoted by Helm-holtz as "unconscious inference." They, like their counterparts in the late 20th century, were far more likely to perceive associationism in a more homely and simple way; James Mill will always have more influence than will his son. What is this simple thing that lived on as associationism in the 20th century?

For most psychologists, biologists, linguists, philosophers, educators, and educated people in general, habit/association is construed in the crud-est possible way, just as James Mill construed it. We see this caricature in the writings of behaviorists and cognitivists—it is the distorted version of Wundt's structuralism that the Gestaltists attacked so fervently. It is the simplified version that has been understood by the casual thinker for over 300 years and that cyclically dominates our theories, is demolished, and re-turns in incarnations only slightly less primitive than their predecessors. Maybe it will not always be with us, but it will for the foreseeable future.

This is so for the same reason that James Mill pointed out; that is, because habit in its crudest form is sufficient to account for those things that we are most interested in explaining. It can give a rough but plausible account for our experience; it can suggest rules for altering our behavior and experience. It may not be sufficient for all things, but it works better than anything else ever proposed.

James Mill (1829) published *Analysis of the Phenomena of the Human Mind*, written during a series of summer vacations. In it he proposed what has appeared in our textbooks since: Experience is comprised of sensations grouped in space (objects) and in time (series of associations), with both kinds of grouping arising from habit. Add to this his strong belief in hedonism and the picture is complete. All that exist are "nodes," or sensations and ideas (past sensations) joined by habitual occurrence in time and space. This accounts for the faculties of the spiritualists; for example, "attention" is not a mental power, it is determined by the power of sensations, ideas, and complexes of both to dominate consciousness and that power is determined by the pleasures and pains associated with them. This interpretation of attention was promoted by James in his treatment of will (Chapter 24), although he strenuously argued against the hedonist explanation for the power of ideas (cf. Malone, 1975b).

This extraordinarily simple version of "mental habit" is associationism for the masses and it is capable of accounting for most of the common aspects of our experience. Given that objects are compounds of ideas, what are *real* objects (as opposed to imaginary ones)? They are compounds that include ideas of muscular resistance that impede our movement and that require us to exert ourselves to remove them. What is patriotism and how may it be taught? It is no more than the idea of "good" or "noble" habitually attached to national emblems, tales of the history of the country, and the like. What is expectation? It is only the noticing of a present sensation that has habitually preceded others, just as the thunder precedes the rain.

HABIT IN THE THEORIES OF THORNDIKE AND WATSON

The fact that habit is so important is another way of saying that simple associationism works and this seems sufficient to account for the rise of theories of learning during the first half of this century. Each of the major theories relied on habit, as do all psychological theories, but each added important aspects that were lost in the translations to general textbook form. By the second half of the century a good deal of progress had been made, but few were aware of it; James's unsatisfactory categories were *still* the only options for most people. The soul/mind alternative was temporarily suppressed during the first half of the century, which was dominated by the behaviorists. And behaviorists seemed to represent the other alternative; their emphasis of habit made them simple associationists and each of them was treated as a minor variation of James Mill, echoing again and again through the century!

This was actually quite true of Thorndike, whose connectionism was close in simplicity to Mill's associationism. Thorndike's chief innovation was emphasizing the association of S-R habits rather than the association of ideas or sensations. Even in *Animal Intelligence* (Thorndike, 1898) he questioned the need to refer to associated ideas and later he strongly criticized the concept of ideo-motor action (Thorndike, 1935). Situations and behaviors are connected and those connections are stamped in by satisfiers, according to the law of effect. This applies both to motor habits and to thinking, seeing, and other mental activities. For example, do we not learn to focus clearly because of the effects that occur when we move around seeing clearly or fuzzily? Traditional behavior therapy methods that emphasize the law of effect do not even take full advantage of all that Thorndike offered in his *Educational Psychology* (1913).

This emphasis on association as motor habit characterized John B. Watson's views as well as Thorndike's and other theorist's and we need not look far to see that James shared this emphasis. As he wrote in "The Sentiment of Rationality" (1962a, p. 164):

> The theory of evolution is beginning to do very good service by its reduction of all mentality to the type of reflex action. Cognition, in this view, is but a fleeting moment, a cross section at a certain point, of what in its totality is a motor phenomenon.

In the same piece he proposed a "motor theory of meaning":

> We are acquainted with a thing as soon as we have learned how to behave towards it, or how to meet the behavior which we expect from it. Up to that point it is still "strange" to us.

John B. Watson's psychology was founded entirely on habit and on the rejection of mentalism. Even these days he is interpreted as arguing that private experience does not exist, an incredible thing to suppose! But what did he mean when he denied the existence of mind, consciousness, sensation, and memory (as typically defined)? He even denied the existence of associations!

Any reader of Watson (e.g., 1919, 1924) can see that he was arguing for what could be called a positivistic view (as we will see later); but mainly he was arguing *against* the introspectionist psychology that was virtually the only psychology at the turn of the century. He proposed that the analysis of consciousness by trained introspectors was futile; the method had not and would not yield anything of value and it was time to throw it out. Along with the *method* of introspection, he urged that we throw out the *terms* that accompanied the method; such entities as sensations, images, and consciousness referred to nothing (in our experience). Watson never denied that we see, hear, feel, and remember; but we see things, not images, and we feel things, not sensations. This radical proposal, Watson's "Behaviorism," was not so radical. William James had reached conclusions similar to Watson's 9 years before Watson's first critique of consciousness (1913, "Psychology as the Behaviorist Views It"). As James wrote: "Consciousness . . . is the name of a nonentity. . . . It seems to me that the hour is ripe for it to be openly and universally discarded" (James, 1962c, p. 208). The "stream of thinking" is really the "stream of breathing"; Kant's "I think" that accompanies experiences . . . "is the 'I breathe' that actually does accompany them."

John B. Watson believed that the introspectionist's mental life was a fiction, that seeing and hearing and remembering did not occur "inside" us. James quoted his colleague Münsterberg, concurring with this opinion:

> The object of which I think, and of whose existence I take cognizance without letting it now work upon my senses, occupies its definite place in the outer world as much as does the object which I directly see.

Nor does memory mean that images are stored as mental states:

> But the interval of time does not in principle alter my relation to the object, does not transform it from an object known into a mental state. (James, 1962c, p. 214)

Sadly, that is a statement that many people will never understand (e.g., Bandura, 1986).

LATER LEARNING THEORIES AND HABIT: MORE THAN SIMPLE ASSOCIATIONISM

Edwin Guthrie, mathematics teacher turned psychologist, adopted the essentials of Watson's position and showed (e.g., Guthrie, 1935) that behaviorism could be charmingly presented. He added the considerable subtlety of one-trial learning and stressed the stereotypy that is the hallmark of habitual activity. Like the writers of the 19th century, he emphasized the practical aspects of habit formation; It is likely that his interpretation of habit better describes current behavior therapy methods than does Skinner's (Malone, 1978; cf. Gardner & Gardner, 1988), although Skinner usually has been given the credit (e.g., Stoltz, Wienkowski, & Brown, 1975).

What of Pavlov? Watson (1919) viewed Pavlovian conditioning as a likely candidate to explain habit formation and most textbooks treat Pavlov's contribution as little more than that. Did Pavlov merely demonstrate what every-one had known for centuries—that habit is important and that new habits are learned because new signals can become attached to old responses?

Until recently that has been the interpretation that has appeared in text-books; bells and food and "laws of learning" of simple habits. This inter-pretation angered Pavlov (e.g., 1932) and writers such as Razran have tried to provide a more accurate picture (e.g., Razran, 1961, 1965). Pavlov's overall view has never been understood; his model for brain functioning, the unity of mind and body, and the dialectical emphasis have not made the textbooks.

Finally, in the 1980s, we may be grateful that visceral conditioning has been "discovered" because of its important implications for pharmacology (e.g., Siegel, 1978) and for the functioning of the immune system (Ader & Cohen, 1982). Pavlovian researchers have reported relevant data for de-cades (e.g., Asratyan, 1965; Bykov, 1957; Razran, 1961), but attention was never paid their reports. Pavlovian conditioning was seen as "stupid learn-ing," only a more precise rendition of the simple associationist version of habit that James Mill had proposed. Pavlov never believed that, but no one reads Pavlov.

A Caricature Solidifies

The popularity of behaviorism during the first half of this century had a number of positive effects, but there were powerful negative effects as well. This arises from the fact that behavioral theories were typically viewed as modern versions of the old associationist theories, such as James Mill's; habit was seen as equivalent to association. Whether true or not, perceived successes of behavioral theories were interpreted as support for a caricature, that is, the simple associationist theory that was one of James's poor alter-natives. The caricature had several salient characteristics:

1. Like the older structuralist theories (e.g., Titchener's), the caricature relied on units of analysis determined in advance. The S-R connection and the CR took the place of Titchener's sensations, images, and affect. Stimuli and responses were always discrete and molecular (i.e., eyeblinks and mus-cle contractions). Although this was true of the caricature, it was not true of all behavioral theories. For example, Watson (1919, 1924) defined stimuli and responses in molecular or molar terms, depending on the phenomenon under consideration. A response could be building a bridge and a stimulus could be a method of education. Habits need not be built of discrete parts.

2. Habits result when connections are made between stimuli and re-sponses. Just as James and many others suggested, these may be linked to-gether as chains.

3. This linkage requires absolute contiguity between stimuli and re-

sponses (or stimuli and stimuli); there can be no time lapses between associated units and apparent lapses are filled with mediators of one kind or another. This part of the caricature is common to many theories—causes and effects must be close in time.

4. Denying the existence of mind must mean that private experience is no longer a part of psychology. This remarkable conclusion was surely part of the caricature and many shallow thinkers have noted that we "must be scientific" and make no reference to thinking, expecting, or other private events. This was a position that was certainly *not* held by Thorndike, Watson, or Guthrie!

Why did this caricature arise? Because of the success of simple associationism in education, psychotherapy, and elsewhere. The same simple associationism that was well known in the 19th century was translated to behavioral theories, most of which emphasized S-R habits. The theories had many individual virtues, but those were lost in the distillation that led to the caricature. The caricature still worked because simple associationism works; at least it works better than the apparent alternative, the mind/soul theories.

Hull's Adoption of the Caricature

The immensely influential theory of Clark L. Hull was presented in relatively complete form in 1943, in his *Principles of Behavior*. As the title implies, it was not as complete a work as was James's *Principles of Psychology*. Rather, it was a gigantic elaboration of the principle of association, defined in the simplest possible way. Hull was a self-admitted opportunist whose interest lay in establishing a reputation and his choice of psychology as the field in which to do that owed to the fact that psychology was ripe for the picking (Hull, 1952).

His "molar behavior theory" was no more than an embellishment of the habit caricature laid out in postulate form with the appearance of quantitative precision. Although over 100 intervening variables were eventually included, the theory can be accurately summarized as a simple associationism, a theory of habit. It was less sophisticated than was Watson's or Guthrie's, but it *appeared* to be far more so. And it was popular for as long as it was (several decades) because the caricature it represented was already widely accepted. Hull's rendition seemed to carry it further than anyone had imagined was possible. Yet, when all the masses of arguments and proofs and equations and variables are broken down, the theory says only that stimuli and responses become associated when they occur close in time. Living things form habits!

Skinner's (1938) theory is different in fundamental ways from the habit caricature; however, because it employs terms such as *stimuli* and *re-*

sponses, it has been treated as a less precise version of Hull's theory and has been attacked by the same critics (e.g., Chomsky, 1959). Differences between Skinner and Hull will be discussed later, but they are not relevant here, because Hull's was assumed to be *the* exemplar of behaviorism and it is what critics still envision when they think of behaviorism.

Were They Really Rebellions?

Rebellions against the gross deficiencies of the "habit caricature" began in the 1960s. On the one hand, its neglect of species-specific behavior spawned the "biological boundaries" movement, spearheaded by data summarized by Seligman (1970) in an influential review, "On the Generality of the Laws of Learning." This was followed by a flurry of activity extending into the 1980s by workers studying taste aversions, autoshaping, language, and other phenomena that did not seem to conform to "laws" associated with the caricature. Ironically, many of these researchers were themselves conspicuous supporters of the caricature prior to the rebellion and their thinking could accurately be described as still "caricature bound" (cf. Malone, 1973, 1975a).

A second, and better known, rebellion took the form of a "new" cognitive psychology that emphasized information processing models. Here too, it was largely the adherents of the simple associationist caricature that participated. (They would typically not have called themselves followers of Hull, and were more influenced by Ebbinghaus and the German associationist tradition, but that is of no consequence; Hull merely represented the caricature, his theory was not *the* caricature.) Researchers who had been studying paired-associate lists now studied "transformations of inputs through processing stages," thus renaming their old associationist viewpoint.

Lachman, Lachman, and Butterfield (1979) traced the development of the "cognitive revolution" and emphasized the dislike these cognitive pioneers had for the neobehaviorist theories that had stifled inquiry for so long. Banded together by this dislike, they developed a strong "esprit de corps"! This shows the magic that labels have; an old form of simple associationism is replaced by a new form, almost identical in every way except for the terminology used. The "inputs" of information processing correspond to Hull's "afferent trace" that includes a short-term memory store; "output" corresponds to "excitatory reaction potential"; the operators that constitute a program correspond to his postulate set; serial processing is precisely the method Hull used in 1930 to provide a mechanical account for knowledge, purpose, and foresight; finally, network models for memory form "habit family hierarchies." Bower and Hilgard (1981) show the great similarity between simple information processing models and Hull's version of associationism by casting the basics of Hull's theory in flowchart form.

CONNECTIONIST MODELS:
THE "NEW" ASSOCIATIONISM

Information processing models are much less popular in the late 1980s; not surprisingly, one replacement appears to be another form of simple associationism that approximates Hull's theory even more closely than do standard information processing models. This "new" way of looking at things is represented by a set of theories collectively called connectionism. This approach consists of the modeling of cognitive processes in the activity of large networks arranged in parallel, with elements assigned different activation values and with the connections between elements differentially weighted. The changing of these weights as the system operates represents what seems to be strengths of associations among connected elements. It sounds like old-time associationism and Hull (e.g., 1930) would have enthusiastically endorsed such models (M. G. Johnson agrees).

Dellarosa (1988, pp. 28–29) also agrees with this assessment, although she shares the mistaken but popular belief that behavioral theories are variations of the same simple associationist caricature:

> The appeal of connectionism has its roots in an idea that will not die. It is an idea that was championed by Berkeley, Hume, William James, Ebbinghaus, and (in a different form) the entire behaviorist school of psychology. Put simply, this idea is that cognition is characterized by the probabilistic construction and activation of connections (or associations) among units: ideas (Hume), habits (James), words (Ebbinghaus), or stimulus-response pairs (behaviorism).

Even a strong proponent of connectionism (Smolensky, 1988) describes connectionist networks as ". . . Humean association with a Master's degree." But Hume's ideas are still seriously discussed two centuries after his death; will connectionist models be seriously considered in 2190? Will Hume be forgotten?

The parallel between Hull's theory and connectionism is striking. We still have the inputs, outputs, and operators of information processing *and* activation values assigned to each element in the network, just as Hull assigned habit strength to each of his elements. And the connections between elements differ in strength and may be positive or negative (excitatory and inhibitory, in Hull's terms). However, whereas Hull was always ready, even eager, to test his model against real data, connectionist models seem less able to do this; as Smolensky (1988, p. 2) put it, the models are ". . . difficult to put into detailed contact with empirical methodologies." Perhaps the parallel with Herbart's "quantitative" associationism is more fitting. This position also had difficulty with experimental data and assumed mental elements varying in attractive and repulsive strength. Equations were proposed to represent interactions among various complexes of elements. James (I: 603) was especially critical of this version of associationism:

> In Germany, the same mythological supposition has been more radically grasped, and carried out to a still more logical, if more repulsive, extreme, by Herbart and his followers . . .

If connectionism is the wave of the future, as it appears to be, then my recent concerns were misplaced. I argued recently (Malone, 1987) that radical behaviorism, of the kind that Skinner represents, has suffered because it has been interpreted as another variant of traditional associationism. I did not foresee that associationism would be transformed from anathema to popular trend.

INTRODUCTORY TEXTBOOK THINKING AND ITS INFLUENCE

Simple associationism appears to have had the upper hand in psychological theory, but both of James's rejected alternatives are commonly mixed in introductory psychology texts; the result is the common sense model of popular psychology, familiar to all of us. It assumes that (a) we consist of a mind in a body, (b) the mind is actually the brain, which is a wonderful computer, (c) our mental content consists of compounds of sensations, and (d) we have faculties of attention, discrimination, memory, and so on.

The faculties are localized in different parts of the brain, of course, and information from the senses arrives via specific labeled receptors and afferent nerves and goes to specific targets in the brain. It is easy to go from a belief in cold receptors in the skin to belief in other "good stories" that seem to verify common sense. The "wonderful computer" that is the mind/brain of introductory psychology has wonderful centers, areas for memory, pleasure, aggression, eating and drinking, and language. There are even cognitive maps in a specific place, the hippocampus, an organ that seems to serve every conceivable function (Buck, 1988).

Students who are presented this model as accurate are unlikely to recognize important data *as* important when they later encounter it. This makes it difficult for instructors in higher-level courses; introductory psychology has either convinced them that psychology is a waste of time or that "the mind/brain is a wonderful computer." Either way, they become less educable and thus introductory psychology serves no good purpose.

The introductory text model is the model of popular psychology, of those whose interest is superficial or who simply want common sense and folk wisdom verified scientifically. But one does not try to verify propositions that are obviously wrong, especially when the methods of verification are very unreliable. The introductory text model, pandering to popular taste, incorporating both of James's poor alternatives, has a contemporary champion in the "Social Cognitive Theory" of Albert Bandura.

Social Cognitive Theory: Combining Poor Alternatives

Bandura (1986) presented a comprehensive theory that has attracted great attention, as examination of a recent citation index testifies. His "Social Cognitive Theory" combines James's rejected alternatives in the form of a simple S-R associationism ("mechanical" and "automatic") with a simple cognitivism (emphasizing thought, capacities and faculties, awareness, and autonomy); both are worse than James envisioned when he rejected such alternatives. How did this unfortunate theory come to be?

Bandura was first known for his demonstrations of the influence of modeling (e.g., Bandura, 1965). In the course of that work, he replicated the findings of Miller and Dollard (1941), who authored the classic *Social Learning and Imitation.* Like Miller and Dollard, who were followers of Clark Hull, Bandura viewed learning theory as the simplest possible S-R associationism; stimuli and responses were discrete things, linked together by contiguity in time and the occurrence of obvious reinforcers. That is the view of learning theory that Bandura still held in his 1986 book, *Social Foundations of Thought and Action.*

Bandura believed that modeling was not well explained by simple associationist learning theory and emphasized what he called "cognitive" determinants. Because subjects exposed to models may not immediately copy their actions and because some models may be imitated without the subject seeing the model rewarded for the specific behavior imitated, Bandura concluded that S-R reinforcement theory was not sufficient to explain modeling. Is that really the case? Miller and Dollard had proposed that imitation may become self perpetuating, acting as an "acquired drive" and Baer and Sherman (1964) suggested that imitation becomes "generalized", which is essentially the same proposal. Hence, a history of imitating models who are rewarded leads to a tendency to imitate such models, whether they are rewarded on the specific occasion where imitated behavior occurs or not.

Bandura rejected this interpretation (for reasons difficult to understand, see Mazur, 1986) and concluded that modeling effects are mediated by cognitive processes. Bandura (1977a, 1977b, 1986) concluded also that modeling was basic to all learning; a solitary learner actually learns by "imitating its own prior behavior" that led to payoffs! This means that the subject must be aware of what it did and what payoffs occurred, so all learning must be accompanied by *awareness,* a point stressed by Bandura (1986).

The insistence that thinking and learning are always accompanied by awareness means that Bandura's popular view parts company with all scholarly views. Current cognitive psychology, whether traditional information processing or current connectionism, clearly does not hold that view. Nor does psychodynamic theory, which has always emphasized the importance of unconscious factors. Recent findings in social psychology show that subjects typically have no awareness of factors that determine their attitudes (e.g., Nisbett & Wilson, 1977) and that "mindlessness" is more common than is awareness (e.g., Langer, 1975). Bandura evidently excludes conditioning of the viscera (e.g., Bykov, 1957; Razran, 1961), including recent American demonstrations of learning by the body's immune system (e.g., Ader & Cohen, 1982). And he discusses, but discounts, Verplanck's (1962) ingenious demonstration of the conditioning of verbal reports and their consequent failure to conform with overt behaviors.

His social cognitive theory proposes that thought mediates all learning. What is thought? According to Bandura (1986, p. 15) thoughts are ". . . brain processes, not disembodied mental events" and they activate the body and direct the brain! Cognition is defined as consciously reasoning, imagining, and reflecting; people analyze, anticipate, plan, and direct. They have basic capacities, including symbolizing, forethought, self regulation, and self reflection. James's soul/mind could not do as much. Ironically, Bandura (1986, p. 2) criticized psychodynamic theory for doing precisely what he proposes:

> . . . inner determinants are often inferred from the very behavior they supposedly caused, creating interpretative circularities in which the description becomes the causal explanation.

What is Wrong With Social Cognitive Theory?

Bandura was led to propose just such a theory of "inferred inner determinants" because he believed that some phenomena of modeling could not be explained by his version of the associationist alternative; that is, by a simple S-R associationism. He seems unaware that what he calls "reinforcement theory" has radically changed over the past decades. "Molar behaviorism" (e.g., Rachlin, 1976) is a far cry from the S-R contiguity theory of Hull, which Bandura sees as radical behaviorism. Radical behaviorism is actually a philosophical viewpoint proposed by Skinner (1945) that has nothing to do with specific theories of learning or cognition. Its counterpart is molar behaviorism, an atheoretical approach derived from Skinner's research, that emphasizes the search for correlations between patterns of behavior extending over time and environmental contingencies extending over time (e.g., Honig & Staddon, 1977). Yet, Bandura (1986, p. 15) believes that the "cardinal rule in operant conditioning theory" is that behavior is controlled by its immediate consequences; "automaticity demands immediacy." If a consequence is not immediate, chains of cues must bridge the delay. Outcomes must be salient, powerful, instant, and regular. As he fails to understand cognitive psychology and so adopts James's mind/soul alternative, he fails to understand "reinforcement theory," as he calls it, and sees only the simple associationist alternative. Unlike Bandura's rendition of the introductory textbook/popular psychology model, molar behaviorism is not easy to understand; see Malone (1987) for a comparison of molar behaviorism and simple associationism.

Bandura's radical behaviorism is Hull's association machine, bearing no resemblance to current behavioral theory. It is as poor a version of behaviorism as is Bandura's rendition of cognitive psychology. His alternatives are no different from the popular versions of the two alternatives James rejected in 1890. But this is a century later and Bandura's views are extremely popular, often viewed by those only superficially knowledgeable as a great achievement, a reconciling of cognitive and behavioral psychology (e.g., McConnell, 1986). James would throw up his hands.

Fortunately, most psychologists do not take Bandura's theory seriously and perhaps it is inevitable that the popular taste requires something that is readily understandable, as social cognitive theory is. But connectionist models, representing the continuation of simple associationist theory into the 20th and 21st centuries, are taken very seriously. Yet, existing data show that these models face grave difficulties.

THE LIMITATIONS OF CONNECTIONISM

If cognitive psychology is to become *connectionism,* we may assume that the mind/soul theory is no longer to be taken seriously; the only serious alternative to behavioral learning theories will be connectionist theories. However, behavioral learning theories are typically expressed as variations of simple associationism, so the alternatives seem of a kind. Behavioral or cognitive elements are joined together in various ways and the only questions to be answered concern the nature of the elements and the ways of assigning strengths and signs to the connections among them!

These alternatives may well suffice, as associationism has for so long, if our only concerns are practical expedience; associationism will work as well as it has for centuries. However, there is a growing body of data, accumulated over the past few decades by basic researchers, that sets severe limitations on any account, behavioral or cognitive, that relies on associations formed among discrete elements. Brief description of these restrictions follows, accompanied by references for the interested reader; space limitations preclude more detail. All of these findings were reported by researchers in the experimental analysis of behavior, guided, more or less, by Skinner's point of view.

To begin with, countless studies have shown that behavior may be maintained by schedules of reinforcement and that a variety of species of subjects, ranging from insects to humans, show strikingly similar patterns of behavior over time on these schedules (e.g., Zeiler, 1977). It has been clear for some time that these schedule performances are not interpretable in conventional associationist terms (cf. Jenkins, 1970).

Further, when subjects are given opportunities to choose among simultaneously presented alternatives differing in value, it is impossible to analyse their behavior in terms of discrete choices of specific items; only an analysis of patterns of choice over time shows any order (e.g., deVilliers, 1977). Surely choice is a fundamental problem for a connectionist account, but simple associationism seems impotent here.

Drug effects are also difficult to explain in ordinary associationist terms. It has become clear that they depend on the history of the organism receiving the drug, the schedule of administration, and, least important, the drug itself. Morse and Kelleher (1977) showed that similar considerations apply to the effects of any agent that is ordinarily called good/bad, pleasant/unpleasant, or reinforcing/punishing. As is the case with schedule behavior and with choice, the associations formed refer to patterns of behavior over time and patterns of stimulation (contingencies), also extending over time.

Associationist theory is also unable to account for avoidance of noxious events (Herrnstein & Hineline, 1966); any analysis that relies on discrete situations, behaviors, and consequences is insufficient. And, as a final example, it is now clear that simple associationism cannot account for the power of acquired (secondary, conditioned) reinforcers; tokens and other symbols do not gain their value because they are paired with or predict things that are already of value (cf. Gollub, 1977).

These and similar findings are more than enough to question seriously the value of simple associationist theory, such as that promoted by Hull and his group. But it seems that Hull's model is virtually identical to the associationism of information processing theories and of the new connectionism. Hence, we know in advance what rocks the connectionists will dash themselves upon; we need only wonder how long it will be before this is pointed out. Ironically, it was a vague awareness of data of this sort that led Bandura (1977a; 1986) to propose his simple cognitive processing theory—if simple associationism is insufficient, mind/soul comes to the rescue, as it has for centuries.

BEYOND ASSOCIATIONISM AND MIND: JAMES'S POSITIVISM

James wrote that this was all that he could claim as original in the *Principles*; what he meant by "positivism" is freedom from the main characteristics of the two poor alternatives. Both simple associationism and the soul/mind theory are rationalistic, in that they begin with fixed models to be applied to phenomena; one assumes elements and laws of association and the other assumes faculties as mental powers. Similarly, both tacitly assume that we already know what it is that is to be explained. But the problem may be that we do *not* well enough understand the phenomena for which our theories are proposed. Readers of Bandura (1986) or of recent connectionist treatments may well wonder whether they commit the same error; are the phenomena they treat really well enough understood so that the main problem lies in explaining them?

James's positivism was described in a philosophical piece, "What Pragmatism Means" (James, 1962b). There he criticized explanatory models fashioned in advance; he turned his back on abstraction, fixed principles, bad a priori reasons, verbal solutions, and closed systems. He turned to concreteness, facts, action, and power. Pragmatism means ". . . looking away from first things, principles, categories, supposed necessities; and of looking toward last things, fruits, consequences, facts . . ." (James, 1962b, p. 183). This positivistic view led him to strange endeavors, such as trying to communicate with the dead (e.g., Stevens, 1989), but it also freed him from the constraints of the accumulation of conformity that is represented in the two poor alternatives.

It would be difficult to defend the proposition that psychology has made real progress over the past century; perhaps the lack of progress owes to the continued domination, in various guises, of the two poor alternatives. They are exemplified in the simple introductory textbooks that present psychology as the study of associations and as the realm of popular categories, such as understanding, comprehension, attention, and processing. Associations and faculties are both names without referents, leftovers from the faculty psychology of 18th-century Scotland.

Someday we may pass beyond introductory textbook models and determine what people and animals do in situations that are of interest to us. Then we can search for explanations. As James wrote to Stumpf a century ago, we may turn away from ". . . psych-mythology and logicalism, and toward a truly empirical and sensationalistic point of view" (Perry, 1935, p. 62).

If we leave the mind/soul and the associationist theories to philosophy, psychology may yet become a "natural science." Like all natural sciences, it may then concentrate on "prediction and control" (James, 1892, p. 149). Although he was no experimenter, James believed that it is facts, and not theories, that we need:

Nevertheless, if the hard alternative were to arise of a choice between 'theories' and 'facts' in psychology, between a merely rational and a merely practical science of the mind, I do not see how any man could hesitate in his decision. (James, 1892, p. 153)

John B. Watson agreed completely, although he lacked the vision to see that James was a kindred soul (Watson, 1924). Others who have seen the virtues of such a "positivistic" view include Skinner (sometimes, e.g., 1931, 1950, 1964) and Gibson (1966). The rest of psychology has, by and large, continued debating which of the two poor alternatives might best be pursued. Will this be true a century from now? What is the use of being a genius, if that is the case?

Applied psychologists need not worry about this. They have relied on the introductory-text models that are based on the two poor alternatives; they will work as well or as badly as they have for centuries. The rest of us may wonder whether psychology will look any different in 2090.

REFERENCES

Ader, R., & Cohen, H. (1982). Behaviorally conditioned immunosuppression and murine systemic lupus erythematosis. *Science, 215,* 1534–1536.

Asratyan, E. A. (1965). *Conditioned reflexes and compensatory mechanisms.* Oxford: Pergamon Press.

Baer, D. M., & Sherman, J. A. (1964). Reinforcement control of generalized imitation in young children. *Journal of Experimental Child Psychology, 1,* 37–49.

Bain, A. (1879). *The senses and the intellect* (4th ed.). New York: Appleton.

Bandura, A. (1965). Behavioral modifications through modeling procedures. In L. *Krasner & L. P. Ullman* (Eds.), *Research in behavior modification* (pp. 310–340). New York: Holt, Rinehart, & Winston.

Bandura, A. (1977a). Self-efficacy: Toward a unifying theory of behavioral change. *Psychological Review, 84,* 191–215.

Bandura, A. (1977b). *Social learning theory.* Englewood Cliffs, NJ: Prentice-Hall.

Bandura, A. (1986). *Social foundations of thought and action.* Englewood Cliffs, NJ: Prentice-Hall.

Bower, G. H., & Hilgard, E. R. (1981). *Theories of learning.* Englewood Cliffs, NJ: Prentice-Hall.

Buck, R. (1988). *Human motivation and emotion.* New York: Wiley.

Bykov, K. M. (1957). *The cerebral cortex and the internal organs.* New York: Chemical Publishing Company.

Carpenter, W. B. (1876). *Principles of mental physiology.* New York: Appleton.

Chomsky, N. (1959). Review of B. F. Skinner, *Verbal behavior. Language, 35,* 26–58.

Dellarosa, D. (1988). The psychological appeal of connectionism. *Behavioral and Brain Sciences, 11,* 28–29.

Descartes, R. (1650). *Les passions de l'ame.* Excerpt translated by R. J. Herrnstein & E. G. Boring (Eds.). (1965). *A source book in the history of psychology* (pp. 205–210). Cambridge, MA: Harvard Press.

deVilliers, P. (1977). Choice in concurrent schedules and a quantitative formulation of the law of effect. In W. K. Honig & J. E. R. Staddon (Eds.), *Handbook of operant behavior* (pp. 233–287). Englewood Cliffs, NJ: Prentice-Hall.

Gardner, R. A., & Gardner, B. T. (1988). Feedforward versus feedbackward: An ethological alternative to the law of effect. *Behavioral and brain sciences, 11,* 429–493.

Gibson, J. J. (1966). *The senses considered as perceptual systems.* Boston: Houghton Mifflin.

Gollub, L. R. (1977). Conditioned reinforcement: Schedule effects. In W. K. Honig & J. E. R.

Staddon (Eds.), *Handbook of operant behavior* (pp. 288-312). Englewood Cliffs, NJ: Prentice-Hall.

Guthrie, E. R. (1935). *The psychology of learning*. New York: Harper & Row.

Herrnstein, R. J., & Hineline, P. N. (1966). Negative reinforcement as shock frequency reduction. *Journal of the Experimental Analysis of Behavior, 9,* 421-430.

Hochberg, J. (1979). Sensation and perception. In E. Hearst (Ed.), *The first century of experimental psychology* (pp. 89-142). Hillsdale, NJ: Lawrence Erlbaum Associates.

Holt, E. B. (1915). *The Freudian wish and its place in ethics*. New York: Holt.

Honig, W. K., & Staddon, J. E. R. (1977). *Handbook of operant behavior*. Englewood Cliffs, NJ: Prentice-Hall.

Hull, C. L. (1930). Knowledge and purpose as habit mechanisms. *Psychological Review, 37,* 511-525.

Hull, C. L. (1943). *Principles of behavior*. New York: Appleton-Century.

Hull, C. L. (1952). Clark L. Hull. In E. G. Boring, H. S. Langfelt, H. Werner, & R. M. Yerkes (Eds.), *A history of psychology in autobiography* (Vol. 4, pp. 143-162). Worcester, MA: Clark University Press.

Hume, D. (1739). *Treatise of human nature*. Excerpt in R. J. Herrnstein & E. G. Boring (Eds.), (1965). *A source book in the history of psychology* (pp. 342-348). Cambridge, MA: Harvard Press.

James, W. (1890). *Principles of psychology*. New York: Holt.

James, W. (1892). A plea for psychology as a natural science. *Philosophical Review, 1,* 146-153.

James, W. (1962a). The sentiment of rationality. In W. Barrett & H. D. Aiken (Eds.), *Philosophy in the twentieth century* (Vol. 1). New York: Random House.

James, W. (1962b). What pragmatism means. In W. Barrett & H. D. Aiken (Eds.), *Philosophy in the twentieth century* (Vol. 1, pp. 179-192). New York: Random House.

James, W. (1962c). Does consciousness exist? In W. Barrett & H. D. Aiken (Eds.), *Philosophy in the twentieth century* (Vol. 1, pp. 207-221). New York: Random House.

Jenkins, H. M. (1970). Sequential organization in schedules of reinforcement. In W. N. Schoenfeld (Ed.), *The theory of reinforcement schedules* (pp. 63-109). New York: Appleton-Century-Crofts.

Joncich, G. (1968). *The sane positivist*. Middletown, CT: Wesleyan University Press.

Lachman, R., Lachman, J., & Butterfield, E. (1979). *Cognitive psychology and information processing*. Hillsdale, NJ: Lawrence Erlbaum Associates.

Langer, E. J. (1975). The illusion of control. *Journal of personality and Social Psychology, 32,* 311-328.

Locke, J. (1700). *An essay concerning humane understanding* (4 vols.). London: Awnsham and John Churchill.

Malone, J. C., Jr. (1973). A note on general process learning theorists. *Psychological Review, 80,* 305.

Malone, J. C., Jr. (1975a). Paradigms of learning. *The Psychological Record, 25,* 479-489.

Malone, J. C., Jr. (1975b). William James and B. F. Skinner: Behaviorism, reinforcement, and interest. *Behaviorism, 3,* 140-151.

Malone, J. C., Jr. (1978). Beyond the operant analysis of behavior. *Behavior Therapy, 9,* 584-591.

Malone, J. C., Jr. (1987). Skinner, the behavioral unit, and current psychology. In S. Modgil & C. Modgil (Eds.), *B. F. Skinner: Consensus and controversy* (pp. 193-206). New York: Falmer Press.

Mazur, J. E. (1986). *Learning and behavior*. Englewood Cliffs, NJ: Prentice-Hall.

McConnell, J. V. (1986). *Understanding human behavior* (5th Ed.). New York: Holt, Rinehart & Winston.

Mill, J. (1829). *Analysis of the phenomena of the human mind*. London: Baldwin and Cradock.

Mill, J. S. (1865). *An examination of Sir William Hamilton's philosophy*. Excerpt in R. J. Herrnstein & E. G. Boring (Eds.). (1965). *A source book in the history of psychology* (pp. 182–188). Cambridge, MA: Harvard Press.

Miller, N. E., & Dollard, J. (1941). *Social learning and imitation*. New Haven, CT: Yale University Press.

Morse, W. H., & Kelleher, R. T. (1977). Determinents of reinforcement and punishment. In W. K. Honig & J. E. R. Staddon (Eds.), *Handbook of operant behavior* (pp. 174–200). Englewood Cliffs, NJ: Prentice Hall.

Nisbett, R. E., & Wilson, T. D. (1977). Telling more than we can know: Verbal reports on mental processes. *Psychological Review, 84*, 231–259.

Pavlov, I. P. (1932). The reply of a physiologist to psychologists. *Psychological Review, 39*, 91–127.

Perry, R. B. (1935). *The thought and character of William James* (Vols. 1–2). Boston: Little, Brown.

Rachlin, H. (1976). *Behavior and learning*. New York: Freeman.

Razran, G. (1961). The observable unconscious and the inferable conscious in current Soviet psychophysiology: Interoceptive conditioning, semantic conditioning, and the orienting reflex. *Psychological Review, 68*, 81–147.

Razran, G. (1965). Russian physiologists' psychology and American experimental psychology. *Psychological Bulletin, 63*, 42–64.

Scudder, V. (1887). The moral dangers of musical devotees. *Andover Review*, January, 46–53.

Seligman, M. E. P. (1970). On the generality of the laws of learning. *Psychological Review, 77*, 406–418.

Siegel, S. (1978). Tolerance to the hyperthermic effect of morphine in the rat is a learned response. *Journal of Comparative and Physiological Psychology, 92*, 1137–1149.

Skinner, B. F. (1931). The concept of the reflex in the description of behavior. *Journal of General Psychology, 5*, 427–458.

Skinner, B. F. (1938). *The behavior of organisms*. New York: Appleton-Century.

Skinner, B. F. (1945). The operational analysis of psychological terms. *Psychological Review, 52*, 270–77.

Skinner, B. F. (1950). Are theories of learning really necessary? *Psychological Review, 57*, 193–216.

Skinner, B. F. (1964). Behaviorism at fifty. In T. W. Wann, (Ed.), *Behaviorism and phenomenology* (pp. 79–97). Chicago: University of Chicago Press.

Smolensky, P. (1988). On the proper treatment of connectionism. *Behavioral and Brain Sciences, 11*, 1–74.

Stevens, J. (1989). When Hodgson spoke from the grave. *Yankee, 53*, 76–81, 114–116.

Stoltz, S. B., Wienkowski, L. A., & Brown, B. S. (1975). Behavior modification: A perspective on critical issues. *American Psychologist, 30*, 1027–1048.

Thorndike, E. L. (1898). Animal intelligence: An experimental study of the associative processes in animals. *Psychological Review, 2(8), monograph supplement*.

Thorndike, E. L. (1913). *Educational psychology*. New York: Teachers College.

Thorndike, E. L. (1935). *The psychology of wants, interests, and attitudes*. New York: Appleton-Century.

Verplanck, W. S. (1962). Unaware of where's awareness: Some verbal operants-notates, monents, and notants. In C. W. Erickson (Ed.), *Behavior and awareness* (pp. 130–158). Durham, NC: Duke University Press.

Watson, J. B. (1913). Psychology as the behaviorist views it. *Psychological Review, 20*, 158–177.

Watson, J. B. (1919). *Psychology from the standpoint of a behaviorist*. Philadelphia: J. B. Lippincott.

Watson, J. B. (1924). *Behaviorism*. New York: Norton.

Wundt, W. (1907). *Lectures on human and animal psychology*. (J. E. Creighton & E. B. Titchener, Trans.) New York: Macmillan.

Zeiler, M. (1977). Schedules of reinforcement. In W. K. Honig & J. E. R. Staddon (Eds.), *Handbook of operant behavior* (pp. 201–232). Englewood Cliffs, NJ: Prentice Hall.

Chapter 7

Association, Cognition, and Neural Networks

Herbert F. Crovitz
Duke University

Poetry is concerned only with the "beautiful show" which makes it possible to contemplate the ideal; how that show is produced is a matter of indifference. Even nature is, in the poet's eyes, but the sensible expression of the spiritual. The natural philosopher, on the other hand, tries to discover the levers, the cords, and the pulleys which work behind the scenes, and shift them. Of course the sight of the machinery spoils the beautiful show, and therefore the poet would gladly talk it out of existence, and ignoring cords and pulleys as the chimeras of a pedant's brain, he would have us believe that the scenes shift themselves, or are governed by the idea of the drama. Hermann von Helmholtz (1852/1962, p. 20)

This chapter concerns the concept of association, which has seen its share of twists and turns. For some present-day psychologists the associationist point of view continues to be, or is once again, attractive. However, for some cognitive psychologists it never was attractive, and we might agree with the sentiment that recent connectionism's "idea that the brain is a neural network motivates the revival of a largely discredited Associationist psychology" (Fodor & Pylyshyn 1988, p. 63). Yet if asked what is happening at the free exciting frontier in psychology now, I would answer: It is the mathematical theory and the emerging technology of neural network modeling of associative memory.

Associationism is a point of view that assumes an understanding of psychological matters can be made in terms of some number of basic units and of relations among them, out of which complex matters can be built, and which allows explanation in terms of mechanism. Furthermore, an associationist "believes that behavior is automatic and for any kind of complex behavior, he relies on memory" (Jenkins, 1974, p. 786). For an illuminating history of associationism see Anderson and Bower (1973, p. 9–39).

Throughout the 100 years since James (1890) a war of words has been fought between the opinions that mechanical laws of association might explain the dance of ideas versus the opinion that we can ignore associationism in attempting to explain the dance of ideas since we are not slaves to automatic association processes. As Cofer (1979, p. 326) has noted, "the associationist-nonassociationist (or cognitive) split runs through most of the century of research on human learning and memory." James believed that automatic mechanical association does describe the normal workings of underlying brain physiology. Yet, as we will see, his views were broad enough to include some cognitive voluntary factors. Association in James's *Principles* relates to current theory both in regard to its attention to associationist ideas as well as to more cognitive ideas, all in the context of faith in explanation in terms of brain function.

James began his vividly written chapter on association with an argument to the effect that although the business of thought is with truth, "reason is only one out of a thousand possibilities in the thinking of each of us" (I: 552).

> If all the categories of thought were logical and the relation between successive thoughts were relations of reason, if pure thought "runs all our trains, why should she run some so fast and some so slow. . . . Why do we spend years straining after a certain scientific or practical problem, but all in vain— thought refusing to evoke the solution we desire? And why, some day, walking in the street with our attention miles away from the quest, does the answer saunter into our minds as carelessly as if it had never been called for— suggested possibly, by the flowers on the bonnet of the lady in front of us, or possibly by nothing that we can discover? If reason can give us relief then, why did she not do so earlier?" (I: 551–552)

What James has done so far, in his uniquely readable manner, is to reject the hypothesis that thoughts follow each other in an order easily interpretable by common sense. Please remember those flowers on the bonnet of that lady: James gave here an instance of the associative cuing of a potential problem-solution. Why hadn't chance encounters with lucky cues earlier led to an answer in a prepared mind? Common sense would suggest that the right associative cue at the right time draws attention back to the quest, and one pays attention to the association long enough for a solution to "click," and for logical critical thought to evaluate the association. For an analogous case see Crovitz (1986).

"It is true that a presiding arbiter seems to sit aloft in the mind, and emphasize the better suggestions into permanence, while it ends by dropping out and leaving unrecorded the confusion. The mode of genesis of the worthy and the worthless seems the same" (I: 552).

James's "presiding arbiter" has been a leading character in romantic accounts of thought. A parallel account of mathematical discovery was later given by the great mathematician Henri Poincare. "Everything happens as if the discoverer were a secondary examiner who had only to interrogate candidates declared eligible after passing a preliminary test" (Poincare, 1914, p. 52); and, "Of the very large number of combinations which the subliminal ego blindly forms, almost all are without interest and without utility. But for that very reason they are without action on the aesthetic sensibility; the consciousness will never know them." (Poincare, 1914, pp. 59–60). A less romantic interpretation of such a state of affairs is possible: Even if all sorts of associations were made in successive iterations in some covert PDP-like internal auto-associator (McClelland & Rumelhart, 1988), the confused ones are unlikely to be perceived and recognized by people with normal consciousness. Things may be different (but not better) in abnormal brain-states in which logical critical abilities may be inaccessible (Daniel, Crovitz, & Weiner, 1987).

The physiological analogy brought in by James to explain the habitual associations between thoughts was a chain of motor reflexes.

> The laws of motor habit in the lower centres of the nervous system are disputed by no one. A series of movements repeated in a certain order tend to unroll themselves with peculiar ease in that order forever afterward. Number one awakens number two, and that awakens number three, and so on, till the last is produced. A habit of this kind once become inveterate may go on automatically. And so it is with the objects on which our thinking is concerned. (I: 554)

We are far enough from James's time so that it is no longer fashionable nor correct to settle for analogies to simple seriality at a physiological level of analysis (but see Sechenov 1863/1965) for the innovative exercise along these lines that led to Pavlov's work on conditioned reflexes, and thence to S-R behaviorist psychology in which a goal was to study the formation and dissolution of associations).

Post-Jamesian views of the serial order of behavior tend to have complicated James's picture. In my laboratory the study of serial associations has centered on Project Alphabet. It involves a method I stumbled upon for playing with simulating anterograde amnesia in oneself with a minimum of appratus and no witnesses.

The method consists of trying to typewrite the 26 letters in alphabetical order while generating, without feedback, the members of a second series between the series of letters. When the second series is difficult, say subtracting sevens from a three-digit number, the series should go "643 a 636 b 629 c 622 d . . . z." Readers might try this now in an easier version, closing both eyes and writing such a series on paper: Errors of an interesting perseverative type will occasionally occur. Several years ago, a sample of 40 intelligent and alert subjects (Duke University graduate students, faculty, and visiting colloquium speakers) did this "double-tracking" task using an electric typewriter (and with their view of what they had typed hidden from sight). Subjects reported that when a letter came to mind it was sometimes unclear whether it was associated with what they had already typed or with what they intended to type. The time it took them to generate number-letter pairs was long (mean = 9.66 sec, sd = 2.61); and, about one-seventh of the letters they typed were wrong. Almost all the alphabetic errors were repetitions (e.g., 643 a 636 b 629 c 622 c . . .).

The significance of this alphabet-game for me is that it exposes the fragility of what common sense would call a simple associative process. It shows an effect of distraction, a sleight-of-mind in which logical critical ability appears to be inaccessible.

Very interesting theoretical work on the problem of the serial order of behavior was done by Karl Lashley. He argued that attempts to express cerebral function in terms of concepts of the reflex arc, or of associated chains of neurons were doomed to failure. Lashley thought that at a physiological level of analysis both serial and parallel processes were involved; the cerebral cortex was "a dynamic, constantly active system, or, rather, a composite of many interacting systems" (Lashley, 1951, p. 526).

Some of Lashley's ideas were expressed in terms of fields of force, which suggests an influence of the Gestalt psychologists, particularly, Köhler (1920). As Boring put the Gestalt idea of the brain, "psychological experience and cortical events are likely to be much more sensibly connected if brain action is mainly a matter of field physics than they would be if brain action consisted only of nerve impulses" (Boring, 1950, p. 691).

These ideas, abstractly conceived and freed from an outmoded view of physics and an erroneous view of biology, appear to have recently resurfaced in some parallel distributed processing ideas of connectionist modeling (e.g., Rumelhart, McClelland, & the PDP Research Group, 1986).

James's Association chapter next presented a section on "the rapidity of association." Reporting that James himself (in a poorly described and rare empirical foray) found he "could name six hundred letters in two minutes on a printed page," and he figured that "five distinct acts of association between sight and sound (not to speak of the other processes concerned) must then have occurred in each second in my mind" (I: 557). He then noted that "The time-measuring psychologists of recent days have tried their hand at this problem by more elaborate means" (I: 557) and reviewed some work by Galton, Wundt, and Cattell. Their work is echoed in the reaction-time studies of information-processing psychologists in recent decades.

We now come to a felicitous error James made when he revised his magazine article "The Association of Ideas" (James, 1880) for inclusion as the association chapter in The Principles. Although he wanted to include habit, recency, vividness, and emotional congruity as factors in association, he apparently misread Francis Galton's Inquiries into human faculty (1883/ 1907), and added a footnote.

> If Shakespeare's plays are mentioned, and we were last night reading 'Richard II.,' vestiges of that play rather than that of 'Hamlet' or 'Othello' float through our mind. Excitement of peculiar tracts, or peculiar modes of general excitement in the brain, leave a sort of tenderness or exalted sensibility behind them in repose. Hence, recency in experience is a prime factor in determining revival in thought. [And now the footnote] I refer to recency of a few hours. Mr. Galton found that experiences from boyhood and youth were more likely to be suggested by words seen at random than experiences of later years." (I: 575).

In fact such remote experiences were retrieved *less* often by Galton than were more recent ones, although they did keep recurring on retests (see Crovitz, 1970). James's error troubled me, and was a factor in doing work trying to replicate the part of Galton's study in which memories came to mind in association with words. The problem of understanding the retention function of autobiographical memory has become more difficult since it was described by Crovitz and Schiffman (1974), a replication-study of Galton's work. College students searched for different personal memories in association with different common English nouns (APPLE, ARM, ARMY, BABY, BIRD, BOARD, BOOK, BOTTLE, BOY, CAT, CHURCH, CLOCK, DOOR, ENGINE, FLAG, HORSE, HOSPITAL, LIBRARY, NAIL, PICTURE, POTATO, PRISON, SHIP, STAR, STREET, TABLE, TICKET, TREE, and WINDOW). See Crovitz (1986) for another use of these common nouns as associative cues for recollection.

The students in the study of Crovitz and Schiffman (1974) then estimated the time-ago of the event to which each autobiographical memory referred. For college-aged subjects the result was a simple power function. The logarithm of the frequency of autobiographical memories is positively and linearly related to the logarithm of the *recency* of the events.. It is interpretable as a retention function on the assumption that people store an equal number of memories each hour of their life (Franklin & Holding, 1977; Robinson, 1976; Rubin, 1982; Rubin, Wetzler, & Nebes, 1986). The retention functions "provide a picture of the relative ease of recall of autobiographical memories across the lifespan" (Rubin et al., 1986, p. 203).

Crovitz and Schiffman (1974) noted that results with college students might not be comparable to Galton's results since Galton was in his mid-50s when he invented the word-association technique and used himself as the subject.

In recent studies of the distribution of autobiographical memories in older adults a complexity does arise (Rubin et al., 1986). Although the same power function with a slope of about 0.8 describes the retention of episodes over the most recent 20 to 30 years in adults 35 to 80 years old, a "reminiscence" component occurs in which episodes referring to times when the subjects were between 10 and 30 years old are over-represented. Thus, it is not surprising that a middle-aged Galton found "a reminiscence component" as he studied his own word-associations. Middle-aged people as well as college-aged people, however, do show recency at work for their personal memories of the last 20 years.

Crovitz and Schiffman (1974) had focused on personal memories that occur as associations to words; Freud had focused on words that occur as associations to words. Nobody denies that associations may occur to words and other stimuli, but how important ought the search for underlying processes of association be in psychological theory?

In Cofer's (Cofer, in preparation) analysis of steps leading to cognitive psychology, James Ward in the Encyclopedia Brittanica of 1886 was credited with reacting against the associationist viewpoint altogether by suggesting that association was relatively unimportant for creatures who can actively deploy their attention as they choose.

William James made the same point, but in the spirit of Georges Braque's great line, that a man should have two ideas, one to kill the other. James's fence-sitting position was that both automatic association existed *and* voluntary cognitive rumination existed. As Myers saw it in his excellent biography, James thought "the process of thinking can be explained by purely physiological principles of association in combination with the thinker's acts of intervention through attention, will, and taking interest, acts that play back upon the brain itself" (Myers, 1986, p. 247). Just how to think about such a combination, and how to establish a scientifically valid two-way relation between "mental events" and "brain events" remains, as it was in James's time, more goal than accomplishment. Yet promising steps in this direction have been made (e.g., Kosslyn, 1987).

From the vantage point of 1990, one can see that James in 1890 might have chosen to guess that separate parts of the brain subserved automatic association and voluntary cognition. However James settled for wittily leaving the challenge for you. "Too much anatomy has been found to order for theoretic purposes. . . . Let us therefore relegate the subject of the intimate workings of the brain to the physiology of the future . . ." (I: 81–82).

ASSOCIATION AND THE BRAIN

I would like to turn now to a consideration of some ideas about how association and cognition have been thought to work.

We begin with Aristotle: "The process of movement involved in the act of perception stamps in, as it were, a sort of impression of the percept, just as persons do who make an impression with a seal" (in wax). Anderson and

Bower (1973) quoted Aristotle in connection with their criticism of the later history of associationism, approving of Aristotle's restraint in arguing that the act of perception alone is a necessary and sufficient condition for the formation of a memory trace. (Aristotle did not bring reinforcement into the game.)

Voluntary recollection, for Aristotle, was *not* automatic. "When one wishes to recollect, here is what he will do: He will try to obtain a beginning of a movement whose sequel shall be the movement he desires to awaken."

A version of Aristotle's distinction between the automatic stamping-in and the voluntary recollection reappears in Hirsh (1974, 1980) who suggests a physiological reconciliation of the wars between associationist and cognitive psychologies.

Aristotle agreed with later associationists in seeing contiguity, similarity and contrast, for example, as standing behind associations between past and current thoughts. Aristotle framed no hypothetical brain-state nor neural network hypothesis to "explain" association.

Descartes did.

> When the mind wills to recall something, this volition causes the little (pineal) gland, by inclining successively to different sides, to impel the animal spirits toward different parts of the brain, until they come upon that part where the traces are left of the thing which it wishes to remember; for these traces are nothing else than the circumstance that the pores of the brain through which the spirits have already taken their course on presentation of the object, have thereby acquired a greater facility than the rest to be opened again the same way by the spirits which come to them; so that these spirits coming upon the pores enter thereby more readily than into the others. (Descartes, quoted in Lashley, 1950/1960, p. 478)

Lashley quoting this, credited Descartes 300 years beforehand with perhaps the earliest brain-model of memory. Lashley noted that if one substitutes nerve impulses for animal spirits, and synapses for pores one has a model of learning as changes in synaptic resistance. Further, action of the pineal gland in bending one way or another even offers a theory of scanning.

John Locke tried hard to avoid making a neural model. Locke wrote:

> I shall not at present meddle with the physical consideration of the mind, or trouble myself to examine wherein its essence consists, or by what motions of our spirits, or alterations of our bodies, we come to have any sensation by our organs, or any ideas in our understandings; and whether those ideas do, in their formation, any or all of them, depend on matter or no. These are speculations which, however curious and entertaining, I shall decline, as lying out of my way in the design I am now upon. (Locke, 1690/1924, pp. 9–10)

When Locke wrote the first edition of his *Esssay Concerning Human Understanding* his intention was to rule innate ideas out of the game. He mentioned association of ideas in the context of faulty associations, but his main empiricist point was that the whole content of the mind was made up of perceptions and reflections on them. Very soon a criticism was published, arguing that allowing non-perceptual "reflections" into the game implies the presence of non-perceptual ideas in the mind and thereby was not consistent with Locke's argument against innate ideas (Locke, 1690/1924, p. 79).

Condillac (1746/1974) also criticized Locke for allowing "reflection" into his system, in a wonderful book that may be the first work on psycholinguistics. Condillac assumed there were perceptions and signs for describing them—namely words: Everything interesting was represented by the associations between words (e.g., recollection and imagination).

In his second edition, Locke added this paragraph in reaction to attacks on "reflection" as an innate intruder.

> Our ideas are said to be in our memories, when indeed they are actually nowhere, but only there is an ability in the mind, when it will, to revive them again, and, as it were, paint them anew on itself, though some with more, some with less difficulty; some more lively, and others more obscurely. (Locke, 1690/1924, p. 83)

This "memory without memory-traces" idea reappears in some modern brain-models. Lashley (1950/1960) did surgical studies and failed to find localized engrams in the brain; that is, memory traces. This led him to insist on the idea of distributed representations of associations between events. Consistent with the spirit of Locke and Lashley, current connectionist models may argue for a memory as not existing locally, and as being realized only on retrieval (Rumelhart et al., 1986).

Now we come to Hartley, and are almost back to James. Here is Hartley's statement of the law of association, in 1749, quoted by James as giving the cause of associations:

> Any vibrations, A, B, C, etc., by being associated a sufficient Number of Times, get such a Power over a, b, c, etc., the corresponding Miniature Vibrations, that any of the Vibrations A, when impressed alone, shall be able to excite b, c, etc., the Miniatures of the rest. (I: 564)

Anderson and Bower (1973) noted Hartley makes no mention of a memory structure; rather . . .

> Hartley argued that remembering was a mental activity "[determined by] the sequencing of association in the mind. . . . The refusal of the British associationists to recognize the existence of memory traces is another instance of the extremeties to which one can be led by an untempered empiricist approach." (p. 25–26)

James took the position that any laws of association were to be understood in terms of action of the brain. From Aristotle's use of Plato's seal-in-wax metaphor all the way to Grossberg's use of a multilevel-networks-of-neurons metaphor (Grossberg, 1982, 1987), models of the association process dot history. However, we must sharply distinguish between "neural network" modeling in its two different current meanings: standard localization-of-function anatomic models of activity in networks of known structures and pathways versus present-day connectionist models that focus on computation in metaphoric networks of abstract "neurons." James would be, I imagine, as ambivalent about the 1980s computer-modeling of the brain as he had been about the mathematical modeling of sensation by early German psychophysicists. A different sort of patience may be needed for designing, performing, and analyzing the results of psychophysical experiments than for writing mathematics and testing computer programs. Patience may be the way of slow and steady progress, but it offends some spirits. But on with the story.

> Association, so far as the word stands for an effect is between THINGS THOUGHT-OF—it is THINGS, not ideas, which are associated in the mind. We ought to talk of the association of objects, not the association of ideas. And so far as association stands for a cause, it is between processes in the brain—it is these which, by being associated in certain ways, determine what successive objects shall be thought. (I: 554)

We now quote James's well-worn-path view of the memory trace: The section "The Law of Contiguity" begins:

> Time-determinations apart, the facts we have run over can all be summed up in the simple statement that objects once experienced together tend to become associated in the imagination, so that when any one of them is thought of, the others are likely to be thought of also, in the same order of sequence or coexistence as before. This statement we may name the law of mental association by contiguity. Whatever we name the law, since it expresses merely a phenomenon of mental habit, the most natural way of accounting for it is to conceive it as a result of the laws of habit in the nervous system; in other words, it is to ascribe it to a physiological cause. . . . Let us assume as the basis of all our subsequent reasoning this law (THE ELEMENTARY LAW OF ASSOCIATION): When two elementary brain-processes have been active together or in immediate succession, one of them, on reoccurring, tends to propogate its excitement into the other. The amount of activity at any given point in the brain-cortex is the sum of tendencies of all other points to discharge into it. (I: 561–567)

> A simple scheme will make the whole cause of memory plain. Let n be a past event; o its 'setting' (concomitants, date, self present, warmth and intimacy, etc., etc., as already set forth); and some present thought or fact which may

appropriately become the occasion of its recall. Let the nerve-centres, active in the thought of m, n, and o, be represented by M, N, and O, respectively; then the existence of the paths M—N, and N—O will be the fact indicated by the phrase 'retention of the event n in memory,' and the excitement of the brain along these paths will be the condition of the event n's actual recall. . . . These well-worn paths of an association are a clear rendering of what authors mean by 'predispositions,' 'vestiges,' 'traces,' etc., left in the brain by past experience. (I: 655)

In mainline American psychology, there followed the well-known shift away from introspection (Lyons, 1986) and toward studying associative processing in presumably non-introspecting animals; for example, Thorndike's work was designed to study association in the animal mind (see Gottlieb, 1979). Subsequently, Tolman (1932) wrote that his book, *Purposive Behavior in Animals and Men*, grew out of an experimental interest in animal learning and "an arm-chair urge towards speculation" (p. iii). Tolman found himself using terms like "cognition" and "purpose," and was well aware that "most readers will persist in believing that I mean by purposes and cognitions entities ultimately subjective in character and metaphysically teleological in import" (Tolman, 1932, p. xii). *Tolman's Association Principle* was:

Whenever one stimulus situation (sign) is followed by another (significate), there is established a relation between them, such that on subsequent occasions the former tends to give rise to an expectation of the latter (sign-significate-relation) . . . sign-significant-expectations are strengthened by confirmation and weakened by nonconfirmation. (Tolman, 1949, p. 145)

When Osgood (1953) quoted this, he complained about Tolman's "originality in the use of language" (p. 386). But it was an evocative originality that forced serious students to keep returning to the glossary in Tolman's 1932 book to reconvince themselves Tolman was as behavioristic as everyone who was respectable at that time. Tolman's impact was in insisting it just will not do to try to hide from complexity; healthy animals and people do act as if they operated on the basis of meaning, over and above stimulus-response reflexes.

As Osgood pointed out, Karl Zener (1937) was one of the first to suggest the apparent associationist simplicity of Pavlovian conditioning was due to the behavioral restrictions imposed on the subject. Sans harness the dog ran to the table and poised "expectantly" over the food pan. Zener saw conditioning as supplying a new "meaning" for the conditioned stimulus, a cognitive meaning.

More recently, cognitive psychology constructed many well-known models of association and memory in terms of an information-processing metaphor of what the brain might be doing. Cautionary critiques exist. My favorite is this:

> If memory is constructive and if "storage" is in the form of schemata . . . then the kind of representation it probably has in the brain is very difficult to characterize. . . . The representation must in some sense be abstract, since it can be manifested in paraphrase and other kinds of productive forms. The notion of an abstract representation somehow operating through brain cells is a sobering one and suggests that perhaps we require much more information about the brain, as well as about memory, before further speculation is indicated. (Cofer, 1973, p. 542)

James's correlational view of association in the brain reappeared in Donald Hebb's "Neurophysiological postulate":

> Let us assume that the persistence or repetition of a reverberatory activity (or "trace") tends to induce lasting cellular changes that add to its stability. The assumption can be precisely stated as follows: When an axon of cell A is near enough to excite a cell and repeatedly or persistently takes part in firing it, some growth process or metabolic change takes place in one or both cells such that A's efficiency, as one of the cells firing B, is increased. (Hebb, 1949, p. 62).

> Hebb introduced his book with some very nice writing; for example: Theorizing at this stage is like skating on thin ice—keep moving or drown. . . . When theory becomes static it is apt to become dogma; and psychological theory has the further danger, so long as so many of its problems are unresolved, of inviting a relapse into the vitalism and indeterminism of traditional thought. (Hebb, 1949, p. xii)

Little did Donald Hebb know that he would become credited with "the Hebb-rule" in the field of connectionist neural computation. The correlational "rule" had already been expressed by William James in the 1890 *Principles*, and so far as I can see, the Hebb-rule could have become known as the James-rule; or indeed, as the Tolman-rule.

I do want to emphasize the charm of the idea of neural association as used metaphorically in modern connectionist neural network modeling. A half-century after James's *Principles* was published, an abstract neural network was developed by McCullough and Pitts (1943). The perceptron network of fully connected neuron-like units was a beautifully simple device for actualizing associative learning (Rosenblatt, 1958). By adding one or more layers of such units to the perceptron network, and adjusting weights between input and output units according to "the Hebb-rule" or "the delta-rule," the new connectionism became the basis of parallel distributed processing models (Anderson & Hinton, 1981; Hinton & Anderson, 1981; Schneider, 1987). Unlike many cognitive psychological theories, such models are grounded in the beautiful mathematics in common usage in theoretical physics. For the mathematics of such models expressed in the terms of statistical mechanics see Hertz and Palmer (in press).

Of course such models have not yet been shown to actually represent the "intimate anatomy" of association in the brain. Such a demonstration seems likely to require the invention of some method for measuring the thresholds and connections of single neurons *in situ*.

Connectionist networks can be fascinating models of associative learning. I have spent weeks hunched over my computer watching the McClelland and Rumelhart (1988) programs "learn" through continuous changes in the representations of things. Each representation is replaced by the next, and there is no better description of this state of affairs than this one, from the *Principles:* "The laws of association to be treated of here might, for aught we can see, be true in a creature wholly devoid of memory or comparison. Each of his ideas would vanish in the act of awakening its successor" (I: 580).

A RESOLUTION OF THE
ASSOCIATIVE-COGNITIVE WARS

James wrote *Principles* in a philosophical tradition that assumed the explanation for psychological matters could be expressed in physiological terms. Rather like some modern neuropsychologists, James hoped to understand the relation between physiological mechanisms and conscious experience. However, the analytic tools available in James's time did not allow much beyond wit and wishing.

James's views of the brain were tentative and imprecise. Much more is known about the brain a century later. The most important relevant developments in physiological knowledge during the past century have concerned changing views of the localization of function in the brain. (See the general review by Phillips, Zeki, & Barlow, 1985; for perception, see Cowey, 1985; for learning and memory, see Mishkin, Malamut, & Bachevalier, 1984).

If associationism is taken as thesis and the cognitive countermovement as antithesis, we may take as synthesis the multiple-systems approach typified in the neuropsychological work of Hirsh (1974, 1980). Hirsh argued that in the absence of the hippocampus, learning is totally a matter of (S-R) habit formation. All that is stored is the changing probability of S → R due to reinforcement contingencies.

Readers familiar with learning theory will realize that the behavior of normal animals is treated in a neo-Tolmanian framework, while that of hippocampally ablated animals is held to be everything for which early S-R theorists could have asked. (Hirsh, 1974, p. 439)

From such work, "both sides in the great debate between behaviorism and cognitivism must ultimately be declared the winners, since the evidence from the study of amnesia demonstrates that both types of processes must be constantly present in normal behavior." (Mishkin et al., 1984)

The idea that an association/habit/learning system exists separately from a cognitive/memory system is consistent with observations concerning source-amnesia (Evans & Thorn, 1966) and with recent descendents of Tulving's (1972) idea of separating semantic from episodic memory (see Sherry & Schacter, 1988). For an example of an unusual amnesia possibly affecting the association/habit/learning system while leaving the cognitive/memory system intact (the opposite of the classical amnesia syndrome) see De Renzi, Liotti, and Nichelli (1987).

What can be expected in the next century? More of the same, with an occasional ironic point of light. I would like to think that the business of studying separate association/habit/learning and cognitive/memory brain systems can be made simple to play with, perhaps by some future discovery along the lines of pharmacology. Perhaps benzodiazepines can be shown to target the association/learning system while drugs such as scopolamine target the cognitive/memory system (see Wolkowitz, Tinkelberg, & Weingartner, 1985).

Or more delightful would be some unlikely future demonstration that separate reversible blockages of blood supply could be arranged to temporarily shut down either the association/habit/learning system or the cognitive/memory system, along the lines of Kenneth J. R. Craik's immortal article proving the retinal locus of visual afterimages by pressing on his eye to temporarily and reversibly separate it in effect from his brain (Craik, 1940).

The argument of this chapter was that the history of the study of association in our field since James (1890) can be tentatively and broadly seen as successive waves of investigation of the psychological output of two hypothesized brain-systems, one of which subserves associative processes (habit and learning) and the other of which subserves cognitive processes (memory).

ACKNOWLEDGMENTS

This work was supported by the Medical Research Service of the Veterans Administration.

REFERENCES

Anderson, J. A., & Hinton, G. E. (1981). Models of information processing in the brain. In G. E. Hinton & J. A. Anderson (Eds.), *Parallel models of associative memory* (pp. 9–48). Hillsdale, NJ: Lawrence Erlbaum Associates.

Anderson, J. R., & Bower, G. H. (1973). *Human associative memory*. New York: Wiley.

Boring, E. G. (1950). *A history of experimental psychology*. New York: Appleton-Century-Crofts.

Cofer, C. N. (1973). Constructive processes in memory. *American Scientist, 61,* 537–543.

Cofer, C. N. (1979). Human learning and memory. In E. Hearst (Ed.), *The first century of experimental psychology* (pp. 323–369). Hillsdale, NJ: Lawrence Erlbaum Associates.

Cofer, C. N. (in preparation). Intimations of cognitive psychology and its emergence. In R. E. Shaw & F. Kessel (Eds.), *The cognitive revolution reconsidered: From empiricism to rationalism*. Hillsdale, NJ: Lawrence Erlbaum Associates.

Condillac, E. B. De. (1974). *An essay on the origin of human knowledge; Being a supplement to Mr. Locke's essay on the human understanding*. New York: AMS Press. (Original work published 1746).

Cowey, A. (1985). Aspects of cortical organization related to selective attention and selective impairments of visual perception: A tutorial preview. In M. I. Posner & O. S. M. Marin (Eds.), *Attention and performance XI* (pp. 41–62). Hillsdale, NJ: Lawrence Erlbaum Associates.

Craik, K. J. W. (1940). The origin of visual afterimages. *Nature, 144,* 512.

Crovitz, H. F. (1970). *Galton's walk: Methods for the analysis of thinking, intelligence, and creativity*. New York: Harper & Row.

Crovitz, H. F. (1986). Loss and recovery of autobiographical memory after head injury. pp. 273–290. In D. C. Rubin (Ed.), *Autobiographical memory*. New York: Cambridge University Press.

Crovitz, H. F., & Schiffman, H. (1974). Frequency of episodic memories as a function of their age. *Bulletin of the Psychonomic Society, 4,* 517–518.

Daniel, W. F., Crovitz, H. F., & Weiner, R. D. (1987). Neuropsychological aspects of disorientation, *Cortex, 23,* 169–187.

De Renzi, E., Liotti, M., & Nichelli, P. (1987). Semantic amnesia with preservation of autobiographical memory: A case report. *Cortex, 23,* 575–597.

Evans, F. J., & Thorn, W. A. F. (1966). Two types of posthypnotic amnesia: recall amnesia and source amnesia. *International Journal of Clinical and Experimental Hypnosis, 14,* 162–179.

Franklin, H. C., & Holding, D. H. (1977). Personal memories at different ages. *Quarterly Journal of Experimental Psychology, 29,* 527–532.

Fodor, J. A., & Pylyshyn, Z. W. (1988). Connectionism and cognitive architecture: A critical analysis. *Cognition, 28,* 3–71.

Galton, F. (1907). *Inquiries into human faculty and its development*. London: Dent & Sons. (Original work published 1883)

Gottlieb, G. (1979). Comparative psychology and ethology. In E. Hearst (Ed.), *The first century of experimental psychology* (pp. 323–369). Hillsdale, NJ: Lawrence Erlbaum Associates.

Grossberg, S. (1982). *Studies of mind and brain*, Boston: Riedel Press.

Grossberg, S. (1987). *The adaptive brain* (Vols. 1–2). Amsterdam: North-Holland.

Hebb, D. O. (1949). *The organization of behavior: a neuropsychological theory*. New York: Wiley.

Helmholtz, H. von. (1962). Goethe's scientific researches. p. 20. in *Popular Scientific Lectures*, New York: Dover. (Original work published 1852)

Hertz, J. A., & Palmer, R. G. (in press). *Neural computation*. New York: Springer.

Hinton, G. E., & Anderson, J. A. (Eds.). (1981). *Parallel models of associative memory.* Hillsdale, NJ: Lawrence Erlbaum Associates.

Hirsh, R. (1974). The hippocampus and contextual retrieval of information from memory: A theory. *Behavioral Biology, 12,* 421–444.

Hirsh, R. (1980). The hippocampus, conditional operations, and cognition. *Physiological Psychology, 8,* 175–182.

Jenkins, J. J. (1974). Remember that old theory of memory? Well, forget it. *American Psychologist, 29,* 785–795.

James, W. (1880). The association of ideas. *Popular Science Monthly, 16,* 577–593.

James, W. (1890). *The principles of psychology* (Vols. 1–2), New York: Holt.

Köhler, H. (1920). *Die physischen Gestalten in Ruhe und im stationaren Zustand* [Physical Gestalten in resting and stationary conditions]. Erlangen, West Germany: Weltkreisverlag.

Kosslyn, S. M. (1987). Seeing and imaging in the cerebral hemispheres: A computational approach. *Psychological Review, 94,* 148–175.

Lashley, K. S. (1950/1960). In search of the engram. In F. A. Beach, D. O. Hebb, C. T. Morgan, & H. W. Nissen (Eds.), *The Neuropsychology of Lashley* (pp. 338–344). New York: McGraw-Hill.

Lashley, K. S. (1951). The problem of serial order in behavior. In L. A. Jeffress (Ed.), *Cerebral mechanisms in behavior* (pp. 112–139). New York: Wiley.

Locke, J. (1924). *An essay concerning human understanding* (A. S. Pringle-Pattison, Ed.). Oxford: Oxford University Press. (Original work published 1690)

Lyons, W. E. (1986). *The disappearance of introspection.* Cambridge, MA: MIT Press.

McClelland, J. L., & Rumelhart, D. E. (1988). *Explorations in parallel distributed processing: A handbook of models, programs, and exercises.* Cambridge, MA: MIT Press.

McCullough, W. S., & Pitts, W. (1943). A logical calculus of ideas immanent in nervous activity. *Bulletin of Mathematics Biophysics 5,* 115–133.

Mishkin, M., Malamut, B., & Bachevalier, J. (1984). Memories and habits: Two neural systems. In G. Lynch, J. L. McGaugh, & N. M. Weinberger (Eds.), *Neurobiology of learning and memory* (pp. 65–77). New York: Guilford.

Myers, G. E. (1986). *William James: His life and thought.* New Haven, CT: Yale University Press.

Osgood, C. E. (1953). *Method and theory in experimental psychology.* New York: Oxford University Press.

Phillips, C. G., Zeki, S., & Barlow, H. R. (1985). Localization of function in the cerebral cortex: Past, present and future. *Brain, 107,* 328–361.

Poincaré, H. (1914). *Science and method.* London: T. Nelson and Sons.

Robinson, J. A. (1976). Sampling autobiographical memory. *Cognitive Psychology, 8,* 578–595.

Rosenblatt, F. (1958). The perceptron: a probabilistic model for information storage and organization of the brain. *Psychological Review, 65,* 386–408.

Rubin, D. C. (1982). The retention function for autobiographical memory. *Journal of Verbal Learning and Verbal Behavior, 21,* 21–38.

Rubin, D. C., Wetzler, S. E., & Nebes, R. D. (1986). Autobiographical memories across the lifespan. In D. C. Rubin (Ed.), *Autobiographical memory* (pp. 202–221). Cambridge: Cambridge University Press.

Rumelhart, D. E., McClelland, J. L., & the PDP Research Group. (1986). *Parallel distributed processing* (Vols. 1–2). Cambridge, MA: MIT Press, A Bradford Book.

Schneider, W. (1987). Connectionism: Is it a paradigm shift for psychology? *Behavioral Research Methods, Instruments, and Computers, 19,* 73–83.

Sechenov, I. (1965). *Reflexes of the brain* (S. Belsky, Trans.), Cambridge, MA: MIT Press. (Original work published 1863)

Sherry, D. F., & Schacter, D. L. (1988). The evolution of multiple memory systems, *Psychological Review, 94,* 439–454.

Tolman, E. C. (1932). *Purposive behavior in animals and man*. New York: Appleton-Century.

Tolman, E. C. (1949). There is more than one kind of learning. *Psychological Review, 56*, 144–155.

Tulving, E. (1972). Episodic and semantic memory. In E. Tulving & W. Donaldson (Eds.), *Organization of memory* (pp. 381–403). New York: Academic Press.

Wolkowitz, O. M., Tinkelberg, J. R., & Weingartner, H. (1985). Psychopharmacological perspective of cognitive functions II. Specific pharmacologic agents, *Neuropsychobiology, 14*, 133–156.

Zener, K. (1937). The significance of behavior accompanying conditioned salivary secretion for theories of the conditioned response. *American Journal of Psychology, 50*, 384–403.

Chapter 8

Imagination

Sohee Park
Stephen M. Kosslyn
Harvard University

I am myself a good draughtsman, and have a very lively interest in pictures, statues, architectures and decoration, and a keen sensibility to artistic effects. But I am an extremely poor visualizer, and find myself often unable to reproduce in my mind's eye pictures which I have most carefully examined.

. . . I can seldom call to mind even a single letter of the alphabet in purely retinal terms. I must trace the letter by running my mental eye over its contour in order that the image of it shall have any distinctness at all.

William James (II: 53, 61)

Although the theories in William James's *Principles of Psychology* have had an enormous impact on certain fields within psychology (e.g., the study of emotion), James's ideas about the sensory-perceptual aspects of the mind have been largely neglected. We argue in this chapter that James's approach to the study of imagery is surprisingly contemporary, and attempt to note areas illuminated by James within this field that have yet to receive their due in contemporary research.

Considering the great emphasis on perception and psychophysics at the time of his writing, and also the fact that he studied in Germany where these areas were being investigated with vigor and enthusiasm, it seems unlikely that James was uninterested in sensory-perceptual processes. James devotes one chapter of his *Principles* to sensation, one to imagination, and two to perception. His treatment of these areas is sophisticated and elegant, yet his influence on contemporary work appears to be negligible. This is in contrast to Helmholtz, whose work on vision and audition has influenced us directly and whose hypotheses we attempt to test and refine to this day. Perhaps this relative lack of influence is due to James's being perceived primarily as a synthesizer of ideas rather than as a theoretician. And in fact, his main contribution to the study of imagery lies in his multidisciplinary review of the state of the art in research on imagination at the end of the 19th century. He gave us a panoramic view of the field and introduced us to the fundamental problems of imagery. James went a long way toward structuring the area of inquiry by elucidating the problems that should be addressed.

James, firmly rooted in biology, begins his discussion of imagery with sensory processes and ends with a neurological model. This model has much in common with many current models, a century later. However, unlike his predecessors, the British Empiricists, and some contemporary theorists, his approach encompasses psychological data, philosophical concerns, and neurological constraints. In this chapter we focus on James's contributions to the way we conceptualize, and attempt to build plausible models of, imagery. We only briefly review his ideas about the role of imagery in concept representation and individual differences in imagery. Our aim is not only to evaluate James's ideas but also to uncover fertile ground as yet unplowed.

In the "Imagination" chapter James divides the main issues into three broad areas: conceptual and philosophical foundations, individual differences, and neurological processes that underlie imagination.

CONCEPTUAL AND PHILOSOPHICAL FOUNDATIONS

James's stance on the nature of concepts is essentially that of a traditional empiricist, although there are differences. James discusses the then-current idea that sensations modify the nervous system, and as a result allow mental copies to arise in the mind. Fantasy or imagination arises from the process of reproducing copies of original sensations that were once experienced. He distinguishes "reproductive" from "productive" imagination. Reproductive imagination involves the recall of literal copies whereas productive imagination involves the integration of elements from different original stimuli. James excludes sensory afterimages from the realm of imagination; he is interested in the mental representation of sensory experience. Hence, he focuses on the idea of a mental "copy" and its relation to concepts.

James begins his discussion of how images and concepts are related with Hume's atomistic view. Hume believed that ideas are copies of the original stimuli and that all ideas originate from sensations. Sensory "impressions" and ideas were thought to differ only in their strength; an image was conceived of as just a weak impression. Hume argued that because a strong impression must have a determinate quantity and quality, so too must its weaker copy. However, James points out that surely Hume himself must have been able to image his own works (books) "without seeing distinctly every word and letter upon the pages which floated before his mind's eye" (II: 46). In other words, James noted that images do not have to be exact copies of the sensory impressions. James then considers Huxley's modification of Hume's position. Huxley argued that our memories are sketches and not exact copies, and complex images are "generic" rather than specific; he equated vague images with abstract ideas. That is, complex images were thought to be prototypical rather than specific. James, however, disagrees with Huxley's position that abstract ideas are the same as vague images: Whether one has a blurred picture in memory (hence, vague) or a sharp one, the image must be a symbol if it is to stand for a whole class of individuals (see Fodor, 1975; Kosslyn, 1983).

In recent years, the idea of prototypes has had a major influence on theories of concept representation. It has been suggested that internal representations of prototypes play an important role in our thought processes and that mental images can serve as such representations (for a review, see Smith & Medin, 1981). However, it is now generally acknowledged that images—like pictures—are "under description"; they must be interpreted in order to have meaning. A picture of a man walking up a hill, for example, could be taken by a Martian as a picture of a man sliding downhill backwards. (Wittgenstein, 1953, pointed out that this ambiguity is unlikely actually to occur for a person, and underlined the importance of our innate mental predispositions to interpret pictures as depicting one thing over all of the other logical possibilities.) The image must be conceptualized in the context of a system of interpretation, which is a view very similar to the one developed by James. As James suggested, it now is clear that not all concepts can be represented by quasi-perceptual images, but images do appear to play a role in at least some forms of thought (cf. Fodor, 1975; Kosslyn, 1983; Shepard & Cooper, 1982).

INDIVIDUAL DIFFERENCES

James then turns to a rather lengthy treatment of individual differences in imagination. He acknowledges that there are great individual differences in imagination abilities (indeed, as quoted at the outset, he professes not to have very vivid visual images himself). James spends the bulk of this section considering lengthy quotes from Galton (1883), which describe Galton's "Breakfast Table Questionnaire" (the grandfather of all imagery questionnaires). Galton began by giving this questionnaire to his friends, who were professionals and eminent men of science. This questionnaire asked the informants to consider how they described what they had eaten for breakfast that morning; this questionnaire had three parts. The first part addressed the "illumination" of the image; was it clear or dim? The second part addressed the "definition" of the images on the breakfast table; were all objects well-defined simultaneously? The third part addressed colors of the images. From the responses, Galton concluded that intellectual men do not use visual imagery because it is antagonistic to abstract thinking. Galton then went on to expand his sample to other sorts of people, and eventually inferred that imagery is used more by "lower" human beings (i.e., lower class men, women, and children) than by intellectual men. From these results, Galton hypothesized that imagery is an inferior and primitive form of mental activity. James's chapter gives some weight to these speculations.

The notion that imagery is an inferior form of thought was not systematically explored until the 1950s, for a number of reasons. First, very little research on imagery was done at all for almost 50 years. The rise of behaviorism in America had as one hallmark a strong anti-introspectionist ideology. As was demonstrated in the 1970s and 1980s, methodologies could be developed for the scientific study of imagery that do not require active introspection; however, there was no impetus to develop them prior to the 1950s. Until then, behaviorism dominated the content of research in academic psychology, and the focus was on input/output relations, not on the internal events that mediated them.

It is curious that during the behaviorist era clinicians studying the effects of brain damage continued to report cases that demonstrated the existence of mental function, including imagery, but these were not incorporated into mainstream psychology. Indeed, even today many, and perhaps most, experimental psychologists are unaware of this body of data. James placed great emphasis on neuropsychological data, and for good reason, as we shall argue shortly.

Modern research on individual differences in mental imagery entered a new phase with Roe's (1951) study of leading scientists. The results of her questionnaire study contradicted Galton's claim that eminent men of science have poor imagery. She found that scientists in different fields use different types of imagery. For example, biologists and experimental physicists reported using visual imagery, whereas theoretical physicists, psychologists, and anthropologists seemed to prefer "verbal" imagery.

The relationship between intelligence and imagery ability has not yet been systematically investigated beyond Galton's speculations. However, if intelligence is defined as performance on an IQ test, then there will be a relation in part if only because certain subsets of the Wechsler Adult Intelligence Tests require some imagery abilities (e.g., the block design task). There are also reports of sex differences in spatial reasoning abilities. Systematic uses of imagery tasks in this context may prove to be useful. Indeed, a research team in our lab has presented 50 adults with an intelligence test and imagery tasks that selectively assessed mental rotation ability, image scanning ability, image generation ability, and image retention ability. The correlations between scores on the intelligence test and scores on the imagery tasks were very low. This is only preliminary research, and needs to be extended further. If these results are robust over a variety of different types of subject populations, then it simply may be that imagery and other forms of intelligence are independent. If so, then Galton's result could reflect small sample size or nonrandom sampling.

Self-reports of great scientists also dampen the generality of Galton's claims. For example, Kekulé's moment of insight into the structure of the benzene molecule reportedly came to him in an image. Kekulé was dozing off, and "saw" a chain of snakes floating. Suddenly, the head of the chain joined the tail of the last snake and formed a ring (Koestler, 1964), inspiring Kekulé to hypothesize that benzene is a ring. Einstein also reported the use of imagery in his thinking, and describes an "imagery simulation" of what a beam of light would look like if one could chase after it and match its speed; Einstein later claimed that this image was one root of his theory of relativity (see Schlipp, 1949; Shepard & Cooper, 1982, discuss many similar examples).

Recently two studies conducted by Kosslyn, Seger, Pani, and Hillger (in press) investigated the ways in which people report using imagery in everyday life. In the first study, the subjects kept a diary for a week, reporting images at the end of the day; in the second study, a detailed questionnaire was given to a group of new subjects, which was filled out hourly or immediately after an image was noted. The results from both studies were extremely similar, lending credibility to the reports. The most surprising result was that most of the images that subjects reported were not formed with an obvious immediate purpose, but often seemed a form of daydream—not unlike some of the anecdotal reports from scientists in their moments of discovery. Not many people reported imagery that was intentionally used for problem solving. It is possible, however, that there are individual differences in the uses of imagery, and that some people tend to use imagery for specific ends more than do other people. This notion is entirely consistent with James's views, particularly if we consider differences in preferred modality of imagery.

James's interest in individual difference is developed further in his discussion of imagination types. Following Binet (1886/1907), he divides people into modality-specific types. For example, those who rely primarily on visual imagery are the visual types whereas those who are very good at imagining sounds are the auditory types. There are also motor types and tactile types. Although there has been some work along these lines in recent times, it has not flowered. For example, Leibovitz, London, Cooper, and Tart (1972) asked subjects to rate the type of imagery evoked by a series of words, and were able to group the respondents according to the modality that predominated. Marsella and Quijano (1974) attempted to find cross-cultural differences in imagery types based on the hypothesis that different cultures stress different sensory modalities. They found no evidence for the hypothesis. After reviewing the literature on individual differences in imagery, White, Sheehan, and Ashton (1977) concluded that more people have and use visual imagery than other types, with the next most common form being auditory imagery. Overall, research in this area has been exploratory and descriptive; unfortunately, there has not been a coherent theoretical framework for approaching individual differences in modality dominance.

Paivio and Ernest (1971) developed one of the few theory-based approaches to studying individual differences in imagery. Paivio's "Dual Code Theory" led them to postulate two distinct ways of representing information in memory: imaginally or verbally. Paivio and Ernest developed the "Individual Differences Questionnaire" (IDQ), which assessed the representational proclivities of a person. This questionnaire produced evidence that some people prefer specific modes of thought, and these preferences predict performance in other tasks (such as speed of identifying briefly presented stimuli).

The most widely used imagery questionnaire in recent times seems to be the VVIQ (Vividness of Visual Imagery Quotient), developed by Marks (1973). Marks found that people who report more vivid images show fewer eye movements when recalling pictures, and Finke (1980) summarizes a variety of behavioral correlations with VVIQ score. These results are interesting, but some of them have proven difficult to replicate. Part of the problem may be that "vividness" is not a simple construct; it could reflect a number of different processing components, some of which may be more relevant for a given task than others. Thus, vividness may be a composite measure, and depending on which components have contributed most in a given sample, the measure will or will not predict performance on other tasks.

Kosslyn, Brunn, Cave, and Wallach (1984) analyzed the underlying processing used in imagery, and provided evidence that people differ in the efficacy of the individual processes. Kosslyn et al. recruited 50 subjects from an advertisement in the local newspaper, ensuring that a varied sample was tested. These people participated in 6 hours of testing, allowing the collection of 13 measures of imagery performance. The first important result was that there were not generally high correlations among the scores for the different imagery tasks; rather, there was a range of correlations, from − .44 to .79. Thus, imagery is not a single ability; if it were, then each person should have performed comparably on all of the tasks. For each measure, a model of the underlying processing subsystems was developed, and the similarity of each pair of tasks was computed using the number of shared processing subsystems posited in the models (the actual method of computing intertask similarity was more complicated than this, but this description serves to convey the gist of what was done). The second result of interest was that the similarities of the models predicted the observed intertask correlations. The correlation between the predicted similarities and actual correlations was r = .56. Another version of this theory of imagery was subsequently developed to be consistent with facts about the neurophysiology and neuroanatomy of the visual system; this version was then used to generate new estimates of intertask similarity, and these estimates proved slightly better, correlating r = .63 (Kosslyn, Van Kleeck, & Kirby, in press).

Neither the theory of Kosslyn et al. (1984) nor that of Kosslyn, Van Kleek, and Kirby (in press) were developed with individual differences in mind; both theories were attempts to devise accounts of basic imagery phenomena that were precise and complete enough to be implemented in a computer simulation model. The attempt, then, to integrate the study of individual differences into the more general study of cognition is exactly along the lines adopted by James. James was not so much interested in individual differences for their own sake, but as a means of gaining insight into the nature of the faculty. This tradition is alive and well.

Most work on individual differences in imagery has focused on visual imagery, including that which attempts to develop the underlying bases of individual differences in information processing. James, however, was interested in modality differences in imagery (partly, it would seem, because of the disparity in the quality of his own auditory and visual imagery). It seems that the time is ripe for renewed attention to the issue of modality-specific processing, especially within an information-processing context. The interaction between different modes of imagery has been reported sporadically, but most of these studies are largely exploratory. For example, Wolpin and Weinstein (1983) studied the effect of olfactory stimulation on visual imagery. They asked people to form visual images with a consistent odor or an inconsistent odor. In the "consistent" condition subjects reported that their visual images became clearer and more vivid. In the "inconsistent" condition, the subjects reported that their visual images became less clear and vivid. (However, only female subjects were tested, which limits the generality of any conclusions one could draw from the study.)

Individual differences in imagery and creativity, another topic that interested James, has not been studied systematically, but there are occasional reports. Luria's (1968) famous synesthesic mnemonist was reportedly able to utilize images in all senses, and often had cross-sensory imagery; he could "feel" the color red, "see" the sound of the flute, "hear" roundness and so on. One may imagine that with such an unusual mind, full of imagery, he was rather artistic or creative. Unfortunately, his vast memory apparently was also a burden on his intellectual functioning. He could never concentrate or attend to one thing at a time. On the other hand, Mozart, who seems to have been endowed with exceptional auditory imagery, reportedly utilized this tool in his moments of creation. He wrote in his letters that when he composed a symphony, he could "hear" all parts in his head simultaneously (Holmes, 1878). Thus, this too is a potentially rich area of research that has yet to be mined.

At present, then, we have more anecdotal accounts than solid data on many facets of individual differences in imagery. If James were alive today, our bet is that he would steer a graduate student or two in this direction, and we see no reason why his modern-day surrogates should not do the same.

NEURAL UNDERPINNINGS

Finally, James considers the possible neural mechanisms that underlie imagery. This is where he tackles the fundamental issues, addressing questions such as: Where does sensation end and imagery begin? What is the nature of imagery? How do we form images? Where is the seat of imagination in the brain? To address these issues he advocates a "backflow" model in which "currents" flow backwards in perceptual pathways in the brain. This idea is very much alive today, and has important implications for the so-called "imagery debate." These ideas are so relevant and central to contemporary concerns that we will focus on them for the remainder of this chapter.

Neuropsychological case studies of imagery have become increasingly popular in recent years (e.g., see Farah, 1984, for a review), almost 100 years after James discussed Charcot's patient (Mr. X) in his chapter on imagination. It was very natural for James to refer to brain functions when discussing cognitive functions, yet mainstream cognitive psychologists have only recently begun to do this without squeamishness.

To orient the reader to James's perspective, we will briefly review his discussion of Mr. X. This patient was a highly educated, multilingual businessman who reportedly had wonderful visual imagery (but inferior auditory memory) prior to his "confusional attack." After the attack, everything seemed foreign and new to him. He could see all things distinctively, but his memory for form and color was gone. For example, he could not recall his wife's or children's faces, and when he saw them they seemed unfamiliar to him. He knew that his wife had black hair, but he did not know what the color black looked like. Moreover, he forgot his own face. When he returned to a well-visited city, it seemed totally new to him. His ability to recognize objects gradually returned, and he came to feel at home again in familiar cities. However, when asked to imagine a well-know landmark in town, he reportedly could not imagine it at all although he knew that it was there. His drawing ability also suffered. His drawings had become very childish, apparently as a result of his inability to imagine what things look like. When he was asked to draw an arcade, he knew it was described as having semi-circular arches, but he could not image what semi-circular things look like! (It is not clear whether he could copy well.) With such loss of visual imagery, he attempted to compensate by relying more on auditory imagery, even though his auditory memory had been clearly inferior to his visual memory prior to his attack. He apparently reported that he began to dream only in words.

In contemporary terms, it seems that Mr. X probably suffered in part from visual associative agnosia (Damasio, 1986), which may have reflected damage to the visual memories themselves or to the means of accessing them. James emphasizes here that the problem was in visual processing, affecting both perception and imagery, and that there are other imagery systems that can partially compensate for the loss of these visual abilities. The idea that imagery and perception share common mechanisms has gained considerable empirical support in recent years (e.g., see Farah, 1988; Finke, 1980; Finke & Shepard, 1986; Shepard & Cooper, 1982, for reviews). However, the idea of compensation across sensory modalities has, to our knowledge, not been studied. Indeed, the role of imagery in drawing is not often examined and is only poorly understood.

Although the idea that imagery and perception share some processes has a long and venerable history, exactly what is shared has never been clear. James's interest lay in the neural pathways that may be shared by imagery and perceptual processes. He took Bain's position that imagery processes occupy the "very same parts" in the brain in the same manner as sensory processes, and analyzed this claim cautiously. What did Bain mean by the "same parts"? Did he mean only the parts inside the brain or also the same peripheral parts? This question is important in addressing the issue of where sensation ends and imagery begins.

At the time, it was commonly believed that imagery is a milder, diluted type of sensation. James uses Bain (1855/1977) to illustrate this viewpoint; to Bain persistence of sensation after the withdrawal of external stimuli suggested continuation of the "same currents," but weaker. Bain then considered "impressions" evoked by mental causes alone and concluded that this "renewed feeling" occupies the very same parts in the same manner as the original impression. James argues that all "currents" tend to run forward (i.e., from sensory organs to brain to motor system) during normal perceptual activity. His question is whether these currents run backwards during imagination processes, and if so, how far. If, James points out, Bain means to include the peripheral parts of the perceptual systems in the imagery systems, then these parts must be somehow excited during the imagination process. James asks, can peripheral sense organs be excited from above during imagination?

James's evidence that currents do run backwards was drawn from personal accounts by Meyer (1843, quoted in James 1890), and by Féré (quoted in James, 1890). Meyer's "experiments" are subjective introspections. For example, he imagined a silver stirrup and after he had "looked" in his mind's eye for a while, he opened his eyes and was able to see an afterimage for a long time. The existence of such a negative afterimage is taken to support James's view. Furthermore, James points out, when external stimulation is very weak it is hard to discriminate images from sensations (Perky, 1910; Segal & Fusella, 1970). More recently, Finke and Schmidt (1977, 1978) demonstrated that orientation-specific color aftereffects (the "McCollough effect") could, under some circumstances, be obtained with imagery. Hence, the borderline between imagination and perception is not clear cut. However, because these sorts of phenomena occur only under unusual circumstances, James concludes that peripheral sense organs are not ordinarily involved in imagery processes; the backflow typically stops before the sensory organs are reached.

Even if the same sense organs (or "low level processes," to use contemporary terminology) are not involved in imagery and perception, the question of whether the two abilities make use of the same types of representations remains. The idea of a top-down activation of perceptual representations has been put forward by Hebb (1968), Shepard & Cooper (1982), and Finke (1980), among others. Farah (1988) reviews the neuropsychological literature and presents a strong case for the use of shared representations. Her evidence includes electrophysiological and cerebral blood flow data collected during imagery tasks, in addition to reports of common effects of brain damage on imagery and visual perception. During visual imagery tasks, normal subjects show activation of the occipital lobe, posterior superior parietal, and posterior inferior temporal areas. These areas show similar activation during normal visual perceptual tasks. In short, there is now good evidence that parts of the brain involved in visual perception are also used in visual imagery.

The next question James considered was, assuming that imagery and like-modality perception share common mechanisms, then how do we discriminate images from sensations under ordinary circumstances? Although James lacked the vocabulary, both literally and conceptually, to state his theory unambiguously, he seems to have been trying to say something like the following: In both perception and imagery there is "current" running bottom-up and top-down (our terms), but the relative intensities are different. In perception, the world is driving most (but not all) of the activity, where as in imagery the activity arises in higher brain centers and currents flow back to the parts of the brain involved in sensory processing (but not to the sense organs themselves). Thus, the way we typically tell which is which is by the "resistance" set up from the backflow relative to the bottom-up currents—by the relative intensities of the two kinds of processing. During perception there is little resistance from backflow.

This sort of theorizing is important for two reasons. First the question of how we distinguish imagery from perception has been neglected in contemporary research. This question is fundamental; if we cannot answer it, we do not really understand the way in which perception and imagery share common processes. Second, and more subtle, the notion of "backflow" has some important implications for the "imagery debate." Before we can discuss these implications, a very brief review is necessary: The debate about imagery began in 1973, with the publication of Zenon Pylyshyn's paper "What the Mind's Eye Tells the Mind's Brain: A Critique of Mental Imagery." This debate was not about the existence or qualities of the experience of "having a mental image." Rather, the debate focused on the way mental images are internally represented, and whether this type of representation is distinct from the "propositional representations" used in language processing. Pylyshyn argued that the pictorial properties of imagery evident to introspection are simply epiphenomenal. That is, just as the heat given off by a lightbulb has no role in allowing one to read, the pictorial properties of imagery putatively have nothing to do with how information is represented or processed. Kosslyn and Pomerantz (1977) summarized and attempted to refute each of Pylyshyn's arguments. Kosslyn and Pomerantz (1977) also summarized the evidence for distinct, non-linguistic imagery representations; for each class of data they compared and contrasted "propositional" and "imagery" account, and argued that the imagery accounts often were more compelling.

Pylyshyn (1981) then put forward an essentially methodological critique, arguing that the experimental results taken to support the claim that images have pictorial properties were flawed. He posited that "task demands" led subjects (often unconsciously) to interpret imagery instructions to require them to mimic what they believed would occur in the analogous perceptual situation. Pinker, Choate, and Finke (1984) and Jolicoeur and Kosslyn (1985) directly addressed this claim, and provided evidence that task demands were not at the root of one imagery result, namely the increased time required to scan increased distance over imagined objects.

There were numerous exchanges in this debate, but it proved largely inconclusive. For the most part, people who initially were convinced that imagery is a distinct form of internal representation stayed convinced, and people who thought imagery representations are in fact like those used in language, continued to think so. This state of affairs is rather depressing from the point of view of cognitive science as science. We need theories that are unambiguous and precise enough to make clear predictions, and we need methodologies that allow disputes to be settled to the satisfaction of all parties. The failure to resolve the debate implies either that the alternative positions were not stated clearly enough to be discriminated empirically, and/or that the appropriate methodology was not available.

James's ideas about imagery have some interesting implications for the debate about the nature of imagery representations if we consider them in a little greater depth. Specifically, what would it mean for "current" to "backflow" during imagery? Recent neuroanatomical studies have revealed that the primate visual system consists of many distinct areas, with the best estimate to date being about 30 (Van Essen, personal communication). These areas are organized roughly hierarchically, with each one projecting fibers to specific other areas. At least so far, every area that projects fibers to another area also receives fibers from that area. And more than that, the sizes of the tracks running in each direction are roughly equivalent—implying that much information is in fact flowing backwards.

A critical insight comes when one asks what the early visual areas are like, that is, those near the end of the "backwards" flow. It turns out that these areas are almost all topographically organized; the cells are arranged to preserve the spatial layout of a stimulus. In a particularly compelling demonstration of this, Tootell, Silverman, Switkes, and DeValois (1982) trained a monkey to look at a pattern and then injected it with a radioactive tracer (2DG); this tracer was taken up into the brain in proportion to how much a given part of the brain was activated. After the animal had looked at the pattern, its brain was (essentially) "developed," allowing one to see which parts had been especially active while the monkey was seeing the pattern. Dramatically, the pattern itself could be seen to be laid out on the primary visual cortex! The pattern was slightly distorted because the foveal areas have proportionally greater representation in the cortex, but its spatial structure was clearly evident.

The primary visual cortex is just one (of some 10 or so) topographically organized area in the brain. Of particular interest is an area called V4, which not only is topographically organized but has cells whose activity is modified by attention and expectation (e.g., Moran & Desimone, 1985). It seems plausible that during imagery a spatial pattern of activation is invoked in this area.

Now, consider the implications of this line of reasoning. If imagery is in fact a consequence of higher cortical centers activating lower ones, then a pictorial representation may in fact be present during imagery. That is, during imagery there may be a representation that is "depictive" in the formal sense developed by Kosslyn (1980), with each part of the representation corresponding to part of the object and with the distances between parts of the representation functioning to preserve the distances between parts on the actual object (when the foveal magnification factor is taken into account). If so, then the debate would be settled once and for all: Imagery would correspond to a distinct form of internal representation, different from that used in language.

There is in fact suggestive evidence that the topographically organized regions of the occipital lobe are activated during imagery (for a review, see Farah, 1988). If it can be shown that patterns of metabolic activity vary systematically with the type of image one is forming—illustrating that the activity is not epiphenomenal—the debate can finally be settled. It is not often that a debate in cognitive psychology comes to fruition, and this possibility underlines why James was interested in how the brain functions; mental activity is, after all, nothing more (or less) than brain function. Thus, following James, it may be useful for cognitive psychologists to consider in greater depth the ways in which their putative processes may actually be carried out in the brain.

CONCLUSIONS

James's chapter on imagery is in large part a synthesis of what was known and speculated at that time. However, in typical James style he did more than simply regurgitate what others thought. James organized the material in such a way as to reveal the underlying issues, and his thinking led him to offer interesting speculations about those issues. Given James's track record in other areas, we should take these speculations very seriously. It would be a real pity if come the next commemorative volume on James at least some of these issues had not been studied in depth.

REFERENCES

Bain, A. (1855/1977). The senses and the intellect. In D. N. Robinson (Ed.), *Significant contributions to the history of psychology: 1750–1920*. Washington, DC: University Publishers of America.

Binet, A. (1886/1907). *The psychology of reasoning*. Chicago: Open Court.

Damasio, A. R. (1986). Disorders of complex visual processing: agnosias, achromatopsia, Balint's syndrome, and related difficulties of orientation and construction. In M. M. Mesulam (Ed.), *Principles of behavioral neurology* (pp. 259–288). Philadelphia, PA: F. A. Davis.

Farah, M. J. (1984). The neurological basis of mental imagery: A componential analysis. In S. Pinker (Ed.), *Visual cognition* (pp. 245–272). Cambridge, MA: MIT Press.

Farah, M. J. (1988). Is visual imagery really visual? Overlooked evidence from neuropsychology. *Psychological Review, 95*, 307–317.

Finke, R. A. (1980). Levels of equivalence in imagery and perception. *Psychological Review, 87*, 113–132.

Finke, R. A., & Schmidt, M. J. (1977). Orientation-specific color after-effects following imagination. *Journal of Experimental Psychology: Human Perception and Performance, 3*, 599–606.

Finke, R. A., & Schmidt, M. J. (1978). The quantative measure of pattern representation in images using orientation-specific color aftereffects. *Perception and Psychophysics, 23*, 515–520.

Finke, R. A., & Shepard, R. N. (1986). Visual functions of mental imagery. In K. R. Boff, L. Kaufman, & J. P. Thomas (Eds.), *Handbook of perception and human performance* (pp. 37-1-37-55). New York: Wiley-Interscience.

Fodor, J. A. (1975). *The language of thought*. New York: Crowell.

Galton, F. (1883). *Inquiries into human faculty and its development*. London: Macmillan. (New York: AMS Press, 1973)

Hebb, D. O. (1968). Concerning imagery. *Psychological Review, 75*, 466–479.

Holmes, E. (1878). *The life of Mozart including his correspondence*. London: Novello, Ewer.

James, W. (1890). *The principles of psychology* (Vols. 1–2) New York: Holt.

Jolicoeur, P., & Kosslyn, S. M. (1985). Is time to scan visual images due to demand characteristics? *Memory & Cognition, 13*, 320–332.

Koestler, A. (1964). *The act of creation*. New York: Macmillan.

Kosslyn, S. M. (1983). *Ghosts in the mind's machine*. New York: W. W. Norton.

Kosslyn, S. M. (1980). *Image and mind*. Cambridge, MA: Harvard University Press.

Kosslyn, S. M., Brunn, J. L., Cave, K. R., & Wallach, R. W. (1984). Individual differences in visual imagery: A computational analysis. *Cognition, 18*, 195-243.

Kosslyn, S. M., & Pomerantz, J. R. (1977). Imagery, propositions and the form of internal representations. *Cognitive Psychology, 9*, 52-76.

Kosslyn, S. M., Seger, C., Pani, J. R., & Hillger, L. A. (in press). When is imagery used in everyday life? A diary study. *Journal of Mental Imagery*.

Kosslyn, S. M., Van Kleeck, M., & Kirby, K. N. (in press). Towards a neurologically plausible theory of individual differences in mental imagery. In D. Marks, P. Hampson, & J. T. E. Richards (Eds.), *Advances in imagery research*. London: Roetledge-Paul.

Leibovitz, M. P., London, P., Cooper, L. M., & Tart, J. T. (1972). Dominance in mental imagery. *Educational and Psychological Measurement, 32*, 679-703.

Luria, A. R. (1968). *The mind of a mnemonist*. Cambridge, MA: Harvard University Press.

Marks, D. F. (1973). Visual imagery differences and eye movements in the recall of pictures. *Perception and Psychophysics, 14*, 407-412.

Marsella, A. J., & Quijano, W. Y. (1974). A comparison of vividness of mental imagery across different sensory modalities in Filipinos and Caucasian Americans. *Journal of Cross Cultural Psychology, 5*, 451-464.

Moran, J., & Desimone, R. (1985). Selective attention gates visual processing in the extrastriate cortex. *Science, 229*, 782-784.

Paivio, A., & Ernest, C. H. (1971). Imagery ability and visual perception of verbal and nonverbal stimuli. *Perception and Psychophysics, 10*, 429-432.

Perky, C. W. (1910). An experimental study of imagination. *American Journal of Psychology, 21*, 422-425.

Pinker, S., Choate, P. A., & Finke, R. A. (1984). Mental extrapolation in patterns constructed from memory. *Memory & Cognition, 12*, 207-218.

Pylyshyn, Z. W. (1973). What the mind's eye tells the mind's brain. A critique of mental imagery. *Psychological Bulletin, 80*, 1-24.

Pylyshyn, Z. W. (1981). The imagery debate: Analogue media versus tacit knowledge. *Psychological Review, 87*, 16-45.

Roe, A. (1951). A study of imagery in research scientists. *Journal of Personality, 19*, 459-470.

Schlipp, P. A. (Ed.). (1940). *Albert Einstein: Philosopher-scientist*. La Salle, IL: Open Court.

Segal, S. J., & Fusella, V. (1970). Influence of imaged pictures and sounds on detection of visual and auditory signals. *Journal of Experimental Psychology, 83*, 458-464.

Shepard, R. N., & Cooper, L. A. (1982). *Mental images and their transformations*. Cambridge, MA: MIT Press.

Smith, E. E., & Medin, D. (1981). *Categories and concepts*. Cambridge, MA: Harvard University Press.

Tootell, R. B. H., Silverman, M. S., Switkes, E., & DeValois, R. L. (1982). Deoxyglucose analysis of retinotopic organization in primate striate cortex. *Science, 218*, 902-904.

White, K., Sheehan, P. W., & Ashton, R. (1977). Imagery assessment: A survey of self report measures. *Journal of Mental Imagery, 1*, 145-170.

Wittgenstein, L. (1953). *Philosophical investigations* (G. E. M. Anscombe, Trans.). Oxford: Blackwell.

Wolpin, M., & Weinstein, C. (1983). Visual imagery and olfactory stimulation. *Journal of Mental Imagery, 7*, 63-74.

Chapter 9

A Look Back at William James's Theory of Perception

Irvin Rock

University of California, Berkeley

I cannot remember what my thoughts were when I first read William James's *Principles of Psychology* as a young student except that I admired the beautiful prose. On rereading it carefully now, however, I came away enormously impressed with James's grasp of the field of perception and with the feeling that we have not made the great strides in our knowledge about this field that might have been expected over a span of 100 years, particularly on a broad theoretical level. Others may disagree with this judgment. However, there have been some important discoveries and there has been some substantial progress in some areas.

What I propose to do in this chapter is first to review what James's theory of perception was, to comment about his theory in the light of present-day thinking, to discuss what we know now about perception that he did not, and finally to discuss one important idea James had about perceptual constancy that may well be right but which has been overlooked. I will end by asking the question about how much progress we have made in this field of inquiry in the 100 years since James's *Principles* appeared.

JAMES'S THEORY OF PERCEPTION SUMMARIZED

Let us begin with a summary of James's theory of perception. To avoid distortion of his views, we will allow him to speak for himself as much as possible. We begin with definitions of sensation and perception:

"*A pure sensation is an abstraction*" (II: 3) and "in popular speech, and in Psychology also" the words sensation and perception "run into each other" (II: 1). Sensation . . . "*differs from Perception only in the extreme simplicity of its object or content*" (II: 2). "The nearer the object cognized comes to being a simple quality like 'hot', 'cold', 'red', 'noise', 'pain', apprehended irrelatively to other things, the more the state of mind approaches pure sensation" (II: 1). "Consciousness of some sort goes with all the [brain] currents, but it is only when new currents are entering that it has the sensational *tang*" (II: 7).

Sensations "are the *immediate* results upon consciousness of nerve-currents as they enter the brain, and even before they have awakened any suggestions or associations with past experience" (1892, p. 12).

But, such *"Pure sensations can* [therefore] *only be realized in the earliest days of life.* They are all but impossible to adults with memories and stores of associations acquired" (II: 7), [but], "To some degree we seem able to lapse into this inarticulate feeling at moments when our attention is entirely dispersed"[1] (1892, p. 13). The mere inarticulate feeling [of the presence of messages from sense organs] conveying qualities such as object colors, sounds, warmth, and the like is Sensation whereas when Ideas *about* the object mingle with these feelings we call it Perception: [However], "every thing of quality felt [even a sensation] is felt in outer space" (1892, p. 15).

"The consciousness of particular material things present to sense is nowadays called *perception"* (II: 76). *"Every perception is an acquired perception"* (II: 78). "Perception is of definite and probable things." Thus even if *"the sensation is associated with more than one reality,* so that either of two discrepant sets of residual properties may arise . . . [the perception] *will be of a probable thing,* of the thing which would most usually have given us that sensation" (II: 82).

We see here that James explicitly endorses what nowadays has come to be called the likelihood principle, which Helmholtz had expressed as follows:

> The general rule determining the ideas of vision that are formed whenever an impression is made on the eye, with or without the aid of optical instruments, is that *such objects are always imagined as being present in the field of vision as would have to be there in order to produce the same impression on the nervous mechanism, the eyes being used under normal ordinary conditions.* (Helmholtz, 1867/1962, p. 2)

A particularly clear statement of James's empiricism, is one he refers to as the general law of perception: *"that whilst part of what we perceive comes through our sense from the object before us, another part* (and it may be the larger part) *always comes . . . out of our own head."* By

---

[1]This last quotation, from James's Psychology (1892), about lapsing into a state of inattention and thereby recovering sensations that otherwise are not experienced by adults, is amazingly prescient. Recent research has shown that inattention seems to have the effect of regressing perception to a level below that of the achievement of constancy (Epstein & Broota, 1986; Epstein & Lovitts, 1985; Rock & Nijhawan, 1989).

"head," James clearly means "brain" (II: 103). The *"brain reacts* by paths which previous experiences have worn, *and makes us usually perceive the probable thing*, i.e. the thing by which on previous occasions reaction was most frequently aroused" (II: 103–104, italics added).

And again, *"Sensational and reproductive brain-processes combined, then, are what give us the content of our perceptions"* (II: 78).

In talking specifically about the perception of space, James says:

> [Although we adults] have a definite and apparently instantaneous knowledge of the sizes, shapes, and distances of the things amongst which we live and move . . . and of the whole great infinite continuum of real space . . . Nevertheless, it seems obvious that the baby's world is vague and confused in all these respects. (1892, p. 335)

> To the babe who first opens his senses upon the world, though the initial experience is one of vastness and extensity, it is an extensity within which no definite divisions, directions, sizes, or distances are yet marked out (1892, pp. 337–338)

How then does the baby actually learn to perceive size and shape? Here again, James subscribes to a Helmholtzian view, in this case concerning the role of the motor system. Points within the retinal image of an object appear to be arranged in a definite order, but this is something we have acquired. What we do have at birth is not the *total absence* of any experience of spatiality (as earlier theorists and some contemporaries of James had it) but rather a sense of extensity or voluminousness.[2] So the baby does perceive an outer field with a certain vastness. What is lacking, however, is a perception of definite divisions, directions, or arrangements in a definite order.

> The muscular sense *has* much to do with defining the *order of positions* of things seen, felt or heard. We look at a point; Another point upon the retina's margin catches our attention and in an instant we turn the fovea upon it, letting its image successively fall upon all the points of the intervening retinal line. The line thus traced so rapidly by the second point is itself a visual object, with the first and second point at its respective ends. It *separates* the points

---

[2]James was adamant and passionate on this point, that the perception of spatiality is not woven out of whole cloth, that, in this regard, the mind is not totally a tabula rasa. Rather we begin life with a sense of extensity or voluminousness, to use his term, including some sense of visual depth, and only because this is true is further learning about spatiality possible. He thus takes pains to separate himself here from other empiristically minded theorists such as Berkeley and Helmholtz. The present writer is puzzled by the fact that virtually all of James's predecessors and contemporaries were so firmly of the opinion that there is no intrinsic sensory basis for the spatiality that characterizes the visual perception of adults and that, therefore, it was derivative (of either touch perception, à la Berkeley, or of the intellect, à la Kant). It is as if there were some enormously important theoretical stake in defending this position and I fail to see what it was. At any rate James attacked it vigorously.

which become *located by its length* with reference to each other . . . Each peripheral retinal point comes in this way to *suggest* a line at the end of which it lies, a line which a possible movement will trace; and even the motionless field of vision ends at last by signifying a system of positions brought out by possible movements between its centre and all peripheral parts. (1892, p. 341)

Presumably then, once every retinal point has come (via such a process of learning, a process of the education of vision by movement) to signify a given direction with respect to all other retinal points, not only is the perceived direction of objects in the scene thus explained but their perceived sizes and shapes are also thus explained. Shape would be the awareness of the set of directions of all retinal points within the objects retinal image in relation to one another, or at least this is how I interpret James's (and Helmholtz's) argument.[3]

SOME INITIAL COMMENTS ON JAMES'S THEORY

What struck me most on rereading James was his phenomenological description of what perception is like. By this I mean an unbiased, naive description of how things look (or sound or feel, etc.) without altering that description on the basis of theoretical preconceptions of how they *ought* to look. It is a superb description that rings true and that in many ways is at odds with the then prevailing analytical introspectionism that Wundt (1907) advocated and it anticipated the phenomenological description of perceptual experiences soon to be offered by the Gestalt psychologists. Here is an example.

So when I get, as now, a brown eye-picture with lines not parallel, and with angles unlike, and call it my big solid rectangular walnut library-table, that picture is not the table. It is not even like the table as the table is for vision, when rightly seen. It is a distorted perspective view of three of the sides of what I mentally *perceive* (more or less) in its totality and undistorted shape. The back of the table, its square corners, its size, its heaviness, are features of which I am conscious when I look, almost as I am conscious of its name. (II: 78)

Another example could easily have been written by one of the Gestalt psychologists several decades later, referring to an event in a railway station:

---

[3]This idea, that may seem so improbable and old-fashioned to some, that the spatial direction of a retinal point is signified by the intended eye movement or, to put in more modern terms, by the efference copy of the command to the eye muscles to move thus and so, has been explicitly entertained, defended by ingenious experiments, and ultimately rejected, in very recent years. Indeed the attempt was made to explain shape perception itself in terms of this kind of mechanism. See Miller and Festinger (1977).

Habitually, when we ourselves move forward, our entire field of view glides backward over our retina. When our movement is due to that of the windowed carriage, car or boat in which we sit, all stationary objects visible through the window give us the sensation of gliding in the opposite directions. Hence, whenever we get this sensation, of a window with *all* objects visible through it moving it one direction, we react upon it in our customary way, and perceive a stationary field of view, over which the window and we ourselves inside of it, are passing by a motion of our own. Consequently when another train comes alongside of ours in a station, and fills the entire window, and, after standing still a while, begins to glide away, we judge that it is *our* train which is moving, and that the other train is still. If, however, we catch a glimpse of any part of the station through the windows, or between the cars, of the other train, the illusion of our own movement instantaneously disappears, and we perceive the other train to be the one in motion. This, again, is but making the usual and probable inference from our sensation. (II: 90–91)

Of course James's *explanation* of this effect, as indicated in the last sentence, is quite different than the one the Gestaltists offered of it based on spontaneous processes of organization and the concept of frame of reference.

Still another example is rather similar to the subsequently uncovered Kinetic Depth Effect by Wallach and O'Connell in 1953:

suppose . . . the object . . . a stick is seen first in its whole length, and then rotated around one of its ends. . . . In this movement the stick's image will grow progressively shorter; its farther end will appear less and less separated laterally from its . . . near end; soon it [the farther end] will be screened by the latter, and then reappear on the opposite side, [the image there finally] will resume its original length; . . . the mind will presumably react upon it after its usual fashion (which is that of unifying all data which it is in any way possible to unify), and consider it movement of a constant object rather than the transformation of a fluctuating one. (II: 215)[4]

James's intent to remain faithful to naive phenomenal experience, the way it is, rather than the way one's theory would like it to be, is nicely illustrated by his insistence that a percept is not simply a fusion of separate sensations and ideas, despite the fact, as we have seen, that in his theory, such a *process* of fusion is precisely what perception is said to be. Thus:

Once more we find ourselves driven to admit that when qualities of an object impress our sense and we thereupon perceive the object, the sensation as such of those qualities does not still exist inside the perception and form a constit-

---

[4]In discussing this effect James indicates how he believes one can achieve the appropriate depth perception without having to argue, as Berkeley had, that this depended upon touch-space. He suggests that the maximum projection of the stick when it is in the frontal plane informs us of how far one end is from the other when, a moment later, the stick is aligned with the line of sight and projects only as a single point.

uent thereof. The sensation is one thing and the perception another, and neither can take place at the same time with the other, because their cerebral conditions are not the same. They may *resemble* each other, but in no respect are they identical states of mind. (II: 81–82)

He illustrates this fact with one of his favorite examples, no doubt making the rounds in the parlors of the day, that the French phrase *Pas de lieu Rhone que nous* will not spontaneously be recognized by the English speaker as *paddle your own canoe*. His point was that when the recognition of the words occurs, the sounds (the sensations) themselves appear to change. As he says "Verbal sounds are usually perceived with their meaning at the moment of being heard" (II: 80). My point then is that James was a good phenomenologist and he realized that the percept did not contain the sensation as a phenomenal ingredient. Rather he realized, correctly I would say, and again anticipating the Gestaltists, that the sensation has no phenomenal reality much of the time and that the stimulus that one might think ought to produce a sensation can give rise to a neural state of affairs that interacts with the neural repositories of other stimuli or of meaning, producing from this interaction an emergent phenomenal quality.[5]

A second reaction I had on rereading James is that although he did distinguish between sensation and perception, as the aforementioned quotations and examples amply document, he did not distinguish between perception and recognition. If by perception we mean the achievement of a representation of objects and events based on proximal stimulation and with regard to properties such as shape, size, depth, lightness, and motion, then should we not distinguish these from recognition, which clearly entails more than just perception?

Apparently James felt no need to make the distinction, undoubtedly because he believed that past experience gave us differing kinds of ideas of associations, some concerning the direction of retinal points, some concerning the depth or motion of objects or the motion of ourselves, and some of the way objects appear as familiar. Thus, as we shall see, although he did realize that not all perceptions are based on past experience, he did not see the need to distinguish a category of perception that was different from sensation on the one hand and from effects based on recognition on the other. Many of James's examples of perception clearly bear on the familiarity and knowledge of the way things look and such appearances are clearly based on "ideas" (as he calls them) based on prior perceptions so that for such cases we can hardly challenge an empiristic explanation. The recognition or identification of things *is* a function of prior experience.

---

[5]The problem about sensation is far from resolved. There are certainly experiences, such as of sensory qualities, which we would want to refer to as sensations. On the other hand it is not the case that we spontaneously experience a particular circumscribed proximal stimulus as a sensation as in James's example of the distorted image of the side of the table.

Still there is a tremendous difference in the claim that past experience determines perception from the claim that it determines recognition. To put the matter in terms of more contemporary language, recognition can be regarded as the last step in a sequence of *bottom-up* processing. The process underlying it would occur *after* the process underlying the perception of the form, color, depth, and size of an object although, phenomenally, perception and recognition may seem to be concurrent. So, for example, on perceiving a red sphere of a certain size, we recognize an apple. But to claim that past experience determines *perception* is to imply *top-down* processing. The memory (or semantic node, in contemporary parlance) is somehow accessed by the incoming stimulus pattern and then affects a lower-level process such as that of form perception. Whether or not such effects occur is an empirical question (fraught with certain logical difficulties). James does point to examples he believes support it, without realizing the difficulties with this claim and without considering possible explanations of it. In my opinion, there are not many clear examples of this kind of effect available.

A third point that struck me about James's account of perception is that despite all of his assertions that I have previously cited, he was not in fact an extreme empiricist. For if Helmholtz was a great influence on him, so was Helmholtz's nativistically-inclined contemporary Ewald Hering (1920/ 1964). Thus, for example, where Helmholtz sought to explain simultaneous color-contrast as an intellectual affair, an unconscious inference, James accepted Hering's explanation of it as the result of the adjacent color exciting a new nerve-process, to which the modified feeling of color immediately corresponds. Where Helmholtz tried to explain various anomalies of motion such as the aftereffect of viewing contours moving in a particular direction in terms of mental suggestion or unconscious inference, or unconscious rotations of the eye, James accepts the view that "*present excitements and after effects of former excitements may alter the results of processes occurring simultaneously at a distance from them on the retina. . . .*" (II: 248)

In fact James is not entirely consistent about the role of past experience in perception even in some of the examples already considered. There are indications throughout the chapters on Sensation, The Perception of Things, and Perception of Space in which James refers to sensations when one might think he should be referring to perceptions. Remember that sensations are presumably innately given whereas perceptions are based on past experience. Thus, for example, he talks about the sensation of lines, of angles between lines, and of the configuration of several lines and angles, as in a pattern such as a triangle. In discussing the phenomena of constancy he refers to the sensation we have of an object when it is *not* in the so-called normal position, as for example a circle at a slant. Such a sensation would then presumably be an elliptical shape, albeit two dimensional. Yet earlier we saw that he implied that shape would be a derivative of the directional sensation produced by the stimulation of retinal loci. At one point, James says:

> for in our perceptions of shape and position it is really difficult to decide how much of our sense of the object is due to reproductions of past experience, and how much to the immediate sensations of the eye. (II: 79)

And in a footnote he says:

> [The reader] may object . . . that in a babe's immediate field of vision the various things which appear are located *relatively to each other* from the outset. I admit that *if discriminated*, they would appear so located. (II: 43)

This seems to contradict his claim that I cited earlier about how location is learned.

WHAT DO WE NOW KNOW THAT JAMES DID NOT KNOW ABOUT PERCEPTION?

This is not the place for a complete discussion of all discoveries and amassing of knowledge about perception over the century since James's *Principles* appeared. In the final section of this chapter I list the many facts and problems concerning which we have "amassed" rather little knowledge and I was struck by some of James's examples which seemed so up to date and which previously I had mistakenly thought were the end result of a good deal of research and observation in recent years. For example, James was aware (as was Wheatstone) that when you view a human face pseudoscopically, so that the reversed images ought to yield a depth reversal, you do not see a hollow face, like a mask seen from the concave side. He pointed out that even the concave side of a hollow mask itself seen normally with both eyes will look convex. He of course regarded this as an example of the power of past experience, in this case with a lifetime of exposure to faces, and many contemporary theorists seem to agree with this interpretation.[6] He was aware of the phenomenon of induced motion of objects (e.g., the moon seen within moving clouds) and of the self (see quotation above of railroad incident); he was aware of reversible figures and their significance; he was aware of a phenomenon much like the Kinetic Depth Effect; he was aware of the proof-readers illusion (as he called it) and of its significance and that children are *more* likely to spot typographical errors than adults when reading in a newly acquired language; he was aware (as was Des-

---

[6]Plausible as this may be, the case is not yet proven. There may be a strong preference for convexity in the third dimension just as we now know there is for convexity in a two-dimensional pattern (Kanizsa & Gerbino, 1976).

cartes) of the relationship between visual angle and perceived distance in size perception; he was aware of the change that occurs in the perception of a word when it is repeated over and over again ("reduced to its sensational nudity" as he puts it) and explained this phenomenon by noting that on repetition of the word the sound no longer accesses the memory we have of it in our minds. He was similarly aware (as was Helmholtz) of the interesting phenomenological changes we experience when we view a landscape (or a painting of one) with our head upside down. He interpreted this, again, as resulting from the decoupling of the incoming sensation from the stored "ideas" by virtue of the unaccustomed point of view and, again, he may well be right about this. I chose those from among many other examples I could have given. In short, James knew a good deal about the important phenomenal facts about perception, and, in my opinion, in many cases interpreted them correctly. Perhaps I should add that much of this knowledge derived from his reading of the work of earlier investigators. However there is also a good deal that we know now that James did not.

Advances in Our Knowledge About Infant Vision

For example, consider the age-old controversy about the relative contributions of innate factors and past experience in perception. The earliest data on this issue came from individuals born blind who later recovered their sight. See Von Senden (1960). But these data were inconclusive. Later experiments sought to rear animals in darkness or in pattern-free homogeneous light but these animals suffered functional impairment of the visual nervous system as a result. For a review of this earlier research, see Zuckerman and Rock (1957). But we now do have a considerable body of knowledge about perceptual capabilities that appear soon after birth and the presumption is, therefore, that such capabilities are innately determined. Some of the data is based on experiments with newly born animals and some is based on experiments with human infants. There is now evidence for the very early presence of the perception of shape, both two-dimensional (Caron, Caron, & Carlson, 1979; Fantz, 1957, 1965; Fantz, Fagan, & Miranda, 1975; Slater, Morrison, & Rose, 1983; Zimmerman & Torrey, 1965), and three-dimensional (Kellman, 1984, Owsley, 1983; Yonas, Arterberry, & Granrud, 1987) and the perception of distance (Campos, Langer, & Krowitz, 1970; Field, 1976; Gibson & Walk, 1960; Granrud, 1986; McKenzie & Day, 1972; Walk & Gibson, 1961). There is also reason for believing that perceptual constancy is present in the first few months of life, in the case of size (Day & McKenzie, 1981; Granrud, 1986; Granrud, Arterberry, & Yonas, 1985; Kellman, 1984) and shape (Caron, Caron, & Carlson, 1979; Cook & Birch, 1984; Day & MacKenzie, 1977; Kellman, 1984). In fact shape constancy seems to be present at birth (Slater & Morrison, 1985) and size constancy as well (Granrud, in preparation). The case for an innate basis of constancy is particularly clear when either the object or the subject is in motion (Gibson, 1987; Kellman & Short, 1987). Certain features of perception that bear on form and organization also seem to be present at a very early age, such as figure-ground perception in which the background seems to lie behind the object when it is occluded by it (Kestenbaum, Termine, & Spelke, 1988; Prather & Spelke, 1982; Termine, Hrynick, Kestenbaum, Gleitman, & Spelke, 1987), the perception of vertical symmetry (Bornstein, Ferdinandsen, & Gross, 1981), the perception of good continuation (Van Geffen & Haith, 1983), and the perception of common fate (Kellman & Spelke, 1983). There is also evidence for a very early responsiveness to intermodal equivalencies such as between vision and touch (Bushnell & Weinberger, 1987; Gibson & Walker, 1984; Meltzoff & Borton, 1979; Rose, Gottfried, & Bridger, 1981) and between looking and hearing (Alegria & Noirot, 1979; Spelke, 1976).

Almost as important as these findings are the methods that have been developed to study perception in infants. As noted earlier, a few decades ago, the question of the innate or learned basis of perception was studied by rearing animals in darkness or without allowing pattern vision and then testing them when they were mature on discrimination problems that required perception of the property under study. The assumption was that one had to wait until maturity before an animal would be capable of learning a discrimination problem and such learning was seen as the only way of probing the perceptual capabilities required (Meyers & McCleary, 1964; Riesen, 1950, 1958; Siegel, 1953). However it was subsequently discovered that these conditions of rearing animals produce severe visual deficiencies if not total blindness (Ganz & Fitch, 1968; Wiesel & Hubel, 1963, 1965a, 1965b) to say nothing of cognitive and emotional impairments. One new method that evolved was to make use of a behavior that appears early in life such as pecking in birds or the preference to view one object over another as manifested in looking behavior (Fantz, 1957, 1965, 1966). If an animal innately prefers (or conversely has an aversion to) one kind of object over another (e.g., oval shaped grains over other shaped particles) then only if that property (shape in this case) can be *perceived* will the preference be manifested in behavior. Another method is to use operant conditioning by contingent reinforcement such as sucking or head-turning in human infants (Bower, 1966; Eimas, Sigueland, Jusczyk, & Vigorito, 1971). It was discovered that infants *can* learn this kind of response and, therefore, it is not necessary to wait until they mature to test their perception.

But the major breakthrough in methodology was the discovery of the habituation method that can be used with human infants. (Fantz, 1966; Horowitz, 1974) It seems to be a fact that even 2-day old infants tend to spend time looking directly at novel objects but soon tire of doing so. As a result, when that object is removed and replaced by another or two others, the direction of their gaze tells an important story. If the original object is presented again, the infant will tend to spend little time looking at it and, if an alternative object is present, will therefore tend to look at that most of the time. But even more important, one can find out about perception in the infant by investigating similarity. If and only if a test object is perceived as similar to the habituated one will habituation now be manifested. Otherwise, if the object is perceived as different, the infant will then tend to look at it again. This, then, is the method that was used in a number of the studies previously cited. It provides us with data about human infant perception that just a short time ago seemed, on the face of it, all but impossible to obtain.

To return to the question of what perceptual properties are present shortly after birth, consider color. There never was any question about its innate basis, but for James and other empiricists this did not constitute a problem because chromatic color was one of the basic sensations. Sensations of course were not learned, and instead constituted the original basis for acquired perceptions. However, achromatic color (or lightness, as it is now called), the perceived shades of grey on the white-grey-black continuum, is another story. Once it was appreciated that the lightness value of a surface remained perceptually constant despite great variation in illumination, investigators such as Helmholtz were aware that this was a problem requiring an explanation, because the luminance reflected to the eye by a surface could not be the stimulus determinant of such unchanging lightness perception. Helmholtz proposed that we take account of the prevailing illumination in assessing the lightness signified by the luminance from a particular surface. But this view has now been universally discarded (for logical more than empirical reasons) and instead the prevailing view is that lightness perception is governed by luminance *relationships* or *ratios* within the retinal image. Although there is still controversy about whether or not a simple ratio hypothesis holds up or whether or not such ratio determination is based on the neural mechanism of lateral inhibition, the common denominator of agreement would seem to be that there is relational information available within the image that makes lightness perception possible and lightness constancy understandable, so that a learning theory is gratuitous (Gilchrist, 1977; Hering, 1920/1964; Jameson & Hurvich, 1964; Wallach, 1948). From what we have seen about James's appreciation of Hering's explanation of contrast, I believe he would have been very comfortable with this present-day analysis.

Advances in Our Knowledge of Neuroanatomy

The empiristic view of Helmholtz and James of how we come to learn the locations of points in the field relative to one another as described earlier has always seemed far-fetched to me. That is, the very belief that such perception of relative location must be learned is what seems far-fetched, not the ingenious theory of how such learning could occur on the basis of eye movements if one believes a learning explanation *is* required. Perhaps the reason why such a theory of learning was proposed was the lack of knowledge, at the time, of a very important anatomical fact; we now know that in the projection of fibers from retina to lateral geniculate body to visual cortex, an orderly relationship is maintained. Thus there is a topological projection of the retina onto the visual cortex so that the spatial relationship among neurons is preserved.

To be sure, the order that is maintained is topological rather than precisely metrical, so that the "map" of the projected image in the cortex is not congruent with the image qua shape or size. Nonetheless such orderly mapping is sufficient reason to expect that the perception of orderly location of the system of positions, discussed by James, can be given directly by the locus of excitation in the cortex. It is true that recent discoveries about cortical feature detectors have modified our understanding about what the firing of various cortical cells signifies, but the fact remains that the features "detected" are localized in regions of the visual field as a function of *where* in the visual cortex the cell is located. A learning theory is gratuitous. It is interesting to note that James *was* aware that the left retinas in both eyes project to the left cerebral hemisphere and the right retinas to the right hemisphere and that damage to either cortical area resulted in hemianopic blindness in the contralateral visual field. I believe, although he does not explicitly say so, that he accepted this fact of determination of perceived location by cortical localization of function as innately given. If so, one can speculate that, had he known about the more refined orderly projection from retina to cortex, he would have accepted perceived location in the field as innately determined. What James had to say about shape is very much dependent on his view (discussed here) about perceived location or direction so that were he to accept directionality as innate he might well have also accepted shape perception as innate.[7]

---

[7]There is a long footnote in the *Principles* which both supports and contradicts my speculations here. James says in part "in the matter of *spatial* feeling, where the retinal patch that produces a triangle in the mind is itself a triangle, etc., it looks at first sight as if the sensation might be a direct cognition of its own neural condition . . . [However] the immediate condition of the feeling is not the process in the retina, but the process in the brain; and the process in the brain may, for aught we know, be as unlike a triangle—*nay it probably is so* (italics added)—as it is unlike redness or rage. It is simply a *coincidence* that in the case of space one of the organic condition viz., the triangle impressed on the skin or the retina, should lead to a representation in the mind of the subject observed similar to that which it produces in the psychological observer." (II: 144) This passage clearly *supports* my speculation that James did not assume any projection from retina to cortex such that a triangular retinal image would project a triangular pattern or excitation in the brain. But it *questions* my interpretation because he emphasizes "process" rather than location and he is of course right that the process underlying the perception of a triangle cannot itself be anything triangular. The fact is that there are quite a few contradictory statements in James.

The Gestalt Contribution on the Necessity of Perceptual Organization

Then there is the impact of Gestalt psychology on the contemporary approach to perception that naturally makes certain aspects of James's theory appear so different to us now. Gestalt psychology in effect offered an alternative to an empiricist theory. The concept of spontaneous organization allowed for the possibility of the achievement of an organized phenomenal world (rather than the "big, blooming, buzzing confusion" that "the numerous inpouring currents of the baby bring to his consciousness" (I: 488) that James described) without the need to assume that such an organized world could only be the product of much prior experience. This aspect of Gestalt psychology is now widely accepted as the origin of the pre-attentive field of experience, and the laws of organization promulgated by Wertheimer (1923) are regarded as the basis of this first stage of the bottom-up processing that results finally in the rich phenomenal world of familiar objects and events (see Beck, 1966; Kubovy & Pomerantz, 1981; Neisser, 1967; Treisman, 1982).

As a matter of fact, James did not even address the problem of perceptual organization because it was not until the Gestaltists (and some of their predecessors such as von Ehrenfels (1890) and Rubin (1921)) pointed it out, that the problem was recognized. Even if one could explain, as James tried to do, how it comes about that the phenomenal directions signified by each retinal point vis à vis that of others is given, it still leaves unexplained the fundamental question of what in the scene is organized as belonging with what else in the scene. It is understandable why he had failed to grasp this problem, because we spontaneously experience different regions as belonging to other regions; thus we incorrectly presume that such belongingness is given in the stimulus input. Köhler (1947) called this the "experience error." Now once this problem *is* grasped the difficulties with an empiricist explanation of it immediately become evident. If one must learn how to organize the field, it follows that, prior to such learning, the field is unorganized. It is difficult to imagine what such a field would look like (James's "blooming, buzzing confusion?"). But some kind of mosaic-like array comes to mind, something like a random-dot pattern. Assuming this to be the case, how does such an impression ever get superseded by the kind of organized one we do experience? There is another point to consider. Suppose at a given moment one does achieve an organized percept (bypassing the problem just discussed). Later on, when the same stimulus impinges again, the empiricist would like to claim that it will lead to the percept achieved on the prior occasion. James is explicit about this, referring to the principle of seeing "the probable thing" on the basis of "the paths which previous experiences have worn" (I: 103). But this kind of theory only makes sense if the stimulus is located precisely where the previous one had been, that is, if it is the same in terms of proximally defined location, size, and orientation. Then the stimulus excitation will start out along the same path. However, we know that such identity of locus is not necessary and would rarely occur anyway and that (as Gestaltists have taught us) transposition of the stimulus is more the rule than the exception. So now he have the problem of explaining why the re-occurring stimulus makes contact with just the right memory trace of that stimulus. If it does not, obviously no past experience effect is to be expected. The answer of how such contact would be expected to occur is the same as for the recognition generally, namely, on the basis of similarity. If similarity is to govern trace access, some degree of organization of perceptual processing must occur bottom-up before such a trace can have its beneficial effect. And if such bottom-up processing gave us the object's shape, for example, then the contribution of the trace to perceived shape is not required. This is the logical difficulty I referred to earlier when distinguishing the empiricist's claim about perception (where the difficulty arises) from the claim about recognition, which is bottom-up (and in which, therefore, no difficulty arises).

To return to the problem of initial organization, if one has to learn to organize the visual field, what information would tell us that region A goes with region B rather than with C or with nothing else at all for that matter? We would need some source of information that was veridical with respect to organization. The obvious candidate is tactile-tactual (or haptic), proprioceptive-kinesthetic, information, which I will collectively and informally refer to as touch. So, had James recognized the problem of organization, he might well have fallen back on the Berkeleyan thesis about the education of vision by touch and maintained that we learn to organize a scene by our touch experiences. James is not clear on this point, at times arguing forcefully (II: 214), as we have seen, for the presence of pure visual sensations of space and, at other times, acknowledging that:

> It is probably the touch-feeling which prevails as real and the sight which serves as sign—a reduction made necessary not only by the far greater constancy of felt over seen magnitudes, but by the greater practical interest which the sense of touch possesses for our lives. (II: 180)

Whether or not James would have argued in favor of the derivation of visual organization from touch perception, there are serious difficulties with such a view. One is that it presupposes that there is no problem of organization within the domain of touch perception and this is a logically unwarranted assumption. Another—and this James would not have known—is that we now know that vision is dominant over touch. That is, given conflicting information from the two sense modalities, as when one looks through a prism or lens that alters the visual appearance or direction of an object while simultaneously touching or grasping the object, not only does vision dominate what is perceived, but it "captures" touch. That is, the very touch "feeling" conforms to what is seen (Harris, 1965; Hay, Pick, & Ikeda, 1965; Rock, 1966; Rock & Harris, 1967; Rock & Victor, 1964). Moreover, if one now extends the experiment in time, so that the subject is given a good deal of experience with the conflicting information, in which case the possibility of learning or adaptation arises analogously to the situation in infancy that Berkeley had in mind, it is not the case that vision begins to change so as to conform with touch. Quite the opposite occurs. What is signified by touch changes in such a way as to conform to vision. Thus, if one tests for judgments via touch alone after the experimental period of adaptation ends, one finds that these judgments have changed. So it seems fair to say that the Berkeleyan thesis has been empirically tested and disconfirmed. In fact, Berkeley had the argument the wrong way around, so that we can now assume that much of how the world of objects feels, with respect to properties such as direction, shape, size, and the like, is a function of prior experience in which vision and touch information are co-extensive. One might speculate that such touch experiences are based on a kind of visualization, at least this is probably true for those of us who are not born blind.

It is for reasons such as these that few investigators believe that perceptual organization must be learned. Rather, the belief is that such organization must be one of the very first processes to occur in a bottom-up direction, the first stage, and that it is a low-level, pre-attentive process. Given such organization, other processes including those based on past experience, can then reasonably be expected to occur. Without it, it would be difficult to understand how veridical perception would be achievable at all. To sum up the position with a catchy phrase, we must see to learn, so that it is unlikely that we must learn to see (Zuckerman & Rock, 1957). As to the principles at work in explaining organization, the Gestalt laws as set forth by Wertheimer (1923) and Rubin (1921) are widely accepted as the correct descriptive generalizations although the neural mechanisms underlying these laws are yet to be uncovered.

If the Gestaltists were correct that an object property such as form resulted from organizational autochthonous processes, then we can now understand even more clearly why we should distinguish perception from recognition. James would be obliged to define the apprehension of an object's form as perception (and not to reduce it to a sensation). But clearly such a perception need not be the result of past experience whereas the recognition of that form when it is seen on subsequent occasions is, by definition, a matter of past experience.

There was another very important theoretical idea about perception that emerged from the Gestalt concept of organization and that challenged in yet another way the widespread belief that James and others held concerning the important role of past experience. When the stimulus is ambiguous,

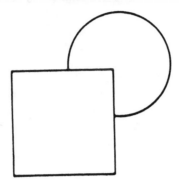

FIG. 9.1   This pattern is perceived as a complete circle occluded by a square rather than as a mosaic representation of a three-quarter circle abutting a square.

it often, if not virtually always, is the case that we tend to perceive it in the way that such a stimulus would most generally be produced. For example, the Necker cube drawing, considered as a proximal stimulus, could conceivably represent a rather complex two-dimensional object but it is virtually impossible to see it that way; rather we spontaneously see it as representing a three-dimensional cube. Or, to give another example, the pattern illustrated in Fig. 9.1 could conceivably represent a mosaic two-dimensional representation of a three-quarter circle abutting a square. But few if any observers will see it that way; rather we see a complete circle behind or occluded by a square.

So these examples and many others certainly seem to lend support to Helmholtz's likelihood principle. After all, what alternative explanation is there for the *preference* on the part of the perceptual system for one perceptual outcome given the fact that the stimulus is ambiguous and itself does not dictate the outcome? The Gestaltists did give us an alternative, the notion of prägnanz. The perceptual system will favor the outcome that is the simplest possible under the prevailing conditions of stimulation. The reader can see why the perception of the Necker cube and of the square occluding a circle are simpler (more regular and symmetrical) than the alternative outcomes in these two examples. The presumption is that a perceptual system that evolved to function on the basis of a simplicity principle would more often than not achieve veridicality. Veridicality of course is crucial for survival. It turns out that the likelihood principle and the prägnanz principle usually make the same prediction. This is not the place to enter into a critique of the concept of prägnanz or to review the by-now considerable literature that has accumulated pro and anti on the subject. For such a recent review, see Hatfield and Epstein (1985). Rather I wanted to provide one more reason why contemporary investigators are loathe to assume what

James was perfectly willing to assume, *faute de mieux*, namely, that likelihood based on prior experience was the source of our perception in so many different cases.

Still more that we know now owes its origin to Gestalt psychology. There are many kinds of perception that are based on certain lawful stimulus relationships and to organization based on a frame of reference. For example, even when a point is moving below threshold, so that in viewing it alone in an otherwise homogeneous field we would not detect its motion, we do detect its motion the moment a stationary point is introduced. Thus object-relative displacement is an important determinant of perceived motion. That this is so, is further evidenced by the fact that the stationary point will equally often be seen as the one that is moving. Now if the moving object is a rectangle surrounding the stationary point, then the outcome is no longer ambiguous. The observer always sees the point moving (provided the rectangle is not moving *too* rapidly). The same outcome occurs if the moving object is simply a larger object than the moving point and it can be adjacent to rather than surrounding the point. Thus such *induced movement* illustrates not only the importance of object-relative displacement but of the role of a frame of reference in resolving a potentially ambiguous stimulus in a particular direction (Duncker, 1929).

Analogous conclusions can be drawn concerning the perception of the upright. A vertical line seen within a tilted rectangle will generally look tilted. The rectangle serves as a frame of reference with respect to which the orientation of the line is gauged. See Asch and Witkin (1948a, 1948b) and Witkin and Asch (1948) on the rod-and-frame effect. If the observer is *inside* a tilted room the effect on truly vertical objects is even greater and the orientation of the body of the observer itself is misperceived. (Such powerful effects on the self by the frame of reference also occur in motion perception, so that induced motion of the self occurs in daily life and in the laboratory whenever the observer is surrounded by a structure that moves. See James's example of the railway station event.)

Must we invoke past experience to explain such lawful examples of relational determination and organization with respect to frames of reference? Gunnar Johansson (1950) has uncovered some dramatic examples wherein the *path* of perceived motion is not governed by the path of an object's image over the retina but rather by the manner in which the motions of the objects relate to one another. What seems to be going on in these examples is that the perceptual system splits the actual retinal motion of each motion into two components. What is most salient is the object-relative change. But the residual retinal motion must also be accounted for, and so the observer also perceives the common motion of all objects. Another way of understanding this kind of effect is in terms of hierarchical organization. An object's motion is related to its immediately surrounding frame of reference and the motion of the frame of reference is seen in relation to the observer.

Thus an insect's vertical motion on a horizontally moving object is seen as vertical despite the fact that its retinal image is moving obliquely (see Rock, 1983). If one maintains that these effects are based on prior experience, the burden of proof is on the investigator who maintains it. As we argued in the case of perceptual organization, it seems intuitively more plausible that these effects do not require prior learning for their existence. For if they are learned, what was perceived before that, and how and why does that perception change?

The Contributions of James J. Gibson

We also now have the benefit of a half-century of theorizing and research by James Gibson and his associates in which a different story about perception has been developed (Gibson, 1950a, 1966, 1979). The claim here is that there is a great deal of potential information about the world that is present in the ambient light that can be picked up by the organism as it moves through the environment. Such information is more subtle (higher order) than had previously been appreciated. Thus, it is maintained, the perceived slope of an entire plane such as the ground can be based on the density gradient in the visual information reaching the eye from such a plane, given the ecological fact that the plane often is uniform in texture. The visual angle of surface objects (e.g., pebbles on the beach), and of the spacing among them, is progressively less as a function of height in the field. The angular velocity of the retinal image of stationary objects on the ground with respect to the observer when the observer moves—as in viewing a scene to the side from a moving vehicle—is an inverse function of their height in the field. Such texture and velocity gradients (or motion perspective as Gibson called the latter) can logically signify the slope of planes but also, Gibson claimed, the size and shape of objects in the scene. (With respect to the latters, size and shape, the argument is a bit more complicated, so that I defer discussion of it for the moment.) Such a theory of "direct perception," as it has been called, implies that there is no need to invoke past experience by way of explanation although Gibson was reluctant to take a stand on the innate versus learned controversy about perception. In fact he and his co-investigator Eleanor Gibson maintained that experience was often necessary to enable one to be sensitive to nuances of information to which otherwise one might not attend or be sensitive (Gibson & Gibson, 1955). Apart from this possibility, however, it seems to this writer that Gibson was propounding a modified stimulus explanation of perception that, therefore, reduces to a theory of innate, wired-in, stimulus-percept couplings.

The fact that, logically, a certain kind of information about the world is potentially available to the perceiver does not prove that in fact the perceiver does use that information or that it is potent information. Some experimental demonstrations have supported the claim (Clark, Smith, &

Rabe, 1956; Gibson, 1950a; Gibson, Gibson, Smith, & Flock, 1959a; Gruber & Clark, 1956) but usually what is perceived in such experiments is not adequate to explain veridical perception in daily life. Moreover it does not necessarily follow that "information" is quite the right term to use here because it may turn out that what is being isolated is a cue to depth and is based on past experience. For example a texture gradient is far less effective when it is inverted or tilted; it should and could represent a ceiling or wall plane but does so less effectively (Rock, Shallo, & Schwartz, 1978; Wallach, 1954). Similarly we have found in our laboratory that a motion gradient is much poorer when it potentially represents a ceiling plane or vertical "wall" plane than a ground plane, again implicating a possible role of past experience.

So much for a consideration of some major ideas that have come along in the century since James wrote the *Principles*. Obviously I have selected only some examples from among a great number of advances that have been made during this period. Of course we now know a good deal more than I have been able to cover in this section. What guided my selection was both the theoretical importance of the work and its reference to James's theory. However, my selection is bound to be idiosyncratic. I left out many developments in our understanding of perception, including important findings concerning sensory and brain mechanisms, advances in experimental methodology and statistical analysis, and substantive discoveries of various kinds. We have also seen the coming and going of various approaches and schools of thought, including the advent of Behaviorism, which dominated the theoretical scene for a good half of the century. This domination of academia by Behaviorism had the very important effect of limiting research on perception, since the very idea of investigating phenomenal or subjective experience was looked upon with suspicion. However, the last quarter century has seen a resurgence of interest in perception as a result of the converging effects of several new disciplines: the renewed respectability of "mind" as a legitimate topic for investigation, based in part on revolutionary developments in linguistics and psycholinguistics; the computational approach to cognitive processes, including perception, the latter being referred to as "machine vision," itself partly a result of technological advances in the development of the digital computer; the new field of artificial intelligence; and the approach to cognition known as information-processing, the central theme of which is that cognition can be understood as successive stages in the processing of information, from "input" (stimulation of sense organs) to "output" (behavior). Paralleling these developments has been an increasing emphasis on the investigation of the brain mechanisms mediating perception, a development that James would have found most congenial.

JAMES ON THE TOPIC
OF PERCEPTUAL CONSTANCY

In keeping with so much of his overall approach to perception, James regarded the achievement of perceptual constancy as based on prior experience. In fact he no doubt would have said that constancy is the hallmark of perception insofar as it transcends sensation by virtue of what we have come to learn about the world. However, the manner in which past experience is brought to bear on the perception of the constant properties of objects is not simply one of learning the equivalence of things seen at different distances or slants. Rather, he argued, there is a *normal position* of viewing that serves as the standard viewpoint and the percept that occurs in this position is the canonical percept of the object. When we are not in the normal position, "*The thing as it would appear to the eye if it were in the normal position* is what we *think of* whenever we get one of the other optical views" (James, 1892, p. 345).

Precisely what is the normal position? In the case of shape, it is when the plane of the object is perpendicular to the line of sight. Thus, for example, if we view a circle that is slanted away from the fronto-parallel (or, as I will call it, the frontal) plane, so that its retinal image is elliptical, we transform or correct the elliptical sensation that might otherwise occur to the perception of a circle, because that is how the object would look were we to be viewing it from a position in which it *would* be in the frontal plane. This formulation makes explicit a claim that has been left out of contemporary thinking on the subject. It is a claim about asymmetry. Thus one would *not* say that as we view a circle in the frontal plane it looks to us or suggests to us an elliptical-like sensation of a circle in a plane slanted away from the frontal plane. Rather what has been emphasized about constancy in the last century has been the perceptual *equivalency* of objects seen under different conditions, which lead to different proximal representations. Typically no mention is made about a unique or special or normal condition of viewing giving rise to a canonical percept.[8]

In the case of size perception, James maintained that the "real" object we think of when we view an object at any distance:

> . . . is that which we get when the object is at the distance most propitious for exact visual discrimination of its details. This is the distance at which we hold anything we are examining. Farther than this we see it too small, nearer too large. And the larger and the smaller feeling [by which James meant vis-

---

[8]The only reference I have ever seen to James's theory of perceptual constancy is that of Epstein (1977). However there have been some references to the concept of "normal viewing" without acknowledgment of James. Katz's (1935) refers to normal conditions of illumination in discussing the concept of lightness constancy. I briefly noted the fact of asymmetry in constancy perception in my book *An Introduction to Perception* (Rock, 1975, p. 73).

ual sensation] vanish in the act of suggesting this one, their most important *meaning*. As I look along the dining-table I overlook the fact that the farther plates and glasses *feel* somewhat smaller than my own, for I *know* that they are all equal in size; and the feeling in them, which is a present sensation is eclipsed in the glare of the knowledge which is merely imagined.[9] (1892, p. 344)

So here again the asymmetry that is claimed means that when we do view an object at arms length, its "normal position," we do not at all think of how it would look were it to be nearer or farther than that.

It may well be that James was correct about this claim and that we have left out something of great theoretical importance in overlooking it. However we should separate the notion of "normal position" from the further claim that this position is learned. It does not necessarily follow that the tendency to correct perception to the canonical one is based on past experience. For that reason the term "canonical view" is to be preferred to the term "normal position" because "normal" presupposes what most typically occurs, empirically. In fact it is not necessarily the case that we have more experience with objects in the so-called normal position. For example, the case where the plane of a circle or square is orthogonal to the line of sight can be thought of as no more likely to occur in daily life than any other case where it is not. Moreover, given the evidence cited earlier on the presence of constancy in the perception of infants soon after birth, it is important to define "normal view" as "canonical view" and not to regard the asymmetry in constancy in daily life as the result of learning. In that way James's idea remains viable. Of course if the canonical view is not the result of prior experience, then we must face the intriguing question about its origin.

There is another point about the canonical or privileged viewpoint that needs to be made. When we view an object that is in the frontal plane, we are seeing it as it is. The diameter of a circle in the frontal plane *is* its objective diameter, whereas the horizontal axis of the elliptical projection of a circle seen at a slant does not represent its veridical width. This fact seems to be implicit in our perception of things. It is as if we know that the measurement that would convey objective values would have to be made in the frontal plane. Similarly, measurement would have to be made at arm's length to ascertain objective size. Although this fact is implicit in our perception, it does not necessarily follow that it is something we must learn.

In my own work I have come across a phenomenon that illustrates and supports the notion of canonical view. Within certain limits we can correctly

---

[9]Note that James regards the *sensation* as "vanishing" or becoming "eclipsed" by what it *suggests*. He subscribes to Berkeley's view of the sensation as a *sign* of something but not to Berkeley's specific view that the visual sensation is a sign of the tactual idea. For James the visual sensation is a sign of the *visual* object suggested by it, generally based on what we know. His use of the term "feeling" in the above quotation and elsewhere it not intended literally.

perceive the shape of an object when we view it from a tilted position of our body or just of our head. Experiments have shown that there is little if any loss of recognition when an object previously seen from an upright position is later viewed from a tilted position (Rock, 1973). So this is a different kind of shape constancy than the one defined in terms of differing slants. However, there is reason for believing that this achievement requires a process of correction in which we must succeed in describing to ourselves (albeit non-verbally and unconsciously) how the object would appear were it to be *egocentrically* upright. The canonical view is thus one in which the top of the object is egocentrically uppermost. When it is in this orientation, we certainly never "think" about what it would look like were it in any other orientation.

Let us assume then that James was correct about the fact that there is an asymmetry in the way perceptual constancy works and that we always correct the impression we receive from any vantage point on the basis of how the object would look from the canonical vantage point. What is the theoretical significance of this fact? The significance is that neither of the two prevailing accounts of constancy can deal with it, so that we would have to revise and extend our theory in order to do so. The classical explanation of constancy that goes back to Helmholtz, and earlier for that mater, is that the perceptual system takes account of the factor that leads to the variability in the proximal stimulus (e.g., distance or slant) in assessing the property signified by the proximal stimulus at the moment (e.g., visual angle or shape of image). Therefore the percept is the joint product of the two factors (e.g., perceived or registered distance and visual angle in the case of size perception). This formulation has no place for the notion of canonical view. Perceived size is constant for varying distances because the product of distance (if veridically represented) and visual angle is constant. Period.[10]

The Direct Perception account of constancy advocated by Gibson (1950b, 1966) is that an invariant is picked up about an object across distances (or slants) so that the object percept will accordingly be invariant. In fact, con-

---

[10]The evidence indicating that constancy characterizes the perception of the infant soon after birth is based on the typical condition in which cues (or information) concerning distance and depth are available. What presumably is innate then is the tendency of the perceptual system to take this information into account in assessing the size or shape signified by the retinal image. But constancy can sometimes occur under conditions in which such information is not available, usually only under special laboratory conditions, as when we view a glowing object with one eye in a dark room. Suppose then one looks at a circle or rectangle slanted in depth which yield images of an ellipse and trapezoid respectively. One will probably perceive a circle and a rectangle (Ames, 1951; Epstein & Morgan-Paap, 1974; King, Meyer, Tangney, & Biederman, 1976). This would be a case of a preferential percept given an ambiguous stimulus and past experience may well be the basis of it, i.e. past experience with these shapes at a slant (although prägnanz cannot be ruled out); the transformation is toward the canonical viewpoint. It is interesting, however, that even when cues to depth *are* present, constancy is better for a circle at a slant (elliptical image) than for an ellipse whose longer axis is at a slant (circular image), (Farné, Andreoli, & Campione, 1974).

stancy is not even a problem to be explained unless one erroneously describes the stimulus in absolute terms. If visual angle is not the proper way to define the stimulus for size and a higher-order definition *is*—in which the relevant feature is invariant—then the problem of constancy is really not a problem at all. In the case of size, what is allegedly invariant is the number of textural elements, in the plane in which the object is located, that are occluded by the object. Thus, since an object will occlude the same number of elements wherever it is *on* the surface of the plane (the texture generally being uniform) the object will appear to be the same size regardless of its distance from the observer. Hence there is also no place in the stimulus-invariance theory for the notion of canonical percept. (See Rock, 1977 for a critique of the invariance theory based on other considerations.[11])

The claim that there is a canonical percept of course implies non-equivalence of *some* kind of perception across viewpoints. But if constancy is achieved for varying viewpoints, how should we characterize the differences in perception? James argued that the *sensations* differ but that these sensations quickly vanish in the act of suggesting this (normal) one. However, if nowadays and for good reason, we generally eschew the concept of sensation, how can we characterize the difference in perception among the differing viewpoints? I and others have argued that there is another mode of perception besides the constancy mode (Gibson, 1950a; Mack, 1978; Rock, 1975, 1983, 1986). Observers are aware of certain absolute features of the proximal stimulus, such as, in the case of size, the experience of extensity, that is correlated with the visual angle of the retinal image. Extensity refers to the impression of the magnitude of the visual field filled by an object. I have suggested that such proximal mode perception occurs as a first stage of processing and leads to the constancy mode of perception as the final stage (Rock, 1983). However the proximal-mode percept lingers on and remains as a *non-* salient aspect of the final perception.

Recent research by Epstein and his coworkers provides evidence in support of this interpretation. When attention is diverted from the object viewed, perception tends to remain at the level that would be expected based on the proximal stimulus, so that size constancy (Epstein & Broota, 1986) and shape constancy (Epstein & Lovitts, 1985) fail to occur. Romi Nijhawan and I have similarly found that the perception of shape is based on the retinal or egocentric coordinates of a figure when the attention of a tilted observer viewing an upright figure is diverted (Rock & Nijhawan, 1989). Thus perception remains at the level of the proximal mode under the conditions of inattention (which incidentally corresponds to James's suggestion

---

[11]One limitation of the invariance theory that I might mention here is that it does not work with objects that are not *on* or in front of a background plane. The rectangular or trapezoidal retinal projections of a rectangular object seen from differing perspectives share no invariant feature that would lead us to predict that they look the same as shapes.

that sensations that ordinarily are no longer consciously available to adult observers can be recovered when attention lapses).

If this theoretical account is correct, it suggests the following story about viewpoint. When the observer is not in the canonical position vis-à-vis the object, the initial stage of processing yields a proximal-mode percept; for example, an ellipse in viewing a circle at a slant, a diminutive person in viewing a person at a great distance, a diamond in viewing a square from a 45-degree tilted position of the head. Based on stimulus information concerning slant, distance, or head orientation, that initial perception is now corrected. This leads to the perception of a circle, a normal-sized person, and a square, respectively, in the examples given. However, when the observer *is* in the canonical position, there is no need to correct the initial perception or, otherwise expressed, the proximal mode and the constancy mode are phenomenologically the same. There is no need to transform the mental representation achieved at the first stage of processing.

[*Note*: The following paragraphs go into further detail on the issue of canonical perception, the related topic of absolute properties in perception, and some relevant research on adaption to optically-altered stimulation. Readers not interested in such detail can skip to the final section of this chapter without losing the thread of the discussion.]

There was one thinker, Merleau-Ponty, who made much of the concept of special viewpoint but apparently had forgotten that James had done so 70 years before, since he does not cite James. In Merleau-Ponty's book *Phenomenology of Perception* (1962), he discusses at length the notion that there is a *privileged perception* that one obtains when one views an object from the optimum distance or direction.

> For each object . . . there is an optimum distance from which it requires to be seen, a direction viewed from which it vouchsafes most of itself: at a shorter or greater distance we have merely a perception blurred through excess or deficiency. We therefore tend towards the maximum of visibility, and seek a better focus as with a microscope. (p. 302)

This notion of a privileged viewpoint is important for Merleau-Ponty's philosophy of perception. He does not believe that what makes a particular viewing distance or direction optimum is its typicality based on frequency, but rather its utility for behavioral commerce with the object, the one that allows us to achieve the optimum "grasp" of the object. Through our bodies we are actively engaged with the world, in Merleau-Ponty's terms "at grips with the world." In fact only for a body involved or coping with the world would it even make sense to speak of constancy. From this it follows that the characteristics of the body are relevant for what is or is not the optimum viewpoint. For a different creature of a different size or set of skills, the optimum distance for optimum perception would be very different. Moreover, when one is not in the optimum position or orientation, a state of tension exists. This tension is of the nature of a force that leads us to seek and, if possible, attain a better "focus."

Although we need not subscribe to Merleau-Ponty's overall theory of perception, there does seem to be something to his observations about privileged viewpoint. What is particularly interesting about his idea is his attempt to explain it in terms other than past experience. Here he clearly parts company with James. My own view is that the body as a phenomenal object in the field is indeed quite important in the perception of certain object properties, but for reasons somewhat different from the ones Merleau-Ponty emphasizes. What we investigators have focused on in considering object perception is the *equivalence* of properties such as size and shape under varying conditions or observation. What we have neglected is the question of absolute properties of objects. Thus it is true that we perceive an apple as the same in size regardless of its distance (up to some limited distance), but what size is that? Surely we can say more about its size than just about its equivalence across distances. What we can say is how large an apple is in relation to ourselves. It is of a size that can fit into the hand. The relationship between object and observer is what gives a thing an absolute size (although it is admittedly odd to define the absolute in terms of the relative!).

My emphasis here is on a size relation of object to body, which is given perceptually and, therefore, although acknowledging the role of the body, does not emphasize its behavioral interaction with the object as does Merleau-Ponty. Now if the appreciation of absolute object size requires comparison of object to body, we can understand why an arms length distance is the one which would best convey that information. Hence an observer would want to translate the appearance of a distant object to one in which it is imagined to be at arms length.

If this reasoning is correct, and certain phenomenally absolute properties are given by the stimulus relationship of object to the body, then the following deduction ought to be valid. It ought not to matter what the absolute size (or orientation) of the entire retinal image is, as far as mediating veridical perception is concerned. As a thought experiment, consider the consequences of viewing the world through an optical device that minifies the retinal image. Where ordinarily an object such as an apple at arms length will subtend an angle of roughly 7 degrees, it now will subtend an angle of, let us say, 3.5 degrees. Ought it to look smaller, half its normal size? If so, that presupposes some necessary, innately determined, connections between the ordinary visual angle for that sized object at arms length and the perception of it as "apple size." Although that is possible, it is not obvious why that should be the case.

If, however, the hypothesis suggested here is correct, then the minifying device ought to have no effect whatsoever. That is, because all objects in the scene will undergo the same reduction in image size, including whatever parts of one's own body that are visible, the seen apple will retain its usual relation to the seen hand; it will fit in it. (Similar reasoning applies to the possibility of viewing the world through an optical device that alters the orientation of the retinal image, such as turning it upside down. All stimulus relationships are maintained, including that of visible body to visible scene, despite the absolute change of orientation.)

In point of fact, I have performed the experiment of minification (Rock, 1965, 1966) and George Stratton (1897) and others since have performed the experiment of image inversion. What happens? The fact is that the world *immediately* appears diminutive (and inverted in Stratton's experiment). This is contrary to the prediction based on stimulus relativity and I have sought to explain it on the basis of a lifetime of experience in which objects of given sizes (at specific distance) have always subtended angles of specific magnitudes. If so, it should be possible to undo this association and substitute a new one by requiring the subject to continue to view the world through the minifying device. In short, perceptual adaptation should be possible. After a while the minified scene ought to appear less diminutive than it does at the outset and that is precisely what we found (by a method of measurement that need not concern us here). The presumption is that, ultimately, a minified scene would appear to be completely normal, but we did not carry out the experiment long enough to confirm this prediction. In the experiment, the observer viewed a few objects on a table through a minifying mirror that allowed sight of him or herself while manually manipulating the visible objects. Control conditions established the important role of sight of the body.

I interpret the results of this experiment to support the theory that objects have absolute phenomenal size (and are not merely seen as equivalent to objects of the same size at differing distances) and that such absolute size is a function of the relationship of object to body. That being the case, we can see why James was right when he suggested that when objects were seen from other than the canonical viewing distance one tends to transform the perception to that one would obtain from such a viewing distance. For it is then that we can perceive its absolute size appropriately.

As to the role of past experience in the canonical perception of absolute size achieved, if my reasoning is correct, it is both relevant and not relevant. It is true that the size that we imagine when we see an object at other than the canonical arm's length distance is based on past experience with it when it is at that arm's length distance. Presumably memory traces are required which include representation of specific visual angle *and* the impression of absolute phenomenal size. These two aspects of the trace are associated. Hence viewing a scene through optical devices that alter the size of the entire image leads to an immediate impression that objects are too small or too large. The visual angle subtended by objects (at specific distances) do not match the corresponding memories. But it is not correct to believe that "normal" viewing distance is *necessarily* linked to past experience. I have suggested a different explanation of the role of arm's length distance, somewhat similar to that favored by Merleau-Ponty, in which the relationship of visual object to visual body is central.[12] If one could abstract from the obfuscating effect of the establishment of memory traces that happen to encode absolute visual angle, then prior experience would not enter in as a causal factor. Thus I would predict that a newborn infant viewing the world through a minifying device would not see it in any way differently than an infant viewing the world normally, that is, without such a device.

PROGRESS IN THE LAST 100 YEARS

It is clear that much has been learned or discovered in the 100 years since James's *Principles* appeared. Yet I believe that progress on a broad theoretical level has been disappointing. We simply do not have a general theory that can deal adequately with the kinds of facts and problems I outline below. In the interim century, in fact, theories that held great promise have come and gone. I refer here to Titchener's extension of Wundt's Structuralism and his core-context theory, to Gestalt theory, to the Transactionalism advocated by Adelbert Ames Jr. and Hadley Cantril, to the Sensory-Tonic theory of Werner and Wapner, to J.J. Gibson's Direct Theory of perception and to various theories that have come out of the Artificial Intelligence approach. Of course not all of these theories have yet "gone."

In my opinion real progress would mean the development of a theory that would provide explanations of the following kinds of fact or problem:

1. An understanding of how perceptual organization works on a pre-attentive level and a clarification of what the parts are in perception, the grouping and concatenation of which, yields the phenomenal world of objects and events. Indeed *are* there such parts?

2. A clarification of those "assumptions" or "constraints" in the form of "knowledge" about the world that are built into the sensory nervous system and with which the perceptual system operates.

3. A clearer understanding of what attention is and how it works, including a clarification of how a given perception is maintained or, conversely, is altered or reversed.

4. An explanation of the perception of form and the perception of similarity and discriminability of forms.

---

[12]James was an important influence on Merleau-Ponty and other phenomenologically-oriented philosophers and psychologists. In emphasizing the "aboutness' or outer directedness of mental states, he along with his contemporary, Brentano, is regarded as a founder of the now widely accepted description of consciousness as "intentional".

5. An explanation of perceptual preference and the question of whether or not past experience and/or achievement of simplicity and object rigidity are factors in such preference.

6. An explanation of how past experience is brought to bear on what is perceived (the top-down problem).

7. An explanation of perceptual constancy or, if it proves to be the case that some constancies are fundamentally different from others, an explanation of each separately.

8. An account of how the various cues to the third dimension interact to give the appropriate distance and depth relationships in the scene. Which, if any, cues to depth are learned and, if learned, how?

9. An explanation of the geometrical illusions including aftereffects that would follow from principles pertaining to the phenomena listed here.

10. A resolution of the question of what kinds of higher-order stimulus information the perceptual system does pick up and utilize. This would presumably include optically given information such as gradients of motion leading to depth perception but also information leading to perceptions such as phenomenal causality and physiognomic qualities.

11. The explanation of the process of recognition on the basis of similarity of percept to memory trace.

12. An account of the role or place of consciousness in perception in the light of the now known fact that perception does sometimes occur that cannot be said to be conscious.

13. An account of how perception gets translated into behavior.

14. The extension of these principles such as to encompass perception in animals at different phylogenetic levels and would thus provide an evolutionary account of how perception evolved to what it is in humans.

Since a theory—or perhaps a set of theories, if it proves to be the case that no single one will do—that would do justice to these problems is not even on the horizon, I feel justified in maintaining that, despite the advances I have summarized, progress has been slow in the century since James gave us his account of perception. Surely though, this amounts to high praise for James's contribution, because his prescience, his penetrating insights, and his ability to summarize in beautiful prose all that was known about perception in his time, gave us such a superb starting point.

REFERENCES

Alegria, J., & Noirot, E. (1978). Neonate orientation behaviour towards human voice. *International Journal of Behavioral Development*, *1*, 192–312.

Ames, A., Jr. (1951). Visual perception and the rotating trapezoidal window. *Psychological Monographs, 65,* Whole No. 324.

Asch, S. E., & Witkin, H. A. (1948a). Studies in space orientation: I. Perception of the upright with displaced visual fields. *Journal of Experimental Psychology, 38,* 325–327.

Asch, S. E., & Witkin, H. A. (1948b). Studies in space orientation: II. Perception of the upright with displaced visual fields and with body tilted. *Journal of Experimental Psychology, 38,* 455–477.

Beck, J. (1966). Perceptual grouping by changes in orientation and shape. *Science, 154,* 538–540.

Bornstein, M., Ferdinandsen, K., & Gross, C. G. (1981). Perception of symmetry in infancy. *Developmental Psychology, 17,* 82–86.

Bower, T. G. R. (1966). The visual world of infants. *Scientific American, 215,* 80–92.

Bushnell, E. W., & Weinberger, N. (1987). Infants' detection of visual-tactual discrepancies: Asymmetries that indicate a directive role of visual information. *Journal of Experimental Psychology: Human Perception and Performance, 13,* 601–608.

Campos, J. J., Langer, A., & Krowitz, A. (1970). Cardiac responses on the visual cliff in prelocomotor human infants. *Science, 170,* 196–197.

Caron, A. J., Caron, R. F., & Carlson, V. R. (1979). Infant perception of the invariant shape of objects varying in slant. *Child Development, 50,* 716–721.

Clark, W. C., Smith, A. H., & Rabe, A. (1956). The interaction of surface texture, outline gradient, and ground in the perception of slant. *Canadian Journal of Psychology, 10,* 1–8.

Cook, M., & Birch, R. (1984). Infant perception of the shapes of tilted plane forms. *Infant Behavior and Development, 7,* 389–402.

Day, R. H., & McKenzie, B. E. (1977). Constancies in the perceptual world of the infant. In W. Epstein, (Ed.), *Stability and constancy in visual perception: Mechanisms and processes* (pp. 285–320). New York: Wiley-Interscience.

Day, R. H., & McKenzie, B. E. (1981). Infant perception of the invariant size of approaching and receding objects. *Developmental Psychology, 17,* 670–677.

Duncker, K. (1929). Über induzierte Bewegung [Induced motion]. *Psychologische Forschung, 12,* 180–259. (Trans. and condensed in W. Ellis (Ed.), *Source book of gestalt psychology.* New York: Humanities Press, Selection 12.)

Eimas, P. D., Siqueland, E. R., Jusczyk, P. W., & Vigorito, J. (1971). Speech perception in infants. *Science, 171,* 303–306.

Ehrenfels, C. von. (1890). Ueber gestaltqualitäten [On form-quality]. *Viertelijahrsch Wissenschatt Philosophie, 14,* 249–292.

Epstein, W. (1977). Historical introduction to the constancies. In W. Epstein (Ed.), *Stability and constancy in visual perception.* New York: Wiley.

Epstein, W., & Broota, K. D. (1986). Automatic and attentional components in perception of size at a distance. *Perception and Psychophysics, 40,* 256–262.

Epstein, W., & Lovitts, B. E. (1985). Automatic and attentional components in perception of shape at a slant. *Journal of Experimental Psychology: Human Perception and Performance, 11,* 355–366.

Epstein, W., & Morgan-Paap, C. L. (1974). The effect of level of depth processing and degree of information discrepancy on adaptation to uniocular image magnification. *Journal of Experimental Psychology, 102,* 585–594.

Fantz, R. L. (1957). Form preference in newly hatched chicks. *Journal of Comparative and Physiological Psychology, 50,* 422–430.

Fantz, R. L. (1965). Ontogeny of perception. In A. M. Shrier, H. F. Harlow, & F. Stollnitz (Eds.), *Behavior of Nonhuman Primates* (Vol. 2), New York: Academic Press.

Fantz, R. L. (1966). Pattern discrimination and selective attention as determinants of perceptual development from birth. In A. H. Kikk & J. F. Rivoire (Eds.), *Development of perception: Vol. 2. The visual system* (pp. 143–173). New York: International Universities Press.

Fantz, R. L., Fagan, J. F., & Miranda, S. B. (1975). Early perceptual development as shown by visual discrimination, selectivity, and memory with varying stimulus and population parameters. In L. Cohen & P. Salapatek (Eds.), *Infant Perception: From sensation to cognition: Vol. 1. Basic visual processes* (pp. 249–346). New York: Academic Press.

Farné, M., Andreoli, A. R., & Campione, F. (1974). Shape constancy in elliptic figures. *Giornale Italiano di Psichologia, I*, 360–376.

Field, J. (1976). The adjustment of reaching behavior to object distance in early infancy. *Child Development, 47*, 304–308.

Ganz, L., & Fitch, M. (1968). The effect of visual deprivation on perceptual behavior. *Experimental Neurology, 22*, 638–660.

Gibson, E. J. (1987). Introductory essay: What does infant perception tell us about theories of perception? *Journal of Experimental Psychology: Human Perception and Performance, 13*, 515–523.

Gibson, E. J., Gibson, J. J., Smith, O. W., & Flock, H. (1959). Motion parallax as a determinant of perceived depth. *Journal of Experimental Psychology, 58*, 41–51.

Gibson, E. J., & Walk, R. D. (1960). The "visual cliff." *Scientific American, 202*, 64–71.

Gibson, E. J., & Walker, A. S. (1984). Development of knowledge of visual-tactual affordances of substance. *Child Development, 55*, 453–460.

Gibson, J. J. (1950a). *The perception of the visual world.* Boston: Houghton Mifflin.

Gibson, J. J. (1950). The perception of visual surfaces. *American Journal of Psychology, 63*, 367–384.

Gibson, J. J. (1966). *The senses considered as perceptual systems.* Boston: Houghton Mifflin.

Gibson, J. J. (1979). *The ecological approach to visual perception.* Boston: Houghton Mifflin.

Gibson, J. J., & Gibson, E. J. (1955). Perceptual learning: Differentiation or enrichment? *Psychological Review, 45*, 300–323.

Gilchrist, A. (1977). Perceived lightness depends on perceived spatial arrangement. *Science, 195*, 185–187.

Granrud, C. E. (1986). Binocular vision and spatial perception in 4- and 5-month old infants. *Journal of Experimental Psychology: Human Perception and Performance, 12*, 36–49.

Granrud, C. E. (in preparation). Visual size constancy in newborn infants. *Journal of Experimental Psychology: General.*

Granrud, C. E., Arterberry, M. E., & Yonas, A. (1985, April). *Size constancy in 3-month-old infants.* Paper presented at the Meeting of the Society for Research in Child Development, Toronto.

Gruber, H. E., & Clark, W. (1956). Perception of slanted surfaces. *Perceptual and Motor Skills, 16*, 97–106.

Harris, C. S. (1965). Perceptual adaptation to inverted, reversed, and displaced vision. *Psychological Review, 72*, 419–444.

Hatfield, G., & Epstein, W. (1985). The status of the minimum principle in the theoretical analysis of visual perception, *Psychological Bulletin, 97*, 155–186.

Hay, J., Pick, H. L., Jr., & Ikeda, K. (1965). Visual capture produced by prism spectacles. *Psychonomic Science, 2*, 215–216.

Helmholtz, H. von. (1962). *Treatise on Physiological Optics* (Vol. 3; J. P. C. Southall, Ed.) New York: Dover. (Original work published 1867)

Hering, E. (1964). *Outlines of a theory of the light sense.* (L. Hurvich & D. Jameson, Trans.). Cambridge, MA: Harvard University Press. (Original work published 1920)

Horowitz, F. D. (Ed.). (1974). Visual attention, auditory stimulation, and language discrimination in young infants. *Monographs of the Society for Research in Child Development, 39*, Serial no.158.

James. W. (1890). *The principles of psychology* (Vols. 1–2). New York: Holt.

James, W. (1892). *Psychology: Briefer course*. New York: Holt.

Jameson, D., & Hurvich, L. (1964). Theory of brightness and color contrast in human vision. *Vision Research, 4*, 135–154.

Johansson, G. (1950). Spacial constancy and motion in visual perception. In W. Epstein (Ed.), *Stability and constancy in visual perception: Mechanisms and processes* (pp. 375–419). New York: Wiley-Interscience.

Kanizsa, G., & Gerbino, W. (1976). Convexity and symmetry in figure-ground organization. In M. Henle (Ed.), *Vision and artifact*. New York: Springer.

Katz, D. (1935). *The world of colour*. London: Kegan Paul, Trench, Trubner.

Kellman, P. J. (1984). Perception of three-dimensional form by human infants. *Perception & Psychophysics, 36*, 353–358.

Kellman, P. J., & Short, K. R. (1987). Development of three-dimensional form perception. *Journal of Experimental Psychology: Human Perception and Performance, 13*, 545–557.

Kellman, P. J., & Spelke, E. S. (1983). Perception of partly occluded objects in infancy. *Cognitive Psychology, 15*, 483–524.

Kestenbaum, R., Termine, N., & Spelke, E. S. (1988). Perception of objects and object boundaries by three-month-old infants. *British Journal of Developmental Psychology, 5*, 367–383.

King, M., Meyer, G. E., Tangney, J., & Biederman, I. (1976). Shape constancy and a perceptual bias towards symmetry. *Perception & Psychophysics, 19*, 129–136.

Köhler, W. (1947). *Dynamics in psychology*. New York: Liverlight.

Kubovy, M., & Pomerantz, J. R. (1981). *Perceptual organization*. Hillsdale, NJ: Lawrence Erlbaum Associates.

Mack, A. (1978). Two modes of visual perception. In M. H. Pick (Ed.), *Modes of perception*. Hillsdale, NJ: Lawrence Erlbaum Associates.

McKenzie, B. E., & Day, R. H. (1972). Distance as a determinant of visual fixation in early infancy. *Science, 178*, 1108–1110.

Meltzoff, A., & Borton, R. W. (1979). Intermodal matching by human neonates. *Nature, 282*, 403–404.

Merleau-Ponty, M. (1962). *Phenomenology of perception*. London and Henley: Rowthledge and Kezan.

Meyers, B., & McCleary, R. A. (1964). Interocular transfer of a pattern discrimination in pattern-deprived cats. *Journal of Comparative and Physiological Psychology, 57*, 16–21.

Miller, J. M., & Festinger, L. (1977). Impact of oculomotor retraining on the visual perception of curvature. *Journal of Experimental Psychology: Human Perception and Performance, 3*, 187–206.

Neisser, U. (1967). *Cognitive psychology*. New York: Appleton-Century-Crofts.

Owsley, C. (1983). The role of motion in infants' perception of solid shapes. *Perception, 12*, 707–717.

Prather, P., & Spelke, E. S. (1982). *Three-month-old infants' perception of adjacent and partly occluded objects*. Paper presented at the International Conference on Infant Studies, Austin, TX.

Riesen, A. H. (1950). Arrested vision. *Scientific American, 215*, 80–92.

Riesen, A. H. (1958). Plasticity of behavior: psychological aspects. In H. F. Harlow & C. N. Woolsey (Eds.), *Biological and Biochemical Bases of Behavior*. Madison, WI: University of Wisconsin Press.

Rock, I. (1965). Adoption to a minified image. *Psychonometric Science, 2*, 105–106.

Rock, I. (1966). *The nature of perceptual adaptation*. New York: Basic Books. (Chap.1, in particular, pp.10–14.)

Rock, I. (1973). *Orientation and form*. New York: Academic Press.

Rock, I. (1975). *An introduction to perception*. New York: Macmillan; London: Collier-Macmillan.

Rock, I. (1977). In defense of unconscious inference. In W. Epstein (Ed.), *Stability and constancy in visual perception* (pp. 321-373). New York: Wiley.

Rock, I. (1983). *The logic of perception*. Cambridge, MA: MIT press.

Rock, I. (1986). The description and analysis of object and event perception. In K. Boff, L. Kaufman, & J. P. Thomas (Eds.), *Handbook of perception and human performance* (Vol. 2, pp. 33.1-33.71). New York: Wiley-Interscience.

Rock, I., & Harris, C. S. (1967). Vision and touch. *Scientific American, 216*, 96-104.

Rock, I., & Nijhawan, R. (1989). Regression to egocentrically-determined description of form under conditions of inattention. *Journal of Experimental Psychology: Human Perception and Performance, 15*, 259-272.

Rock, I., Shallo, J., & Schwartz, F. (1978). Pictorial depth and related constancy effects as a function of recognition. *Perception, 7*, 3-19.

Rock, I., & Victor, J. (1964). Vision and touch: An experimentally created conflict between the senses. *Science, 143*, 594-596.

Rose, S. A., Gottfried, A. W., & Bridger, W. H. (1981). Cross-modal transfer in 6-month-old infants. *Developmental Psychology, 17*, 661-669.

Rubin, E. (1921). *Visuell Wahrgenommene Figuren* [Visually perceived figures]. Copenhagen: Glydendalske.

Senden, M. von. (1960). *Space and sight: The perception of space and shape in the congenitally blind before and after operation* (P. Heath, Trans.). London: Methuen.

Siegel, A. I. (1953). Deprivation of visual form definition in the ring dove: I. Discriminatory learning. *Journal of Comparative and Physiological Psychology, 46*, 115-119.

Slater, A., & Morrison, V. (1985). Shape constancy and slant perception at birth. *Perception, 14*, 337-344.

Slater, A., Morrison, V., & Rose, D. (1983). Perception of shape by the new-born baby. *British Journal of Developmental Psychology, 1*, 135-142.

Spelke, E. S. (1976). Infants' intermodal perception of events. *Cognitive Psychology, 8*, 553-560.

Stratton, G. (1897). Vision without inversion of the retinal image. *Psychological Review, 4*, 341-360 and 463-481.

Termine, N., Hrynick, T., Kestenbaum, R., Gleitman, H., & Spelke, E. S. (1987). Perceptual Completion of Surfaces in Infancy. *Journal of Experimental Psychology: Human Perception and Performance, 13*, 524-532.

Treisman, A. (1982). Perceptual grouping and attention in visual search for features and objects. *Journal of Experimental Psychology; Human Perception and Performance, 8*, 194-214.

Van Geffen, K., & Haith, M. (1983). Infant visual response to gestalt geometric forms. *Infant Behavior Development, 7*, 335-346.

Walk, R. D., & Gibson, E. J. (1961). A comparative and analytical study of visual depth perception. *Psychological Monographs, 75*, whole no.519.

Wallach, H. (1948). Brightness constancy and the nature of achromatic colors. *Journal of Experimental Psychology, 38*, 310-324.

Wallach, H. (1954). *Memory effect in perception*. Paper read at the *International Congress of Psychology*, Montreal.

Wallach, H., & O'Connell, D. N. (1953). The kinetic depth effect. *Journal of Experimental Psychology, 45*, 205-217.

Wertheimer, M. (1923). Untersuchungen zur Lehre von der Gestalt, II. [Laws of organization in perceptual forms]. *Psychologische Forschung, 4*, 301-350. (See a condensed trans. in W. Ellis (1950) *A Source Book of Gestalt Psychology*, Selection 5, New York: Humanities Press; see also the condensed trans. in D. C. Beardslee and M. Wertheimer (1958) *Readings in Perception*, Selection 8, Princeton, NJ: Van Nostrand Reinhold.)

Wiesel, T. N., & Hubel, D. H. (1963). Single cell responses in striate cortex of kittens deprived of vision in one eye. *Journal of Neurophysiology, 26,* 1004–1017.

Wiesel, T. N., & Hubel, D. H. (1965a). Comparison of the effects of unilateral and bilateral eye closure on cortical unit responses in kittens. *Journal of Neurophysiology, 28,* 1029–1040.

Wiesel, T. N., & Hubel, D. H. (1965b). Extent of recovery from the effect of visual deprivation in kittens. *Journal of Neurophysiology, 28,* 1060–1072.

Witkin, H. A., & Asch, S. E. (1948). Studies in space orientation: IV. Further experiments on perception of the upright with displaced visual fields. *Journal of Experimental Psychology, 38,* 762–782.

Wundt, W. (1907). *Outlines of psychology* (4th German ed.) (C. H. Judd, Trans.). Berlin: Stechert.

Yonas, A., Arterberry, M. E., & Granrud, C. E. (1987). Four-month-old sensitivity to kinetic and binocular information for three-dimensional shape. *Child Development, 58,* 910–917.

Zimmerman, R. R., & Torrey, C. C. (1965). Ontogeny of learning. In A. M. Schrier, H. F. Harlow, & F. Stollnitz (Eds.), *Behavior of nonhuman primates* (Vol. 2; Chap. 11). New York: Academic Press.

Zuckerman, C. B., & Rock, I. (1957). A reappraisal of the roles of past experience and innate organizing processes in visual perception. *Psychological Bulletin, 54,* 269–296.

Chapter 10

Space Perception and the Psychologist's Fallacy in James's *Principles*

Edward S. Reed
Drexel University

The theory of space perception presented in *The Principles of Psychology* is one of the most coherent and developed arguments of that important book. Space perception was of great significance for James as a test case for his doctrine of psychophysiological unity (to be much more provocatively developed in his account of the stream of consciousness and of the emotions). James considered himself to be a sensationalist, by which he meant that all of perception and even all of thought had to have its origin in the mind's reaction to the body's physiological condition. He opposed those whom he called "psychological stimulists"—many of whom, such as Wundt or Helmholtz, we might, confusingly, dub sensationalists—those who believed that sensations were punctate and meaningless mental atoms. If sensations were mere punctate mental states in this way, then all meaningful psychological states would have to involve something in addition to sensation, and it was this idea that James opposed. If one were to erect a real psychology of thought or emotion on a sensationalist basis, then sensations had better be much richer and more interesting than James's opponents were willing to allow. Space perception thus became a battleground: Is our knowledge of space based on attending to spatial properties already found in sensations, as James would argue, or is it the result of adding spatial structure to originally non-spatial sensory awareness, as the psychical stimulists thought? As I shall show, James believed his opponents were factually incorrect about the spatial character (or lack of it) of sensations. He also thought they had fallen prey to the most pernicious methodological problem in psychology: the psychologist's fallacy. I shall trace both the empirical and methodological aspects of James's argument, and then suggest ways in which James's ideas still have relevance for modern psychologists.

JAMES'S THEORY OF SPACE PERCEPTION

James's account of space perception is a typical example of his general approach to the explanation of psychological states. For James, all knowledge comes from our ability to locate information about what we consider to be reality within the complex stream of experience. As James puts the matter in his chapter on sensation, "we are constantly selecting certain of our sensations as *realities* and degrading others to the status of *signs* of these. When we get one of the signs we think of the reality signified" (II: 41). The sensations that count as signs are just as much experiences as those that count as reality, but our consciousness focuses on the reals and leaves the others out of account, as sub- or unconscious (although James does not use such terms).

The idea that our minds pick out one sensation (or perhaps one complex of sensations) as reality, James applied to every sense modality. In the case of sight, for example, he claims:

> Out of all the visual magnitudes of each known object we have selected one as the REAL one to think of, and degraded all the others to serve as its signs. This "real" magnitude is determined by aesthetic and practical interests. It is that which we get when the object is at the distance most propitious for exact visual discrimination of its details. (II: 179; cf. II: 237)

James thus believed that the visual idea of an object in thought is the most vivid sensation of form it produces, what some modern writers have called "canonical form" (II: 184, 260; cf. Hochberg, 1978).

Throughout his account of perception—and indeed all forms of cognition and emotion—James places a heavy burden on the concept of sensation. If the perception of space or of an object ultimately comes down to an experience derived from one or a few sensations, then these sensations must contain significant amounts of information. When James wrote, this was a radical position, because the received view was that sensations are themselves meaningless and, especially, pointillistic, lacking in all spatial properties. For James, on the contrary, sensations were much richer than this (as was true also for Mach and Stumpf, to whom James often appealed). The function of sensation, James wrote, is of "acquaintance with a fact" and this fact is an "immediately present outward reality" (II: 2). Whereas the majority of psychologists and physiologists, following Johannes Müller, held sensations to be nothing more than fragments of subjective experience, James held them to be objectively based, and far more directly functional to the life of the observer. Although the Müllerian view has continued to dominate the field, there has also been a countervailing tendency in perceptual psychology whose proponents (e.g., the Gestalt school) have followed James in trying to locate the rich sources of information in sensory perception.

James viewed his theory as a kind of physiological psychophysical proposal. He believed that spatial sensations were mental correlates of sensory impressions (precisely what the dominant Müllerian school denied). James repeatedly objects to those who seek "psychical" as opposed to "cerebral" antecedents of space perception (e.g., II: 278). A sensation for James is the first stage of psychical functioning, "its antecedent is directly physical, no psychic links, no acts of memory, inference, or association intervening" (II: 218). The difficulty with such a theory is that, apparently, identical stimuli give rise to different spatial awarenesses—which is precisely what led many writers, Helmholtz chief among them, to conclude that "the organic eye process pure and simple . . . is incapable of giving us any sensation of a spatial kind at all" (II: 219). On this view, nonspatial visual sensations are *transformed* into spatial knowledge by acts of association and inference, relating visual, tactile and kinesthetic sensations to each other and to memories as well. This is still a dominant theory of space perception (e.g., Haber, 1985; Marr, 1982), but James rejects it. He claims that there really are sensations of space and that, although other sensations and mental processes can *alter* these spatial sensations (or at least enter into relations with them) these sensations are, nevertheless, the basis of all spatial awareness and knowledge. If an identical stimulus yields now one perception and later a different perception, James argues (with Hering) that the reason must be that some different *physiological* result of the situations has occurred. He disagrees with Helmholtz that the explanation is due to some (unconscious) different *mental* interpretation of the two situations (II: 4). "Retinal sensations are spatial; and were they not, no amount of 'synthesis' with equally spaceless motor sensations could intelligibly make them so" (II: 277-8).

It is scarcely an exaggeration to say that these contrasting explanations of space perception still haunt the field today (see Haber & Hershenson, 1980, for a good review). Many writers want to explain the fundamental visual spatial constancies (e.g., position, line of sight) at least partially in terms of non-visual inputs. The reasoning behind this is two-fold: First there is an *assumption* that monocular visual inputs are intrinsically non-spatial; and, second, there are cases when a constant visual stimulus seems to yield variable effects on spatial awareness (Epstein, 1977; Matin, 1986). Yet there are other modern perceptionists, most notably James Gibson (1950; Hagen, 1985) who would seem to agree with James that no amount of information processing can create spatial knowledge from non-spatial inputs. (Although, it should be pointed out, Gibson would strongly disagree with James that it is sensation that is the source of spatial information, see Gibson, 1966.) Given the contemporary flavor of the issues, and the undecided status of the arguments, James's thinking on the role of unconscious inferences in perception may be of interest to modern psychologists.

JAMES ON UNCONSCIOUS INFERENCE

From James's perspective, the problem with hypothetical psychological processes like "unconscious inferences" (the paradigm of all information processing mechanisms) is not that they invoke the unconscious, but how they treat the unconscious. James himself was keenly interested in unusual forms of consciousness, lapses of consciousness, and pre- and subconscious states, as is more than evident from his chapter on the Stream of Consciousness and his lectures on *The Variety of Religious Experiences*. For James, the stream of consciousness is nothing more than a well defined current in a larger river of experience. Consciousness as a cognitive state, as a knowing that thus and such is my current circumstance, emerges from less explicit forms of awareness. All of James's explanations of cognitive states, of perception, conception, and feeling, require that consciousness be a sort of articulation of one stream of thought amidst a much vaster and murkier river of experience. Having spent so much effort trying to distinguish cognitive conscious states from non-cognitive non-conscious states, James was decidedly unwilling to accept Helmholtz, Wundt, and others' (including Freud's?) disregard for the functional distinctiveness of these two modes of experience. Explanations invoking unconscious inference typically treat unconscious sensations and other unconscious states as if they were identical to explicit cognitive conscious states, but merely hidden from awareness. (That this is still the case is well illustrated in Pylyshyn's, 1984, recent discussion of so-called "cognitive impenetrability.") For example, because I sense unconsciously the increasing "blueness" of light from those distant hills, I consciously perceive them as further off. James was happy to believe that all lookers, not just trained artists like himself, inarticulately sense such "aerial perspective." But James condemned as absurd the idea that these less-than-conscious sensations could function in any way as *knowledge*, as an explicit step in an inference, or, as one would now say, a stage in a computational process. For James, a subconscious state was precisely the sort of experience that was *not* articulate knowledge, and it was a confusion of the first order to treat unconscious sensations as explicit stages in processing information.

According to James, perception is a process in which one or a cluster of sensations stands out as the most explicit, the best, the clearest evidence of some fact of the environment. There is no Kantian machine-shop, as he liked to put it, in which the mind performs inferences. James does not deny that many more sensations are had than come to consciousness in perception. But the status of these not-quite-conscious sensations is as a fringe of awareness, as a background that is uncertain, vague, and of which we are unaware or, at best, partially aware. He is surprised that anyone could believe that unconscious states could be as cognitive as Helmholtz or Wundt (or modern cognitive scientists) claim.

All the hypothetical processes for establishing relations among sensations are unnecessary, according to James, because, if one assumes (as he did) that relations themselves can be stimuli for sensations, then the hypothetical relation-creating processes are superfluous. Instead of searching for hypothetical mental processes of inference that unites, combines, and relates stimuli, James argued that we should look for physical and physiological processes which produce relational stimuli that then give rise to complex sensations. The idea of relational stimuli was important not only in the rise of Gestalt psychology (Köhler, 1929/1947), but also for Tolman's (1932) purposive behaviorism, and for Boring (1933), Troland (1929–1931), and Gibson's (1933, 1937) dimensionalist theory of perception.

James is quite adamant in his development of this concept of relational stimuli, and it is worth quoting him at length on this topic. The first example James used to prove his case is that of brightness contrast (following Hering's critique of Helmholtz), but:

> There are many other facts beside the phenomena of contrast which prove that when two objects act together on us the sensation which either would give alone becomes a different sensation. A certain amount of skin dipped in hot water gives the perception of a certain heat. More skin immersed makes the heat much more intense, although of course the water's heat is the same. A certain extent as well as intensity in the quantity of the stimulus is requisite for any quality to be felt. Fick and Wunderli could not distinguish heat from touch when both are applied through a hole in a card, and so confined to a small part of the skin. Similarly, there is a chromatic minimum of size in objects. The image they cast on the retina must needs have a certain extent or it will give no sensation of color at all. . . . It is not easy to explain any of these results as illusions of judgment due to the inference of a wrong objective cause of judgment due to the inference of a wrong objective cause for the sensation which we get. No more is this easy in the case of Weber's observation that a thaler laid on the skin of the forehead feels heavier when cold than warm. (II: 28–29)

After enumerating a number of further examples where changes in the extensity of a multi-dimensional stimulus produces qualitative changes in perception, James concludes:

> Probably every one will agree that the best way of formulating all such facts is physiological: it must be that the cerebral process of the first sensation is reinforced or otherwise altered by the other currents which come in. No one, surely, will prefer a psychological explanation *here*. Well, it seems to me that

all cases of mental reaction to a plurality of stimuli must be like these cases, and that the physiological formulation is everywhere simplest and best. (II: 30)

When James wrote—and the situation is not much different today—it was simply assumed that sensations are "devoid of all spatial content" (II: 31). If this were so, then some process of mental "compensation" would certainly be needed to explain spatial awareness. Such unconscious mental processes would seem to be unnecessary for the basic facts of spatial perception, the so-called "projection" of visual sensations "out" from the retina and of tactile sensations "out" from the skin into objects. This is an instance of Wundt's law, at which James pokes fun: The law "can only be defined as a tendency to feel all things in relation to each other. Bless its little soul! But why does it change the things so, when it thus feels them in relation?" (II: 28). Whereas it is plausible that changes in physical extensity or intensity of relational stimuli cause alterations in experience, why should unconscious sensations change when other sensations occur alongside of them? This kind of mentally caused change can be asserted to occur, as with Wundt's law, but this is just to assert that of which we are ignorant, as James's crack suggests.

ATTACK ON TWO-STEP THEORIES

One of the least acceptable consequences of the unconscious inference theory was, for James, the nature of the "two-step" process usually hypothesized in such theories. According to this style of explanation, the process of perception is inherently dual. First, some sensation is registered. Second, this sensation is related to other sensations, and/or memories, and/or other mental contents. From these quasi-inferential processes of establishing relationships, a perception is supposedly produced. We have seen that James objected to describing these relationships as unconscious mental processes, preferring to locate the relationships in the stimuli themselves, or in the patterns of stimulation in the nervous system. But James had other objections to this theory as well.

Most importantly, the theory of unconscious inference encourages one to believe that the first stage in the perceptual process (i.e., the sensation or, in modern jargon, the output of a sensory transducer) is not easily accessible to consciousness. (This is because no one has ever been able to find introspective evidence in favor of two-step theories.) Because of this, one can describe the sensation stage in many ways, without the constraint of having to match the hypothetical sensation to observable feelings. James objected to this forcefully. For example, he objected to describing muscle sensations as spatial for, according to his own observations, muscles give a feeling of effort or strain, but not of bigness or shape (the latter coming from touch and articulatory sensations from joints). In arguing this way, James opposed the then-dominant British theory, first expounded in detail by Thomas Brown (1820) that the infant's trial and errors at movement are the first stages in a process whereby sequences of muscle movement sensations are unconsciously interpreted in terms of their resultant behavioral (spatial movement of the limbs) consequences.

In a reply to Ford's (1893) critique of the account of space perception in *The Principles*, James (1893/1920) spelled out his thinking on muscle sense very clearly. He attacks the "usual explanation" that we see space because, when we look from one thing to another there is a "muscular sweep," which produces a spatial sensation. James objects: "One does not see why the end of a muscular feeling should appear separated in space from its beginning. . ." (1893, p. 331). Why should muscle sensations be any more or less spatial than, say, visual or auditory sensations? In *The Principles* (II: 243–266) James carefully analyzed Wundt's and Helmholtz's arguments against the claim that visual sensations are spatial and rejects them. James argues that visual spatial sensations are not the result of bringing visual and muscle sensations into an apperceptive unity, they are "retinal" exclusively. The movements of the eyeballs play a great part in educating our perception, it is true; but they have nothing to do with *constituting* any one feeling of form" (II: 266). If visual sensations lack spatial properties, then muscle sensations will not be able to help them out in any way: "Wundt's theory is the flimsiest thing in the world. It starts by an untrue assumption, and then corrects it by an unmeaning phrase. Retinal sensations *are* spatial; and were they not, no amount of 'synthesis' with equally spaceless motor sensations could intelligibly make them so" (II: 277–278). James would be appalled that this "flimsiest thing in the world" is still a popular account of spatial awareness, even though his own cogent objections to it have hardly been met.

Retinal sensations are spatial, James was convinced, because the stimuli for them are relational. (This was an idea developed around the same time by Hering, Mach, and Stumpf, all known to James, and vice versa.) Add this one new idea and the plausibility of two-step theories evaporates. Specifically, James (and his German colleagues) would counter Helmholtz and Wundt at several points. First, the psychological stimulists' account of the *content* of sensations was questioned. Muscle sensations were sensations of effort, not of space; retinal sensations included spatial properties. Second, James's opponents' refuge in the concept of unconscious sensations was attacked in two ways: that the contents of sensations were accessible to consciousness, and that unconscious mental states could not function as explicit, articulate stages in a process of inference. Third, the psychological stimulists' model of mental relationships were dismissed as fictions, to be replaced by an analysis of relational stimuli, and an analysis of relational physiological processes, along with a psychological process of attending to and fixing the most important informative sensations.

THE PSYCHOLOGIST'S FALLACY

James's theory of space perception was one of several sensationalistic theories that emerged (in partial reaction against Helmholtz and his followers) at the end of the 19th Century. The fundamental idea behind all these novel theories was that stimuli could be complex and relational. Hering had studied complexes of brightness contrasts as stimuli; Mach and Exner had begun to look at motion patterns as stimuli; and Stumpf had drawn important connections between auditory and visual space perception that relied on an analysis of relational stimuli. Thus the sensationalist aspect of his work was not innovative, either when his articles on space perception appeared in *Mind* in 1887 or when the *Principles* appear in 1890. (It should be noted that James's sensationalism in his account of cognition and emotion *was* innovative.) However, James had probably thought more deeply about touch, muscular sense, and vestibular sensibility than had his European allies—Mach and Exner not excepted—thus placing him in good position to challenge those "eye men" who liked to fall back on the "skin men" for explanations, as James (II: 279) teasingly put Helmholtz's position. Unbeknownst to James, also in 1890, Christian von Ehrenfels published an important essay in an obscure journal in which he argued that relational stimuli produce not sensations but *"Gestalt qualität"* as he put it. Over the next two decades, there was to be intense discussion as to whether these *Gestalts* were the result of a one-step or a two-step process. Just after 1910, two students of James's friend Stumpf—Köhler and Koffka—launched a concerted attack on two-step theories of the production of *Gestalten*, as they were now being called. Out of this attack on two-step theories of Gestalt awareness was born the "Berlin school" and what we now know as the Gestalt movement (see Gurwitsch, 1936/1966). Although James played a very minor role in discussions of space perceptions after 1890, his model and influence surely had some effect on Stumpf's students, but the details of this history have yet to be written.

In *The Principles* James himself had advanced beyond merely asserting the superiority of his sensationalism to the psychical stimulists' theory. James's phenomenology of the stream of consciousness, with the unconscious as deep currents, had made him realize that the psychical stimulists' claims about unconscious sensations were not merely wrong, but were in fact evidence of a serious methodological flaw. In working through his critique of two-step theories, James came to believe that a deep fallacy lay beneath the many diverse attempts to derive spatial awareness from non-spatial sensory elements. In short, he claimed that all the psychological stimulists had commited what he called the "psychologist's fallacy" (I: 196; II: 281).

In its most general form, the psychologist's fallacy is the confusion of knowledge by acquaintance with knowing about something, of tacit with explicit knowing (I: 220f). James's critique of all versions of the unconscious inference theory is that the knowledge-base, which such theories assume drives the inference process, is treated as if it were explicit knowledge about the world, when the whole purpose of the explanation is to account for knowledge by acquaintance. A particularly egregious form of this fallacy can be found in the recent and popular theory of vision expounded by David Marr (1982). Marr's explanations of how one sees even a very simple shape presuppose that the mind interprets the retinal image by using extraordinarily sophisticated knowledge about what is in the environment, and remarkably complex processes of extrapolation and inference. James's objection to this would surely be exactly the same as his objection to Helmholtz's theory: One cannot explain the apprehension of the spatial properties of the world by appealing to sophisticated geometrical knowledge—surely the precise opposite is true! And, to the rebuttal that this knowing-about geometry is tacit and unconscious, James's rejoinder, as we have seen, is that then one has to abandon the "Kantian machine shop" with its explicit logic, inferences, and the like, for this is surely a misrepresentation of the nature of subconscious awareness.

The distinction between knowledge-by-acquaintance and knowing-about is a difference between feeling and thinking. This is not an absolute distinction, because thoughts (cognitive states) in James's view are articulations of feelings (sensations). For example, when we visualize an object we may do so by "picturing" it; that is, imagining it from a specific point of view, usually not quite in front of it and from a distance suitable for seeing all the object's features in reasonable detail. James's analysis of this is that our thought of the object selects one sensation or one group of sensations (those from this special viewpoint) as being the most real representation of the object. Practically speaking, then, knowledge-by-acquaintance and knowing-about are correlative states (I: 221–222). The fact that the two kinds of knowledge form a sort of continuum makes it quite easy to fall prey to the psychologist's fallacy. Nevertheless, James insists, there is a clear distinction between "feeling and thought . . . through feelings we become acquainted with things, but only by our thoughts do we know about them. Feelings are the germ and starting point of cognition, thoughts the developed form" (I: 221–222).

The whole study of space perception has been undermined by repeated instances of the psychologist's fallacy. Even today there are perceptual psychologists who would agree with Spencer (as cited by James, II: 281) that, because extension "consists" of a series of relations among co-existing positions (according to knowledge-about space, i.e., geometry), then the perception of space cannot arise from the simultaneous activity of different cells in a receptor array "unless there is knowledge of their relative positions." It is safe to say that the majority of theories of space perception have assumed, with Spencer, that information about these relative positions is crucial to the apprehension of space. "Similarly, because movement is analyzable into positions occupied at successive moments by the mover, philosophers [and psychologists] . . . have repeatedly denied the possibility of *its* being an immediate sensation" (II: 281). But what is perceived in "spatial" awareness need not be space as known to geometers (Gibson, 1979), and what is perceived when we are aware of motion need not be the displacement of a stimulus across a receptive field (Gibson, 1968; Wertheimer, 1912). The fallacy that James attacks is the *assumption* that space must be known through first knowing the loci of body parts and then the loci of parts of the layout. There would be no fallacy if this assumption were expressed as an *hypothesis*; it would just turn out to be a falsified hypothesis, as there are clear cases of both space and motion perception where no particular bodily loci are apprehended.

James is thus wholly out of sympathy with the doctrine of "projection," the assumption that sensations are felt first as bodily realities and then "projected outwards" into perceived space. The tactile stimulation from the pen with which I am writing is, on this view, felt in my fingers subconsciously and then (with the help of sensory data from the joints and muscles of my hand and arm) projected outwards, so that I feel the pen as an external implement, not as a series of pressures on my fingers. The very idea that sensations have a bodily locus is an example of the psychologist's fallacy: "To say that we feel a sensation's seat to be 'in the brain' or 'against the eye' or 'under the skin' is to say as much about it and to deal with it in as non-primitive a way as to say that it is a mile off" (II: 42).

One might extend James's critique to the study of spatial cognition as well as spatial perception. For instance, the theory of cognitive maps might well be considered a good example of the psychologist's fallacy. An animal or a person that is acquainted with a layout may have knowledge *about* that layout, and that knowledge might even take on map-like forms. But in what sense is the knowledge about layout a basis for acquaintance with it? To treat perceptions as if they inhere into cognitive maps is just as muddled as to treat sensations as if they inhered in the body. The perception of a layout is part of acquaintance with: To think about the layout one may (but need not) develop a mental map, but that map would be derived from spatial awareness, not the other way around. Again, the fallacy here lies in *assuming* that acquaintance with a layout has a knowing-about (map) structure. One could treat this as an hypothesis and ask whether direct experience with a layout and mediated experience with the same layout produce similar kinds of spatial cognition. A few such experiments have been done, and they seem to show that direct and mediated experience with the same layouts yield rather different cognitive results (Thorndyke & Hayes-Roth, 1982).

RESUMÉ OF JAMES'S THEORY
OF SPACE PERCEPTION

James's theory of space perception thus offers few novel facts, but a number of novel interpretations. James repeatedly and insightfully reexamined the received account of what information is available in sensation for spatial awareness—covering touch, kinesthesis, vision, and even audition—and he showed that what he called sensation carries much more spatial information than had previously been realized. He diagnosed this failure to understand that sensations were spatial as being due to the psychological stimulists' disbelief in relational stimuli. The psychological stimulists were also wrong about unconscious states and processes, which, James insisted, are in no way like their conscious, explicit, counterparts. According to James there is no unconscious inferencing or information processing (as we would now put it), although the complex, relational processes of the central nervous system do yield a fringe of unarticulated subconscious feelings. The spatial illusions that the psychological stimulists claim reveal the inappropriate workings of unconscious mental processes in certain situations are due in fact to incorrect associations among the sensations themselves, not to incorrect changes made to the sensations (II: 219f.). The widespread appeal of visual perceptionists to the powers of touch and muscle sensation in explaining space perception are a muddle: *All* sensations provide *some* spatial qualities. Thus, sensations do not have to be projected outward from the body, and one does not learn about the loci of body regions first, and then infer external spatial positions (II: 31, 35).

For James, perceived space is a system of possible relations among sensations (II: 36), including motion sensations as well as spatial sensations from all sense modalities (II: 171). The totality of space is just the sum of all our spatial impressions. What is immediately seen, before thought analyzes it—the space with which we are acquainted, not that which we know about—is not a three-dimensional world, but a world that has a variety of more or less definite spatial properties (II: 78). As we receive more spatial sensations, and associate some of the sensations with one another, we build up an articulated experienced space that becomes increasingly definite and which becomes more a space that is known about than one that is experienced.

CONCLUSION:
THE MEANING OF THE PSYCHOLOGIST'S FALLACY
FOR MODERN PSYCHOLOGY

James believed that it was easy to confuse feelings with thoughts, and that, therefore, the psychologist's fallacy is "the *great* snare of the psychologist" (I: 196). What happens is that psychologists know the facts of which their observers are aware and, if the psychologist is not careful, he or she will confuse her own knowledge with the observers' mere acquaintance with the same fact. Yet why should psychologists, and especially the psychological stimulists, like Wundt (James's personal *bete noir*) fall such easy prey to this rather crude confusion? A proper answer to this question is one of the most urgent tasks facing theoretical psychology even today. All I can do here is to offer several tentative suggestions, as hypotheses worthy of further investigation.

The psychologist's fallacy is a legacy of the Cartesian ontology in which sensations for the first time appeared in modern form. In this ontology there must exist a class of entities that are both physical and mental, which have both bodily reality and mental significance. Descartes called such entities the "second grade of sense" (Cottingham, 1986; Reed, 1982). Later, Thomas Reid (1785/1969) introduced the modern terminology, distinguishing between sensations and perceptions. Nevertheless, the problem of what could count as a sensation has plagued scientists since the 17th Century. At first, the stimuli for sensations were assumed to be physical entities (primary qualities, Descartes' matter in motion), but by the end of the 18th Century it was realized that many physical stimuli give rise at best to *unconscious* sensations (Leibniz's *petites perceptions*) which was a contradiction in terms for the Cartesian school. The Scots school of medical physiology, and especially the important experimental medical scientist Robert Whytt (1768) resolved this contradiction by defining stimuli as the activities of nerves, themselves affected by specific physical agencies. Sensations thus became the physical response of the nervous system and the mental state (conscious or not) accompanying that response. This in turn raised the question of why different nerves had varying responses to the same stimulus, and why only certain nerves responded at all to particular stimuli (Physiological specificity). At the same time, Whytt wondered why the psychical responses to physical stimuli were specialized (psychological specificity) (see Wright, in preparation, for a review of the Scots school's thought).

Influenced by the earlier Scots, and by his near contemporaries, Charles Bell and Marshall Hall, and also by German *naturphilosophie*, Johannes Müller's *Handbook of Physiology* (1833–5/1838–40) articulated these problems of specificity in a way that still is relevent for psychology and neuroscience. For Müller, the specific physical responses of nerves (nerve "energies" as he, a vitalist, called them) were lawfully correlated with specific mental sensations. The sensory qualities of light, Müller argued, are a result of the specific physical responses of the retina and optic nerve, not of the electromagnetic energy we call light and which presumably causes those responses. Many scientists understood Müller to be arguing for a particularly powerful method for investigating sense perception: control one's physical stimulation, isolate particular receptors and nerves, and study their specific responses to the controlled stimulation, then use psychophysical methods to correlate the physiologically specific receptor behavior to specific sensations. With this method one was supposed to be able to deduce a finite number of specific sensations from which all perception might be built up. Helmholtz's two great masterpieces, *On the Sensations of Tone* and the *Physiological Optics*, followed this psychological stimulist method explicitly, but the method is a failure. Conceptually, it is full of holes, as James showed. Historically, no one has ever been able to decide on just what specific sensations exist, tied to what stimuli, or how those sensations might cohere into perceptions (Gibson, 1985).

Toward the end of the 19th Century, William James and others began arguing that complex physical relations could be stimuli for sensations, self-consciously opposing this psychological stimulist tradition, in which simple physical variables had been supposed to specifically correlate with sensation via the mediation of single nerves. But none of these thinkers—not Hering, Mach, Stumpf, or James—challenged the prevailing Müllerian doctrine of specificity. They all assumed that particular physical stimuli did yield specific sensations, they just wanted to expand the list of possible correlations. But this expansion brought peril, for it began to seem as if there were no order in psychophysical relations yet, unless one challenged Müller, it would be impossible to explain how a relation, which necessarily was received by more than a momentary nerve impulse, could yield a specific response. Wundtian psychophysics was a narrow discipline in which trained observers attempted to measure in as precise a way as possible how particular variations in physical stimulation mapped quantitatively into psychological states. James's psychophysics was also psychophysical, but had little of Wundt's introspective quantitative rigor—indeed, even the physicist Mach's new psychophysics lacked this quantitative side. Wundt therefore claimed that the higher psychological processes, such as cognition, could not be studied experimentally at all, but must be approached through historical and comparative methods (Blumenthal, 1985).

The critics of the psychical stimulists did not rest with Wundt's attempt to limit quantitative experimental psychology. Köhler (1913/1971) fought back with a powerful critique of Helmholtz, in which he showed that Müllerian specificity could be salvaged only by the most gratuitous ad hoc hypotheses. One had to appear to the existence of whole series of unnoticed sensations each of which would be altered by equally unconscious processes of judgment. No independent method had been offered for verifying the existence of either the specific sensations or their correlated judgments. Would it not be better to abandon Müller's sensationalistic notion of specificity and instead to explore empirically in what ways the mind and brain are "isomorphic," as Köhler (1929/1947) liked to put it? Although Gestalt psychologists did turn their experiments to trying to prove this point, they never succeeded in formulating a working hypothesis about the specific relations between physical stimuli and mental response. While Köhler (1940) attempted to study both stimulus structures and their allegedly corresponding brain fields, this was not a widespread activity in Gestalt research (see Koffka, 1935), and it did not succeed. The great successes of Gestalt theory came from their descriptions of both the behavioral and phenomenal fields, descriptions which were, by and large, not connected with any serious attempts to analyze the physiological or physical fields to which the phenomenal ones were correlated.

To my knowledge, only one student of James's, Edwin Bissell Holt pursued the critique of the psychical stimulists and searched for an adequate account of psychological specificity. Holt (1915) developed a theory of "cognition as specific response." By this he meant that what was cognized by an animal or person was embodied in the specific environmental factor or object toward which the agent's behavior, as a whole, was directed. Holt argued that response in this integrated sense was consistent with both Freudian and Sherringtonian thinking. What Freud called a wish was nothing more than a single coherent course of action in which one was prepared to engage. Many wishes might compete at one moment, but only one could emerge as the specific response. Holt believed that Pavlov's and Sherrington's ideas of nervous integration could explain what he saw as a progression from an embryological state in which the nervous system responded with local reflexes (i.e., not to environmental properties but to Müllerian physical stimuli) to a mature state in which the agent showed "recession from the proximal to the distal stimulus"—reacting to environmental happenings, not to physical stimuli at the body. Although many modern cognitive scientists might have some sympathy for the claim that cognition is the capacity to understand and deal with the objective features of one's environment, few would be in sympathy with Holt's belief that this claim might emerge from a primitive reflex state on the basis of classical conditioning and integrated nervous functioning.

More recently, James Gibson, himself a student of Holt's at Princeton in the 1920s (Reed, 1988), has proposed another novel account of specificity. Explicitly rejecting Müllerian doctrine, Gibson (1979, p. 115) argued that there exists *ecologically* specific information on which both perception and action are based. This information is external to an observer because it is contained in the fields of energy distributed around an animal's body and throughout its habitat. Gibson (1966) claimed that such information is detected by an active, exploratory process, in which a variety of regions of the nervous system are so coordinated as to "resonate" to the same informative structure. For instance, one can feel an object's shape and solidity with one finger, with several fingers on one hand, or even with all ten fingers on both hands. The reason why a unified, constant object is felt (as indeed it is, see Gibson, 1962) is that the information (patterns of mechanical deformation of the fingers and hand, resistance offered to the skin, angles of approach available to the joints, etc.) is constant, even though external. There is still considerable controversy concerning Gibson's proposals for explaining perception, much less cognition. Moreover, Gibson was forced to abandon sensationalism entirely because of his emphasis on the pickup of external information. The specificity James, like Müller, sought in sensation, Gibson sought in ecological laws (Turvey, Shaw, Reed,& Mace, 1981).

All these attempts to replace or transform Müller's notion of specificity have in common the desire to prevent psychologists from falling into the psychologist's fallacy. If we did know precisely what it was to which an observer was responding, be it a Gestalt pattern, Holtian wish, or Gibson's ecological information, we would then be able to infer in a proper way what was the state of mind of that organism. That is, we would be able to infer in what an observer's acquaintance with things consisted. Theories of psychological specificity are attempts to account for acquaintance on its own terms, and to avoid reducing knowledge by acquaintance to knowledge-about. It is unfortunate that James's cogent critique of the psychological stimulists, and their inadequate account of specificity is not more widely known. Even today, many theories of perception, cognition, and action do not have within them a principled means for determining to what, specifically, an experimental subject is responding. Without a principled theory of specificity many untrue assumptions are made about the units of awareness, behavior, and thought. The processes of perceiving, acting, and knowing are then confused with these hypothetical units, "the conditions of the latter are demanded of the former state of mind, and all sorts of mythological processes are brought into help" (II: 281). If modern information processing psychology is not to flounder in a sea of unjustified assumptions and unverifiable processes, we had better seek to use knowledge about James's psychologist's fallacy as a life raft to get us to *terra firma*.

ACKNOWLEDGMENTS

The research and writing of this essay was supported by a Drexel University Research Scholar's Award (1986–1987) and by a Mary E. Switzer Research Fellowship from the National Institute for Disability and Rehabilitation research (NIE) (1987–1988).

246   REED

REFERENCES

Blumenthal, A. L. (1985). Shaping a tradition: Experimentalism begins. In C. E. Braxton (Ed.), *Points of view in the modern history of psychology*. New York: Academic Press.

Boring, E. G. (1933). *The physical dimensions of consciousness*. New York: Century.

Brown, T. (1820). *Lectures on the philosophy of the human mind*. Philadelphia: John Grigg.

Cottingham, J. (1986). *Descartes*. London: Blackwells.

Ehrenfels, C. von (1890). Ueber gestaltqualitaten [On form-quality]. *Vierteljahrsch Wissenschatt Philosophie, 14*, 249–292.

Epstein, W. (Ed.). (1977). *Stability and constancy in visual perception*. New York: Academic.

Ford, E.B. (1893). The original datum of space-consciousness. *Mind*, (New Series) *2*, 217–218.

Gibson, J. J. (1933). Adaptation, aftereffect, and contrast in the perception of curved lines. *Journal of Experimental Psychology, 16*, 1–31.

Gibson, J. J. (1937). Adaptation with negative aftereffect. *Psychological Review, 44*, 222–244.

Gibson, J. J. (1950). *The perception of the visual world*. Boston: Houghton Mifflin.

Gibson, J. J. (1962). Observations on active touch. *Psychological Review, 62*, 477–491.

Gibson, J. J. (1966). *The sense considered as perceptual systems*. Boston: Houghton Mifflin.

Gibson, J. J. (1968). What gives rise to the perception of motion? *Psychological Review, 75*, 335–346.

Gibson, J. J. (1979). *The ecological approach to visual perception*. Boston: Houghton Mifflin.

Gibson, J. J. (1985). Conclusions from a century of research on sense perception. In S. Koch & D. Leary (Eds.), *A century of psychology as a science*. New York: McGraw-Hill.

Gurwitsch, A. (1986). *The field of consciousness*. Pittsburgh: Duquesne University Press. (Original work published 1936)

Haber, R. (1985). Perception: A one hundred year perspective. In S. Koch & D. Leary (Eds.), *A century of psychology as science* (pp. 250–283). New York: McGraw-Hill.

Haber, R., & Hershenson, M. (1980). *The psychology of visual perception* (2nd ed.). New York: Holt.

Hagen, M. A. (1985). James J. Gibson's approach to visual perception. In S. Koch & D. Leary (Eds.), *A century of psychology as science*. New York: McGraw Hill.

Hochberg, J. (1978). *Perception* (2nd ed.). Englewood Cliffs, NJ: Prentice-Hall.

Holt, E. B. (1915). *The Freudian wish and its place in ethics*. New York: Holt.

James, W. (1890). *The principles of psychology* (Vols. 1-2). New York: Holt.

James, W. (1893). The original datum of space-consciousness. *Mind*, (New Series 2), 363–365. (Reprinted in William James (1920) *Essays and Reviews*. London: Longmans Green)

Koffka, K. (1935). *Principles of Gestalt psychology*. New York: Harcourt.

Köhler, W. (1913). Ueber unbemerkte Empfindigung und Urteilstäuschungen [On unnoticed sensations and errors of judgement]. *Zeitschrift für Psychologie, 66*, 51–80. (Reprinted in M. Henle (Ed.). (1971). *The selected papers of Wolfgang Köhler*. New York: Liveright.)

Köhler, W. (1940). *On dynamics in psychology*. New York: Liveright.

Köhler, W. (1947). *Gestalt psychology* (2nd ed.). New York: Liveright. (Original work published 1929)

Marr, D. (1982). *Vision*. San Francisco: Freeman.

Matin, L. (1986). Visual localization and eye movements. In K. Borr, L. Kaufman, & J. Thomas (Eds.), *Handbook of perception and performance Vol. 1: Sensory processes*. New York: Wiley.

Müller, J. (1838–40). *Elements of physiology* (Vols. 1-2; W. Baly, Trans.). London: Murray. (Original work published in German in 1833–5)

Pylyshyn, Z. (1984). *Computation and cognition*. Cambridge, MA: MIT Press.

Reed, E. S. (1982). Descartes' corporeal ideas hypothesis and the origin of scientific psychology. *Review of Metaphysics, 35*, 731–752.

Reed, E. S. (1988). *James J. Gibson and the psychology of perception.* New Haven, CT: Yale University Press.

Reid, T. (1969). *The intellectual powers of man* (Reprint ed.). Cambridge, MA: MIT Press. (Original work published 1785)

Thorndyke, P., & Hayes-Roth, B. (1982). Differences in spatial knowledge acquired from maps and navigation. *Cognitive Psychology, 14*, 560–589.

Tolman, E. (1932). *Purposive behavior in animals and men.* New York: Century.

Troland, L. T. (1929–1931). *Psychophysiology* (Vols. 1–3). New York: Van Nostrand.

Turvey, M., Shaw, R., Reed, E., & Mace, W. (1981). Ecological laws of perceiving and acting. *Cognition, 9*, 237–304.

Wertheimer, M. (1912). Experimentelle studien uber das Sehen von Bewegung. [Experimental studies on the seeing of motion]. *Zeitschrift fur Psychologie, 61*, 161–265.

Whytt, R. (1768). An essay on the vital and other involuntary motions of animals. Reprinted in *The Works of Robert Whytt.* Edinburgh: Balfour, et al.

Wright, J. (in preparation). *Metaphysics and physiology: Mind, body and the animal economy in 18th Century Scotland.*

Chapter 11

Consciousness and Comparative Psychology

Ronald Baenninger
Temple University

When *The Principles of Psychology* was published academic psychologists considered subjective experience as data for scientific examination. William James's readers encountered thoughtful analyses of mental life—his own and that of others. For James, the irreducible data of psychology included the psychologist, "the thought studied," the "thought's object," and the "psychologist's reality" (I: 184). A century later experimental psychology has weathered a period when such matters were officially relegated to "armchair" psychology, when human subjective experience was removed from the respectable concerns of scientific psychology by the precepts of Wittgenstein (1921/1961), Bridgman (1936), and Watson (1913).

As sciences mature they become increasingly arcane to lay persons. When scientific problems are explained and enigmatic phenomena become better understood by scientists, their vocabulary inevitably becomes more specialized and inaccessible to outsiders. The conceptual frameworks and the problems studied become different from what lay people expect specialists in the science to be studying. Physicists no longer study falling bodies, electricity and magnetism, or heat transfer because Newton, Faraday, Rumford, and Joule were so successful in explaining such everyday phenomena. The problems that initially defined the field have been satisfactorily dealt with and are studied by freshmen; current research has to do with questions that only knowledgeable specialists would think of asking. The science becomes defined by questions that are quite different from those that originally defined it. There is a kind of scientific "recency effect," and only those who teach the introductory course can recall the early concerns of their field.

Psychology has been a bit different. We have never really answered the basic questions, those that most lay people think we are studying. The mind, mental life, and conscious experience are what students of introduc-

249

tory psychology expect to learn about. As a rule they do not, but are treated instead to the arcane matters that we have gone on to study. Fascinating as so much contemporary psychology is, there is a way in which it appears as a diversion from what William James pointed out as the territory for us to explore. Perhaps as a result of not answering those basic questions about the mind and conscious experience we have a kind of "primacy effect" in which we cannot forget them. Or perhaps it is more correctly termed a "Zeigarnik effect"—uncompleted tasks are not forgotten until they are completed.

Another consequence of never answering our original questions may be that scientific psychology is largely ignored by intellectuals and scholars outside our field. Jacques Barzun pointed out, in *A Stroll with William James* (1983), the extent to which James has been revered by intellectuals as diverse as Bertrand Russell, Oliver Wendell Holmes, Alfred North Whitehead, and Gertrude Stein. William James and Sigmund Freud were the only psychologists selected by Robert M. Hutchins for his series of Great Books of the Western World.

During much of academic psychology's history few psychologists studied subjective phenomena, not because we had dealt satisfactorily with them, but because we had not. The introspective analysis of subjective phenomena fell into disrepute early in the 20th century for scientifically valid reasons (Lyons, 1986). The data of such investigations are neither public nor reliable, and thus they violate the requirements of objective, nomothetic science. Ten years after publication of the *Principles of Psychology*, Jacques Loeb could write that "what the metaphysician calls consciousness are phenomena determined by the mechanisms of associative memory" (Loeb, 1900, p. 214). By the middle of the 20th century scientific psychology (based on observable data like operant responses, reaction times, histological sections, and microelectrode recordings) clearly occupied the high ground in our field.

Gentner and Grudin (1985) examined the kinds of metaphors used by eminent psychologists to describe mental processes. During the middle decades of the 20th century psychology was, above all, objective. Between 1894 and 1975 there was a clear shift away from early use of animate or spatial metaphors toward the neural and systems metaphors characteristic of biology, mathematics, and physical science. From 1935–1955 few metaphors of any kind were used. In William James's 1905 APA presidential address he used 29 distinct metaphors for mental processes, a total not surpassed until 1975, when the resurgence of cognitive psychology was well underway (Gentner & Grudin, 1985).

JAMES AND METHOD

Although he had doubts about its trustworthiness, the primary method of psychology for William James was introspective observation (I: 185). He grudgingly accepted the utility of the experimental method, and was unenthusiastic about the achievements of Wundt, Fechner, and their colleagues, asserting that their method

> could hardly have arisen in a country whose natives could be bored . . . The simple and open method of attack having done what it can, the method of patience, starving out, and harassing to death is tried: the mind must submit to a regular siege, in which minute advantages gained night and day by the forces that hem her in must sum themselves up at last into her overthrow. There is little of the grand style about these new prism, pendulum and chronograph-philosophers. They mean business, not chivalry. What generous divination, and that superiority in virtue which was thought by Cicero to give a man the best insight into nature, have failed to do, their spying and scraping, their deadly tenacity and almost diabolic cunning, will doubtless some day bring about. (I: 192)

But in addition to introspection and the experimental method William James relied on what he called the "comparative method," although he meant something a bit different from modern comparative psychology. "So it has come to pass that instincts of animals are ransacked to throw light on our own, and that the reasoning faculties of bees and ants, the minds of savages, infants, madmen, idiots, the deaf and blind, criminals, and eccentrics, are all invoked in support of this or that special theory about some part of our own mental life" (I: 194).

Laboratory animals may be as useful as humans for research in psychology, since their inability to describe their experience directly is irrelevant in much behavioral research. Descriptions by human subjects may be equally irrelevant if the goal is complete objectivity. Especially in his chapter on "Instinct" in *Principles of Psychology* James relied on observations and anecdotes about other animal species, and assembled a fascinating list of universal human tendencies that are: (a) not the result of habit and (b) occur only in certain situations. The modern reader will find these similar to contemporary definitions of instinctive behavior. Although his emphasis was on interactions among and between instincts and habits, James was reluctant to explain behavior on the basis of instincts, a trap that led many later psychologists and ethologists into problems of circularity.

There is a modern sound to much of James's discussion of instinct. For example, his description of the "opposite instincts" of attachment and fear (II: 396, based on Spalding's 1873 paper) is remarkably similar to Eckhart Hess's (1962) analysis of imprinting and the termination of critical periods. In fact, James's "Law of Transitoriness" is quite similar to that old ethological concept—"Many instincts ripen at a certain age and then fade away" (II: 398).

Although James was primarily concerned with human psychology, the breadth of his reading on the natural history of other species led him to some surprising conclusions. He asserted that humans have many more instincts than any other animal species so that they are not even especially useful in understanding ourselves (II: 393). In any event, James used animal observations tactically rather than strategically. His view of comparisons between humans and other creatures seems to have been closer to Aristotle's than to the scientific psychologists of the 20th century. Aristotle took as an obvious truth that we know humans better than other species of animals, and should therefore base our understanding of animals on our knowledge of our own species, a strategy that justifies anthropomorphism.

Later psychologists have often been guilty of zoomorphism, the uncritical application to humans of facts that we know about other animals. Half a century after James, many laboratory psychologists argued that understanding the behavior of rats, pigeons, dogs, or monkeys was a prerequisite for understanding our own behavior. Spence (1956), for example, argued that we must study the simpler behavior of simpler creatures before we can hope to understand the complexities of ourselves. James and Spence at least had in common an unwillingness to attribute any mental life to members of other species. For James this discredited them as models for the psychological research that he had in mind, whereas for Spence it made them perfectly satisfactory, if not superior.

PSYCHOLOGY AND ANIMALS

Despite his use of animal examples to illuminate our own instincts, it is clear that William James did not believe there was any necessary relationship between other species and our own. James used the subjunctive case in referring to Charles Darwin's theory of evolution by natural selection, a theory that emphasized essential continuity between the behavior or mental life of different species. This was not an idea that James publicly espoused. The doctrine of Special Creation was probably much closer to his views, as it was to most of those raised in the "Genteel Tradition" during the Victorian era.

For some contemporary psychologists, other species of animals are inherently fascinating. Discovering things about their behavior, their varieties of social organization, ecological relationships, and evolutionary antecedents is a worthy scientific goal even if nothing at all is learned about humans during the process. The majority of psychologists do not espouse this "pure science" view and are interested in animals to the extent that they help in understanding humans. I can think of four basic reasons why animals are professionally interesting to such people:

Homology.   In some limited situations, the behavior of humans and other species may be homologous, that is, we and they both show a particular behavior because we descended from a common ancestor who also showed the same behavioral trait. Atz (1970) has argued that examples of behavioral homologies are rare because we have few animal relatives with whom we share common ancestors. Humans and laboratory rats cannot have homologous behaviors because we do not share any unique common ancestors from which we both descended; ancestral rats were rodents, and ancestral humans were hominid primates. Since all mammals trace their lineages back to primitive reptiles, any behavioral similarities between us and rats would have to be found also in the orders of rodents, primates, carnivores, lagomorphs, cetaceans, chiropterans, insectivores, ruminants, and so on in order to qualify as homologous. As a result, it would be unlikely to find homologous behaviors in any order other than the primates. Possible examples include such expressive gestures as smiling (von Hooff, 1972), yawning (Baenninger, 1987; Redican, 1982), or tongue showing (Smith, Chase & Lieblick, 1975).

Convergence and Analogy.   Species that are unrelated may have a trait in common because it is an effective solution to a problem that the several species have in common, not because they derived it from a common ancestor. For example, several species have evolved predator defenses in the form of quills, and hedgehogs (insectivores), porcupines (rodents), and echidnas (monotremes) all share this form of defense against predators although the three species belong to different orders, and are unrelated except for their common membership in the class Mammalia. People and rats use their forepaws to manipulate food into their mouths, not because of common ancestry but because it is a useful solution to a common problem. When another species has a behavioral trait that is similar to ours only in a functional sense, then the trait is referred to as analogous. For example, baboons establish and maintain their social relationships with other individuals by picking insects and other matter out of each other's fur, an activity known as grooming. People at social gatherings have verbal interactions about the weather, current events, or other innocuous topics. The behavior looks very different, but its function is (apparently) similar to the grooming among baboons: It establishes or maintains relationships. In science or medicine, traits that are homologous, convergent, or analogous can provide a sound logical basis for the modeling of humans by studying the similar traits in other animals.

Generality.   Principles of psychology may seem more firmly grounded and legitimate if they can be found in a variety of different species. For example, the effects of positive reinforcement have been found to be similar in many vertebrate species, and this very ubiquity provides reason to predict such effects in still other species. Such effects may even be universal, but the logic supporting this contention is not compelling, and is similar to that found in many legal arguments. Lawyers seek to establish that a previous decision is relevant and establishes a precedent; if a particular decision has repeatedly been made in the past, then it is considered correct and applicable in the future. But the mere repetition of a legal decision does not make it correct from a scientific, moral, or legal standpoint. A great many legal decisions were made during the era of slavery, for example, and precedents were established in which people were treated as the property of American slave owners. These precedents did not establish the universal validity of the principles underlying slavery. Similarly, the mere repetition of instances in which a psychological principle appears valid does not establish it as a universal law, applicable in all species.

We humans have conflicting reactions to the discovery that other species are similar to us. If we are proud of a human trait, like our linguistic ability, then there are many who object vigorously if that trait is demonstrated in "lower" animals (Premack, 1986). On the other hand there is often relief when a human trait that we decry, such as aggression, is reported to be universal in other species (Lorenz, 1966). The mere observation of a superficial similarity among species means little scientifically. It may be entertaining, as demonstrated by the popular success of writers like Lorenz, Robert Ardrey, and Desmond Morris who often emphasized the similarities between humans and other species while ignoring the differences. In *The Territorial Imperative* (1966, pp. 165-173) Ardrey described the territorial aggressiveness of male bowerbirds, callicebus monkeys, and Italians as if their superficial similarities had an evolutionary basis. This may provide wry amusement, but the differences among species cannot be ignored by respectable scientists. My reading of William James suggests that he was not above this sort of thing. His descriptions of instincts in other species (II: 24) are anthropomorphic, and presumably were intended to establish the generality of such "instincts" as play, cleanliness, and parenting. They are also touching, and induce warm feelings of kinship with other species of animals. James's descriptions do not match those of his popular contemporaries such as Seton-Thompson (1901) for sentimental anthropomorphism.

People often seem reassured when they discover that some other species may be as bad as we are. For example, in my early studies of predatory aggression I found that laboratory rats frequently killed mice without eating them, and carnivorous species may also engage in this "surplus killing" (Baenninger, 1978; Kruuk, 1972). To those who believe that only humans kill in the absence of dire necessity, these facts may be reassuring. Being unique can feel lonely, especially if we are uniquely wicked.

Pedagogy.   Teaching often makes use of animal examples as a way of communicating. The fables of Aesop, the Bible, medieval bestiaries, and modern children's books all include animal stories that instruct while entertaining and providing moral injunctions. Even introductory psychology texts usually rely on Pavlov's salivating dogs to communicate the basic concepts of classical conditioning.

Which of these four justifications for talking about animals did William James implicitly believe? Like many modern psychologists, James did not specify his precise reasons for talking about animals. My guess is that generality and pedagogy were paramount, because scientifically valid reasons based on homology, convergence, or analogy would have required a greater acceptance of Darwin's ideas than James expressed. For example, in discussing the human instinct for sociability he quoted Galton's description of the apparent delight with which South African cattle returned to the company of their kind after an enforced absence (II: 431). In arguing that we have an instinct for construction James suggested, "As for habitation, there can be no doubt that the instinct to seek a sheltered nook, open only on one side, into which he may retire and be safe, is in man quite as specific as the instinct of birds to build a nest" (II: 426). Surely James was not suggesting that the human tendencies to seek companionship or build shelters were homologous with functionally similar behaviors in cattle or birds. Cattle and birds are not ancestral humans, even for ardent Darwinians.

Most of our behavioral similarities with other species result from converging or analogous evolution and form the basis for much animal research. Modern scientific psychologists, for example, study avoidance learning in laboratory rats because the phenomena they discover may provide new insights into human learning; they examine learning processes in rats as a way of modeling humans, just as swine provide models for human pulmonary phenomena, or armadillos provide models for leprosy. James does not seem to have been using animals as models of humans. As far as I can tell he never explicitly stated that a particular behavior or mental event is likely to occur in people because it is found in some other species. William James was a fine teacher, and was much in demand as a speaker. I suspect his references to animals were simply a way of communicating with audiences both outside and inside academia. I find no evidence that he believed in the essential continuity of behavior or mind among species.

Why did Hull, Spence, Watson, and other objective behaviorists study animals? Their ideas of ecology, evolution, and our relationships to other species seem no more advanced than those of William James. Hull (1945) asserted, for example, that species differences could be accounted for by changing some values of constants and exponents in his behavioral "laws." For him, behavior was behavior regardless of which species showed it, and animal models provided the means for discovering general laws of behavior and learning. Since such behaviorists were not interested in consciousness or experience, there was no reason to ignore animal models because laboratory rats obviously learned and behaved. For James there was good reason to be reluctant in ascribing consciousness or mental experience to other species. Animals make poor models if their validity as models can be tested only indirectly. If we have no way of knowing whether their experience is like ours, then it is pointless to draw parallels in the realm of experience.

A similarity of behavioral outcomes does not prove that the processes underlying those outcomes were similar. Bitterman (1960) found that performance on certain reinforcement schedules was virtually identical in rats, goldfish, monkeys, and college students. Presumably there were differences in the complexity of mental experiences that mediated such remarkably similar behavioral outcomes, but we have not yet discovered what they are.

During the period when Hull and Spence were household names among American psychologists, we were self-consciously scientific (in the sense that only public, objective data were permissible). Phenomena like mental processes and experience were almost pejorative terms and were not considered appropriate for scientific examination. Hypotheses that sounded mentalistic were suspect, as Krechevsky discovered during his acrimonious printed controversy with Spence about whether laboratory rats formed "hypotheses" during discrimination learning (Krechevsky, 1933; Spence, 1936). Tolman's soundness was questioned because of his insistence that rat behavior was purposive and guided by expectations. Morgan's Canon was strictly adhered to by psychologists, and the attribution of human feelings (Anthropomorphism), thoughts (mentalism), or purposes (teleology) to other species—or even to other people—were generally eschewed with little attempt to establish the existence (or non-existence) of such concepts in laboratory animals. The simplest mechanistic explanations came to be preferred in trying to understand behavior.

MORGAN'S CANON

One of Charles Darwin's basic premises was that a quantitative, but not a qualitative, gap existed between the minds or abilities of humans and other species of animals. Logically, there are two alternatives in demonstrating continuity among animal species: (a) one can reduce humans to the level of other species, or (b) one can raise other species to our level. Much of the modern debate about the relevance of sociobiology and evolution to human behavior results from choosing the first alternative. Objections to the second alternative have contributed to the controversy over animal language capabilities (Premack, 1986). Many of us are guilty of fond, well-meaning attempts to document the sophisticated mental ability of our pets, but scientists are supposed to know better. Some of Darwin's early supporters, such as Romanes, attributed complex motives, insights, and feelings to other mammals—and even to fish, birds, reptiles, amphibians, and invertebrates.

These attributions got out of hand. Among the examples of fanciful anthropomorphism was the suggestion that the increased buzzing and social disintegration of a beehive after removal of the queen was due to mourning by the bereaved bees. In response to such unrestrained theorizing in the absence of supporting data, C. Lloyd Morgan suggested that "In no case may we interpret an action as the outcome of the exercise of a higher psychical faculty, if it can be interpreted as the outcome of the exercise of one which stands lower in the psychological scale" (Morgan, 1894, p. 53). This admonition became known as Lloyd Morgan's Canon of Parsimony, and is now a basic attitude of ethologists, comparative psychologists, and animal behaviorists.

Morgan's Canon is a special case of Ockham's razor, which urges us to seek the simplest solutions, arguments, or explanations; in science this generally means that only objectively falsifiable causal methanisms are employed as explanations. Instead of positing a mourning buzz, most animal behaviorists would now explain the behavior of bereaved beehives in terms of a process called trophallaxis, or mutual feeding of certain chemicals that regulate aspects of behavior. Without the queen and her regulating chemicals there is disruption of normal interactions in the hive, with buzzing as a side effect. The bees may feel morose and troubled but we cannot falsify such an anthropomorphic hypothesis. The mechanistic explanation is complex in its details but is surely "lower on the psychological scale" than the more poetic hypothesis. There is no doubt that Morgan's Canon cleared away much scientifically unproductive anthropomorphizing.

But Morgan's Canon may have had unintended inhibitory effects on the willingness of scientists to entertain complex hypotheses. Simple mechanistic explanations may be preferred just because they are simple, and not because they are superior to complex ones. We may reject on faith (without any evidence) the possibility that complex mental phenomena can occur at all in other animals. Explanations of animal behavior that attribute complex psychological processes to them may be rejected out of hand, just because they are complex, hard to imagine, and difficult to test. This may occur even when simple explanations turn out to be inadequate.

Many experimental psychologists, for example, are uncomfortable with the concept of expectancy. The idea that an animal might, on the basis of its past experience, expect to find a particular stimulus in a particular place may be regarded as mentalistic, fuzz-minded and unnecessarily complex. But a fuller understanding of behavior may result if we accept the possibility that a mental event, an expectancy, underlies the animal's movement to a particular place. For example, positive or negative reinforcement may be adequate to explain a dog's movement to a place where food or safety have previously occurred. But what of the responses that were not even present during acquisition trials? Why does the dog perk up its ears, whimper, turn its head and eyes toward the learned location, and prepare to spring toward it? These responses appear only on subsequent trials, and persist into extinction trials. One might account for their appearance by positing a number of stimulus-response chains of acquisition for each, in the manner of the goal response chains hypothesized by Spence, but surely it is simpler and less cumbersome to posit the existence of a single mediating mental event called an expectancy. It is entirely possible that an expectancy explanation would satisfy Ockham's Razor (which calls for the simplest solution), while violating Morgan's Canon (which calls from the lowest level of psychological functioning). This paradoxical possibility has not been considered by psychologists very often.

Tinklepaugh (1928) placed banana pieces under inverted cups in a delayed response experiment on memory in monkeys. When bananas were secretly replaced by lettuce (not a preferred item for monkeys) the monkey

> . . . rushes to the proper container and picks it up. She extends her hand to seize the food, but her hand drops to the floor without touching it. She looks at the lettuce but (unless very hungry) does not touch it. She looks around the cup . . . stands up and looks under and around her. She picks up the cup and examines it thoroughly inside and out. She has on occasion turned toward the observers present in the room and shrieked at them in apparent anger. (p. 210)

To deny that a mediating mental state underlies the appearance of such behavior complicates our explanation of it. New responses appeared when bananas were replaced with lettuce, responses that were not present during acquisition trials. What are they responses to?

To non-psychologists it must appear that we handicap ourselves in quixotic ways. Our attempts to understand human or animal behavior by ignoring mediating effects of conscious experience seem like seeking the Holy Grail with bags over our heads. There are costs to such scientific handicaps, as exemplified by two major difficulties encountered in the study of aggression.

Intent and Aggression

All those who have studied aggressive behavior have had difficulty defining it (Zillmann, 1979). Definitions that are scientifically respectable, that avoid mentalism, anthropomorphism, and teleology must leave out intention, a concept that implies some kind of conscious or unconscious mental experience. Aggression is objectively defined as "the attempt to deliver noxious stimuli, regardless of whether it is successful" (Buss, 1971, p. 10). But an aggressor's experienced anger, hostility, and intentions may be crucial for distinguishing between aggression and phenomena like play, predation, accidental injury, or surgery in which noxious stimuli are delivered without aggressive intent. Conversely, aggressive threats and threat displays imply an intent to deliver noxious stimuli, even when there is no attempt to do so.

Catharsis and Aggression

The ancient Greeks believed that one consequence of powerful emotional experiences was catharsis, defined as "the state of feeling produced by dramatic tragedy." It meant "the stillness at the center of one's being which came after pity or fear had been burned out. The soul is purified and calmed, freed from the violent passions" (Schaar, 1961, p. 320). The argument over whether real or vicarious aggressive acts lead to catharsis has persisted for millennia, and is still present in recent debates about the effects of observing violence on television or in sports events. Physiologically (Hokanson, 1970) or psychologically (Feshbach, 1984) there is reason to believe that behaving aggressively, even at second hand, decreases subsequent aggression. But there is also considerable evidence that the reverse is true, and that aggression may escalate in self-reinforcing, positive feedback loops (Baenninger, 1974). Presumably, either consequence may occur but we are hampered in specifying the circumstances by our ignorance of the experiences consequent to aggressive acts. If behaving aggressively is followed by pleasurable experiences organisms will likely repeat aggressive responses; if they are followed by peaceful, cathartic states then subsequent aggressive responses may be reduced instead.

A RETURN TO MIND IN ANIMALS

Difficulties such as the roles of intent and catharsis in aggression would no doubt have appeared perverse to William James, as they surely must to non-scientists now. Early psychologists described psychology as the study of behavior and mind in humans and other animals (Yerkes, 1913). Despite epistemological difficulties we may be returning to this viewpoint. Current introductory psychology texts frequently define psychology as the study of behavior *and* mental functioning (Henley, Johnson, Herzog, & Jones, 1989).

In recent years there has been a resurgence of interest in animal minds (Burghardt, 1985; Candland & Kyes, 1986; Gallup, 1985; Griffin, 1985; Walker, 1983). Donald Griffin, a widely-respected biologist best known for his discovery of bat echolocation, has argued that scientific blinders have prevented us from discussing consciousness in animals. Latto (1986) distinguished between two distinct aspects of animal consciousness: (a) the ability to mentally represent stimuli and events and (b) awareness of ongoing mental processes, whether perceptual, emotional or cognitive. By avoiding the second aspect we may have limited our understanding of animals and complicated our explanations of their behavior. When we treat animals as mechanical robots without awareness we alienate ourselves from them. We also violate a belief held by most scientists and lay people. As Mason

(1976, p. 930) asserted, "That animals are aware can scarcely be questioned."

The question is really what we can do about animal consciousness scientifically. We avoid attributing conscious awareness to other species because we fear opening a Pandora's box from which all sorts of mentalistic bogeymen will emerge. When Pandora's curiosity got the better of her she opened the box and all the world's ills escaped from it. But we should remember that the only thing that Pandora was able to keep inside the box was Hope. The hope that currently unverified concepts (like animal awareness) will eventually increase our understanding is one aspect of scientific progress. Genes, protons, black holes, and "animal electricity" resisted objective verification for a long time, and are still not experienced directly, and certainly not without elaborate equipment and procedures. We are still awaiting our Leewenhoek to give us a microscope of the mind.

Griffin (1984) suggested that consciousness in animals is likely to be present in situations where they are showing versatile problem solving or learning, where there is evidence of their anticipation or intentions, and when they are communicating with each other (or with us). Cooperative dam building by beavers, web building by spiders, or migration of small passerine birds over vast distances are magnificent achievements that fill us with wonder. But the ability to construct things, solve problems, or even reason logically does not necessarily imply that conscious awareness of those processes is occurring. Computer programs have been written to do all those things successfully, and presumably neither the software nor the hardware are consciously aware of doing them.

The study of animal cognition is a thriving area of research currently (e.g., Hulse, Fowler, & Konig, 1978; Roitblat, 1987); it has been apparent to naturalists and animal owners for centuries that other species of animals could do clever and even creative things. Separating edible grain from sand by dropping the mixture in water would not necessarily occur to me, but it did occur to a lowly female member of a Japanese macaque troop on Koshima Island, and other troop members were smart enough to recognize and adopt a good idea (Kawai, 1965). But we do not know whether the monkey had an "Aha" experience.

William James believed that the evolution of consciousness was a central problem for psychology, but the modern comparative work of cognitive scientists is based on objective observation of behavior and tells us little or nothing about mental experience or awareness that may accompany cognitive feats such as perception of rhythm, problem solving, or sentence construction. The work on communicative abilities of apes by the Gardners (1985), Savage-Rumbaugh (1986), and Premack (1986) has suggested to some the possibility of communicating with other species so that they can tell us of their mental experience in the same way that other humans can give us introspective reports. Would introspective data from apes be comprehensible to us if the ape could describe its own mental processes? Would we have "windows on other minds," as Mason put it? Or might it be that conscious awareness and mental experience are species specific?

Conscious experiences must always precede their description. Thus, by its very nature, a psychology of human mental experience can discover nothing that is new to all human beings. Someone must have an experience before they can introspect or describe it to a psychologist: the description may be novel for humanity but the experience is not novel because the experiencing individual(s) already had it. For example, a common experience involves seeing little, moving, "nonsense" shapes while gazing at the empty sky. The "things" are apparently small hyaline cells that slough off and float across the path of light between the lens and retina; they are referred to as "floaters." There is usually a kind of embarrassed relief when they are described because most people have never told anyone else about their repeated experience of floaters. The description is new, whereas the experience is not. Toward the end of Mahler's "Lied von der Erde" there is a soprano note that always produces a pleasant tingling, prickling sensation on the back of my neck. Other people may recognize that they have the same feeling when I describe mine to them but nothing new has been discovered by either of us, except that others have the same experience.

When coelacanths or quarks or Saturn's rings were discovered we all become aware of genuinely novel phenomena. Before their discovery these concepts were not a part of anyone's conscious experience, even though they existed already. Special measuring devices had to be invented, and hypotheses that suggested what to look for had to be formulated to permit these discoveries. Can we devise a mental telescope or microscope for the minds of other species when we do not know what we are seeking? The conscious experiences of our fellow primates would be genuinely new discoveries, in the sense that no human being had ever experienced them before, but there is no compelling reason to believe they would correspond to our own. The ethologist Jakob von Uexkull (1934) proposed that our knowledge of other creatures depended on understanding their Umwelt (i.e., the world surrounding them as they perceived it). But how can we know how other creatures perceive the world? We know that houseflies have compound eyes, but does it necessarily follow that their visual perception is of an array of facets, each viewing a scene slightly differently? Primates with two eyes have two overlapping views of objects so that perception of three dimensions is possible by stereopsis. Perhaps flies perceive some sort of hyperspace because of their multifaceted receptors. These are fascinating questions at a neglected frontier of science. But we cannot answer them if we continue to despair of examining the consciousness of other species.

Rychlak (1986) identified three meanings of consciousness, associating each one with the types of causes proposed by Aristotle (i.e., material cause, efficient cause, formal cause, and final cause):

1. The "Living wakefulness" meaning, in which consciousness emerges as the assembled outcome of physical matter, that is, neurons and their synaptic pathways. Sperry (1969, 1970) used this meaning in arguing that consciousness is an emergent property of the human brain, a property that must be grasped to permit a thorough causal understanding of how the brain works. In this sense, members of all large-brained mammals would likely be conscious. Rychlak argued, however, that this material cause of consciousness was too limited because the "logic of consciousness" cannot emerge from lower level neuronal substrates, and is not patterned on a one:one correspondence of neuron assemblages. Humans (or computers) can formulate problems in alternative ways with the same "wiring." Probably most neurobiologists, ethologists, and comparative psychologists would grant the possibility that other animals may be conscious in this material, reductionist sense.

2. Rychlak's second meaning of consciousness builds on the first but also includes awareness of experience. Like Hebb, he suggested that consciousness includes both brain processes and "a cognition or awareness of the object perceived" (Hebb, 1968, p. 468), an idea similar to Aristotle's efficient cause. Awareness of their experience by animals is a topic that has intrigued ethologists and comparative psychologists (Burghardt, 1985). But Rychlak argued that such awareness implies the capacity to appreciate that something else "could be relevant, applicable, or actually taking place . . . other than what is actually occurring" (p. 259). To be aware of what *is* we must know what else *might be*. This raises a fascinating question that has become important to those studying animal behavior and sociobiology, namely to what extent other species communicate deceptive messages. The capacity to lie may be evidence of consciousness awareness, according to this criterion.

Many species of invertebrates and vertebrates provide deceptive signals that may be structural or behavioral, but they are generally not communicated *voluntarily*. Camouflage; Batesian or Mullerian mimicry; injury-feigning displays that distract predators from nests; threat displays that intimidate opponents or that falsely signal an intent to attack—these all are deceptive in their effect, but not necessarily in their intent. To the extent that these deceptions involve instinctive acts they fail to satisfy Rychlak's criterion because the deceiver cannot do otherwise. We cannot conclude that the animal is aware if it is unable to *not* perform the display. On a species level we can speak of deception, but the individual is not choosing to deceive by performing the display. Commission or omission of an act must both be available possibilities for an individual if we are to draw conclusions about its conscious awareness.

3. Rychlak's third meaning of consciousness involves the continuity or organization of experience toward some end, an idea similar to Aristotle's final cause. For an animal to organize experience in this teleological sense implies an awareness of the self, the end toward which experience is organized. An implication of consciousness in this sense is that a conscious organism actively operates on its environment in a coherent way so that its needs can ultimately be met. When psychologists have studied the behavior of animals the usual approach has been to look at one aspect of behavior at a time. Perhaps as a result we have seldom paid attention to the coherence, continuity or internal consistency of behavior.

The physical sciences have advanced beyond the study of material and efficient causes, with their mechanical pushes and pulls of the Newtonian era, and now emphasize the importance of formal or final causes that embody context, pattern, order, and organization. One form that this shift has taken in psychology is a renewal of interest in the "self" as an organizing principle, or set of interactive constraints (Gallup & Suarez, 1986). The term need not imply an homunculus, and perfectly respectable journals of the American Psychological Association now publish papers with the term in their titles. In a survey of the twelve 1986 issues of *The Journal of Personality and Social Psychology* I found that 46 out of 281 articles had "self" in the title, usually in hyphenated form. In the twelve issues of the *Journal of Experimental Psychology* the term appeared in a title only once in 143 articles, but introspection by the experimental subjects was reported in either the Results or Discussion of thirteen articles.

Another form that the shift to formal explanations of behavior has taken can be seen in the work of psychologists and behavioral ecologists such as Caraco, Shettleworth, Kamil, and Collier who have used a variety of optimality models in studying the foraging of squirrels or nectar-feeding birds in natural patches (Kamil, 1978; Newman & Caraco, 1987) or pigeons in the laboratory (Shettleworth, Krebs, Stephens, & Gibbons, 1988). The fact that these animals behave in complex and varying environments *as if* they had systematic strategies that maximize the satisfaction of their needs while minimizing their losses and energy expenditure does not prove that they do have such strategies. But economists have been attributing intelligent strategies to humans for generations without direct proof that individuals maximize, optimize, or "satisfice." The fact is that "economic man" often behaves as if he engages in certain rational strategies for investment, allocation of resources, and so forth. The finding that laboratory rats' meal size and frequency is predictably governed by ambient temperature, distance to food sources, its protein content, the work requirements, and handling costs of food *in the absence of deficiencies* is surely evidence that these animals are actively operating on their environmental circumstances, rather than passively responding to them (Collier, 1982, 1986).

Wittgenstein asserted, "Whereof one cannot speak thereof one must be silent." (Wittgenstein, 1921/1961, p. 151). This dour dictum is now flouted in both human and nonhuman psychology largely because the things of which we cannot yet speak (objectively) are thought to be important for our explanation and understanding. Baars (1986) interviewed 17 eminent psychologists including behaviorists, cognitive psychologists, and cognitive psychologists who used to be behaviorists. No behaviorists who used to be cognitive psychologists could be found. The Zeitgeist no longer relegates problems of the mind and consciousness to philosophers, and many would agree with Robert M. Yerkes (1913): ". . . if we throw overboard, as Prof. Watson does, the method of self-observation, together with everything that has been claimed to be distinctive of the psychologist's point of view and purpose, we should consider the science merely a fragment of physiology. . ." (p. 581). In comparative psychology we cannot use self-observation (except as a way of generating hypotheses about animals), because other species may differ from us in qualitative ways, and their sense of self may be quite different from ours.

AN EPISTEMOLOGICAL CODA

Logically, there are four possible ways in which conscious minds and neural structures interact in behavior:

1. *Dualism*. Mind and body can be independent and autonomous, although normally there is interaction and mutual influence of the mental and the material entities. Obviously the hormones, neurotransmitters and neuromodulators of our bodies, influence our conscious experience in some ways. But the ways in which our conscious experiences influence such bodily events are more difficult to probe. The dualist position asserts a correlation between mental and bodily events, and thereby implies that causality may go in either direction.

2. *Mentalism*. The position that only mental events are real limits us to talking exclusively about mind and conscious experience. This view liberates psychology from physiological, reductionist explanations because mental events are interpreted as uniquely psychological. Mental events are also, in a sense, uniquely accessible to us as individuals. Unfortunately for objective science the mental events of other people are not readily accessible, so that hypotheses about mental activity of others are difficult to falsify.

3. *Materialism*. If only bodily events are real then mental events such as consciousness are nothing more than the bell on the clock, not the mainspring of action, as T. H. Huxley put it. Jackendoff (1987) unhappily arrived at Huxley's conclusion after admitting that he found it every bit as incoherent to speak of conscious experience as a flow of information as to

speak of it as a collection of neural firings, and that it is completely unclear how computations, no matter how complex or abstract, can add up to experience. Is conscious experience an epiphenomenon, a bit of decoration on the machinery of life? It is easier to be a materialist with regard to nonhuman species. We have never had their experiences, so we have no conception of what we are leaving out.

4. *The Double-Aspect View.* From this perspective, mental and bodily events are two aspects of the same reality, for example, our experience of the color green is simply the internal aspect of an external stimulus with a wavelength of 550 nm. The pictures we experience on a TV screen are not identical to the electrical signals that are broadcast, but result from the TV set's way of expressing those signals. If the causal direction is implicitly from the material to the mental, and never the reverse, this view can degenerate to the kind of "nothing but" reductionism that asserts (like Ebenezer Scrooge in Dickens' *Christmas Carol*) that a dream is nothing but an underdone potato or a piece of cheese.

How can we study conscious awareness and experience, particularly in creatures incapable of introspection, however fallible that method may be? Latto (1986) suggested several possibilities, including examination of patterns of overt behavior that seem to imply the active operation of an organism on its environment. He also held out some hope for physiological methods that involve recording of evoked potentials such as the N100 and P300. The latter is believed to occur only when subjects report awareness of the presence or absence of stimuli, but these methods must ultimately rely on correlations of introspective reports with brain recordings.

Traditional objective science has proceeded on the assumption that the goal of science is to cut through or clear away the chaos or flux of matter or events. By this means, science is supposed to arrive at the underlying stable propositions, laws, or explanations governing matter, events, or other phenomena. *Epistemological realism* refers to the position that the laws or propositions discovered by science exist independently of the cognitive or perceptual activity of scientists. To the realist, the scientific process is reminiscent of the sculptor who claims that there is a horse hidden inside his block of marble, and that his task as a sculptor is to chip away until he finds it. In its extreme form, realism is absurd, since fact and theory are always intertwined. As Charles Darwin put it: "How odd it is that anyone should not see that all observation must be for or against some view if it is to be of any service!"

Epistemological rationalism is an alternative to realism. This view of how scientists move from common sense to scientific knowledge begins by accepting the primacy of human activity in achieving order, organization, and knowledge. In particular, the human activity of constructing interpretations is seen by the rationalist as central to science, just as constructing and interpreting is central to creating a sculpture from a block of marble. In the rationalist view, interpreting by scientists is what generates both order and organization, and the interpretations constitute explanations (Overton, 1984). Evidence that William James was a rationalist in this sense derives from his inclusion of the psychologist and the "psychologist's reality" as basic data of psychology (James, I: 184).

To an epistemological realist interpretations are like scaffolding, temporary structures for the sculptor to stand on which are discarded as the scientific sculpture emerges from the block of stone. For the realist, the final form of scientific truth includes no interpretation at all, just hard "descriptive" facts, whereas the rationalist includes interpretation as an integral aspect of scientific knowledge. An example from physics may help to clarify the distinction.

Light was initially interpreted as energy waves by Huygens, Newton, and other 17th-century scientists. We use this interpretation when we teach psychology students about the visual stimulus. But by the 20th century it had become clear that light could also be interpreted in quite different terms. What is the truth, the "real" nature of light?

Einstein postulated in 1902 that the energy in a beam of light, instead of being spread out over a wave surface, as in the classical theory proposed by Huygens in 1670, was concentrated in packets that are now called light quanta or photons. Both interpretations are "true" in the sense that when light is propagated it behaves as if it were an electromagnetic wave, whereas in the interaction of light with matter it behaves as if it were an assemblage of photons. De Broglie suggested that this dual nature of light might also be true of matter; for example, electrons and protons might behave like waves as well as having a corpuscular quality.

Psychologists have frequently taken physics as the model for their science. We have done this without always recognizing that physics has moved from its earlier epistemological realism to a more rationalist paradigm, from an emphasis on material causes to an emphasis on formal (or final) causation. In rationalist explanation, order and organization are not found in direct observations (or in descriptions of them) but in the construction of principles of order and organization. Quantum mechanics, or entropy, or natural selection are principles of organization, but are not directly observable; nor are kinship structures, reinforcement, mental structures, the id and ego, language structures, mental operations, or the instincts that James discussed in *Principles of Psychology*.

It may be time to include consciousness (whether human or nonhuman) in this list of interpretive constructs. We will never observe consciousness directly, but it may aid us in perceiving organization and explaining the behavior of animals. Whether we define it in terms of awareness or a sense of self, our problem will be one of characterizing the precise roles of consciousness in explaining directly observable behavior. And it is nothing less than "speciesism" (Singer, 1975) to exclude consciousness from our explanations of animal behavior, if we are willing to use the concept in explaining human behavior.

REFERENCES

Ardrey, R. (1966). *The territorial imperative*. New York: Atheneum.

Atz, J. W. (1970). The application of the idea of homology to behavior. In L. R. Aronson, E. Tobach, D. S. Lehrman, & J. S. Rosenblatt (Eds.), *Development and evolution of behavior* (pp. 53–74). San Francisco: W. H. Freeman.

Baars, B. J. (1986). *The cognitive revolution in psychology*. New York: Guilford.

Baenninger, R. (1974). Some consequences of aggressive behavior: A selective review of the literature on other animals. *Aggressive Behavior, 1*, 17–37.

Baenninger, R. (1978). Some aspects of predatory behavior. *Aggressive Behavior, 4*, 287–311.

Baenninger, R. (1987). Some comparative aspects of yawning in *Betta splendens, Homo sapiens, Panthera leo,* and *Papio sphinx. Journal of Comparative Psychology, 101*, 349–354.

Barzun, J. (1983). *A stroll with William James*. New York: Harper & Row.

Bitterman, M. E. (1960). Toward a comparative psychology of learning. *American Psychologist, 15*, 704–712.

Bridgman, P. W. (1936). *The nature of physical theory*. Princeton, NJ: Princeton University Press.

Burghardt, G. M. (1985). Animal awareness: Current perceptions and historical perspective. *American Psychologist, 40*, 905–919.

Buss, A. H. (1971). Aggression pays. In J. L. Singer (Ed.), *The control of aggression and violence: Cognitive and physiological factors*. New York: Academic Press.

Candland, D. K., & Kyes, R. C. (1986). Introduction: The human primate's theory of the primate mind. In J. G. Else & P. C. Lee (Eds.), *Primate ontogeny, cognition, and social behavior*. Cambridge: Cambridge University Press.

Collier, G. (1982). Determinants of choice. In D. J. Bernstein (Ed.), *1981 Nebraska Symposium on Motivation* (pp. 69–127). Lincoln: University of Nebraska Press.

Collier, G. (1986). The dialogue between the house economist and the resident physiologist. *Nutrition and Behavior, 3*, 9–26.

Feshbach, S. (1984). The catharsis hypothesis, aggressive drive, and the reduction of aggression. *Aggressive Behavior, 10*, 91–101.

Gallup, G. G. (1985). Do minds exist in species other than our own? *Neuroscience and Biobehavioral Reviews, 9*, 631–641.

Gallup, G. G., & Suarez, S. D. (1986). Self awareness and the emergence of mind in humans and other primates. In J. Suls & A. Greenwald (Eds.), *Psychological perspectives on the self* (Vol. 3, pp. 3–26). Hillsdale, NJ: Lawrence Erlbaum Associates.

Gardner, B. T., & Gardner, R. A. (1985). Signs of intelligence in cross-fostered chimpanzees. *Philosophical Transactions of the Royal Society of London*, Series Bs, *308*, 159–176.

Gentner, D., & Grudin, J. (1985). The evolution of mental metaphors in psychology: A 90 year retrospective. *American Psychologist, 40*, 181–192.

Griffin, D. R. (1984). *Animal thinking*. Cambridge, MA: Harvard University Press.

Griffin, D. R. (1985). Animal consciousness. *Neuroscience and Biobehavioral Reviews, 9*, 615–622.

Hebb, D. O. (1968). Concerning imagery. *Psychological Review, 75*, 466–477.

Henley, T. B., Johnson, M. G., Herzog, H. R., & Jones, E. M. (1989). Definitions of psychology. *Psychological Record, 39*, 143–152.

Hess, E. H. (1962). Ethology: An approach toward the complete analysis of behavior. In R.

Brown, E. Galanter, E.H. Hess, & G. Mandler (Eds.), *New directions in psychology*. New York: Holt, Rinehart, & Winston.

Hokanson, J. E. (1970). Psychophysiological evaluation of the catharsis hypothesis. In E. I. Megargee & J. E. Hokanson (Eds.), *The dynamics of aggression*. New York: Harper & Row.

Hooff, J. A. R. A. M. von (1972). A comparative approach to the phylogeny of laughter and smiling. In R. A. Hinde (Ed.), *Non-verbal communication*. Cambridge: Cambridge University Press.

Hull, C. L. (1945). The place of innate individual and species differences in a natural science theory of behavior. *Psychological Review, 52,* 55–60.

Hulse, S. H., Fowler, H., & Honig, W. K. (1978). *Cognitive processes in animal behavior*. Hillsdale, NJ: Lawrence Erlbaum Associates.

Jackendoff, R. (1987). *Consciousness and the computational mind*. Cambridge, MA: MIT Press.

James, W. (1890). *The principles of psychology* (Vols. 1–2). New York: Holt. (Unabridged and unaltered republication in two volumes by Dover Publications, 1950).

Kamil, A. C. (1978). Systematic foraging by a nectar-feeding bird, the Amakihi. *Journal of Comparative and Physiological Psychology, 92,* 388–396.

Kawai, M. (1965). Newly acquired pre-cultural behavior of the natural troop of Japanese monkeys on Koshima Islet. *Primates, 6,* 1–30.

Krechevsky, I. (1933). Hereditary nature of "hypotheses." *Journal of Comparative Psychology, 16,* 99–116.

Kruuk, H. (1972). Surplus killing by carnivores. *Journal of Zoology, 166,* 233–244.

Latto, R. (1986). The question of animal consciousness. *Psychological Record, 36,* 309–314.

Loeb, J. (1900). *Comparative physiology of the brain and comparative psychology*, New York: G. P. Putnam.

Lorenz, K. (1966). *On aggression*. New York: Harcourt, Brace and World.

Lyons, W. (1986). *The disappearance of introspection*. Cambridge, MA: MIT Press.

Mason, W. A. (1976). Windows on other minds. *Science, 194,* 930–931.

Morgan, C. L. (1894). *An introduction to comparative psychology*. London: Walter Scott.

Newman, J. A., & Caraco, T. (1987). Foraging, predation hazard and patch use in grey squirrels. *Animal Behavior, 35,* 1804–13.

Overton, W. F. (1984). World views and their influence on psychological theory and research: Kuhn-Lakatos-Laudan. In H. W. Reese (Ed.), *Advances in child development and behavior* (Vol. 18). New York: Academic Press.

Premack, D. (1986). *Gavagai*. Cambridge, MA: MIT Press.

Redican, W. K. (1982). An evolutionary perspective on human facial displays. In P. Ekman (Ed.), *Emotion in the human face* (2nd ed.). Cambridge: Cambridge University Press.

Roitblat, H. L. (1987). *Introduction to comparative cognition*. New York: W. H. Freeman.

Rychlak, J. F. (1986). The logic of consciousness. *British Journal of Psychology, 77,* 257–267.

Savage-Rumbaugh, E. S. (1986). *Ape language: From conditioned response to symbol*. New York: Columbia University Press.

Schaar, J. H. (1961). *Escape from authority: The perspectives of Erich Fromm*. New York: Basic Books.

Seton-Thompson, E. (1901). *Wild animals I have known*. New York: Charles Scribner's Sons.

Shettleworth, S. J., Krebs, J. R., Stephens, D. W., & Gibbons, J. (1988). Tracking a fluctuating environment: A study of sampling. *Animal Behavior, 36,* 87–105.

Singer, P. (1975). *Animal liberation*. New York: New York Review Press.

Smith, W. J., Chase, J., & Lieblick, A. K. (1975). Tongue showing: A facial display in man and gorilla. *Semiotica, 11,* 201–246.

Spence, K. W. (1936). The nature of discrimination learning in animals. *Psychological Review,* *43*, 427–449.

Spence, K. W. (1956). *Behavior theory and conditioning.* New Haven, CT: Yale University Press.

Sperry, R. W. (1969). A modified concept of consciousness. *Psychological Review, 76,* 532–536.

Sperry, R. W. (1970). An objective approach to subjective experience: Further explanation of a hypothesis. *Psychological Review, 77,* 585–590.

Tinklepaugh, O. L. (1928). An experimental study of representative factors in monkeys. *Journal of Comparative Psychology, 8,* 197–236.

Uexkull, J. von (1934). *Streifzuge durch die Umwelten von Tieren und Menschen* [A stroll through the environment of animals and men]. Berlin: Springer.

Walker, S. (1983). *Animal thought.* London: Routledge and Kegan Paul.

Watson, J. B. (1913). Psychology as the behaviorist views it. *Psychological Review, 20,* 158–170.

Wittgenstein, L. (1961). *Tractatus, logico-philosophicus* (D. Pears & B. McGuinness, Trans.). London: Routledge, Kegan, Paul. (Original work published 1921).

Yerkes, R. M. (1913). Comparative psychology: A question of definitions. *Journal of Philosophy, 22,* 580–582.

Zillmann, D. (1979). *Hostility and aggression.* Hillsdale, NJ: Lawrence Erlbaum Associates.

Chapter 12

The Stream of Consciousness Since James

Howard R. Pollio

University of Tennessee

Mention the phrase stream of consciousness, and you are soon likely to find yourself talking about James Joyce, Marcel Proust, Virginia Woolf, William Faulkner, or even Edward Dujardin. If the surname *James* occurs at all, it is as likely to be attached to Henry as to William. This seems an odd, if predictable, state of affairs since the term stream of consciousness was coined by William James in his attempt to describe the nature of mental life, as he put it, "from within." Over the years, and they were not all that many, the concept of stream of consciousness was lost to psychology once James Joyce turned Leopold Bloom loose in the quasi-real, quasi-mythic city of Dublin and gave Molly Bloom license to engage in a soliloquy on practically everything.

How is it psychology lost, or gave up, its claim to the Jamesian stream of consciousness? Perhaps the major reason concerns James's view that the stream of consciousness was designed to describe the flow of psychological phenomena "from within." Except for a brief flirtation with the study of consciousness by the introspectionists (whom James chided for chopping it up into analytic fictions known as mental elements) psychology from about 1916 until at least 1960 was ruled by the view that the view "from within" was subjective and unscientific. The only valid perspective for psychology was "from without," and the only proper subject matter was that which is viewable from without: behavior. Both the topic of mental life and the concept of stream of consciousness fell into disfavor and were lost to psychology in a long half-century of Watsonianism.

Stream of consciousness, however, is not an empty term. Everyone understands what is meant by it even if they are unable to provide a point-at-able referent. Perhaps it was for this reason that the study of consciousness prospered in a number of settings not quite so constrained by Bridgeman's operationism as was early psychology. In addition to the Joycean odyssey in literature, psychoanalysis increasingly came to deal with an aspect of consciousness not unknown to James: what Freud called the un-conscious. Philosophy also took up the challenge of consciousness in the form of a philosophy known as phenomenology. Although the program originally envisioned by Husserl never reached fulfillment, it became quite influential when combined with the existential thought of Heidegger in Germany and Merleau-Ponty in France. These developments, especially in France, were strongly influenced, and even foreshadowed, by Proust in literature and Bergson in philosophy.

The seemingly subjective nature of a psychology predicated on stream of consciousness thinking was not the only problem with the Jamesian program. Consciousness considered as a stream seems neither to sit still nor to have a specific location: Sometimes it is experienced in the head, at other times in an object of the world, at still other times in a world brought about by printed words bearing little similarity to the world created through and by their agency. William James (1890) acknowledged these difficulties when he wrote that it would be better to say "it consciouses" by analogy with the French "it rains." By this maneuver he hoped to avoid describing human consciousness as a noun-like thing bound to a specific location. Instead, he hoped consciousness would be considered as a restless, invisible, and unlocatable process that we unequivocally experience but cannot point at nor stop for more leisurely examination.

CONTEMPORARY PSYCHOLOGY AND THE STREAM OF CONSCIOUSNESS

Beginning in the 1960s psychology took on a new direction in the form of cognitive psychology, and the idea of studying mental life again seemed possible. In the 25 or 30 years since the first stirrings of the cognitive revolution, the study of mental phenomena has moved again to the center of psychology becoming, as Kuhn (1970) would style it, the dominant concern of the dominant paradigm of contemporary psychology.

One of the best ways, according to Kuhn, of discovering how a paradigm sees itself is in terms of how its introductory texts treat formerly problematic topics. To learn what has become of the Jamesian stream, all we need is look at a collection of contemporary introductory texts and see how consciousness is presented. To provide some empirical grist for this analysis, 20 different introductory texts, having publication dates no earlier than 1984, were examined to see whether (and if) they had a chapter with the word "consciousness" somewhere in the title. All 20 did, with the majority also using the phrase "altered states of" somewhere nearby. Although there are many ways to examine this body of data, the most obvious is to note the location of the chapter in the text and to identify the major topics covered.

TABLE 12.1
Location of the Chapter on Consciousness In Introductory Texts

Preceded by	%	Followed by	%
Psychological Processes:	75%	Processes	75%
Perception	50	Learning	55
Motivation	15	Perception	10
Emotion	5	Sensation	5
Learning	5	Meaning	5
Biology	20%	Biology	10%
Brain	5	Brain	5
Foundation	10	Physiology of Emotion	5
Nervous System	5	The Person	15%
Other		Development	10
Sexuality	5%	Personality	5

Table 12.1 describes where the chapter on consciousness occurs in terms of chapters that precede and follow it. By and large, the chapter on consciousness occurs in the first third of the text and is preceded by chapters concerning psychological processes (largely, perception) or biological foundations. The chapter on consciousness is followed most frequently by those falling under the general rubric of learning. Some small number of texts follow the chapter on consciousness by one on development or personality; an even smaller number follow it by one on emotion or brain function. The topic of consciousness usually falls somewhere between perception and learning. In a former day, we might have said it falls between a stimulus and the habit yielding a response; in the present day, between pattern reception and output.

Where, as a point of contrast, did James locate his chapter on consciousness? Here there are two different volumes to consider: the larger *Principles of Psychology* (1890) and its reduction to the briefer *Psychology* (1893). Stream of consciousness occurs in the major text as Chapter 9 (of 26) and is titled "The Stream of Thought" (although James quickly indicates this term is interchangeable with stream of consciousness). Within the briefer text, the title is the more familiar one ("The Stream of Consciousness") and occurs as Chapter 11 (of 27). Within the original text the chapter is preceded by "The Relationship of Minds to Other Things" and followed by "The Consciousness of Self." Within the briefer *Psychology*, the chapter falls between a discussion of "Habit" (the chapter's title) and "The Self."

In both texts, James follows his chapter on stream of consciousness by one on self. For James, there is an extremely close connection between self and consciousness, and this relationship is developed quite directly at the outset of his chapter on self in the brief text:

Whatever I may be thinking of, I am always at the same time more or less aware of myself, of my personal existence. At the same time it is I who am aware; so that the total self of me, being as it were duplex, partly known and partly knower, partly object and partly subject, must have two aspects discriminated in it of which for shortness we may call one the Me and the other the I. (James, 1893, p. 176)

What topics do contemporary texts include in their chapters on consciousness? Table 12.2 presents a list of 13 topics that occurred at least once in each text. With the exception of right left hemisphere differences, biological rhythms, and, perhaps, day-dreaming, all topics concern—as the chapters themselves announce—altered states of consciousness. Over half of the chapters are explicitly entitled alternate states of consciousness and avoid issues of wake-a-day consciousness altogether. When consciousness is covered in contemporary texts, it is covered from the vantage point of non-ordinary events; ordinary consciousness is of little interest in and of itself.

Two implications that can be drawn from this analysis are that consciousness is an issue only when it is extra-ordinary and that we have a good pragmatic grasp of ordinary, wake-a-day, consciousness. Although sleep and dreams are viewed as "ordinary" phenomena, they are usually discussed in terms of non-obvious findings—more REM after sleep deprivation, for example—or as a triumph of operational definition over subjective experience. Daydreaming is treated in terms of questionnaires, for example, the Singer-Antrobus Imaginal Process Inventory (1970). The vast majority of texts also include topics discussed by James: hypnosis, peak- experiences, drugs, and hallucinations. What is missing, however, is a description of human conscious experience in any way other than as an introduction to more extra-ordinary states of consciousness. What is also missing is the relationship of consciousness to self.

THE VIEW OF ORDINARY CONSCIOUSNESS
FROM EXPERIMENTAL PSYCHOLOGY

Unlike Anglo-American psychology of the same period, Wolfgang Köhler began his classic text with a description of wake-a-day experience: that of his own attempt to describe his experiences as he began to write *Gestalt Psychology* (Köhler, 1947/1975). From this beginning, he progressed to a description of direct experience, and from there to a critique of Behaviorism, which banished the study of direct experience as "subjective." But Kohler did more than chide Behaviorism for its attitude toward direct experience: He offered a clear description of what such experience is like. Although contemporary psychology views Gestalt theory as having to do with perception and, perhaps, secondarily with other psychological processes, Köhler did not so limit his domain. The major Gestalt principle of ordinary, wake-a-day consciousness is that of figure/ground. In one sense, fig-

TABLE 12.2
Major Topics In Twenty, Current Introductory Psychology Texts

Concept	% Occurrences
Sleep and/or Dreams	100%
Hypnosis	90%
Drugs	90%
Meditation	50%
Day Dreaming (fantasy)	30%
ESP/telepathy/psycho kinesis	15%
Right-Left hemisphere differences	10%
Biological Rhythms	10%
Peak Experiences	10%
Near Death Experiences	10%
Biofeedback	5%
Sensory Deprivation	5%
Hallucinations	5%

ure/ground, is an extremely simple concept to grasp: Every event is always experienced within some context, against some ground. In another sense, the concept is extremely subtle and far-reaching: There are no events independent of grounds and what is experienced depends as much on the context as on the figure. Experience is a field event that includes not only its perceptual ground but also grounds provided by other relevant contexts such as socio-historical era, social setting, personal history, the current situation, and so on. The analytic context of the laboratory (or the psychological test) does not offer a condition of zero field but that of a special field, and to see the laboratory (or test) as providing a context-free rendering of an event is not only misleading but wrong.

Wake-a-day conscious experience is a field event in which different events emerge as figural for some particular person, in some particular setting. Although the number of grounds may be extended to include language, any attempt to locate consciousness in the "head" misses the significance of the figure/ground concept. Wake-a-day consciousness is a relational event that ties together the current figural event with all of those ground conditions that give it its particular experiential properties. Wake-a-day consciousness is never isolated from the world; consciousness always achieves its figures within the setting of the world and of the person.

Although gestalt psychologists drew other implications, the important points for a psychology of consciousness seem to be that individual conscious awareness always has a focal and a non-focal structure to it, and that such a structure emerges only within the context of person-world relationships. If the "self" appears at all, it is always contextually situated. The curious conclusions to all of this must be that the self is no less a relational event than other figures of direct experience and, for Gestalt psychology, situational aspects of the person are no less significant than historical ones.

The self is a relational event that depends for its shape (boundaries) on the field within which it is presently lived and/or described.

Once we grant that direct, wake-a-day, experience is a viable topic, many different modes of study become possible. In one attempt to describe the normal flow of conscious experience, Klinger (1978) used a naturalistic self-report procedure in which student volunteers were "beeped" as they went about their ordinary, extra-laboratory lives for a 24-day period. These studies (and others by Hurlburt, 1979, 1980) offer a number of interesting facts about everyday experience: (a) wake-a-day experience is constantly changing (coherent laboratory segments have a median duration of about 5 sec.); (b) most reports of wake-a-day experience concern everyday, present tense, contextually related descriptions that are specific and unfanciful; (c) most sequences contain directed and associated elements, although more directed sequences were reported; (d) most reports (about 69%) relate to the setting in which they occurred whereas 21% were not, and 10% were hard to place.

In a different attempt to describe wake-a-day experience, Pollio (1984) interrupted students during the course of lectures and asked them to write down what they were thinking of prior to the interruption. Results were similar to those reported by Klinger, including the potentially disturbing fact that students were off-target with respect to lecture content some 39% of the time. When off-target responses were examined more carefully, it was found that the largest percentage (27%) were concerned with time. The second most frequent category (25%) concerned other people who were either in the present context or imagined. Many of these other-focused remarks concerned the lecturer. What might not have been gratifying about this concern was that students were concerned more with non-teaching issues ("I never noticed how much the instructor looks like a chip-munk") than with the lecturer's dynamic style or charismatic personal bearing. The third (18%) and fourth (13%) most frequent categories included a focus on bodily events and on mood.

What these data suggest is that events in the college lecture hall (as elsewhere) are experienced against a background supplied by the world of everyday reality. Within the context of the college classroom, this means that students come into the lecture halls not as disembodied minds waiting to be filled with knowledge but as fully embodied human beings having a full compliment of experiences against which college lectures must compete for focal awareness. The structure of human experience, as Gestalt psychology stressed, is always one in which some event stands out against some background, within some context.

Students not only experience things in class, they also do things and it is reasonable to wonder if there is any relationship between what students experience and do in lecture classes? To answer this question individual students were continuously monitored for a complete 50-minute lecture hour. At random intervals the student was interrupted and asked to fill out a self-

TABLE 12.3
Percent Concordance Between Behavioral Records and Self Report

	Self Report	
Behavioral Record	On-target	Off-target
On-target	.64	.29
Off-target	.03	.04

report. Both self-report and observational protocols were coded into two major categories: on-target and off-target.

One way of looking at these results concerns the degree of concordance between being on- or off-target in terms of both behavioral record and self report. When this was done, the data can be described in terms of Table 12.3. In the best of all possible worlds—best, that is, for researchers and lecturers—the two cells On/On and Off/Off would comprise close to 100% of the responses. This means that instructors would know, by looking, which students were on or off-target. Unfortunately, this turned out to be the case only 68% of the time. In 32% of the cases, behavior tells us little about self-awareness (and, it is important to note, vice versa: Being on target in terms of awareness does not tell us unequivocally what students are doing).

These data replicate and extend Klinger's results: The stream of wake-a-day conscious experience constantly changes focus, is sometimes related to concurrent behavior and sometimes not, is not always functionally related to its current context, and, in general, provides a good confirmation of James's description of ongoing classroom consciousness offered some 90 years earlier in his lectures to teachers (James, 1921):

> In most of our fields of consciousness there is a core . . . that is very pronounced. You, for example, now, although you are also thinking and feeling, are getting . . . sensations of my face and figure, and . . . voice. The sensations are the *centre* or *focus*, the thoughts and feelings the *margin*, of your actually present conscious field.
>
> On the other hand, some object of thought, some distant image, may have become the focus of your mental attention even while I am speaking—your mind, . . . may have wandered from the lecture; and, my face and voice, although not absolutely vanishing from your conscious field, may have taken up there a very faint and marginal place. Again, some feeling connected with your own body may have passed from a marginal to a focal place, even while I speak.
>
> In the successive mutations of our fields of consciousness, the process by which one dissolves into another is often very gradual . . . sometimes the focus remains but little changed, while the margin alters rapidly. Sometimes the focus alters, and the margin stays. Sometimes focus and margin change places. Sometimes, again, abrupt alterations of the whole field occur. (p. 16–17)

THE VIEW OF CONSCIOUSNESS FROM
PSYCHOANALYSIS

Although usually concerned with other matters, psychoanalysis also had something to say about the stream of normal, human conscious experience. It is well to remember that two of Freud's earliest books—*The Psychopathology of Everyday Life* (1905/1938) and *Wit and Its Relationship to the Unconscious* (1905/1932)—have a clear footing in ordinary wake-a-day consciousness, even if the major theoretical principles are derived from an analysis of dreams.

The single most significant principle assumed to apply to all of human experience is that of the unconscious, which includes wake-a-day consciousness as a subset. A number of methods provide access to this domain, including an analysis of dreams and the technique of free-association. For Freud, symbols represent disguised bits of unconscious concerns held together by a similarity in personal meaning. A major principle of symbolization is that of condensation, in which a number of images or ideas coalesce into a single symbol such that their "unconscious" meaning is masked by being distorted (or displaced) to a different aspect of content.

Although we may think of surrealist painting à la Dali, Magritte, or Max Ernst as a major artistic representation of the Freudian Unconscious, more ordinary poetry and poetic devices seem at least as good a choice as surrealistic art. Whereas Dali and company juxtapose (condense) odd images and may even make use of figure/ground principles, poetic diction intrinsically uses allusion, synecdoche, displacement, and so on in attempting to enhance the experience created by a poem. Early Freudian theory viewed metaphor as a prototypic linguistic device designed to abet hiding unconscious material (Sharpe, 1940), although recent empirical work offers a more benign interpretation (Pollio, Barlow, Fine, & Pollio, 1977). We may well agree with the literary critic, William Friedman (1955), who wrote, "Freudian psychology tends to make poetry indigenous to the constitution of the unconscious mind; the dream fabric is essentially [the product of] a poetry-making organ" (p. 102).

The Freudian analysis of jokes, similarly, implicates the unconscious as a crucial element. Although psychoanalytic theories of humor (see Wolfenstein, 1954, for example) usually focus on the distortion of disturbing themes by the joke facade, fully half of Freud's original monograph concerned issues of technique. For Freud, the technique of the joke, the dream, and the metaphor all partake of some combination of condensation and displacement, and these techniques form the bedrock of ongoing mental activity. Whereas dreams may yield insight into how the stream of consciousness progresses during sleep; jokes, poems, myths, and other symbols provide insight into the wake-a-day world. Rational thought may be what we strive for in daytime activity; such thought, however, is not all that goes on, either by day or night.

The primary legacy of Freudian theory is that the stream of conscious experience is a multi-leveled phenomenon, with deeper levels related to more primitive impulses and with higher levels related to more rational ones. As our fondness for myths, jokes, poems, and slips of the tongue indicates, rational processes are scarcely ever in total control. The stream of human experience consists of items that frequently are opaque to oneself and others, unless considerable effort is expended to decipher them. It also consists of items that are transparent to oneself and others. In between the two is the preconscious, which is both more opaque than wake-a-day consciousness and more transparent than the Unconscious.

If Freud endowed consciousness with a depth and a darkness, Jung endowed it with a history. The concepts of archetype, collective unconscious, myth, and persona all served to convert the Freudian unconscious from a biological storehouse of impulses into a cultural storehouse of mythic images and recollections. For Jung, the job of symbolization is not only to bring forward what is forbidden but to express what is mythic. Symbols have the peculiar property of belonging both to the individual and to the species. Although it is always possible to seek the meaning of a symbol in the personal experiences of a single individual, such explanation is incomplete until it makes contact with the larger meanings characterizing human consciousness in general.

If Freud's literary prototype is poetry, Jung's primary form is myth. Many of the most original speculations deriving from Jungian theory attempt to demonstrate the universality of certain mythic elements and motifs. If Sophocles motivates the Freudian view of consciousness, Joyce presents the Jungian view. Friedman (1955) has gone so far as to identify *Finnegans Wake* as a representation not only of an individual stream of consciousness but also as "The Jungian abstraction, the collective unconscious. . . . Not only is this book a direct transcript of Jung's conception of the dreamer as myth maker, but the intended ambiguity of the relationship gives the dreamer the universal aspect of being 'everyone' since the beginning of time" (pp. 14–15).

THE VIEW OF CONSCIOUSNESS FROM LITERATURE AND MUSIC

Stream of consciousness writing takes place largely within the 50-year period from 1880 to 1930. Although earlier foreshadowings appear in different literary traditions (e.g., Sterne in English, Stendahl in French, Dostoyevsky in Russian), the major works are all coincident with, or shortly following, James's characterization of the stream of consciousness in *The Principles*. It is as if something was in the air that equally affected James, Proust, Joyce, Richardson, Stein, Faulkner, and others. Despite a common concern with stream of consciousness phenomena, there are great differences between the abstract description provided by James and the more concrete-literary ones provided by Joyce, Proust, et al.

Three of the most well known authors of stream of consciousness novels are Marcel Proust, James Joyce, and William Faulkner. For Proust, the major question is one of time and meaning; for Joyce, the distinction is between inner and outer experience; for Faulkner, the focus is on who speaks and when. Each author renders consciousness in a different way: Proust's narrator, Marcel, uses an interior monologue in which the character speaks to himself in a coherent, if complicated, form of discourse. Sentences, although long and filled with parenthetical remarks, asides, and metaphoric images, are nonetheless still sentences. The prose is a monologue, and the monologue is structured in terms of the ordinary rules of (long) sentences.

Proust's theme is also significant: the attempt to recapture the past as re-evoked by some material object in the present field of the person. Sometimes it is a cookie, the spices of a city, an odor, a musical refrain, a brick wall, the sound of spoon against a plate, and so on. Each of these incidents is offered as an example of what Proust calls "involuntary memory" in which the past overwhelms the present and the person gives him or herself over to the change in time. Involuntary memory is contrasted with more linear (or clock-based) memory in which events have a unique location and a unique starting and finishing point. For Proust, involuntary time is closer to the way time is experienced in consciousness as we freely go back and forth in a complexly inter-related mental event.

Although Proust describes examples of involuntary memory in a number of places in *Swann's Way*, and other volumes of *Remembrances of Things Past*, there is usually no break in the narrative or in the technique by which the monologue is rendered.

> The past becoming one with the present is an illusion Proust does not faithfully carry out. He speaks about the process in elaborate terms but fails to reproduce its effect for the reader. When the author completely identifies his own style with that of his character's meditations, he fails to render states of consciousness in their most convincing terms. (Friedman, 1955, p. 94)

If Proust fails to change his style from a narrative that unfolds in clock time to one unfolding in involuntary memory, there is no such failure in Faulkner, especially in the novel *The Sound and the Fury*. Although the reader is completely adrift as to what is going on at the beginning of the first chapter, successive chapters allow for the emergence of a more coherent narrative line. The first three sections of the novel all offer first-person streams: that of Benjy (Part I) and that of his brothers Quentin (Part II) and Jason (Part III). The fourth part is a more ordinary narrative and is told from the standpoint of the family maid.

Benjy is a retarded adult (to whom the title refers), and his chapter offers the least articulate level of consciousness. Benjy's monologue is not Marcel's monologue: The sentences are short and do not follow one another in a clear way. When the past is introduced, it is a fragmented past evoked by a relevant aspect of the present, and the reader is quickly drawn into that world. The stream capturing these memories becomes progressively less well defined until events from vastly different time periods are presented in the same segment. As the chapter progresses, there is a decrease in sentence control and words exhibit a disorganized polysemy. Anything is likely to occur next to anything else, and items are juxtaposed rather than organized within the grid of either ordinary language or spatio-temporal reality.

Quentin's section deals with a much more emotional stream of consciousness, that of a late adolescent. The centerpiece is Quentin's memory/ recollection of a fight during which he passed out. It is during this section that both content and prose lose their ordinary syntactic control as Faulkner omits punctuation and capitalization. The chronology is also confused although there are two clear temporal foci to the chapter: the present and the day of Quentin's sister's marriage. Within most of the chapter Quentin's stream of consciousness is presented as a straightforward interior monologue and, except for the dream sequence, the writing is articulate (even ornate) as befits an intelligent college student. Time, however, is a problem for Quentin, and this is reflected in the difficulty the reader has in recovering an orderly chronology.

The third major section (by Jason) stays mainly at the level of interior monologue. Although there is some movement between present and past, there is enough contact with clock time to keep the stream both within the present and the narrative. The content is clearly the wake-a-day world (there are frequent references to clock time), although the episode does go back and forth in providing its unique perspective on the events of the novel. Sentence structure is a little looser in Quentin's section than in the final, more narrative, section. The stream is related to the world, as both move back and forth across the events of Jason's life. Events in time past are rendered by the use of italics and while narrative flow is sometimes unclear, this stylistic device is relatively easy to follow once the reader gets the hang of it.

Stream of consciousness technique reaches a high level of development in Faulkner. Despite this, the author usually associated with this technique is James Joyce. In three novels, *Portrait of the Artist, Ulysses*, and *Finnegans Wake*, Joyce explores stream of consciousness technique as his characters move from the level of everyday (in *Portrait* and to some degree in *Ulysses*) to that of mythic intelligence and memory (parts of *Ulysses* and most of *Finnegans Wake*). Since the stream of consciousness as a psychological phenomena is of primary concern, it seems best to deal only with parts of *Portrait* and *Ulysses*, especially since the same character, Stephen Daedalus, appears in both.

The first stream of consciousness in *Portrait* occurs on the very first page, which begins, without any indication such as quotation marks, with us listening to a story from the perspective of a very young child. As this mode of presenting personal experience continues, the reader is provided with examples of the streams of consciousness of a 6-year-old arriving at school and meeting a bully, of an adolescent watching a young woman bathe, and of a young man entering post-college life. Although a number of techniques are used to convey Stephen's experiences, most of the writing is in the third person. The only concession made to stream of consciousness style occurs when transitions in the text are not explicitly signaled: for example, when the child Stephen moves back and forth from the world of the present (an encounter with a bully) to that of the past (remembrances of sitting with mother by the fire). If there is an impression to be gotten from *Portrait* it is that of change: change in perspective (present/past, author/ character, old/young), change in language and style (child/adolescent/ college-age), and change in locale (the various way-stations of Stephen's life). The novel is not difficult to follow, and the reader seldom has trouble discerning whose stream of consciousness is whose.

The situation in *Ulysses* is less clear. Altogether the book opens easily enough, with Stephen observing his friend, "Stately, plump, Buck Milligan," the remainder of the chapter concerns Stephen including a long and rambling recollection by Stephen of his life from the end of *Portrait* until now. The remainder of *Ulysses* is given over to three separate sets of experiences: one from the life of Leopold Bloom, another from his wife Molly, and the third from Stephen. Each stream has its own cadence and vocabulary, and each reaffirms the character of its respective creator: Stephen, the estranged intellectual; Leopold, the Jew in search of a homeland; and Molly, the unfortunate wife of Leopold, who holds a passionate view of herself, others, and the world.

Perhaps the most famous stream of consciousness in all literature is Molly Bloom's reverie on which *Ulysses* ends. Molly begins by being impatient and then angry at having to wait for Leopold. Having nothing to do, and unable to fall asleep, she looks around the apartment. She notices the clock, the wallpaper, and other objects at hand. Each object serves as a starting point for a sequence of thoughts. Ultimately, the images melt together until Molly returns to the days of her courtship with Leopold, most particularly to the first time she said yes, and on this note she drifts off to sleep.

When I put the rose in my hair like the Andalusian girls used or shall I wear a red yes and how he kissed me under the Moorish wall and I thought

well as well him as another and then I asked him with my eyes to ask again
yes and then he asked me would I yes and drew him down to me so he could
feel my breasts all perfume yes and his heart was going like mad and yes I
said yes I will Yes. (p. 783)

As a counterpoint to Molly's monologue, consider Leopold's stream of
consciousness. The following example is taken from a section in which
Bloom is reading newspaper headlines, specifically, "AND IT WAS THE
FEAST OF THE PASSOVER."

He stayed in his walk to watch a typesetter neatly distributing type. Reads it
backwards first. Quickly he does it. Must require some practice that. mangiD.
kcirtaP. Poor papa with his hagadah book, reading backwards with his finger
to me. Pessach. Next year in Jerusalem. Dear, O dear! All that long business
about that He brought us out of the land of Egypt and into the house of
bondage alleluia. Shemay israel Adonai Elohenu. No, that's the other. Then
the twelve brothers, Jacob's sons. And then the lamb and the cat and the dog
and the stick and the water and the butcher and then the angel of death kills
the butcher and he kills the ox and the dog kills the cat. Sounds a bit silly till
you come to look into it well. Justice it means but it's everybody eating everyone else. That's what life is after all. How quickly he does that job. Practice
makes perfect. Seems to see with his fingers. (p. 121)

The first few sentences set the context: Bloom is watching type being set.
The next sentence contains the name *Patrick Dignam*, a man whose funeral
Leopold had just attended. Thoughts of Dignam's death, combined with
the right to left reading of the name required by its being set in type, remind
Bloom of Hebrew writing and of his deceased father. Bloom then gets to
thinking about the Passover service in his home. The remainder of the
monologue, down to the phrase "and the dog kills the cat," refers to memories of the service Hebrew phrases included. The monologue ends with a
reflection of social power as eating—both from the song in the Hagadah
and from dietary aspects of the Passover meal. The last three sentences return the reader to the typesetter's shop.

Leopold and Molly's soliloquies reveal that not only is Leopold's stream
rendered by an interior monologue but that it is relatively easy to follow if
one understands the allusions. Molly's daydream is much less well formed
syntactically, as one thought runs together with another without much in
the way of a transition. Although sentencing is unique, the sequence is not
difficult to follow, especially if read aloud. Finally, both excerpts offer similarities important for a psychological understanding of the stream of consciousness: First, there is no distinction between inside and outside (the
printer's shop vs. Leopold's memory) or between past and present (Molly in
the room now, Molly daydreaming about a prior time), and second, all aspects of the stream are experienced in the present. A final aspect to both

quotes, but most especially to the one by Molly, concerns its rhythm and flow, what could be called its rhythmic or musical properties. Reading Molly's soliloquy aloud indicates just how musical a rendering Joyce gives it.

This aspect of Molly's reverie suggests that there might be a more-than-casual relationship between music and stream of consciousness writing. Anyone listening to symphonic music cannot help but be struck by its flow, the different pacing of its parts, the distinctions introduced by various instruments, and by the various themes within a given section. These aspects of the music emerge for even the most unsophisticated listener, and one wonders if other aspects of musical composition might serve as a useful analogy for understanding stream of consciousness writing.

Friedman (1955) has noted that there are three major aspects to such an analogy:

1. There is a rhythm in both language and music. Although each character in Faulkner has his or her own rhythm (Benjy vs. Quentin—slow vs. agitated), the most clear cut use of rhythm is in Joyce. Consider the powerfully rhythmic phrase on which *Ulysses* begins: "Stately, plump, Buck Milligan . . ."
2. Leitmotifs occur in both novels and musical compositions. Within music, a leitmotif is a short musical phrase that continually reoccurs in a composition and is used to suggest important themes or characters. This technique occurs in stream of consciousness writing, most especially in Proust, where leitmotifs are meant to intimate and signal past incidents.
3. Counterpoint, more natural to music than literature, is the adding of a second melody to highlight or contrast with a basic melody. Musically, it occurs at the same time as the melody; in stream of consciousness writing it is expressed by successive renderings of the same situation by the same character(s) or by a rendering of the same situation by a different character(s).

How seriously should the analogy between music and stream of consciousness writing be taken? No more or less lightly than any analogy should be taken. As such, it suggests that aspects of consciousness involve techniques common to music and writing: sound, rhythm, pace, imagery, leitmotif, counterpoint. What the analogy does not require is a one-to-one mapping of one domain onto the other. There is no way in which to capture chords or strict temporal simultaneity. There also is little or no way writing could map onto the harmonic structure of music. What we must be content with is the usual recipe for analogy: similarity (or resemblance) in difference. If this were not the case, literary and musical compositions would be the same, and Wagner could be Joyce.

One conclusion to be drawn from literary renditions of human consciousness is that level is an important aspect. Some renditions occur at the level of fully accomplished speech in the form of monologue, others occur at the level of dream and symbol, including those cultural dreams we call myth. A second aspect concerns the locus of the event described: Is it in the person or in the world? The boundary between person and world is tenuous in these descriptions, as characters express events that come as easily from personal pasts or futures as from the current life situation. Images merge, change, and transform as the stream encompasses one and then another event. It is here that rhythm and tempo are crucial. Even if the person is not totally comprehensible to the reader (as in the first chapter of *The Sound and the Fury*) what is comprehensible is change and the unique rhythm of that change.

Time is significant in still another way: Past, present and future do not align themselves one after the other as clock and calendar suggest they should. The temporal organization of consciousness is content-based, with the character equally involved in the event as it now occurs, as it anticipates a future, and/or as it was foreshadowed by and in some past. Certain threads of a life—its themes or leitmotifs—tie the present focus to other events and meanings; no event is unconnected from the rest. At any moment, the stream is of a single piece, and if such coherence defies the grid of rational expectation, this seems to be the way consciousness is. The temporal qualities described by steam of consciousness technique clearly defy the linear qualities of ordinary historical or narrative time.

Finally, there is language. Sometimes it is syntactically well formed and filled with image and allusion; at others, it is fragmentary with an almost literal rendition of events and sensations; at still others, it is lyric and poetic. In the latter case, the stream is both linguistically powerful and confusing and a reader is never quite sure if Joyce is offering a simple play on words or one steeped in the mysteries of character or culture. Language is used to suggest, arouse, and ultimately confound the reader; it is seldom used to enumerate events or denote a reality apart from itself.

Each monologue has a distinctive signature, whether of a 33-year-old retarded man/boy or of an effete mid-life Frenchman, and such uniqueness gives each rendition an ability to provide a singular perspective on narrative events. If there is one aspect to the human world unassailably rendered by stream of consciousness technique it is that of personal perspective: Each character renders the world in unique terms. This is as true for a character in the midst of a myth (Bloom in *Ulysses*) as for one stridently engaged in everyday reality (Jason in *Sound and Fury*). It is at this point the literature of consciousness makes contact with the literature of character, for in this mode of writing, personal consciousness *is* character. If we take the lead offered by stream of consciousness novels, William James is clearly correct in placing his chapter on self immediately after the chapter on consciousness.

THE VIEW OF CONSCIOUSNESS FROM
PHILOSOPHY

Like literature, 20th-century philosophy also concerned itself with consciousness. Some schools, such as logical positivism, attempted to overcome the vagaries of consciousness by strict definition. Other schools, such as the later Wittgenstein, simply accepted the difficulties posed by consciousness and suggested we content ourselves with an analysis of language. Still other schools, such as those founded by Bergson and Husserl, suggested taking consciousness as the starting point for setting philosophy on a new and more rigorous foundation. When combined with the existential thought of Heidegger and Merleau-Ponty, Husserl (and to a lesser extent, Bergson) offered a new conceptual foundation for contemporary analyses of consciousness both in philosophy and in psychology.

Bergson's philosophy relates to issues of conscious experience largely in terms of his approach to the problems of time and intuition. For Bergson there are two types of time: one that is represented spatially, say by the movement of a hand on a clock or by our attempt to describe time as a line, and a second that cannot be so represented. Only the latter form, called pure time or duration, is important for the study of consciousness. In contrast to metric time, duration is concerned with succession and not similarity, intensity and not quantity, simultaneity and not sequence. Duration is an immediately given aspect of experience; it is not measurable by a clock, calendar, or digital summator.

These two modes of time implicate and are supported by two modes of knowing: a spatial, analytical mode and a duration-based, intuitive mode. Intuition is the more complicated of the two modes, and Bergson views it as that type of awareness involved in all creative acts, but most especially in those of the artist. Intuition is a direct awareness of things; analytic reflection is a more distant mode in which person and world are separate, and the best the thinker is ever able to experience is a re-presentation of some object, event, or person.

A good deal of Bergsonian theory comes together in his short book *Laughter* (1900/1956). In this work, he describes the essential aspect of what is laughable as a direct experience of the contrast between what is mechanical and what is spontaneous. It is not difficult to see that "mechanical" refers to analytic modes of perceiving and knowing and that "spontaneous" refers to more direct, intuitive modes of perceiving and knowing. What is crucial is the experience of one masquerading as the other—a jack-in-the-box, a puppet, a falling clown, a rigid person, a tic or mannerism, a recurring vice, and so on. Laughter attempts to convert the mechanical into the human. It is a human action designed to move the person from an analytic mode to a more intuitive, and, hence, more genuinely human one.

These ideas sound like James. Whether the concepts of stream of consciousness and duration were developed independently of one another is unclear; what is clear is that both struggle against the dominant view of consciousness as thinking and of thinking as spatial and analytic. Edmund Husserl, also concerned himself with this issue. His opponent was not Kant, as seems to be the case for Bergson, but Descartes, and his point of departure was not time but mind. Like Descartes, Husserl sought to place philosophy on a new foundation by finding a secure starting place. Using a procedure analogous to the Cartesian doubt, Husserl tried to "bracket" all prior knowledge as so to determine the essential aspects of consciousness. In this attempt, he borrowed (and modified) Brentano's concept of intentionality and hoped to re-constitute human knowledge from this starting point.

What does Husserl mean by intentionality? For both Brentano and Husserl, intentionality means that human experience and the world are never separate—they mutually implicate each other. Intentionality is the foundational structure of human experience and is best rendered by the assertion that there is no consciousness *in general*; consciousness is always *consciousness of something* (Pollio, 1982). Descartes, and even Bergson, makes a distinction between subject and object, between an experiencer and something experienced. Ihde (1977) describes the fundamental rule of Husserl's philosophy as: "Every experiencing has its reference or direction toward what is experienced, and, contrarily, every experienced phenomena refers to or reflects a mode of experiencing to which it is present (pp. 42–43)."

Husserl offered a number of descriptions of the relationship between the object experienced, the mode of its being experienced, and the person experiencing it. Borrowing from Ihde, this situation may be diagrammed as follows:

(I)(mode of experiencing)→(object experienced)
3   2   1

What this diagram is meant to capture is that all three aspects of consciousness-as-intentional are always co-present. The numbers 1, 2, and 3 suggest that the correlation between self and world begins with a direct experience of the "object" pole—what Husserl would call with "the thing itself." The second aspect of the relationship between what we usually call self and world concerns its mode of experiencing and includes activities as diverse as hearing, touching, seeing, or thinking. The third stage in any reflection on the nature of experience concerns the experiencer. Unlike Cartesian or introspective views of self, the I is not first, the mode second, and the world third. In phenomenology the "I" appears on the basis of phenomenon that are usually called the world. "The philosophical 'I' takes on its significance through its encounter with things, persons, and every type of otherness . . . (Ihde, 1977, p. 51)."

This description applies not only to things but to the ways in which we experience ourselves as an "I" different from other "I's". In coming to this understanding, phenomenology distinguishes two different modes of experiencing: what the philosopher refers to as unreflected (or direct) and reflected (or thought-about) experiencing. In describing his experience of chopping wood, Ihde notes that during the act of chopping he does not attend to "what is going on in the experience" (Ihde, 1977, p. 47); he is simply involved in the act of chopping. Following Merleau-Ponty (1962), he describes his experience as follows: "I am outside myself in the world of my project." After finishing his chore, and returning to the typewriter, Ihde notes that there are two different ways of talking about wood-chopping. In the unreflected, or direct mode, Ihde reports his experience as "actual, involved, immersed in the project of the moment; narrowly focused and concentrated" (Ihde, 1977, p. 45). In the reflected mode, Ihde thinks back on the unreflected experience of chopping wood. Reflected experience presupposes direct experience—chopping wood—as its theme. Since reflecting is also a direct experience, we are lead to the possibility of using reflected experiencing as a topic of further reflection, as in the phrase "Thinking (3) about thinking (2) about thinking (1)." In the case of thinking (3), what is reflected on is thinking about thinking. In the case of thinking (2), What is reflected on is thinking. In the case of thinking (1), what is reflected on is some activity that is not thinking.

The scope and power of reflected experiencing provide it with the appearance of being more significant than the thinking person. Since we are able to think about anything—including thinking itself—is it possible to see how Descartes could have been led to assume thinking defines what it means to be human: "I think, therefore, I am." What Descartes did, and Western thought agreed to, was to remove thinking from the thinking person. Regardless of what it is about, thinking is unreflected and, therefore, takes place only within the world of person, time, history, language, society, and so on. Like all human experiencing, reflection is never context-free. Although the context may be as narrow as a philosopher contemplating chopping wood or as broad as a mathematician contemplating infinity, both topics, as well as the situations in which they occur, constitute the life world (or *Lebenswelt*) of the thinker. Husserl intended his philosophy to provide a foundation on which to base a context-free (i.e., a transcendental) philosophy of knowledge. Unfortunately, the problem of the human life world could not be bypassed and came to engage him more frequently as he pursued Cartesian meditations throughout his life.

Although Husserl posed the problem of the human life world, it remained for Heidegger to describe consciousness within the world as lived; to transform phenomenological philosophy into existential philosophy. Heidegger viewed philosophy as a method of attaining a human understanding of human phenomena such as consciousness, and to define consciousness as consciousness-in-the-world or, as Heidegger and the later existential-philosophers would put it more generally, as being-in-the-world. Since Heidegger's philosophy is extremely rich it is probably best to focus on a few major concepts such as *Dasein, Mitsein,* and Time.

Dasein, which may be understood as Heidegger's attempt to describe self, is presented in the following sentence: *"Das 'Wesen' des Daseins liegt in seiner Existenz"* (1927/1972, p. 42). Taking the words in their everyday sense, the sentence could be translated, "The 'essence' of existence lies in its existence." It is better not to translate *Dasein,* since it is both an everyday word compounded of the words *da* and *sein*—"being" and "there"—and the center of Heidegger's thought. Under this reading, the sentence becomes: "The 'essence' of *Dasein* lies in its existence." Since existence is *ek-sistere,* how a thing stands out, and *essence* is a form of the Latin verb 'to be,' it seems best to retranslate the sentence as: "The being of *Dasein* is as it appears."

Heidegger's use of *Dasein* indicates that personal experiences of self always "appear" in some particular place, at some particular time. Place and time are not attributes, like color or size, or even spatial location; they are fundamental modes of being. They are the recognition that human being is always situated. One situation in which *Dasein* finds itself is the world of other people. Being-in-the-world, therefore, is also a being-with-others—A *Mitsein.* It is well to remember that other people are not objectified elements of the environment; they, too, are centers of a self-world with its own history and future. Fundamentally isolated, we live in *Mitsein* through shared activity and meaning, most especially as these are given by language and culture.

The human world is the world as experienced. Although Heidegger never makes mention of James, it is clear that James's understanding of self and its derivation from the stream of consciousness is congenial to Heidegger's thoughts. If Husserl restored consciousness to the world, Heidegger attempted to describe the world in which consciousness makes its way. It is no longer possible to talk about "consciousness" or even "consciousness of"; it is now necessary to locate consciousness in the context of other people, time, society, and the natural world. What starts as a heuristic rule in Husserl yields clear and significant existential contexts in Heidegger.

Unlike Heidegger and Husserl, Merleau-Ponty does not worry about relationships between being and world but about relationships between doing and experiencing. These reflections lead him to assign the human body a position of centrality in his philosophy. There are two perspectives an individual can take on the human body, his or her own included: that of personal experience (what Merleau-Ponty terms first-person experience) and that of reflection or perception (what Merleau-Ponty terms third-person experience). Under these perspectives, each person has the possibility, as Plessner (1970) put it, of both being a body (first-person) *and* of having a body (third-person). Merleau-Ponty described the difference between being and having a body as the distinction between the body-as-lived and the body-as-object. The former is experienced directly; the latter is a result of "objective" third-person experiences of the body by disciplines such as biology or medicine. With Merleau-Ponty, the separation of mind and body suggested by Descartes is finally addressed. There are bodily experiences of having and of being, and both sets of experiences are always in-the-world. (See MacGillevray, 1985, for a phenomenological analysis of the ways in which adults describe their experiences of the body.)

Merleau-Ponty's philosophy treats human consciousness both as embodied *and* abstract, and his philosophy attempts to overcome the separation of mind, body, and world prevalent in contemporary thought. "Movement is not though-about movement; bodily space is not space thought of or represented . . . Movement is not the handmaiden of consciousness . . . Each instant of a movement embraces its whole space [and] institutes the link between a here and a there, a now and a future . . . Consciousness is not a matter of 'I think that' but 'I can' . . . (Merleau-Ponty, 1962, pp. 88–147).

These quotes indicate that consciousness is not described as a search light illuminating the world of some distant thinker; rather, consciousness is both a perceptual/conceptual process *and* an embodied/motor one. Personal existence is rooted in the world, and human existence lives the temporal, spatial, and interpersonal aspects of its world long before it reflects on these aspects separate from its being-in-that-world. The whole of the conceptual world does not precede nor even co-occur with embodied activity; rather it rests upon reflections of prior experiences in the world as well as on experiences of others in that world. All human being is social, all human being is temporal, all human being is embodied, all human being is worldly, and each of these great contexts is a starting point for our more separated reflections on them. Time, space, others, and world derive from reflections on our experiences long after we have lived and acted in the worlds of time, space, and others without having thematized them. Human experience is lived before it is known.

This description of human experience is crucial for any psychological analysis of consciousness. It is no longer enough to make consciousness into a faculty and separate it from behavior and the world. Together consciousness-*and*-behavior define human existence as it unfolds in-the-world. Modern philosophical analyses best conceptualize consciousness as a patterned event, a field, in which experience is not subject to any reified boundary such as mind separate from body, person separate from other people, this moment separate from that moment, and so on. Although it is true that individual contexts may yield such experiences, we should not be misled into assuming that the structure of the phenomenological field at any one moment, in any one situation, is the way it will be at some other moment, in some other situation. The self considered as *Dasein* is situational and temporal.

This description suggests a close affinity between gestalt psychology and modern existential–phenomenological thought. Aside from Kohler's infatuation with isomorphism, much of gestalt psychology is directly translatable into phenomenological terms and vice versa. As such, both define consciousness as a field event that is always structured by a variety of significantly human grounds: that of the body (both as action and as object), that of time (both as duration and as measured), and that of other people and the world. Events emerge and disappear, are remembered or forgotten, facilitate or interfere with change, and are thought about or ignored in accordance with a unique first-person field structured on the basis of these near and far grids of human experience. Each personal field is unique and changing and there is no separation between experience, behavior and the world; all co-define the concrete nature of some specific consciousness at some specific moment.

METAPHORS OF CONSCIOUSNESS

Lakoff and Johnson (1980; Johnson, 1987; Lakoff, 1987) point out that it is possible to discern the general outlines of a theory in terms of the metaphors it uses to present its ideas. This approach seems quite applicable to theories of human consciousness since James himself coined one of the earliest metaphors in the modern analysis of this topic, that of a stream. Sometimes the metaphors are not quite so explicit: For example, Proust talks of *leitmotifs* and *themes*, and such metaphors make sense only if consciousness is considered a musical composition of one sort or another. In other theories, the metaphors are quite explicit as, for example, in the case of phenomenological *field*.

Table 12.4 provides a list of metaphors frequently used to describe consciousness in the years since James. If we compare sets 1-4 with 5-8, a very obvious difference emerges: Members in the first set imply motion or change whereas members in the second set are relatively static. Sets 1, 3, and 4 are themselves ongoing events whereas Set 2 is more concerned with the transmission of change than with change itself. For the train or chain metaphor, change progresses along pre-established tracks or linkages, with the present direction depending more on the past than on the present or future.

The nature of time in Sets 1, 3, and 4 is different from that in Set 2. Whereas items in Set 1 include an understanding of time in which direction is not fixed, items in Sets 3 and 4 involve an understanding of time in which its direction is set by the formal properties of the metaphor itself. In one case, the vehicle is musical (and Joyce takes the fugue metaphor almost literally in certain parts of *Ulysses*) whereas in the other, it is in terms of lin-

TABLE 12.4
Major Metaphors Used in the Modern Study of Consciousness

Metaphor Set	Theorist(s)
(1) Stream, bird's flight	James
(2) Train, chain	Freud; earlier Associationist philosophers
(3) Symphony, fugue, musical composition	Joyce, Proust, Bergson
(4) Monologue, Soliloquy, Tale, Story	Faulkner, Proust
(5) State(s), Mode(s)	Academic Texts in Psychology
(6) Level(s), Depth(s)	Joyce, Freud, Jung
(7) Field, Pattern	Köhler, Merleau-Ponty,
(8) Horizon, Perspective, focus/fringe, figure/ground, Reflected/Unreflected	Husserl, Köhler, Heidegger, James, Merleau-Ponty

guistic or narrative conventions: *The Sound and the Fury* is a tale told by, and about, an idiot. The order of literary and musical composition sets constraints unique to these domains; only the stream metaphor has the movement, freedom, and unpredictability of a natural phenomena in a natural context.

There seem to be other systematic differences among sets. Although these differences are, perhaps, not as clear, they appear quite strongly in the contrast between Sets 5 and 6 and Sets 7 and 8. The major difference seems to be one of contrasting a wholistic organization of conscious experience (i.e., as a field or pattern) with one composed of distinct types, components, or pieces (states or modes of consciousness). This latter distinction may be divided even further: For example, the metaphors comprising Set 5 simply posit a distinction among types of consciousness—a horizontal organization if you will. The metaphors defining Set 6 posit a more vertical organization in which there are higher and lower levels of consciousness. The psycho-analytic triad of conscious, pre-conscious, and unconscious reveals such a top-to-bottom organization, whereas the Jungian metaphor of racial unconscious is at once "below" personal unconsciousness and more profound or significant. Even the double-entendre on *deep*, as is in *below* and *profound*, describe a vertical ordering of states.

In contrast to this emphasis on "real" differences, the difference between right and left hemispheres (Set 5) or between unconscious and conscious processes (Set 6), the metaphors comprising Sets 7 and 8 do not describe ontologically distinct categories. What Sets 7 and 8 attempt to capture is the configuration of a patterned event and to provide a way of talking about relationships among aspects of the totality. The use of visual metaphors in Set 8 has the same meaning in philosophical discussions of consciousness as in Gestalt psychology where a complete range of psychological phenomena were discussed in terms of perceptual prototypes. This overlap is not accidental, and the reciprocal influences between gestalt psychology and existential-phenomenological philosophy reach their sharpest articulation in the writings of Merleau-Ponty; writings that make frequent references to Wertheimer, Goldstein, Koffka, and Lewin. Only the terms reflected and unreflected are meant categorically; focus and fringe and figure/ground are relational concepts quite general in application.

The eight sets of metaphors seem to embody two major themes: mobility (or stasis) and wholism (or categorical components). Each of the 8-item sets may be located in the 2×2 partition brought about by these categories. So, for example, *field* is static and wholistic; *train* is mobile and componential. Since all metaphors of consciousness may be uniquely located in this table, any proper metaphor of human conscious experience must be concerned with components, organization, and rules for change and continuity. If we look at this list with only a slightly prejudiced eye, it seems clear that the Jamesian metaphor encompasses the greatest number of possibilities, especially if we remember that he endowed his stream with both a focus and a fringe.

One final point deserves comment concerning the stream metaphor: namely, that components, organization, and change-in-continuity also characterize two other significant aspects of the human life world: time and self (see Dapkus, 1985, for a further discussion on this point). Within these contexts, the stream metaphor not only suggests change and continuity and components and unities, it also suggests a coherence to these domains such that as they change we (and others) are able to recognize them as continuous with what went before. Although it is perhaps going too far to see the topics of consciousness, time, and self merging into a new definition of what it means to be a human being, as Heidegger seems at points to suggest, it does not seem to be going too far to see these topics as more intimately related than current views usually allow. By his very ordering of chapters—with the chapter on self following the one on stream of consciousness—James reminds us of this possibility. Because of these implications, and others yet unexplicated, it is no wonder the Jamesian metaphor has lasted longer than others and continues to be productive after a century of examination and use. Although 100 years is not long for a useful idea to last (Descartes' *Cogito* is going on 350) it seems clear that the more we learn about consciousness, the stronger the stream metaphor becomes. For this insight we must be grateful to the master, William James.

REFERENCES

Bergson, H. (1900/1956). *Laughter*. New York: Doubleday.

Dapkus, M. (1985). A Thematic analysis of the experience of time. *Journal of Personality and Social Psychology, 49*, 408–419.

Faulkner, W. (1946). *The sound and the fury*. New York: Modern Library. (Original work published 1929)

Freud, S. (1905/1932). *Wit and its relationship to the unconscious.* In *The basic writings of Sigmund Freud.* New York: Random House.

Freud, S. (1905/1938). *The psychopathology of everyday life.* In *The basic writings of Sigmund Freud.* New York: Random House.

Friedman, W. (1955). *Stream of consciousness: A study in literary method.* New Haven, CT: Yale University Press.

Heidegger, M. (1927/1972). *Being and time.* New York: Harper & Row.

Hurlburt, R. T. (1979). Random sampling of cognitions and behavior. *Journal of Research in Personality, 13,* 103–111.

Hurlburt, R. T. (1980). Validation and correlation of thought sampling with retrospective measures. *Cognitive Therapy and Research, 4,* 235–238.

Ihde, D. (1977). *Experimental phenomenology.* New York: SUNY Press.

James, W. (1890). *The principles of psychology* (Vols. 1–2) New York: Holt.

James, W. (1893). *Psychology.* New York: Holt.

James, W. (1921). *Talks to teachers on psychology.* New York: Holt.

Johnson, M. (1987). *The body in the mind.* Chicago: University of Chicago Press.

Joyce, J. (1934). *Ulysses.* New York: Modern Library. (Original work published 1922)

Joyce, J. (1947). *A portrait of the artist as a young man.* New York: University Press. (Original work published 1916)

Joyce, J. (1947). *Finnegans wake.* New York: University Press. (Original work published 1939)

Klinger, E. (1978). Modes of normal conscious flow. In K. S. Pope & J. L. Singer (Eds.), *The stream of consciousness* (pp. 226–258). New York: Plenum Press.

Köhler, W. (1947/1975). *Gestalt psychology.* New York: Mentor Books.

Kuhn, T. (1970). *The structure of scientific revolutions.* Chicago: University Press.

Lakoff, G. (1987). *Women, fire and dangerous things.* Chicago: University of Chicago Press.

Lakoff, G., & Johnson, P. (1980). *Metaphors we live by.* Chicago: University of Chicago Press.

MacGillevray, W. (1985). *Embodiment and Ambiguity: A Phenomenological Description of the Human Experience of the Human body.* Unpublished Dissertation, University of Tennessee, Knoxville.

Merleau-Ponty, M. (1962). *The phenomenology of perception.* London: Routledge and Kegan Paul.

Plessner, H. (1970). *Laughing and crying.* Evanston, IL: Northwestern University Press.

Pollio, H. R. (1982). *Behavior and existence.* Monterey, CA: Brooks/Cole.

Pollio, H. R. (1984). *What students think about and do during college lectures.* Knoxville, TN: Teaching-Learning Issues, Learning Research Center.

Pollio, H. R. Barlow, J. M., Fine, H. J., & Pollio, M. R. (1977). *Psychology and the poetics of growth.* Hillsdale, NJ: Lawrence Erlbaum Associates.

Proust, M. (1927). *Swann's way.* New York: Modern Library.

Proust, M. (1928). *The past recaptured.* New York: Modern Library.

Sharpe, E. (1940). An examination of metaphor. *International Journal of Psychoanalysis, 21,* 201–213.

Singer, J. L., & Antrobus, J. S. (1970). *Dimension of daydreaming: A factor analysis of imaginal processes and personality scales.* NIMH Report.

Wolfenstein, M. (1954). *Children's humor.* Bloomington: Indiana University Press.

Chapter 13

James on the Will

James Deese

University of Virginia

No topic has more completely disappeared from modern psychology than that of the will. It barely survived in the mainstream of psychology into the 1920s, perhaps even then only because it was one of the voices of resistance to the behavioristic revolution. McDougall treats of it at length in his famous book, *Social Psychology* (1908), but it scarcely figures in his later textbook, *Outline of Psychology* (1924). In that book there are but a scant three or four pages devoted to the topic, and this is almost the last mention of the topic in anything that could properly be designated as a textbook in psychology. True enough, the will hung on in textbooks, usually written by those in holy orders, especially designed for Catholic colleges well into the 1930s. It is still a topic of concern in certain philosophical and theological circles, and there it centers on the vexatious question of freedom of the will. But it is very hard to find any reference to the will in the psychological textbooks of the last 40 years. The will has disappeared from official psychology.

Psychological textbooks are, for all practical purposes, the invention of the 19th century. The early texts often follow the tradition established by Kant of labeling what we now call psychology by the term anthropology. Neither Kant nor those who followed in his tradition use the term anthropology in its modern sense. Rather it describes what we now call psychology. The first textbook published in America with the title of *Psychology* (Rauch, 1841) carried the subtitle *A study of the Human Soul Including Anthropology*. The section of that book labeled *Anthropology* includes hints of what later in the 19th century came to be that discipline, but mainly the topics discussed in this part of Rauch's book are those to be found in the mainstream of psychology. The author, Frederick A. Rauch, an immigrant from Germany who died at much too early an age, had the potential to transform American life. In a scant decade, from his mid-twenties to his untimely death at 35, he founded what was to become Franklin and Marshall College, hammered out a theological code, and wrote his textbook on psychology, a work much ahead of its time. He does discuss the will, but mainly to put to rest certain theological doubts that might have arisen from a reading of the balance of the book.

On the other hand, the textbook, *Psychology*, written by John Dewey (1887), published just 3 years before the publication of James's book, makes the topic of will central. Dewey's text is more old-fashioned both in form and substance than either Rauch's or James's. It is built out of the intellectual tradition, mainly Calvinistic, that in curious ways shaped many of Dewey's ideas, even into his old age. Dewey's text is predicated on the medieval principle that the study of the mind is, like Gaul, divided into three parts—cognition, feeling, and conation. Cognition is a very fashionable word nowadays, but in Dewey's time it was on the verge of going underground. It only resurfaced in psychology 50 years later. *The Cognitive Powers* (McCosh, 1886) was the subtitle for one of the two volumes of the influential text written by James McCosh, sometimes President of Princeton. Dewey is only a little less antique than McCosh, but to his credit he mainly uses the plainer word, knowledge, for cognition, and he largely foreswears the use of conation for the term will.

James's discussion of the will, compared with that of Dewey's, occupies a very small portion of the massive *Principles*. Furthermore, James's discussion of the topic, as one might suppose, is idiosyncratic. It must have been very difficult to comprehend for someone like Dewey who was not completely at home in the new German psychology. It is, in its way, tortured and, for James, unusually obscure. This is not to say that the topic was unimportant or unfamiliar for James. Many of his writings both before and after the *Principles* testify to that fact. But he does wrestle with strange demons in this chapter. It is, in the context of the *Principles*, a whale among fishes. In order to understand this, we must examine not only that particular chapter, but we must look elsewhere in the *Principles* as well as in the widely scattered writings James addressed to the topic of the will.

My first task will be to provide the reader with a summary of Chapter 26 of the *Principles*. This is not an easy thing to do. Although it occupies but a small fraction of the *Principles*, we must remember that the *Principles* is a very long book. Chapter 26 occupies more than 100 pages of Volume 2. Those 100-plus pages are devoted to many issues, often dealt with, characteristically, in James's indirect (I almost wrote devious) style. He, unlike Dewey, deals with the new experimental psychology. He must also express his own views on the topic of the will (often more boldly expressed elsewhere), and he must at least touch on the theological issue of the freedom of the will, an issue central to Christian and, only to a lesser extent, Jewish theology. This concern clearly makes James most uncomfortable.

WHAT JAMES HAD TO SAY

Fashions in the production of books (not necessarily in the writing of books) sometimes puts obstacles in the way of the scholarly reader. My frustration at reading books with "end notes" rather than footnotes would be relieved if copyeditors would list the end notes not just by chapter number but by chapter title, so that it would not be necessary to go back to the text to see what number, as opposed to what topic, one was reading. In the *Principles* no such problem occurs. There are real footnotes. They are, by the way, fascinating, and they have often sent me on an excursion to a library (usually the Health Sciences Library, a fact that reveals volumes about what James read) to trace down a reference.

But one fashion in the production of books has changed for the better since James's *Principles*. Headings in the *Principles* are few and, given the length of the text, remarkably far between. Rather, the various topics covered in the separate chapters are only listed in the table of contents. So, if you want to find a particular topic, you must refer back to the table of contents. Fortunately, in the *Principles*, there are page references in the topical entries in the table of contents. I make this comment mainly to warn the reader of the difficulty in tracing down the particular topics on which I comment.

James tells us at the outset (II: 487) that he is going to tell us how voluntary movements presuppose a memory of involuntary movements. This is one of the most curious aspects of James's theory of the will, and although it makes little sense to late 20th-century psychology, it may well find its way into the mainstream as a kind of anticipation of Yoga-like control of the body. Be that as it may, James begins by making a distinction between movements that are automatic and reflexive and those which are desired and intended. So far so good. He gives us a learned account of the reflex (as, of course, famously did Dewey). He tells us that "*voluntary movements must be secondary, not primary functions of our organism*" (II: 487). Good enough. This may be a reflection of the synthesis of 19th-century evolutionary theory and reflex physiology, or, on the other hand, it may simply be an aside (one never knows with James).

James goes on, however, to give us an example of reflexive actions that suggests he did not understand the distinction between voluntary action and reflexes as well as did the unmedically trained Dewey. It is that of a child who runs to James to hide his face when an express train roars by the station platform. To be sure, all of the physiological reactions (the tears, etc.) were reflexive in the broadest modern sense, but, although we may describe the child's reaction as impulsive, it lacked the characteristics of the true reflex as physiology understands that notion. In fact, one could imagine circumstances under which the child might have stood its ground, however frightened and however beset its body may have been by the reflexive actions of fear.

James's point appears to be that voluntary action is secondary to reflexive action. The act must be foreseen, and thus the result of experience, in order to be deliberately ordained. James then goes on to say something very strange: "*When a particular movement, having once occurred in a random, reflex, or involuntary way, has left an image of itself in the memory, then the movement can be desired again, proposed as an end and deliberately willed*" (italics added; I have adopted a most Jamesian prodigality with the use of italics, II: 487).

Surely James did not mean to imply what at least one reading of this passage would imply, namely that a reflex could be converted into a voluntary action simply by being repeated with some sense of deliberation. James is often maddeningly obscure, and that is certainly part of the charm we all experience in reading James. His texts cry out for explications. But whose explication is to be judged correct? Certainly, James might have agreed, not his own.

James goes on to tell us that we build up a storehouse of ideas about the various movements left by the memories of their involuntary performance. The important implication of this idea is not, as we might suppose on a casual reading, for developmental psychology. James, in his view, is simply pointing to how we produce voluntary movements. This notion of the production of voluntary actions is borrowed wisdom, and it is not, unfortunately, borrowed wisdom from the physiology which James knew but from the new experimental psychology, which, if it had any central idea at all, was rooted in the pervasive 19th-century notion that all voluntary actions must be conscious. James goes on to tell us that we have residual effects of the motion, namely kinesthetic impressions. He tells us that there is an absolute need for sensations of some sort to guide us in the memory of movements (II: 490).

On page 492 of Volume 2 James asks a question obviously of central importance to him: "Is there anything else in the mind when we will to do an act?" He uses this question to enter into the thicket of controversies then raging over certain findings of the new psychology. He tells us that there is a "powerful tradition" in psychology that says there is something else. By this James means to refer to Wundt's notion of the feeling of innervation. James wisely chooses to disbelieve in it, I suspect because it does not appeal to James's impatient mind. The feeling of innervation is simply an unnecessary construct, as a mid 20th-century psychologist might put the matter.

All of the discussion up to page 522 of Volume 2 will strike the modern reader as being irrelevant and more than a bit obscure (despite the charm of James's prose). That is because it concerns many of the issues of the new psychology (mainly Wundt's introspectionism) that provide only a puzzle for the modern mind. James, for all of his disdain of the new psychology, shows us that he knows what it is about. Dewey did not, and Dewey's text of 3 years earlier, for all that they might have disagreed, would not have mystified McCosh or Rauch. But James would have, for he was when he wrote the *Principles*, clearly *au courant* with all that was going on in German academic psychology. He was full of the controversies of the era. He even took the Pflüger-Lotze quarrel seriously. This controversy was, the reader will recall, over whether or not the spinal cord had certain primitive qualities of consciousness. More importantly, James was concerned with testing the limits of introspection. He was interested in the kind of thing that would lead, a few years later, to the imageless thought controversy.

In this section there are some typical Jamesian asides that make it always a delight to read him. He tells us (II: 496) that it is a general principle in psychology that consciousness deserts all processes for which it can no longer be of use. The tendency of consciousness to a minimum of complication is a dominant law. Thus, the act of willing turns out to be void of sentience (Does James contradict himself?).

In this same context we must forgive James for giving us a long-winded and complicated argument to the effect that we are not conscious of the act of willing. Given the new psychology from Germany, however, this was something very necessary to do, and it does, as I alluded to earlier, anticipate the objections of the Würzburgers. James was vastly more familiar with the literature on the pathology of neurophysiology and its implications for psychology, but he still takes more seriously the arguments of the introspectionists. Some years later, this introspective view of the problem of the sensations of the will gets transformed into concern over the sensations of motivation. James's respect for introspection lingered on in the views of Cannon and others about the sensations of hunger and thirst and how they disappeared when food or water was ingested. So the introspective analysis of the will did not end as abruptly as did the notion of the will itself; rather it continued on into the early work on the physiology of motivation.

The first heading of this long chapter appears on page 522 of Volume 2. It is "ideomotor action." To put the matter simply, ideomotor action is about an issue which is hard for the late 20th-century mind to understand. When the idea is explained to us, we are likely to exclaim "but there aren't any, or if there are, they are unimportant in the regulation of behavior." The way James puts the idea (italics his) is: *"Is the bare idea of a movement's sensible effects its sufficient mental cue, or must there be an additional mental antecedent, in the shape of a fiat, decision, consent, volitional mandate, or some other synonymous phenomenon of consciousness, before the movement can follow?"* (II: 522). This issue, depending on how one interprets the text, has been either declared by modern psychology to be moot or has been decided in favor of the "additional mental antecedent." It is probably moot because the whole issue has disappeared for many modern psychologists. It has been decided by some in favor of the additional mental antecedent as the result of some strange combination of the ideas of Freud and Chomsky, or, to give the matter more proper due, by the ideas of the Würzburg psychologists, with whose ideas James may or may not have been eventually familiar. He could not have been familiar with them when he wrote the *Principles*, for the views of the Würzburgers did not exist then, but it is not clear to me that his later writings reflect any familiarity with the strange ideas coming out of Würzburg. But surely the phrase (II: 522): "Wherever movement follows *unhesitatingly and immediately* the notion of it in the mind, we have ideomotor action" expresses a similar idea. Did any of the Würzburgers say it more succinctly? Although the Würzburg psychologists discovered the unconscious as truly as did Freud, James did not, and his reference to ideomotor action should not lead us to suppose that he did. All that can be said in the centennial year of the *Principles* is that the notion of the unconscious—unconscious *will* if you please—was in the air in the 1890s. Chomsky's notion of the unconscious creation of ordinary sentences was 70 years away, and we may excuse James for not being, as were the Würzburg psychologists, the anticipators of Chomsky's insight. But James, as always, was aware that there was a problem here.

Next in this chapter James comes to a very modern problem: conflict. If there is only ideomotor action it is only because there is no conflicting notion (for the action) in the mind. In support of this assertion James places himself ahead of his time. He invokes, informally, what most 19th-century psychologists chose to ignore, hypnotism. Somehow, James seems to have believed, the hypnotic state bares the mind in such a way as to make direct ideomotor action possible.

McDougall in his *Social Psychology* (1908) published nearly two decades later, expands on the notion of conflict and the will (without, it must be said, citing James). He (McDougall) says that an act of will occurs (my words) when the whole personality throws itself on the side of some weaker motive in a conflict. This is generally regarded as one of McDougall's central ideas, but it was James who invented it. One of his most charming illustrations is invoked to defend the idea: How hard it is to get out of bed on a frosty morning. But nowadays, who would admit to the weaker motive? James does not use McDougall's locutions, but in his example he is clearly arguing for the will throwing itself on the side of the weaker, morally right side of the conflict.

In fact, the theory of conflict is more explicit in James than it is in McDougall. "A waking man's behavior is thus at all times the resultant of two opposing neural forces" (II: 527). From here on, James appears to be committed, as was McDougall, to the modern notion of motives and the rich possibilities of conflicting motives warring for control of the psyche. James sits at the nexus of modern psychology and all that preceded him. Motives, not in the older, nearly legal sense, but in the modern sense, are the powers

of the mind. Here is modern psychology in the making. The will, to characterize it in its usual way, is reserved for conscious acts, and, like consciousness itself, is, for James, perilously close to being an epiphenomenon.
There is a conscious derivative of the conflict of motives or of the will with
a motive. But decision *characterizes* the will. Decision, indeed, is the conscious will. The five types of decision that James describes are but an exem-
plification of this characteristic of the will (see II: 531–535).

The section that follows represents a real transition to the notion of motive and conflict among (or between) motives. James's determination to do
an introspective analysis of this question gives the passage a slightly old-
fashioned flavor, but who knows; the problem may return. If the discussion
that follows on types of personality (e.g., the explosive will) does not have a
modern ring to it, it could at least be adapted for modern tastes.

The whole of his middle part of the chapter is meaty, but I pass over it
hastily partly to seduce the modern reader into looking into it and partly
because it ends up being a defense of the notion of the will as a mere epiphenomenon of the resolution of the decision. James is clearly unhappy
here. He cannot bring himself to give the notion of will the central position
that it held in, say, medieval psychology, but he cannot bring himself to dismiss it as a mere epiphenomenon. His similar shilly-shallying on the question of consciousness is well known.

On page 549 of Volume 2, we come to that most characteristic of 19th-
century topics: "Pleasure and Pain as Springs of Action." Here James's
most banal behavioristic tendencies surface. "If a movement feels agree-
able, we repeat and repeat it as long as the pleasure lasts. If it hurts us, our
muscular contractions at the instant stop" (II: 550). Note the words: "If a
movement . . ." and "our muscular contractions at the instant stop." Even
Watson could not have been more explicit in reducing psychology to muscle
twitches.

But James, as always, manages to rescue himself from a simple-minded
behaviorism. "Important as is the influence of pleasures and pains upon
our movements, they are far from being the only stimuli" (II: 550). He goes
on to his celebrated argument to the effect that pleasures and pains might
seem to be the only *comprehensible* and *reasonable* motives for action, as
the only actions on which we *ought* to act. Here, of course, he shows his
debt to the British empirical moral tradition, but he does not appear to me
to take the argument as seriously as does McDougall as an ethical principle.
Such a point of view becomes evident in its starkest simplicity only in the
work of B. F. Skinner.

In the ordinary course of things, ethical acts—that is to say acts guided
by pleasure or pain—are only intermittent. Most of our comings and go-
ings, to paraphrase James, are ideomotor. Throughout this section, James
wrestles mightily and to little avail with British hedonism. He cites Bain
and Spencer at great length, and he gives evidence of manifest discomfort

with where they are leading him. Such vacillation, as we all know, is common in James, and it is one of the things that makes him so appealing and causes us to distance him from the dogmatic psychologists, Watson and Freud, to name two.

Despite the almost perilous flirtation with ideas that were to become the foundation stones of behaviorism, as well as the basis for the ethics of much of modern psychology—behavioristic or not—James does not succumb to the error of identifying will with action. Volition stops with the idea that initiates the action. "The movements which ensue are exclusively physiological phenomena" (II: 560). Thus, the will of the aphasic conjures the image of a word, but that unfortunate individual cannot make the correct movements to form the word (James's example, and an excellent one). Effort of attention is at the heart of the will, says James. And he would be very pleased by the modern finding that a cortical-evoked potential precedes the actual performance of a willful act by about a fifth of a second. There is no need to suggest that there is simply a sensory-motor connection, as the later behaviorists would assume. Will only arrives when there is an effort to execute the idea. So, although will properly remains purely ideational and does not spill over into the motor act itself, it has the special characteristic of demanding something—most probably a motor act. But "the whole drama is a mental drama" (II: 564). The will is idea. It is hardly possible to find a proposition that places a greater distance between James and modern psychology than this.

Throughout the *Principles* James makes a strong and generally successful effort to keep faith with the hard-fought divorce between psychology and philosophy (and especially in America, theology). But he cannot resist dealing with that philosophical—nay, theological—question of the freedom of the will. He reminds us that certain issues are beyond empirical psychology. Thus, he tells us (in Vol. 1) that he has said, and believes that he could not give a coherent account of how we come to an "unshakeable belief," that thinking is immaterial (a belief thoroughly shaken in the generation that followed James), but that it must remain as a postulate essential to making psychology (or anything else, James might have added) intelligible. He goes on to say that if we admit that our thoughts exist, we ought to admit that they exist just in the form in which they appear. This is an argument dangerously close to that invoked by A. O. Lovejoy in his *Revolt Against Dualism* (1930).

Thoughts appear, sometimes with effort and sometimes without. The object of thought is sometimes determined and sometimes not. But the appearance of indeterminacy is only an appearance. Remorse over some protracted sequence of thoughts, which give rise to an act, is real, but is it justified? James waivers, but he finally comes down on the side of a pragmatic but not philosophical determinism. "My own belief is that the question of free-will is insoluble on strictly psychological grounds" (II: 572). A preference for free will is "ethical," a preference elected by James, but that preference must be excluded from psychology. James is eloquent in the best Jamesian way about free will. "Freedom's first choice should be to affirm itself. We ought never to hope for any other method of getting at the truth if indeterminism be a fact" (II: 572). Deterministic arguments can never be coercive. James falls back at this point on a psychological argument out of his time about the difficulty of distinguishing among decisions without effort and ideomotor actions (to say nothing of the merely reflexive). He comes to his most celebrated statement on the matter:

> Psychology will be Psychology and Science Science, as much as ever (as much and no more) in this world, whether free will be true in it or not. Science, however, must be constantly reminded that her purposes are not the only purposes and that the order of uniform causation, which she has use for, and is therefore right in postulating may be enveloped in a wider order, on which she has no claims at all. (II: 576)

Thus, something like the freedom of will may be a useful idea for some intellectual exercises and cannot be condemned altogether just because it does not suit the psychological sciences. James, no doubt, had in mind theology and perhaps even some branches of philosophy. It is very unlikely, however, that he had anything in mind like the problems created for the philosophy of the law by the introduction of the social sciences and particularly psychology into the justice system. In our time, when there is an intense interest in the relation between psychology and the law, some of us have begun to appreciate that the philosophical underpinings of the law require a certain respect for the freedom of judgment and for individual responsibility (see Robinson, 1980). But there is still a powerful current of opinion among the majority of psychologists that we must, to preserve psychology as psychology and science as science, insist that all human actions are determined by the circumstances surrounding them. Such a view is implicit in the shift from the will to motivation, and it lies at the bottom of our discomfort with where to draw the line in the insanity defense.

JAMES AND THE SHIFT TO MOTIVATION

The Principles is not the last textbook to have a whole chapter devoted to the will. There is, as I have noted, a chapter on the subject in William McDougall's sensationally successful book, *Social Psychology* (1908). But McDougall's chapter is very different from James's. First of all, McDougall is not obsessed, as James is, with consciousness being almost the whole of psychology. Even more to the point, McDougall's chapter is almost a fulfillment of James's view that psychology should be psychology and science science. The will, for McDougall, does not belong in a true psychological science, for it negates the idea of causation.

The important aspect of McDougall's book is, of course, the celebrated list of instincts, which, if it had not been overwhelmed by the Freudian flood, might well have provided us with the major 20th-century theory about the nature of personality. McDougall's arguments about replacing will with motivation simply do not occur in James. James's chapter on instinct and the chapter on the will scarcely acknowledge one another. But even more than James, McDougall is at pains to reject the theological foundations of the will.

James discussed the will in the context of the new German psychology of the day. Thus, he takes seriously the importance of the idea of a feeling of innervation, and a good portion of his chapter on the will is directed toward the introspective evidence for and against it. McDougall, on the other hand, tackles the theological and moral problems forthrightly and not just as an afterthought as in James's chapter. McDougall tells us that any "libertarian" (McDougall's word) view of volition is incompatible with any "science of society." But he goes even further than James in the matter. He says that punishment would make no sense if voluntary actions were outside of the psychologically determined nature of human beings (McDougall, unlike B. F. Skinner, clearly believes in the efficacy of punishment). So, McDougall is more direct than James, and he is closer to that contemporary position that limits voluntary actions to their control by *systems* of rewards and punishments.

McDougall does have a theory of volition that, antique diction aside, has a ring of the behavioristic theories of conflict that emerged in the 1930s. The sense of the will happens when the totality of the personality throws itself on the side of a weaker motive in a conflict. As we have seen, this is a notion close to that of James. In discussing the will, McDougall invokes motives and conflict among motives. It is here that McDougall reveals himself as a genuine transitional figure from the psychology of the will to the psychology of motivation.

McDougall's notion, however, makes the single-dimensioned theory of the behaviorists (approach–avoidance, approach–approach, etc.) comparatively simple minded. McDougall's notion is much more complicated. Various motives can interfere with one another, and a collection of motives can, so to speak, gang up on a single motive.

As I have already noted, James does anticipate the modern theory of motives in his chapter on instinct. McDougall's theories about the matter are more modern than James's, but the examples James gave us lend a distinctly (from the perspective of the 1980s) more sophisticated air to the matter. James is a better ethologist than McDougall. He does not present us with a rationally derived list of instincts. Rather he simply discusses some examples of instinctive actions that come to his mind, and he moves easily back and forth, in the manner of a modern teacher of animal behavior, between human and animal examples. It is here that James's famous broody hen and her never-too-much-to-be-sat-upon-eggs occurs (II: 387). And human beings, James tells us, are not simply animals bereft of instinct, rather we have more of them and in more complex combinations than other creatures. For psychological reasons, James is clearly more at home in this chapter than he is in the chapter on the will. James is famous for the openness of his mind, but the difference between his various philosophical writings on will and his psychological one (in the *Principles*) tells us that he was tortured by the various stances his beliefs caused him to assume. The result is that the chapter on instinct is both more modern than the chapter on the will and is easier for the psychological mind to follow.

We may conclude that James is in the mainstream in which the idea of the will died and was replaced by motivation. But all the same, James devotes more space to the will in the *Principles* than to instinct. We modern interpreters can put two and two together—there is more space and more anguish. James the philosopher is uncomfortable with James the psychologist. And even James the psychologist is uncomfortable with James the orthodox psychologist. Instinct (the modern reader should read motivation) is that which determines our emotions, our decisions, and our lives. Here James and McDougall come together. But our task is not to understand James on motivation, but James on the will, and in order to grasp James's struggles with the will in the *Principles* we must look elsewhere in James's writings.

JAMES AND THE PHILOSOPHY OF THE WILL

I have said that James, in the *Principles*, is much too concerned with the new German psychology to really deal with the idea of the will in the way in which he would like. In various other works, mostly written after the *Principles*, he does so. The psychology of *The Varieties of Religious Experience* (James, 1902) is suffused with concern over the will (particularly in the sections on conversion and the conversion experience). But the central document, aside from the *Principles*, by which we can understand James on the will is in *The Will to Believe*. *The Will to Believe* was conceived as early as 1896 and published in 1905. Whatever the date, the *Principles* had absolved James of the responsibility of explaining the new psychology to the world. In *The Will to Believe*, James could get on with the task of telling us what the real function of the will is. It is clear that despite science will be science, and so forth, James has a sense of the central psychological reality of the will (insofar as anything for James could be said to be central). In fact, the heart of pragmatism lies in the will. After all, we are not compelled, either by God, by implacable historical destiny, or by history's iron laws of economics, to believe in either this or that. Rather we are free to choose this or that, and we may, furthermore, flaunt our freedom by believing this or that depending on the circumstances of the moment.

James, in this essay, is concerned with the vexatious problem of freedom and determinism. It is, however, in the essay, "The Dilemma of Determinism" (James, 1905) that he makes his celebrated distinction between soft and hard determinism (revised in a psychological context by D. N. Robinson, 1985). James knows about the passions, but there is also reason. James is not much given to comment on secular law and its relations with psychology (the love affair between law and psychology is a long way in the future), but in one place in *The Will to Believe* (1905, p. 20) he gives away his stance on the matter: "Few cases are worth spending much time over: the great thing is to have them decided on *any* acceptable principle, and got out of the way." Could anything be more Jamesian? But notice that it is not that things are decided for us by psychological principles or laws. We simply decide them on whatever principles are at the moment acceptable.

However, the full Jamesian position on freedom and determinism occurs in the essay, "The Dilemma of Determinism." This essay was a long time in the making. It was first delivered before a group of students at the Harvard Divinity School. It was then published in the *Unitarian Review* in 1884, and it was finally published as one of the essays collected under the title *The Will to Believe*.

Here he completely abandons the freedom versus determinism issue as a psychological one. He makes the problem one of nature in general. Is nature determined or free? But he says: "But there are two *words* which usually encumber these classical arguments, and which we must immediately dispose of if we are to make any progress. One is the eulogist word *freedom* and the other is the opprobrious word *chance*. The word 'chance' I wish to keep, but I wish to get rid of the word 'freedom' " (James, 1905, pp. 148–149).

But then James characteristically turns around and he says:

"Now, all this is a quagmire of evasion under which the real issue of fact has been entirely smothered. Freedom in all these senses presents simply no problem at all. No matter what the soft determinist mean by it,—whether he mean the acting without external constraint; whether he mean the acting rightly, or whether he mean the acquiescing in the law of the whole,—who cannot answer him that sometimes we are free and sometimes not?" (James, 1905, p. 149)

In other words, yes, we all know about freedom, but the important question is whether the universe is built on chance or not. Thus, years before it became a real issue in metaphysics, James is concerned about chance in the universe—not freedom of decision, but chance in the universe. He goes on to toy with the idea of alternate universes (a consequence of what James calls "loose play" in the system).

Then he, inexplicably, brings us back to psychological determinism.

> The question relates solely to the existence of possibilities, in the strict sense of the term, as things that may, but need not, be. Both sides admit that a volition, for instance, has occurred. The indeterminists say another volition might have occurred in its place: the determinists swear that nothing could possibly have occurred in its place. (James, 1905, pp. 151-152)

From thence James comes back to his celebrated pluralism. We are divided by what we have faith in, but like our faith in monism or dualism, it matters only in the particular instance on which side we come down.

He then, in this most crucial essay, goes on to say that indeterminism rightly means chance (in the metaphysical sense, evidently not in the psychological sense). The problem, in the long run, is not a psychological one but a metaphysical one, and one which bears on our conception of the relation between the Creator and the universe. In short, James *does* in this essay tackle the theological question of the freedom of the will—and not merely in the sense of whether we really are free but in the sense that has worried Christian theologians for 1,500 years as to whether our Creator would or could allow such a thing.

Thus, James on the will tells us more about James than it does about that vexatious topic. James wants to be both the psychologist and the moral philosopher, but he recognizes that in order to keep his integrity as psychologist he must foreswear moral philosophy. Would that a legion of modern psychologists would have the same scruples. It is easy to point to B. F. Skinner in this respect, but the murky confusion of psychology and moral philosophy that has characterized Skinner of the last 40 years is more than matched in the ideas of many a lesser figure.

In a letter written in 1870 James says: "My first act of free will shall be to believe in free will" (H. James, 1920). Yet, as psychologist, "Psychology will be Psychology and Science Science." There is no place for free will, because the notion of freedom, apart from chance, lies utterly outside the boundaries of psychological science. James appears to hope against hope that chance will rescue him from his dilemma (James, 1905, p. 178-179, written when the *Principles* was underway). Chance is, he says, "altogether good" (James, 1905, p. 178). Thus chance is given the role of rescuing James from an implacable psychological determinism. But it is a poor solution, for James knows that a universe of chance is no better a place for moral philosophy than a universe of rigidly enforced mechanical laws. And it deprives him of the medieval solution to the problem—faith and reason. James is a stalwart about faith all right: "I myself believe that the evidence for God lies primarily in inner personal experiences" (James, 1907, p. 109). But James has a deep distrust of reason. There is a relatively short chapter in the *Principles* on reasoning, but it is mainly a charming essay full of such Jamesian wisdom as that the main "sagacity" in solving syllogisms lies in the minor premise, and that the major premise is largely a matter of "fulness of learning" (II: 332). The chapter is heavily influenced by British associationism, and there is no hint of the basis for human reasoning in language or a notational system of some sort (unlike Rauch's text of 50 years earlier, there is no chapter on language in the *Principles* and precious little discussion of it). If we look up cognition in the index, we are referred, in a very medieval way, to knowing, but once again there is little in the way of discussion of processes, save in the chapters on perception. If we look up reason in the index we are referred to logic, but the pages on logic (II: 647–659) are few relative to the total devoted to what we would now call cognition and perception, and they are neither strong Jamesian psychology nor Jamesian philosophy. I am, in reading these pages, reminded that James once described algebra as a form of low cunning.

Thus, in the end, we must conclude that pointing the way to the solution of the problem of the will in psychology was not one of James's great achievements. He was compelled by the psychology of his time to deal with the will as a process in consciousness, and he realized that human decisions—political, legal, and moral—required an assumption of human freedom. But he could never quite bring himself to say that psychology must face its own limitations, if we are to accept such an assumption as given.

James is one of the great minds of the modern world, but he is frustrating to someone who wishes to impose a grand order on intellectual history. He might have, in a few pages, brought psychology the great insight that Skinner later gave us in the distinction between operant or voluntary processes and respondent or involuntary processes. That Skinner himself fails to see the full implications of that distinction gives us even more regret that James did not, in the convoluted chapter on the will, come to full grips with the distinction between the willed and the unwilled.

REFERENCES

Dewey, J.(1887). *Psychology*. New York: Harper & Brothers.

James, H. (Ed.). (1920). *The letters of William James*. Boston: Atlantic Monthly Press.

James, W. (1890). *The principles of psychology* (Vols. 1-2). New York: Holt.

James, W. (1905). *The will to believe and other essays in popular philosophy*. New York: Longmans, Green.

James, W. (1907). *Pragmatism: A new name for old ways of thinking*. Longmans, Green.

James, W. (1902). *The varieties of religious experience*. New York: Longmans, Green.

Lovejoy, A. O. (1930). *The revolt against dualism*. Chicago: Open Court.

McCosh, J. (1886). *Psychology: The cognitive powers*. New York: Charles Scribner's Sons.

McDougall, W. (1908). *An introduction to social psychology*. Boston: Luce.

McDougall, W. (1924). *Outline of psychology*. New York: Charles Scribner's Sons.

Rauch, F. A. (1841). *Psychology or a view of the human soul including anthropology*. New York: M. W. Dodd.

Robinson, D. N. (1980). *Psychology and the law: Can justice survive the social sciences?* New York: Oxford University Press.

Robinson, D. N. (1985). *Philosophy of psychology*. New York: Columbia University Press.

Author Index

Subject Index